DEVELOPMENTAL PSYCHOLOGY

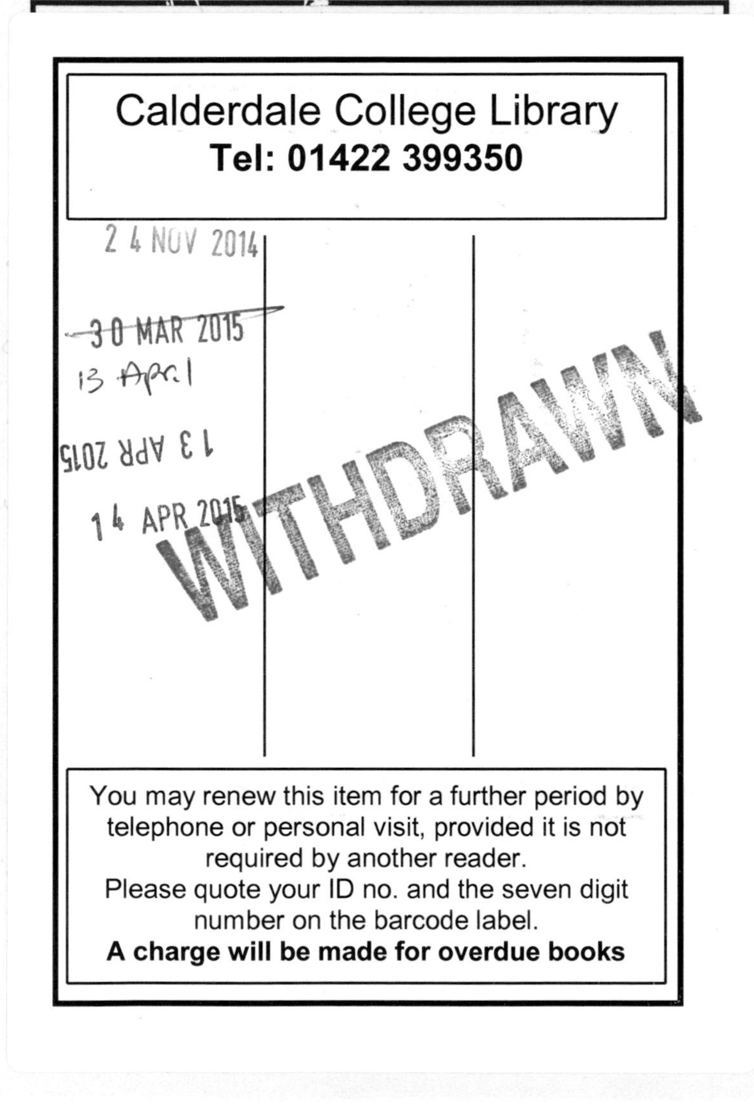

DEVELOPMENTAL PSYCHOLOGY

Rob McIlveen and Richard Gross

Hodder & Stoughton

A MEMBER OF THE HODDER HEADLINE GROUP

British Library Cataloguing in Publication Data
A catalogue record for this title is available from The British Library

ISBN 0 340 69099 2

First published 1997
Impression number 10 9 8 7 6 5 4 3 2 1
Year 2002 2001 2000 1999 1998 1997

Typeset by Wearset, Boldon, Tyne and Wear.
Printed in Great Britain for Hodder & Stoughton Educational, a division of Hodder Headline Plc, 338 Euston Road, London NW1 3BH by Redwood Books, Trowbridge, Wilts.

CONTENTS

Part 3: Social behaviour and diversity in development

Part 4: Adolescence, adulthood and old age

PREFACE

Our aim in this book is to provide an introduction to the area of developmental psychology. In order to do this, we have divided the book into four parts. The first, *Early socialisation*, comprises three chapters. In Chapter 1, we look at the development of sociability and attachments, including a discussion of theories of the attachment process. In Chapter 2, we consider the short-term and long-term effects of deprivation (separation) and privation, and examine the extent to which the effects of extreme early privation can be reduced. Chapter 3 considers classifications of child-rearing, the possible effects of different child-rearing styles on children's development and similarities and differences between cultures in their child-rearing styles.

Part 2, *Cognitive development*, also comprises three chapters. Chapter 4 is devoted to Piaget's theory, which has probably been more influential than any other single theory of cognitive development. The application of Piaget's theory to education, together with discussion of three other influential theories of cognitive development and their application to education, makes up Chapter 5. Chapter 6 is concerned with the influence of genetic and environmental factors on the development of measured intelligence.

The third part of the book, *Social behaviour and diversity in development*, again consists of three chapters. Chapter 7 discusses theories of moral development including Freud's psychoanalytic theory, social learning theory and Kohlberg's cognitive-developmental theory. Chapter 8 deals with the development of gender, beginning with discussion of the relationship between sex and gender, then going on to consider a number of different theories of gender development. In Chapter 9, after identifying the major components of the self-concept, there is discussion of how the self-concept develops and theoretical approaches to the self.

Part 4, *Adolescence, adulthood and old age*, comprises four chapters. Chapter 10 is concerned with personality change and social development in adolescence, including the influential theory of Erik Erikson. Chapter 11 discusses theories of personality change in early and middle adulthood, while Chapter 12 considers the impact of critical life events (such as retirement, marriage and bereavement) in adulthood. Chapter 13 focuses on late adulthood or old age, with discussion of major theories of adjustment to this final period of the life cycle.

We believe that this book covers the major aspects of developmental psychology as it would be taught on most courses, including A level and undergraduate courses. While the sequence of chapters and much of the content is based on the revised AEB A level syllabus, the general issues and major theories that are discussed represent the core of this important and increasingly popular area of psychology. For the purposes of revision, we have included detailed summaries of the material that is presented in each chapter. Although we have not included a separate glossary, the Index contains page numbers in **bold** which refer to definitions and main explanations of particular concepts for easy reference.

DEDICATION

To my mother, and late father, for giving my development that crucial kick-start, to Jan, my wife, Tanya and Jo, my daughters, for helping me, in their different ways, to give and to receive love, crucial aspects of my continuing development.

R.G.

To Katie. Daddy's Wonderwall.

R.M.

ACKNOWLEDGEMENTS

Many thanks to Tim Gregson-Williams and Liz Lowther at Hodder & Stoughton for their (usual) patience, help and guidance. Liz, welcome aboard!

PART 1
Early socialisation

EARLY SOCIAL DEVELOPMENT

Introduction and overview

One of the most important challenges faced by human beings is learning to relate to other people. Normally, the first people with whom the new-born interacts are its parents. In early childhood, relationships are formed with brothers and/or sisters, and other children beyond the immediate family. As development continues, so the child's network of relationships increases, with teachers, classmates, neighbours and so on becoming an important part of social development.

Our aim in this chapter is to look at theories and research relating to the process of social development in the first years of life. We will concentrate on the processes of *sociability* and *attachment*, beginning the chapter by looking at what sociability and attachment are, how attachments develop and the factors that affect the quality of attachment between a caregiver and infant. However, the majority of this chapter will be devoted to a critical examination of the explanations that have been advanced to explain the attachment process.

What is sociability?

According to Buss and Plomin (1984), sociability refers to one of three dimensions of temperament (the others being emotionality and activity), which are taken to be present at birth and inherited. Specifically, sociability refers to the seeking of and being especially gratified by rewards from social interaction, preferring to be with others, sharing activities, being responsive to others and seeking responsiveness *from* others. Whilst babies differ in terms of their degree of sociability (it is a source of individual differences), it represents a general human tendency to want and seek the company of other human beings. As such, it can be regarded as a prerequisite for the development of attachments, and corresponds to the pre-attachment and indiscriminate attachment phases of the attachment process (see below).

What is attachment?

Kagan et al. (1978) have defined attachment as:

> 'an intense emotional relationship that is specific to two people, that endures over time, and in which prolonged separation from the partner is accompanied by stress and sorrow'.

Whilst Kagan and his colleagues' definition applies to the formation of an attachment at any point in the life cycle, the first attachment we form is widely accepted by psychologists as being crucial for healthy development since it acts as a *prototype* for all later relationships.

Attachment, then, can be seen as a close emotional bond that will last for many years. Although affectionate relationships may be established with any consistent caregiver, the most intense relationship that usually occurs in the early stages of development is between mother and child. As a result, most research interest has focused on that particular attachment.

STUDYING THE DEVELOPMENT OF ATTACHMENTS

One way in which attachment can be studied in the psychological laboratory was devised by Mary Ainsworth and her colleagues (e.g. 1971, 1978) and is called the *Strange Situation*. In this, an infant and its mother (and/or sometimes its father) are taken to an unfamiliar room in which the infant is free to explore while the mother sits passively. After three minutes, a female adult stranger enters the room. Following one minute of silence, the stranger speaks to the mother for one minute, and then approaches the infant. At this point, the mother leaves, and the stranger and infant are left alone for three minutes. The mother then returns and the stranger leaves. After the mother has tried to resettle the baby, she leaves again and the baby is left alone in the room. After about three minutes, the stranger returns and begins to interact with the baby. When a further three minutes (or less) have elapsed, the mother returns and the stranger leaves unobtrusively. In all, there are eight increasingly stressful episodes. The episodes may be curtailed (if the baby is unduly distressed) or prolonged (if more time is needed for the baby to become reinvolved in play). The Strange Situation and the eight episodes, which are the same for all children, are shown in Figure 1.1 and Table 1.1.

Research has shown that the attachment process can be divided into a number of *phases*. The first or *pre-attachment phase* lasts until about three months of age. From about six weeks, babies develop an attraction to other human beings in preference to inanimate features of the environment. At about six weeks, the infant engages in behaviours such as nestling, gurgling and smiling which are directed to just about anyone (indeed, for this reason, smiling is referred to as the *social smile*).

At about three months, infants begin to distinguish between people and can tell the difference between familiar and unfamiliar people (Maurer and Salapatek, 1976). Although the social smile disappears, the infant will allow strangers to handle and look after it without becoming noticeably distressed, provided that the stranger gives adequate care. This phase, which lasts until the age of seven months or so, is called the *indiscriminate attachment phase* or, to use Ainsworth's (1985) term, the *attachment-in-the-making phase*.

From around seven months, infants begin to develop specific attachments and actively seek the proximity of certain people (particularly the mother). They become distressed when separated, a distress which is termed *separation anxiety*. This *discriminate attachment phase* occurs when the infant can reliably distinguish its mother from other people and has developed *object permanence*, that is, the awareness that things continue to exist even when they cannot be seen (see Chapter 4, page 42). At around seven or eight months, the baby avoids proximity with unfamiliar people and some, though not all, infants display the *fear of strangers response* (Schaffer, 1966), which includes crying and/or trying to move away. Note that the fear response is not elicited by the simple physical presence of strangers. Typically, it will be elicited only by direct contact with a stranger.

From about nine months onwards, the child becomes increasingly independent from its caregiver. This is called the *multiple attachments phase*, and strong additional bonds are formed with other major caregivers (such as the father, grandparents and siblings) and with peers. Although the fear of strangers response typically diminishes, the strongest attachment continues to be the discriminate attachment subject of the previous phase. Figure 1.2 (page 4) summarises the major milestones in the social development of infants.

The quality of attachment

Using the Strange Situation, Ainsworth et al. (1978) discovered that infants form one of three basic attachments to the mother. The crucial feature determining the quality of attachment is the mother's *sensitivity*. Sensitive and insensitive mothers differ in terms of the ways in which they respond to their babies' needs. The sensitive mother sees things from her baby's perspective, correctly interprets its signals, responds to its needs, and is accepting, co-operative and accessible. By contrast, the insensitive mother interacts almost exclusively in terms of her own wishes, moods and activities. Ainsworth and her colleagues' research indicated that sensitive mothers have babies that are *securely attached* whereas insensitive mothers have *insecurely attached* babies. The insecurely attached babies fell into one of two categories. Some were *anxious-avoidant* (or *detached*) whilst others were *anxious-resistant* (or *ambivalent*). The typical behaviours of these three types of baby are shown in Table 1.2 (page 5).

Figure 1.1 The 'Strange Situation' devised by Mary Ainsworth and her colleagues

Table 1.1 The eight episodes in the 'Strange Situation'

Episode	Persons Present	Duration	Brief Description
1	Mother, baby and observer	30 seconds	Observer introduces mother and baby to experimental room, then leaves.
2	Mother and baby	3 minutes	Mother is non-participant while baby explores; if necessary, play is stimulated after 2 minutes.
3	Stranger, mother and baby	3 minutes	Stranger enters. First minute: stranger silent. Second minute: stranger converses with mother. Third minute: stranger approaches baby. After 3 minutes, mother leaves unobtrusively.
4	Stranger and baby	3 minutes or less*	First separation episode. Stranger's behaviour is geared to that of baby.
5	Mother and baby	3 minutes or more†	First reunion episode. Mother greets and/or comforts baby, then tries to settle the baby again in play. Mother then leaves, saying 'bye-bye'.
6	Baby alone	3 minutes or less	Second separation episode.
7	Stranger and baby	3 minutes or less	Continuation of second separation. Stranger enters and gears her behaviour to that of baby.
8	Mother and baby	3 minutes	Second reunion episode. Mother enters, greets baby, then picks up baby. Meanwhile, stranger leaves unobtrusively.

* Episode is curtailed if the baby is unduly distressed.
† Episode is prolonged if more time is required for the baby to become reinvolved in play.

(based on Ainsworth et al., 1978, and taken from Krebs and Blackman, 1988)

Ainsworth et al.'s findings have been challenged by some researchers. Vaughn et al. (1980), for example, have shown that attachment type may change depending on variations in the family's circumstances, suggesting that attachment types are not necessarily permanent characteristics. Other researchers have proposed that *innate differences* between babies could also explain differences in the quality of attachment. Asher (1987), for example, has proposed that some human (and non-human) infants are more intense and anxious than others. According to Larsen and Diener (1987), such differences in *temperament* apparently persist into young adulthood at least. Accounting for such temperamental differences is difficult; however, it could be that a *reactive sympathetic nervous system* might be responsible for them (Kagan, 1989).

It has also been claimed that there are attachment types other than those proposed by Ainsworth and her colleagues. Main (1991), for example, has proposed the existence of an *insecure-disorganised/disoriented* attachment type (or Type D). This term refers to a baby that acts as if the attachment figure (as well as the environment) is fear-inducing. To increase attachment behaviour, the baby must seek closer proximity to one of its sources of fear (namely the attachment figure). This,

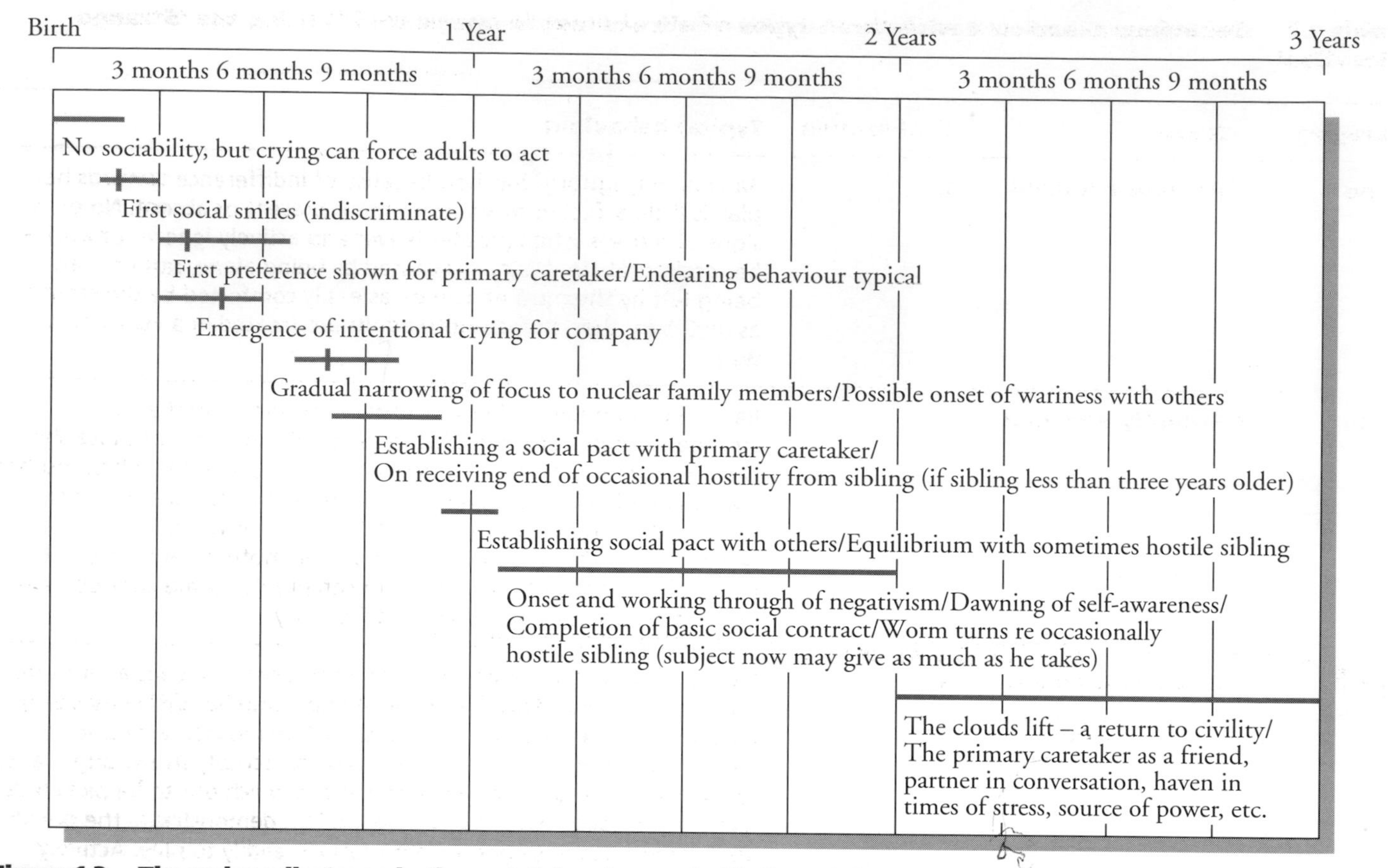

Figure 1.2 The major milestones in the social development of infants (after White, 1985, and taken from Houston et al., 1989)

argues Main, produces a conflict between seeking and avoiding proximity which are, of course, incompatible behaviours. We should also note that cross-cultural research suggests that there are marked differences in the distributions of Ainsworth et al.'s three types of attachment (see, for example, Takahashi, 1990). Although Type B appears to be universally the most common, Type A is relatively more common in Western European countries, whereas Type C is more common in Israel and Japan.

Despite the various empirical, methodological and ethical criticisms that have been made of Ainsworth and her colleagues' research (see, for example, Durkin, 1995), their Strange Situation is generally considered to be a powerful and useful procedure for studying socioemotional development in infancy (Lamb et al., 1985). Indeed, there is evidence to suggest that secure attachment appears to *predict* future social competence. Sroufe et al. (1983), for example, found that securely attached infants at 12 to 18 months functioned more confidently at age two to five, in that they were enthusiastic and persistent when given challenging tasks. They were also more outgoing and responsive with other children, suggesting that they had developed what Erikson (1963) has termed a sense of *basic trust* (see page 125). Additionally, Bretherton (1985) found that three- to five-year-old children with insecure attachments found it difficult to get on with other children in nursery school and were often hostile, isolated and socially inept.

HOW ATTACHMENT FORMS: THEORIES OF THE ATTACHMENT PROCESS

'Cupboard love' theories of attachment

According to psychoanalytic accounts of attachment, infants become attached to their caregivers (usually the mother) because of the caregiver's ability to satisfy *instinctual needs*. For Freud (1926):

> 'the reason why the infant in arms wants to perceive the presence of its mother is only because it already knows by experience that she satisfies all its needs without delay'.

Table 1.2 Behaviour associated with three types of attachment in one-year-olds using the 'Strange Situation'

Category	Name	% of sample	Typical behaviour
Type A	**Anxious-avoidant**	15	Baby largely ignores mother, because of indifference towards her: play is little affected by whether she is present or absent. No or few signs of distress when mother leaves and actively ignores or avoids her on her return. Distress is caused by being alone, rather than being left by the mother; can be as easily comforted by the stranger as by the mother. In fact, both adults are treated in a very similar way.
Type B	**Securely attached**	70	Baby plays happily while the mother is present, whether the stranger is present or not. Mother is largely 'ignored' because she can be trusted to be there if needed. Clearly distressed when mother leaves and play is considerably reduced. Seeks immediate contact with mother on her return, is quickly calmed down in her arms and resumes play. The distress is caused by the mother's absence, not being alone. Although the stranger can provide some comfort, she and the mother are treated very differently.
Type C	**Anxious-resistant**	15	Baby is fussy and wary while the mother is present; cries a lot more and explores much less than types A and B and has difficulty using mother as a safe base. Very distressed when mother leaves, seeks contact with her on her return, but simultaneously shows anger and resists contact; e.g. may approach her and reach out to be picked up, but then struggles to get down again. This demonstrates the baby's ambivalence towards her. Doesn't return readily to play. Actively resists stranger's efforts to make contact.

(based on Ainsworth et al., 1978, and taken from Gross, 1996)

Freud believed that healthy attachments are formed when feeding practices satisfy the infant's needs for food, security and oral sexual gratification. Unhealthy attachments are held to occur when infants are *deprived* of food and oral pleasure or are *overindulged*. As a result, psychoanalytic accounts of attachment emphasise the significance of feeding practices, especially breast-feeding, and the importance of the *maternal figure* whose status Freud saw as being:

> 'unique, without parallel, (and) established unilaterally for a whole lifetime as the first and strongest love-object . . . the prototype of all later love-reactions'.

The behaviourist view of attachment also sees infants as becoming attached to those who satisfy their need for nourishment and tend to their other physiological needs (and note that this a very rare example of agreement between the psychoanalytic and behaviourist perspectives!). Infants associate their caregivers (who act as *conditioned reinforcers*) with gratification, and they learn to approach them in order to have their needs satisfied. This eventually *generalises* into a feeling of security whenever the caregiver is present.

However, neither the behaviourist nor the psychoanalytic account of attachment as 'cupboard love' is likely to be true, as was demonstrated in a series of experiments conducted by Harry Harlow and his associates (e.g. Harlow, 1959; Harlow and Zimmerman, 1959). Harlow was actually interested in learning in rhesus monkeys and, in order to control for experience and to prevent the spread of disease, he separated new-born monkeys from their mothers and raised them in individual cages. Each cage contained a 'baby blanket', and Harlow found that the monkeys became intensely attached to the blankets and showed great distress when the blankets were taken away to be laundered. The fact that the monkeys appeared to have formed an attachment to their blankets, and displayed behaviours comparable to those of infant monkeys actually separated from their mothers, appeared to contradict the view that attachment comes from an association with nourishment.

In order to determine whether food or the close comfort of a blanket was more important, Harlow placed infant rhesus monkeys in cages with two 'surrogate mothers'. In one experiment, one of the surrogate mothers was made from wire and had a baby bottle attached to 'her'. The other surrogate mother was made from soft and cuddly terry cloth but did not have a bottle attached to 'her'. Harlow reported that the infants spent most of their time clinging to the cloth mother, even though there was no nourishment to be gained from 'her'. On the basis of this finding, Harlow concluded that monkeys (at least) have an unlearned need for *contact comfort* which is as basic as the need for food.

The surrogate mother made of terry cloth also served as a 'secure base' from which the infants could explore their environment. When novel stimuli were placed in the cage, the infants would gradually move away from the 'mother' for initial exploration, often returning to 'her' before exploring further. When 'fear stimuli', such as an oversized wooden insect or a toy bear loudly beating a drum, were placed in the cage, the infants would cling to the cloth mother for security before exploring the stimuli. However, when the infants were alone or were with the wire surrogate mother, they would either 'freeze' and cower in fear or run aimlessly around the cage. Figure 1.3 (a–c) shows some of the behaviours exhibited by the infant monkeys in Harlow's experiments.

Later research showed that when the cloth 'mother' had other qualities such as rocking, being warm and feeding, the attachment was even stronger (Harlow and Suomi, 1970). There are clearly parallels between Harlow's experimental manipulations and what often happens when human infants have contact with warm-bodied parents who rock, cuddle and feed them.

Although it is clear that attachment does not depend on feeding alone, the rhesus monkeys reared exclusively with their cloth 'mothers' did *not* develop normally. As adults, they were extremely aggressive, rarely interacted with other monkeys, made inappropriate sexual responses, and were difficult (if not impossible) to breed. In monkeys, at least, then, normal development would seem to depend on other factors as well. Harlow and Suomi's (1970) research indicates that one of these factors is interaction with other members of the species during the first six months of life.

Research on attachment in humans also casts doubt on 'cupboard love' theories. In a longitudinal study of Scottish infants, Schaffer and Emerson (1964) found that infants *do* become attached to people who do not perform caregiving activities. For Schaffer (1971), 'cupboard love' theories of attachment see infants as passive recipients of nutrition rather than active seekers of stimulation. In Schaffer's view, babies do not 'live to eat', but rather they 'eat to live'.

Ethological theories of attachment

The concept and label of attachment were actually introduced to psychology by *ethologists*, that is, students of the behaviour of non-human animals in their natural environments. In a series of classic experiments, Lorenz (1935) showed that some non-humans form a strong bond with the first moving object they encounter (which is usually, but not always, as Lorenz himself showed, the mother). In the case of *precocial species* (that is, species in which the newborn is capable of locomotion and possesses well-developed sense organs), the mobile young animal needs to learn rapidly to recognise its caregivers and to stay close to them. Lorenz called this phenomenon *imprinting* and, since it occurs through mere exposure without any feeding taking place, it too casts doubt on the plausibility of 'cupboard love' theories of attachment, at least in non-humans.

The response of following a moving object indicates that a bond has been formed between the infant and the individual or object on which it has been imprinted. Ethologists see imprinting as an example of a *fixed-action pattern* of behaviour which occurs in the presence of a species-specific releasing stimulus (also known as a *sign stimulus*). Lorenz saw imprinting as being unique because he believed that it only occurred during a brief *critical period* of life and, once it had occurred, was irreversible. Figure 1.5 (page 8) shows the relationship between imprinting and the critical period. Support for this comes from the finding that when animals that have imprinted on members of other species reach sexual maturity, they may show a sexual preference for members of the species on which they have imprinted (Krebs and Blackman, 1988).

Bornstein (1989) has defined a critical period as a restricted time period during which certain events must take place if correct development is to occur. Lorenz saw imprinting as being genetically 'switched on' and then 'switched off' at the end of the critical period, and

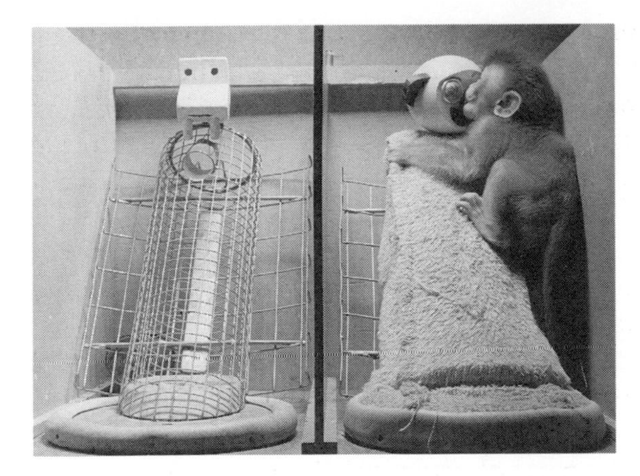

Figure 1.3 Behaviours exhibited by infant monkeys in Harlow's experiments

(a) Even when the wire monkey is the sole source of nourishment, infant monkeys showed a marked preference for the terry-cloth 'mother'

(b) Infant monkeys frightened by a novel stimulus (in this case a toy teddy bear banging a drum) retreat to the terry cloth-covered 'mother' rather than to the wire 'mother'

(c) When placed in strange situations without their surrogate mothers, infant monkeys displayed intense fear reponses

Figure 1.4 Konrad Lorenz with one of the greylag geese which, as a gosling, had become imprinted on him

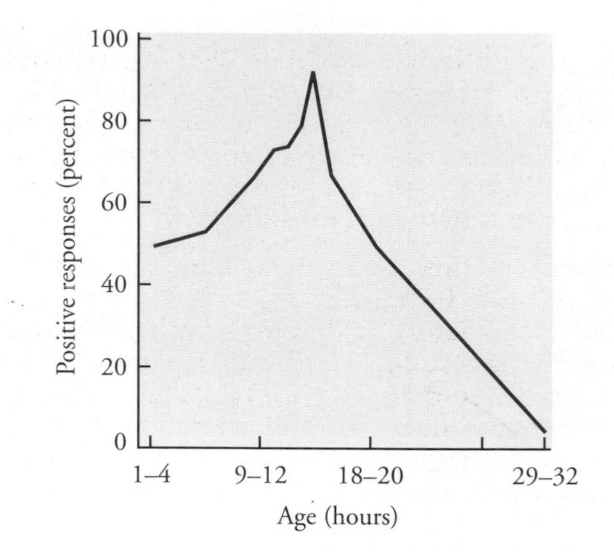

Figure 1.5 The graph represents the relationship between imprinting and the age (hours after hatching) at which a duckling was exposed to a moving model of a male duck. Imprinting was measured in terms of the percentage of trials on which the duckling followed the model on a later test. Imprinting reached a peak at between 12 and 17 hours after hatching (adapted from E.H. Hess, 'Imprinting in animals'. Copyright © 1958 by Scientific American, Inc. All rights reserved.)

research shows that in some animals the critical period appears to be bounded by the age at which they are first able to move and the age at which they develop a fear of strangers. However, the view that the critical period is under genetic control has been disputed by studies which show that the period of imprintability can be extended (e.g. Sluckin, 1965). This has led researchers to talk about imprinting in terms of there being a *sensitive period*, that is, one in which learning is most likely to happen and will happen most easily, but which is not absolutely critical. We should also note that imprinting *can* be reversed (at least in the laboratory). Imprinting of the sort that occurs in geese, for example, clearly does not occur in humans since new-born children separated from their mothers will not attach to a mannikin. Moreover, as we noted on page 2, not all children develop a fear of strangers and, when they do, it appears *before* they are capable of independent movement.

Bowlby's theory of attachment

The most comprehensive theory of attachment formation is that offered by John Bowlby. Bowlby was influenced by ethological theory in general and Lorenz's concept of imprinting in particular. In his books *Child Care and the Growth of Love* (1953) and *Attachment and Loss* (1969, 1973, 1980), Bowlby argued that because the new-born human infant is entirely helpless at birth, babies are *genetically programmed* to behave towards their mothers in ways that ensure their survival. The important *species-specific* behaviours displayed by babies are shown in Box 1.1.

Box 1.1 The important ways in which infants shape and control the behaviour of their caregivers

Sucking: Whilst sucking is important to obtain nourishment, not all sucking is nutritive (Piaget, 1952). Non-nutritive sucking, which is also seen in non-humans, appears to be an innate tendency which inhibits a new-born's distress. In Western societies, babies are often given 'soothers' to pacify them when they are distressed.

Cuddling: Human infants adjust their posture to mould themselves to the contour of the parent's body. The reflexive response that encourages front-to-front contact with the mother plays an important part in reinforcing the caregiver's behaviour. The importance of close physical contact was clearly demonstrated by Harry Harlow, whose work is described on pages 5–6.

Looking: Looking serves as a signal to parents. When parents do not respond to an infant's eye contact, the infant usually shows signs of distress (Tronick et al., 1978). The looking behaviour of an infant thus acts as an invitation for the mother to respond. If she does not, the infant is disturbed and avoids further visual contact. Mutual gazing, by contrast, is rewarding for the infant (Stern, 1977).

Smiling: Smiling appears to be an innate behaviour, since babies can produce smiles shortly after birth. Infant smiles are very rewarding for adults, who view the smiling infant as a 'real person'.

Crying: Young infants usually cry only when they are hungry, cold or in pain. In such circumstances, crying is most effectively terminated by picking up and cuddling the infant. Caregivers who respond quickly to crying during the first three months tend to have babies that cry *less* during the last four months of their first year than infants with unresponsive caregivers (Bell and Ainsworth, 1972). Thus, babies with responsive caregivers learn to cry only when they need attention from their caregiver. Moreover, such infants learn to communicate effectively by means of behaviour other than crying (e.g. gestures and pre-speech sounds).

(adapted from Carlson, 1988)

Bowlby argued that the baby's mother also inherits a genetic blueprint which programmes her to respond to the child. The result of these genetic programmes is attachment. Bowlby argued for the existence of a critical period during which the *synchrony* of action between mother and infant produces an attachment. In Bowlby's (1951) view, mothering is almost useless if delayed until after two and a half to three years for all children and useless for most children if delayed until after 12 months. Once the attachment between mother and baby has been formed, it activates an internal system that regulates how far away from the mother the child will move and the amount of fear the child will show towards strangers (Krebs and Blackman, 1988). For Bowlby (1969):

'No form of behaviour is accompanied by stronger feelings than is attachment behaviour. Infants greet those with whom they are attached with joy, and become anxious, angry and sorrowful when they leave or threaten to leave'.

According to Bowlby (1969), infants display a strong innate tendency to become attached to one particular individual, a tendency he termed *monotropy*, an attachment that is *qualitatively* different from any subsequent attachments. As he wrote in 1951, the relationship with the mother is different in kind from that of relationships with others, and:

'mother love in infancy is as important for mental health as are vitamins and proteins for physical health'.

Bowlby's theory has attracted much research interest. As we will see in the following chapter, his view that there is a critical period for the development of attachment is almost certainly untrue. The evidence also suggests that a related view, the existence of a *maternal-sensitive* period during which mother-child bonding is most likely to occur, is also unlikely to be true, at least in humans. The idea that there might be a maternal-sensitive period was first proposed by Klaus and Kennell (1976). According to them, if the infant was taken away from the mother during the maternal-sensitive period, a period which they believed might be governed by the release of maternal hormones, bonding between the mother and infant would not occur.

Klaus and Kennell's *extended contact hypothesis* suggested that mothers who had large amounts of contact with their newborns were more likely to cuddle, soothe and enjoy their babies than were mothers who had only brief periods of contact. Although there were several methodological flaws in Klaus and Kennell's research (see Myers, 1984, for a review), their views were influential in changing hospital practices: prior to the publication of Klaus and Kennell's findings, most hospitals tended to separate new-borns from their mothers after delivery. Research has shown, however, that 'bonding' can take place if mothers see their babies one day or even several months after birth (Durkin, 1995). Moreover, Lamb (1976) has suggested that the father's caregiving can be just as effective as that of the mother, and there seems to be little difference in the way children form attachments to their mothers and fathers despite the absence of what Parke and Swain (1980) have called 'bonding hormones' (see also Box 1.2).

Bowlby's views on monotropy have also been the subject of much criticism, with several lines of evidence casting doubt on his claims. For example, Rutter (1981) has reported that several indicators of attachment can be shown for a variety of attachment figures other than the mother. Although Bowlby did not dispute the formation of *multiple attachments*, he saw attachment to the mother as being unique in that it is the first to appear and the strongest of all. Research conducted by Schaffer and Emerson (1964), however, disputes this. They showed that whilst not all the child's attachments are of equal strength, multiple attachments seem to be the rule rather than the exception to the rule, and that the mother is not always or necessarily the main attachment figure.

In Bowlby's view, the father is of no direct emotional significance to the young infant, but only of indirect value as an emotional and economic support for the mother. Whilst, as contemporary sociobiology suggests, mothers may have a greater *parental investment* in their offspring and hence are better prepared for child rearing and attachment (Kenrick, 1994), Bowlby's views on fathers as attachment figures are disputed by the findings of several studies, including that conducted by Lamb (see above). Box 1.2 summarises some of the other findings that have been reported.

Figure 1.6 According to Bowlby, the father is of no direct emotional significance to the infant/young child. But the evidence suggests that fathers are capable of caregiving which is comparable to that of mothers – both in quantity and in quality

Box 1.2 The father-child bond

- Many fathers form close bonds with their offspring shortly after the offspring's birth (Greenberg and Morris, 1974).
- Some 12-month-old (or older) infants are equally or more attached to the father than the mother (Kotelchuck, 1976).
- Fathers tend to spend less time with their children than mothers. The time they do spend is typically related to play rather than to care (Easterbrooks and Goldberg, 1984).
- When fathers become primary caregivers, they interact with their infants in the nurturing, gentle fashion which is more typical of mothers (Field, 1978).
- In general, whilst there may be differences in the style of interaction, there are no differences in the quantity or even quality of mothers' and fathers' caregiving (Yogman et al., 1977).

(adapted from Crooks and Stein, 1991)

On the basis of the various findings concerning the role played by the father in the attachment process, Parke (1981) has suggested that:

> 'both mother and father are important attachment objects for their infants, but the circumstances that lead to selecting mum or dad may differ'.

As Box 1.2 shows, rather than being a poor substitute for a mother, the father makes his own unique contribution to the care and development of infants and young children.

Cognitive-developmental accounts of attachment

Instead of looking at attachment in terms of the emotional bonds it involves, cognitive-developmental theorists emphasise the *cognitive* relationships between parents and offspring. According to Krebs and Blackman (1988), cognitive-developmental theory focuses on the ability of the infant to distinguish between itself and others. Once that ability has been acquired, cognitive-developmental theorists look at the ability of the infant to distinguish between strangers and primary caregivers. Cognitive-developmental theorists are also interested in the ways in which caregivers stimulate the infant's *growth of knowledge*.

Schaffer's (1971) research is fundamentally cognitive-developmental in nature, since it shows that infants only become attached to a specific individual when they are able to distinguish that person from other people. For cognitive-developmental theorists, infants become attached to their caregivers because they provide the most interesting, informative and cognitively challenging events in their lives (Krebs and Blackman, 1988). The satisfaction the infant derives from securing an attachment can thus be explained in terms of its growing sense of competence and mastery as well as the effective mutual stimulation of caregiver and infant. Rather than being due to the satisfaction of instinctual needs, then, cognitive-developmental theorists see attachment as coming from the development of increasingly organised and integrated conceptions of the social world.

Conclusions

In this chapter, we have looked at theories and research relating to the process of social development in the first years of life. Our discussion has largely concerned the process of attachment, and we have reviewed several theories which seek to explain this process. Each theory focuses on a particular aspect of attachment, with some emphasising innate factors and others emphasising learning. The evidence suggests that no one theory is correct, and that all of the factors the various theories identify are implicated in the attachment process.

Summary

- Learning to relate to other people represents one of the most important challenges human beings face. From birth onwards, the individual's network of relationships expands.
- **Sociability** and **attachment** represent two major aspects of social development.
- **Sociability** refers to one dimension of temperament, namely the general human tendency to want/seek the company of other human beings. It is an innate source of individual differences and can be regarded as a prerequisite for the development of attachments.
- An **attachment** is an intense emotional relationship, specific to two people, that endures over time, and in which prolonged separation from the partner is accompanied by stress and sorrow. Our earliest attachment is crucial for healthy development since it acts as a **prototype** for all later relationships. The child's most intense early attachment is usually with its mother, and that is where most research interest has concentrated.
- Ainsworth et al. devised the **Strange Situation** as a method for studying attachment in the laboratory. This comprises a series of eight pre-determined episodes, each lasting about three minutes, involving an infant, its mother (and/or sometimes its father) and a female adult stranger, in an unfamiliar room. The episodes become increasingly stressful. The episodes may be shortened or prolonged, depending on the baby's reaction.
- The attachment process can be divided into a number of **phases**. In the **pre-attachment phase** (six weeks to three months), babies develop a preference for other human beings over inanimate objects, as shown through their nestling/gurgling/**social smiling**.
- During the **indiscriminate attachment/attachment-in-the-making phase** (three to seven months), infants distinguish between familiar and unfamiliar people. They allow strangers to handle and care for them without becoming obviously distressed, provided the care is adequate.
- During the **discriminate attachment phase** (seven to nine months), infants begin to develop specific attachments and actively seek the proximity of certain people (especially the mother). This is based on the ability to reliably distinguish the mother from other people and on **object permanence**. While all babies display **separation anxiety**, only some will display the **fear of strangers response**, which is typically only triggered by direct contact with a stranger.
- During the **multiple attachments phase** (nine months onwards), the child becomes increasingly

independent of its caregiver and forms strong additional attachments with other major caregivers. However, the strongest attachment remains the discriminate attachment figure of the previous phase.

- Using the Strange Situation, Ainsworth et al. found differences in the **quality of attachment** of infants to their mother, with the mother's **sensitivity** being the crucial determining factor. The sensitive mother sees things from her baby's perspective and tends to have a **securely attached** baby, while the insensitive mother interacts almost exclusively in terms of her own wishes/moods/activities and tends to have an **insecurely attached** baby.
- **Insecurely attached** babies are either **anxious-avoidant/detached (Type A)**, largely ignoring the mother out of indifference towards her, their play affected little by her presence or absence, or **anxious-resistant/ambivalent (Type C)**, fussy and wary while the mother is present, very distressed when she leaves, seeking contact with her on her return but simultaneously showing anger and resisting contact.
- While the **securely attached (Type B)** baby uses the mother as a safe base and is distressed by her absence, the anxious-avoidant baby is distressed by being alone. The anxious-resistant baby has difficulty using the mother as a safe base and explores much less than the other two types.
- There is evidence that attachment type may change if the family's circumstances change, suggesting that attachment types are not necessarily fixed characteristics. There may also be **innate differences** in **temperament** between babies, which could account for differences in the quality of attachment and which could persist at least into young adulthood.
- Main has found evidence of an **insecure-disorganised/disoriented (Type D)** attachment type, in which the baby acts as if the attachment figure/the environment is fear-inducing. This creates a conflict between seeking and avoiding proximity with the attachment figure.
- Cross-cultural research suggests that while Type B appears to be universally the most common, Type A is relatively more common in Western European countries, while Type C is more common in Israel and Japan.
- Despite the various criticisms made of Ainsworth et al.'s research, the Strange Situation is generally considered to be a powerful and useful procedure for studying socioemotional development in infancy. Secure attachment seems to **predict** future social competence, corresponding to Erikson's **basic trust**. Insecurely attached children are often hostile/isolated/socially inept.
- According to Freud's psychoanalytic theory, infants become attached to their mother because she satisfies their **instinctual needs**. Healthy attachments depend on feeding practices (in particular breast-feeding) satisfying the infant's need for food/security/oral sexual gratification, while unhealthy attachments occur when infants are **deprived** of these or **overindulged**. The **maternal figure** is the first and strongest love-object, the prototype of all later love relationships.
- Behaviourists also see infants as becoming attached to those who satisfy their needs for food/other physiological needs. Caregivers act as **conditioned reinforcers** who become associated with gratification; this **generalises** into a feeling of security whenever the caregiver is present.
- Both the psychoanalytic and behaviourist accounts are **'cupboard love' theories**. The limitation of such theories was demonstrated by Harlow in a series of experiments involving rhesus monkeys.
- In one experiment, newborn monkeys separated from their mothers were placed in individual cages with two 'surrogate mothers', one of which was made from wire and fitted with a baby bottle, the other made from soft/cuddly terry cloth but with no bottle. The babies spent most of their time clinging to the cloth mother, which led Harlow to conclude that monkeys have an unlearnt need for **contact comfort** which is as basic as the need for food.
- The cloth mother also served as a secure base from which the infants could explore their environment, providing security when faced with novel or fear stimuli.
- When the cloth mother rocked, was warm and provided food, the attachment was even stronger. This has parallels with human infants' contact with warm-bodied parents who rock/cuddle/feed them.
- The rhesus monkeys reared exclusively with cloth mothers became very aggressive adults, rarely interacting with other monkeys and difficult/impossible to breed. It appears that interaction with other monkeys during the first six months is necessary for normal development.
- Schaffer and Emerson's longitudinal study of Scottish infants found that infants become attached to people who do not perform caretaking functions, casting doubt on 'cupboard love' theories, which see infants as passive recipients of food rather than active seekers of stimulation.

- It was **ethologists** who introduced the term **attachment** into psychology. Lorenz showed that some non-human animals form a strong bond with the first moving object they encounter (usually the mother). The young of **precocial species** need to learn quickly to recognise their caretakers and to stay close to them, a process called **imprinting**. This occurs through mere exposure without any feeding taking place, again casting doubt on 'cupboard love' theories.
- The following response indicates that a bond has been formed between the infant and the individual/object on which it has been imprinted. Imprinting is an example of a **fixed-action pattern** which occurs in response to a species-specific releasing stimulus/**sign stimulus**. It only occurs during a brief **critical period** and is irreversible.
- According to Lorenz, imprinting is genetically 'switched on' and then 'switched off' at the end of the critical period. However, studies showing that imprintability can be extended suggest that imprinting involves a **sensitive period** in which learning is most likely to happen/will happen most easily, but which is not absolutely critical. Also, imprinting can be reversed and the kind of imprinting that occurs in geese clearly does not occur in humans.
- Bowlby's theory of attachment was influenced by ethological theory, especially Lorenz's concept of imprinting. Babies are **genetically programmed** to shape/control the behaviour of their caregivers in **species-specific** ways that ensure their survival, in particular sucking/cuddling/looking/smiling/crying.
- According to Bowlby, the mother also inherits a genetic blueprint which programmes her to respond to the baby, and there is a critical period during which the **synchrony** of the mother and baby's behaviour produces an attachment. This period lasts up to two and a half to three years for all children and up to 12 months for most children. Once the attachment has been formed, it activates an internal system that regulates proximity to the mother and fear of strangers.
- According to Bowlby, infants display a strong innate tendency to become attached to one particular person (**monotropy**) and the attachment to the mother is **qualitatively** different from any subsequent attachments.
- Bowlby's claim regarding a critical period is almost certainly untrue, as is the related claim regarding the existence of a **maternal-sensitive** period for the development of the mother's bond to the baby. This was first proposed by Klaus and Kennell in their **extended contact hypothesis**.
- Klaus and Kennell's views influenced hospital practices, whereby newborns used to be separated from their mothers after delivery. However, bonding can occur even if mothers first see their babies several months after birth.
- According to Lamb, the father's caregiving can be just as effective as the mother's, and there is little difference in how children form attachments to both parents, despite the fathers' lack of 'bonding hormones'.
- According to Rutter, several indicators of attachment can be shown for a variety of attachment figures other than the mother. While not disputing the formation of **multiple attachments**, Bowlby saw attachment to the mother as unique. Schaffer and Emerson's research showed that, although not all the child's attachments are of equal strength, multiple attachments seem to be the rule and the mother is not always/necessarily the main attachment figure.
- Bowlby sees the father as having only indirect emotional significance for the infant. While sociobiology sees the mother as having greater **parental investment** in her offspring, studies have shown that some 12-month-olds (or older) are equally or more attached to the father than the mother and, when fathers are the primary caregivers, they interact with their infants in a 'maternal' way and to the same degree as mothers do. These findings suggest that the father is an important attachment figure in his own right.
- **Cognitive-developmental** theorists emphasise the **cognitive** as opposed to the emotional relationships between parents and offspring, such as the ability of the infant to distinguish between itself and others, which is required for the ability to distinguish between strangers and primary caregivers. These theories are also interested in how caregivers stimulate the infant's **growth of knowledge**.
- Schaffer has shown that infants only become attached to a specific individual when they are able to distinguish the person from others. Caregivers provide the infant with the most cognitively challenging events in their lives; attachments stem from the satisfaction derived from a growing sense of competence/mastery/understanding of the social world, rather than from satisfaction of instinctual needs.

THE EFFECTS OF EARLY DEPRIVATION

Introduction and overview

In the previous chapter, we described the research conducted by Harry Harlow and his colleagues on infant rhesus monkeys. The original purpose of the experiments was to explore the claim made by 'cupboard love' theories of attachment that the provision of nutrition is a crucial element in the formation of attachments. As well as dispelling 'cupboard love' theories, Harlow's research also provided information about the effects on infant rhesus monkeys of being raised without a real mother. As we noted in the previous chapter, the monkeys in Harlow's experiments did not appear to develop normally as a result of their experiences. For example, when the females reached maturity, most of them rejected the advances of male monkeys and only four out of 18 females conceived as a result of natural insemination. Those who produced offspring either rejected their young, by pushing them away, or behaved in an 'indifferent' way towards them.

The interesting question that arises from Harlow's research concerns the effects that being deprived of nurturing caregivers has on *humans* and whether any effects that do occur are permanent. Our aim in this chapter is to consider critically research into the effects and permanence of certain types of deprivation in human children.

Bowlby's maternal deprivation hypothesis

As we saw in the previous chapter, Bowlby argued for the existence of a critical period in the formation of attachments. This, along with his theory of monotropy, led him to claim that attachment between mother and infant could not be broken in the first few years of life without serious and permanent damage to social, emotional and intellectual development. For Bowlby (1951):

> 'an infant and young child should experience a warm, intimate and continuous relationship with his mother (or permanent mother figure) in which both find satisfaction and enjoyment'.

Bowlby's maternal deprivation hypothesis was based largely on studies conducted in the 1930s and 1940s of children brought up in residential nurseries and other large institutions (such as orphanages). The findings of some of these early studies are briefly described in Box 2.1.

Box 2.1 Some early research findings on the effects of institutionalisation

Goldfarb (1943): Fifteen children raised in institutions from about six months until three and a half years of age were matched according to genetic factors and mothers' education and occupational status with 15 children who had gone straight from their mothers to a foster home. The institutionalised children lived 'in almost complete social isolation during the first year of life'.

Tests showed that at age three, the institutionalised group were behind the fostered group on measures of abstract thinking, social maturity, rule-following and sociability. Later testing, between the ages of ten and 14, showed that the institutionalised group continued to perform more poorly on the various tests. Additionally, their average IQ was 72 as compared with 95 for the fostered group. Although the children were not assigned randomly to the institutionalised and fostered 'conditions', with the result that important differences could account for the findings, Goldfarb concluded that *all* the poorer abilities of the institutionalised children could be attributed to the time spent in the institutions.

Spitz (1945, 1946) and Spitz and Wolf (1946): These studies focused on the *emotional* effects of institutionalisation. Spitz found that in some very poor South American orphanages, the orphans received only minimal attention from the staff. The orphans were apathetic and displayed *ana-*

clitic depression, a severe disturbance involving such symptoms as a poor appetite and morbidity. After three months of unbroken deprivation, recovery is rarely, if ever, complete. Spitz also believed that *hospitalism*, a similar set of symptoms involving physical and mental deterioration, was caused by separation from the mother as a result of long-term hospitalisation. In their study of 91 orphanage infants in the United States and Canada, Spitz and Wolf found that over one-third died before reaching their first birthday, despite good nutrition and medical care.

Unfortunately, neither Bowlby nor the researchers whose findings are described in Box 2.1 recognised that the *understimulating nature* of the institutional environment as well as (or instead of) the absence of maternal care could be responsible for the effects observed in the children. As Rutter (1981) has noted, in order to implicate *maternal deprivation* in developmental retardation, it is necessary to disentangle the different *types* of deprivation and the different kinds of retardation they produce.

Rutter has also pointed out that Bowlby's use of the term 'deprivation' covers 'a most heterogenous range of experiences and outcomes due to quite disparate mechanisms'. By this, Rutter means that Bowlby failed to distinguish between the effects of being separated from an attachment figure and the effects of never having formed an attachment at all. Deprivation (de-privation) is properly used to describe the *loss* through separation of the maternal attachment, and Bowlby's theory and research were mainly concerned with this aspect. In contrast, the term *privation* is properly used to refer to the absence of an attachment figure. In the remainder of this chapter, we will look at the effects of deprivation and privation and consider whether such effects that have been found are permanent.

SHORT-TERM EFFECTS OF DEPRIVATION (OR SEPARATION)

One example of short-term deprivation is when a child goes into a nursery while its mother goes into hospital. Another is when the child itself goes into hospital (cf. the research of Spitz described in Box 2.1). Although it is difficult to define how short a short-term separation is, we can conceive of it in terms of days or weeks rather than months. Bowlby's research showed that when young children have to go into hospital, they display *distress*, a response which is characterised by three important components or stages as shown in Box 2.2.

Box 2.2 The components or stages of distress

Protest: The initial immediate reaction takes the form of crying, screaming, kicking and generally struggling to escape, or clinging to the mother to prevent her leaving. This is an outward and direct expression of everything the child feels – anger, fear, bitterness, bewilderment and so on.

Despair: The struggling and protest eventually give way to calmer behaviour. The child may seem to have become apathetic, but internally still feels all the anger and fear that were previously displayed. The child keeps such feelings 'locked-up' and wants nothing to do with other people, appearing depressed and sad. The child may no longer anticipate the mother's return and barely reacts to offers of comfort from others, preferring instead to comfort itself by rocking, thumb sucking and so on.

Detachment: If the separation continues, the child begins to respond to people again but will tend to treat everybody alike and rather superficially. However, if reunited with the mother at this stage, the child may well have to 'relearn' the relationship with her and may even 'reject' her (as she 'rejected' her child).

The evidence suggests that not all children go through the three stages of distress and that there are differences between them in terms of how much distress they experience. Maccoby (1980) has reported that separation is likely to be most distressing between the age of seven to eight months (when the infant has just formed an attachment: see Chapter 1, page 2) and three years, with the period between 12 and 18 months being associated with maximum distress. It seems that the child's ability to hold an image in its mind of the absent mother (that is, to think of her) is one of the variables associated with age, as is its limited understanding of language. Thus, because young children do not understand the meaning of phrases like 'in a few days' time' or 'next week', it is difficult to explain to them that the separation is only temporary. It may well be that children believe themselves to have been abandoned completely, that their mother no longer loves them, and that they are in some way to blame for what has happened ('Mummy is going away because I've been naughty').

Although there are wide differences within the two genders, the evidence also suggests that boys are generally more distressed and vulnerable than girls. Additionally, and irrespective of gender, any behaviour problems that existed before the separation are likely to be accentuated. A child who is aggressive before the separation occurs, for example, is likely to become more aggressive and be most disturbed by the separation. Children appear to cope best if their relationship with the mother is stable and relaxed, but not too close. An extremely close and protective relationship, in which the child and mother are rarely apart and the child is unused to meeting new people, may produce extreme distress simply because the child has not experienced anything like it before (see Figure 2.1).

Stacey et al. (1970) have found that 'good' previous separations help the child to cope with subsequent separations and become more independent and self-sufficient generally. Stacey et al. studied four-year-old children who had gone into hospital to have their tonsils removed. The children were in hospital for four days, and their parents were not allowed to stay overnight. The researchers found that those children who coped best had experienced separations before, such as staying overnight with their grandparents.

The existence of *multiple attachments* has also been shown to make separation less stressful. For example, Kotelchuck (1976) found that when the father is also actively involved as a caregiver, children in the Strange Situation (see Chapter 1, page 2), are more comfortable than is the case when only the mother acts as the main caregiver. The quality of the substitute care is also influential in terms of the amount of distress a child experiences. Even institutions can provide high-quality care, as was shown in Burlingham and Freud's Hampstead nursery in which stability, affection and active involvement were encouraged.

Unfortunately, many institutions are run in such a way that it is extremely difficult for substitute attachments to develop. Things like a high staff turnover, a large number of children competing for the attention of a small number of staff, and the sometimes deliberate policy of no special relationships being formed in order to avoid claims of favouritism and consequent jealousy, can all act against the development of high-quality substitute attachment (Tizard and Rees, 1974).

The evidence concerning *day care* seems to indicate that, contrary to the views of Bowlby, the consequences are not necessarily detrimental to the child (Kagan et al., 1980). What does seem to be important is the *quality* of the substitute care (such as how well staffed the day-care centre is: see above) and how *stable* the arrangement is. When a centre is well staffed and well equipped, there are very few negative effects. A poor centre, however, can have harmful effects. This also seems to be the case with day nurseries (Garland and White, 1980) and child-minders (Mayall and Petrie, 1983). In the case of child-minders, Mayall and Petrie found that the quality of British child-minding was variable, with some minders being highly competent and others failing to provide a stimulating environment. So, whilst child-minding need not be disruptive, it sometimes may be.

According to Dario Varin of the University of Milan (cited in Cooper, 1996a), babies who spend long periods in day-care nurseries *are* more likely to behave badly than those who stay at home with their mothers and are less likely to make friends. In a series of studies, Varin and his colleagues found that, contrary to expectations, children who attended day centres from their first or second years displayed less co-operative behaviour than children cared for at home. Varin argues that:

> 'these results suggest that at least for some children an early and extended group experience does not ... foster socio-moral development, even if the quality of group care is "good enough" '.

In Varin's view, governments should bring in measures promoting more flexible employment patterns so that children could be cared for at home by their parents in the early stages of life, 'a unique type of care which cannot be substituted for by any education'.

LONG-TERM EFFECTS OF DEPRIVATION (OR SEPARATION)

Long-term separation includes the permanent separation resulting from the *death* of a parent and the increasingly occurring separation caused by *divorce.* Possibly the most common effect of long-term deprivation is what Bowlby calls *separation anxiety*, a term he used to describe the fear that separation will occur again in the future. Box 2.3 shows some of the ways in which separation anxiety may manifest itself.

Box 2.3 Characteristics associated with separation anxiety

- Increased aggressive behaviour and greater demands towards the mother.
- Clinging behaviour – the child will not let the mother out of its sight. This may generalise to relationships in general, so that a man who experienced 'bad' separations in childhood may be very dependent on, and demanding of, his wife.
- Detachment – the child becomes apparently self-sufficient because it cannot afford to be let down again.
- Some fluctuation between clinging and detachment.
- Psychosomatic (psychophysiological) reactions.

According to Bowlby, *school phobia/refusal* is an expression of separation anxiety, and because the child fears that something dreadful will happen to its mother while it is at school, it stays at home in order to prevent it. Two of the major sources of such fear are *actual events* (such as the recent illness of the mother or death of a relative) and *threats* made by the mother that she will leave home, 'go mad' or 'kill herself' if things do not improve.

Figure 2.1 John (17 months) experienced extreme distress while spending 9 days in a residential nursery when his mother was in hospital having a second baby. According to Bowlby, he was grieving for the absent mother, while for the Robertsons (who made a series of films called *Children in Brief Separation*) it was bond disruption that caused John's disturbance (i.e. he was prevented from forming a substitute attachment)

The effects of divorce

A large number of studies have shown that divorce has serious effects on the children who are affected by it, and that marital breakdown causes more problems for children than marital discord. Additionally, the more disruption a child suffers, the worse the adjustment (Cockett and Tripp, 1994). Richards (1995) has reviewed the effects of parental divorce on children. Some of the major findings are shown in Box 2.4.

Box 2.4 Some of the major effects on children of parental divorce

Richards (1995) reports that compared with children of similar social backgrounds whose parents remain married, those whose parents divorce show consistent but small differences throughout childhood. They also have different life courses as they move into adulthood. The differences include:

- Lower levels of academic achievement and self-esteem.
- A higher incidence of conduct and other problems of psychological adjustment during childhood.
- Earlier social maturity with some transitions to adulthood (such as leaving home, beginning sexual relationships, entering cohabitation or marriage, and childbearing) typically occurring at earlier ages.
- A tendency in young adulthood to more changes of job, lower socioeconomic status, and indications of a higher frequency of depression and lower scores on measures of psychological well-being.
- More distant relationships in adulthood with parents and other kin.

Note that the differences refer to *average* scores for children of divorced and non-divorced parents. The variation is wide, particularly for those whose parents have divorced.

(based on Richards, 1995)

The research findings summarised by Richards (1995) are *correlational*, and it may be that divorce is not the only factor producing the differences described in Box 2.4. Richards suggests a number of hypotheses, which are unlikely to be mutually exclusive, that might be implicated. For example, it could be that *divorce-prone couples*, that is, couples who are most likely to divorce,

Figure 2.2 It is not divorce as such that makes children whose parents split up more likely to become maladjusted, but *inter-parental conflict*, especially when the child becomes the focus of the conflict, as in *Kramer vs Kramer*, starring Dustin Hoffman and Meryl Streep

have particular styles of child rearing which account for the differences. This hypothesis is supported by Elliott and Richards' (1991) finding that some of the effects associated with divorce can be seen *before* couples separate. However, and as Booth and Amato (1994) have pointed out, this hypothesis cannot account for all the effects seen *later*.

Another hypothesis suggests that the amount of contact and styles of parenting after separation are important factors. Downey and Powell (1993), for example, have shown that children reared in a single-parent household with a parent of the same sex do less well than other children. Although growing up in a single-parent household may not necessarily be disadvantageous (provided there is a reasonable level of financial support), the *change* from two parents to a single residential parent might be significant (Richards, 1987).

Inter-parental conflict may also lead to maladjustment. Amato (1993), for example, has shown that conflict between parents who live together is associated with low self-esteem in children, and low self-esteem may lead to other difficulties including lower achievement at school and difficulties in forming relationships. Other hypotheses concerning *economic factors*, *life changes*, *relationships with wider kin* and *relationship patterns* have also been advanced to explain the detrimental effects of parental divorce on children. As Richards (1995) has observed:

> 'we need to seek to test these hypotheses. All of them have implications for social policy and at a time when divorce law, mediation and the welfare system are all under active debate and review, it seems particularly important that we should have a good base in evidence for intentions'.

Although most research into the effects of divorce on children has focused on its negative impact, there is some evidence to suggest that divorce can *benefit* both parents and children by increasing self-reliance and giving them control over their lives. Research conducted by Ann Woollett and Patsy Fuller at the University of East London (cited in Laurance, 1996) does *not* indicate that divorce is a 'good thing'. However, their data do suggest that children experience a sense of stability as a result of a feeling of love being focused on them. We shall examine the effects of divorce on parents and children further in Chapter 12.

The effects of parental death

As Flanagan (1996) notes, parental death is a special kind of separation because, unlike divorce, it is unlikely that there was a history of discord, although in some cases the period prior to death may have been difficult. At least one study (Bifulco et al., 1992) has shown that children who experience the death of their mother have higher rates of anxiety and depression in adulthood as compared with children whose mother separated from them for longer than a year. As is the case with divorce, a number of factors can modify the effect of parental death. These include the degree of substitute care which is subsequently provided and the effect the death has on the other members of the family (Flanagan, 1996).

Privation

As we noted earlier (see page 15), the term *privation* refers to the failure to develop an attachment to any individual. In humans, it is usually (but not necessarily) associated with children reared either from or shortly after birth in institutions. In the light of the obvious importance of the child's first relationship, it is not unreasonable to expect that the failure to develop an attachment of any kind will adversely affect all subsequent relationships.

Harlow's research (see pages 5–7) showed that monkeys brought up with only surrogate mothers were very disturbed in their later sexual behaviour and had to be artificially inseminated because they would not mate naturally. Also, the unmothered females became very inadequate mothers. In humans, privation has been shown to have a variety of physical, intellectual and social effects. It is to some of these that we now turn.

Affectionless psychopathy

According to Bowlby, separation experiences in early childhood cause affectionless psychopathy, that is, the inability to have deep feelings for other people and the consequent lack of meaningful interpersonal relationships. Bowlby's claim was based in part on the findings he reported in his 1946 book *Forty-four Juvenile Thieves*. Bowlby reported that of the 44 thieves, 14 showed many affectionless characteristics (such as an inability to experience guilt). By contrast, none of the children in a control group of emotionally disturbed juveniles not guilty of a crime showed such characteristics. Seven of the juvenile thieves had suffered complete and prolonged separation from their mothers, or established foster mothers, for six months during their first five years of life. A further two had spent nine months in hospital, unvisited, during their second year (which, as we saw in Chapter 1, is when attachments are normally being consolidated). Only three of the 30 other, non-affectionless thieves had suffered comparable separations.

Bowlby interpreted his findings in terms of deprivation, but it is more likely that privation was the major cause of the affectionless character. According to Rutter (1981), the general picture is of multiple changes of the mother-figure and home during the children's early years making the *establishment* of attachments very difficult. Even if we accept this conclusion, the study itself has a number of methodological problems. For example, it was a *retrospective* study in which the children and their mothers had to remember past events, and they may have done this less than accurately. Also, Bowlby did not offer any explanation for the remainder of the children (who were, in fact, the majority) who had *not* suffered complete and prolonged separations.

In a later study, Bowlby and his colleagues (1956) looked at 60 children aged seven to 13. These children had spent between five months and two years in a tuberculosis sanitorium (in which no substitute mothering was provided) at various ages up to the age of four. About half of the children had been separated from their parents before they were two years old. Bowlby and his colleagues found that there were few significant differences in terms of IQ scores or teachers' ratings when these children were compared with a group of non-separated 'control' children from the same classes at school. Although the separated children were more prone to 'daydreaming', showed less initiative, were over-excited, rougher in play, less able to concentrate and less competitive, the *overall* picture was that the two groups were more similar than different. Certainly, the sanitorium children showed no more evidence of affectionless psychopathy than the control group children, regardless of whether the separation had occurred before or after two years of age.

Referring to the fact that illness and death were common in the families of the sanitorium children (ten per cent of the mothers had died by the time of follow-up), Bowlby and his colleagues were forced to conclude that 'part of the emotional disturbance can be attributed to factors other than separation'. The claim for a link between affectionless psychopathy and *separation* (or bond disruption) is therefore largely unsubstantiated. However, unwittingly, Bowlby may have provided evidence to support the view that *privation* may be associated with the affectionless character. This is certainly the view of Rutter (1981), who suggests that a failure to form bonds in early childhood is likely to lead to:

> 'an initial phase of clinging, dependent behaviour, followed by attention-seeking, uninhibited, indiscriminate friendliness and finally a personality characterised by lack of guilt, an inability to keep rules and an inability to form lasting relationships'.

Developmental retardation

According to Dennis (1960), there is a *critical period* for intellectual development before the age of two. Dennis's claim was based on his study of orphanages in Iran, in which he found that children adopted after the age of two appeared to be incapable of closing the gap between themselves and average children, whereas those adopted before the age of two were capable of closing the gap. The evidence for the existence of such a critical period is, however, weak. For example, the possibility of *reversing* the effects of privation on intellectual functioning *after* the age of two (as well as the long-term effects of early privation in the absence of any intervention) were dramatically shown in a study originally conducted by Skeels and Dye (1939) and followed up nearly 30 years later by Skeels (1966).

Figure 2.3 Children raised in large institutions are not only denied the opportunity of forming an attachment with a mother-figure but also experience poor, unstimulating environments that are associated with mental subnormality and retarded linguistic development

The original study looked at 25 children raised until the age of two in an American orphanage which offered a minimum of social interaction and stimulation. At age two, 13 of the orphans (average IQ 64.3) were transferred to a school for the mentally retarded. Individual care for the orphans was provided by older, subnormal girls. These 13 children also enjoyed superior play facilities, intellectual stimulation, staff-child ratios and so on. The other 12 children (average IQ 86.7) remained in the orphanage.

At the age of about three and a half, the 13 who had been transferred to the school (the 'experimental' group) either returned to the orphanage or were adopted. Whilst the experimental group's average IQ had risen from 64.3 to 92.8, the average IQ of the other 12 children (the 'control' group) had fallen from 86.7 to 60.5. At the age of seven, the average gain for members of the experimental group was 36 points whereas the average loss for members of the control group was 21 points.

Skeels followed up the children into adulthood. He found that all of the experimental group had had more education than the control group. Indeed, all of the experimental group had finished high school, and about one-third had gone to college, married, had children of normal intelligence, and been self-supporting through their adult lives. The control group members had mostly remained in institutions, were unable to earn enough to be self-supporting and were still mentally retarded.

Skeels and Dye's findings suggest that a crucial variable for intellectual development is the amount of *intellectual stimulation* a child receives rather than the amount of mothering (as claimed by Spitz, Goldfarb and Bowlby). In general, the evidence suggests that poor, unstimulating environments are associated with mental subnormality and retarded linguistic development (the latter being crucial for intellectual development generally). As well as intellectual development, researchers have looked at the long-term effects of privation on other aspects of human development. We examine some of the findings below.

ARE THE EFFECTS OF LONG-TERM PRIVATION REVERSIBLE?

From what we have seen, privation can have harmful long-term effects. The permanence of such effects has, however, been questioned. For example, Harlow and his colleagues found that the effects of early environmental impoverishment in rhesus monkeys *could* be reversed, or at least moderated, by providing them with extensive contact with 'therapist monkeys' (Novak and Harlow, 1975; Suomi and Harlow, 1977; Novak, 1979). In humans too, research has shown that babies deprived of early bonding can recover from such deprivation. For example, Kagan and Klein (1973) studied a

Guatemalan Indian society in which infants routinely spend the first year of their lives confined to small, windowless huts because of the parental belief that sunlight and fresh air are harmful to babies. As judged by standards of normal development, these infants, who are rarely cuddled, played with or talked to by their parents, are listless, unresponsive and intellectually retarded. After their first birthdays, the infants are allowed out of the huts and rapidly become involved in play and exploration, and they form attachments just like children who have not been similarly deprived.

In a major review of research in the area, Clarke and Clarke (1976) claimed that the effects of early privation are much more easily reversible than studies such as that of Dennis (1960) would suggest. Support for this claim comes from research conducted by Tizard (1977) and Tizard and Hodges (1978). These researchers looked at a number of children who, on leaving care, were either adopted or returned to their own families. Although the institutions responsible for the children provided good physical care and appeared to provide reasonably adequately for their cognitive development, staff turnover was high, and the institution operated a policy against allowing too strong an attachment to develop between the staff and children (see Tizard and Rees, 1974, page 16). As a result, the children had little opportunity to form close, continuous relationships with an adult. Indeed, by the age of two, they had been looked after for at least a week by an average of 24 different caregivers. By age four, this average had risen to 50. The children's attachment behaviour was very unusual and, in general, their first opportunity to form a long-term attachment came when they left the institutions and were placed in families. This occurred between the ages of two and seven.

The adoptive parents very much wanted a child, and Hodges and Tizard found that, by the age of eight, the majority of adopted children had formed close attachments to their parents, despite their lack of early attachments in the institutions. At the same age, however, only *some* of those children returned to their own families had formed close attachments. In contrast to the adoptive parents, the biological parents were ambivalent about having the child and often had other children and material difficulties competing for their attention. As reported by their parents, the ex-institutional children as a whole did not display more problems than a comparison group who had never been in care. According to their teachers, however, they tended to display attention-seeking behaviour, restlessness, disobedience and poor peer relationships.

Hodges and Tizard (1989) reported that, at age 16, the family relationships of most of the adopted children seemed satisfactory, both for them and their parents, and differed little from a non-adopted comparison group who had never been in care. Thus, early institutional care had not necessarily led to a later inability to form a close attachment to parents and become as much a part of the family as any other child. However, those children returned to their families still suffered difficulties and poor family relationships. These included mutual difficulty in showing affection, and the parents reported feeling closer to siblings than to the returned child.

Outside the family, the picture was very different, and both the adopted and returned children showed similar relationships with peers and adults. The children were still more often oriented towards adult affection and approval than a comparison group. They were also still more likely to have difficulties in peer relations, less likely to have a special friend or to see peers as a source of emotional support, and more likely to be friendly to any peer rather than choosing their friends.

On the basis of Hodges and Tizard's research, we can conclude that children who are deprived of close and lasting relationships with adults in the first years of their life *can* make such attachments later. However, these do not arise automatically if the child is placed in a family. Rather, they depend on the adults concerned and how they nurture such attachments. Hodges and Tizard's research also shows that whilst attachments can be formed, such children do experience a number of difficulties in their social relationships. These do not appear to be related to the kind of family they join, but seem to originate in the children's early institutional experience. Moreover, since they affect relationships with peers, as well as adults outside the family, they may have implications for future adult relationships (see, for example, Gross, 1994).

Other research into adopted children has also shown that the outcome for them is much better than might have been expected on the basis of their early history of neglect, multiple changes of foster parents, and late ages of adoption (e.g. Kadushin, 1970; Triseliotis, 1980). In the Triseliotis study, for example, 40 people born in 1956 or 1957 who had experienced long-term fostering (between seven and 15 years in a single foster home before the age of 16) were interviewed at the age of 21. On the basis of the interviews, Triseliotis concluded that if the quality and quantity of care and relationships are adequate, the effects of earlier disruptions and suffering can be reversed and normal development achieved.

Another way of studying the long-term effects of privation is to examine the context in which the deprivation is embedded, which means following up the children closely in order to trace the *developmental pathways* that lead by multiple steps from early experience to outcome in maturity (Schaffer, 1996). This approach was used by Quinton and Rutter (1988), who set out to determine whether children deprived of parental care in turn become depriving parents. The researchers observed women, brought up in care, interacting with their own children. Compared with a non-institutionalised group of women, these mothers were, as a group, less sensitive, supportive and warm towards their children.

According to Quinton and Rutter, this difference can be explained in terms of a variety of subsequent experiences the women had as a result of being brought up in care (such as teenage pregnancy, marrying an unsupportive spouse, and marital breakdown) as well as in terms of their deprived childhoods. However, there was also considerable variability *within* the group brought up in care, and by no means all of them exhibited deficient parenting skills. One way of explaining the variability is in terms of developmental pathways. For example, some of the women had much more positive school experiences than others, making them three times more likely as adolescents or young adults to make proper plans and choices for their career and marriage partner. As a result, they were 12 times more likely to marry for positive reasons, which in turn increased by five times the chances of their marital relationship being supportive. This itself increased their chance of good social functioning (including being a caring parent) by a factor of three (Rutter, 1989). This represents a route for escaping early adversity; similar adverse experiences in childhood can give rise to multiple outcomes (Schaffer, 1996), as shown in Figure 2.4.

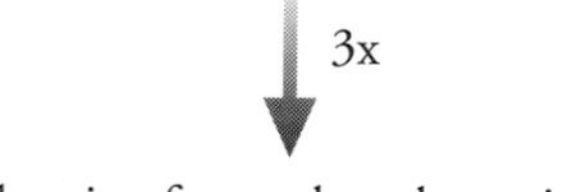

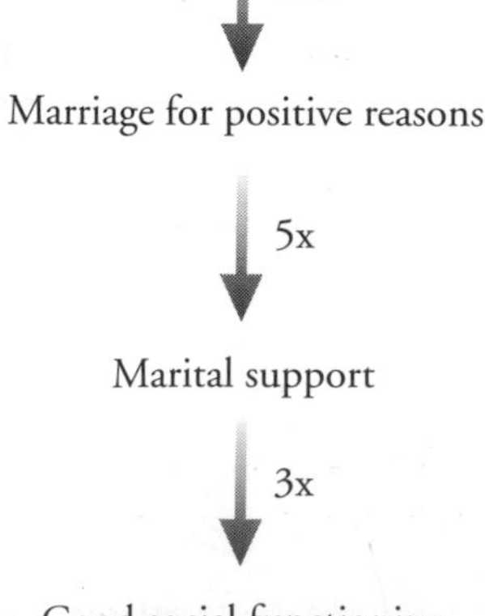

Figure 2.4 A simplified adaptive chain of circumstances in institution-reared women (based on Quinton and Rutter, 1988, and Rutter, 1989)

THE REVERSIBILITY OF EXTREME EARLY PRIVATION

A number of studies have looked at the long-term effects of *extreme* early privation in which the children concerned have endured years of isolation. Such studies include those of Anna (Davis, 1940), Isabelle (Mason, 1942), survivors of concentration camps (Freud and Dann, 1951), P.M. and J.M. (Koluchova, 1972), L.H. (Koluchova, 1976), Genie (Curtiss, 1977) and Mary and Louise (Skuse, 1984). Box 2.5 describes the findings of one such study.

Box 2.5 The case of P.M. and J.M.

Koluchova (1972) reported the case of identical twin boys in the former Czechoslovakia who were cruelly treated by their stepmother. The boys were found in 1967 when they were aged seven. They had grown up in a small, unheated closet, had been often locked in the cellar, and suffered harsh beatings. Following their discovery, the boys spent time in a children's home and a school for the mentally retarded. In 1969, they were fostered.

At first, the boys were terrified of many aspects of their new environment, communicated largely by gestures, and had little spontaneous speech. However, they gradually made progress, both socially and intellectually. When followed up seven years after their discovery (when they were 14), the twins showed no psychopathological symptoms or unusual behaviour. By the age of 20, the boys had completed a quite demanding apprenticeship (in the maintenance of office machinery) and were of above average intelligence. They still had very good relationships with their foster mother and her relatives and their adopted sisters. Additionally, the twins had developed heterosexual relationships and had both recently experienced their first love affairs.

As with other studies of the effects of extreme privation, this study seems to highlight the importance of having somebody (not necessarily a mother-figure) with whom it is possible to form an emotional bond. The study also shows that the effects of long-term extreme privation *can* be reversed.

According to Skuse (1984), victims of extreme privation show a characteristic clinical picture when first discovered. This picture is one of motor retardation, absent or very rudimentary vocal and symbolic language, grossly retarded perceptuomotor skills, poor emotional expression, lack of attachment behaviour, and social withdrawal. Apart from profound mental retardation and childhood autism, this clinical picture is unlikely to be found in any other condition. Language is undoubtedly the most vulnerable cognitive faculty. In all of the cases studied, language was profoundly retarded at first, even when other features of mental development were apparently unaffected. The early combination of profound language deficit and apathy/withdrawal from social contact leads to special difficulties in developing a normal range and quality of relationships later on.

Despite this apparently bleak picture, however, the various studies into the long-term effects of extreme early privation do suggest that the view that early experience is of overriding importance for later growth is inadequate (cf. Clarke and Clarke, 1976). Whilst adverse early life experiences may have serious lasting effects on development in some circumstances, it is not invariably the case that they will. Some children are more resilient than others, and there does not seem to be a straightforward connection between cause and effect.

The evidence suggests that if recovery of normal ability in a particular faculty is going to occur, rapid progress is the rule. However, the evidence also suggests that further progress can be made several years after discovery, even in cases where the obstacles to success were thought to be genetic/congenital, as in Skuse's (1984) study of Mary and Louise. After their discovery, both Mary and Louise received speech therapy. In the case of Mary, however, the therapy was abandoned because of poor progress. Mary was subsequently placed in a variety of children's homes and received consistent, intensive speech therapy. Four years later, a remarkable transformation had occurred, and Mary's poor social communication and language (which were reminiscent of autism) had improved dramatically. In Skuse's view, in the absence of genetic or congenital abnormalities, victims of extreme privation have an excellent prognosis.

Conclusions

This chapter has reviewed research into the effects of early deprivation on the child. Although short- and long-term deprivation and privation can have detrimental effects, the evidence suggests that such effects are not irreversible and that recovery from both deprivation and privation is possible.

Summary

- Harlow's research involving infant rhesus monkeys demonstrated the falsity of the claim made by 'cupboard love' theories that feeding is a crucial element in the formation of attachments. It also showed that infant monkeys raised without a real mother failed to develop normally, such that when females reached maturity, they rejected the advances of a male and most had to be artificially inseminated. Those who produced offspring either rejected them or were indifferent towards them.
- As far as humans are concerned, Bowlby's **maternal deprivation hypothesis** claims that attachment between mother and infant cannot be broken in the first few years of life without serious/permanent developmental damage being

done. This combines the concept of a critical period for attachment formation and his theory of monotropy.

- The maternal deprivation hypothesis was based largely on studies in the 1930s and 1940s, like those of Goldfarb, Spitz, and Spitz and Wolf, of children raised in institutions. Goldfarb compared a group of children raised in institutions with a group raised in a foster home. At age three and also between the ages of 10 and 14, the former were behind on measures of abstract thinking/social maturity/rule following/sociability, and their average IQ was also lower. Goldfarb attributed **all** these deficits to the time spent in the institutions.
- Spitz and Wolf focused on the **emotional** effects of institutionalisation, such as **anaclitic depression** and **hospitalism**. They found that over one-third of orphanage infants in the USA and Canada died before their first birthday, despite good nutrition and medical care.
- Neither Bowlby nor Goldfarb, Spitz and Wolf recognised that the **understimulating nature** of the institutions, as well as or instead of **maternal deprivation**, could have produced the observed effects. According to Rutter, different types of deprivation need to be separated along with the different kinds of developmental retardation they produce.
- Rutter argues that Bowlby's use of 'deprivation' fails to distinguish between the effects of being separated from an attachment figure and the effects of never having formed an attachment in the first place (i.e. **privation**). **Deprivation** (de-privation) strictly refers to the loss through separation of the maternal attachment, and this is what Bowlby's theory and research was mainly concerned with.
- Examples of **short-term deprivation/separation** are a child going into a nursery while its mother goes into hospital, or the child going into hospital itself. A typical response by the child is to display **distress**, which comprises **protest**, **despair** and **detachment**.
- Not every child will go through all three stages of distress, and there are important individual differences regarding the degree of distress experienced. Distress is likely to be most intense between 12 and 18 months, and boys are generally more distressed and vulnerable than girls. Irrespective of gender, behaviour problems that pre-date the separation are more likely to be accentuated. Children seem to cope best if they have a stable and relaxed relationship with the mother.
- Stacey et al.'s study of four-year-olds entering hospital to have their tonsils removed found that those who coped best had experienced previous 'good' separations, such as staying overnight with grandparents. This helps to make the child more independent and self-sufficient.
- The existence of **multiple attachments** also makes separation less stressful. Kotelchuk found that when the father is also an active caregiver, children are more comfortable in the Strange Situation than when only the mother is the main caregiver.
- The quality of substitute care influences the amount of distress the child experiences. Many institutions make it very difficult for substitute attachments to develop, due to high staff turnover, competition for the attention of a small number of staff and/or a deliberate policy against any special relationships.
- Contrary to Bowlby's views, **day care** is not necessarily detrimental to the child. What matters are the **quality** of the substitute care and the **stability** of the arrangement. A poorly staffed and equipped centre can be harmful, as can incompetent child-minders who fail to provide a stimulating environment.
- According to Varin, babies who spend long periods in day-care nurseries are more likely to behave badly than those who stay at home with their mother and are less likely to make friends. Contrary to expectations, children who attended day-centres from their first or second year were less co-operative than those who were cared for at home, suggesting that early, extended group experience does not promote socio-moral development.
- **Long-term deprivation/separation** includes the permanent separation caused by the **death** of a parent and **divorce**. Perhaps the most common effect is **separation anxiety**, which can manifest itself as increased aggressiveness, greater demands towards the mother, clinging behaviour, detachment, some fluctuation between clinging and detachment, and psychosomatic or psychophysiological reactions. According to Bowlby, separation anxiety can take the form of **school phobia/refusal**.
- Many studies have shown that **divorce** has serious effects on children and that marital breakdown causes more problems for children than marital discord. According to Richards, children whose parents divorce **on average** have lower levels of academic achievement and self-esteem, and higher incidence of psychological adjustment problems during childhood compared with those

of similar social backgrounds whose parents remain married.

- They also achieve social maturity earlier and experience some adult transitions earlier. As young adults, they tend to change jobs more often, achieve lower socioeconomic status, become depressed more often and score lower on measures of psychological well-being. In adulthood, they have more distant relationships with parents and other relatives.
- These data are **correlational**, so that divorce may not be the only factor producing the differences. Another possibility is that **divorce-prone couples** have particular child-rearing styles. The amount of contact and styles of parenting after separation may also be important, such as being reared in a single, same-sex parent household.
- Maladjustment may be caused by **inter-parental conflict**. The harmful effects of divorce may also be associated with **economic factors**, **life changes**, **relationships with wider kin** and **relationship patterns**. These various hypotheses are not mutually exclusive and they all have implications for social policy.
- There is also some evidence that parental divorce can **benefit** both parents and children by increasing self-reliance and giving them control over their lives. Research by Woollett and Fuller suggests that children may experience a sense of stability as a result of feeling loved.
- **Parental death** is unlikely to have been preceded by discord, unlike divorce. Children who experience the death of their mother have higher rates of anxiety and depression in adulthood compared with children whose mother separated from them for more than a year. Several factors can modify the effect of parental death, including the substitute care provided and the effect of the death on the rest of the family.
- **Privation** in humans is usually associated with being raised in institutions and, given the importance of the first relationship, failure to develop an attachment of any kind is likely to adversely affect all subsequent relationships.
- Harlow's research showed that monkeys reared with only surrogate mothers were very disturbed in their later sexual behaviour and would not mate naturally. The unmothered females also became very inadequate mothers.
- According to Bowlby, separation experiences in early childhood cause **affectionless psychopathy**. This was based partly on his study of 44 juvenile thieves. While Bowlby interpreted his findings in terms of deprivation, Rutter sees privation as the more likely cause of the affectionless character, with the **establishment** of attachments having been the major difficulty.
- Bowlby et al.'s study of children who had spent up to two years in a tuberculosis sanatorium found few significant differences in IQ or teachers' ratings between them and a group of non-separated controls from their own classes. Despite some behavioural and emotional differences, the **overall** picture was that the two groups were more similar than different; the sanatorium children showed no more evidence of affectionless psychopathy, regardless of whether the separation had occurred before or after the age of two.
- Bowlby et al. admitted that any emotional disturbance shown by the sanitorium children could be attributed to factors other than **separation**, such as illness or death in their families. So while there is little evidence to support Bowlby's claim that affectionless psychopathy is linked to separation, Rutter believes that **privation** is likely to produce a personality characterised by lack of guilt, an inability to keep rules and an inability to form lasting relationships.
- According to Dennis, there is a **critical period** for intellectual development before the age of two. This was based on his study of Iranian orphanages, in which he found that children adopted after age two were **intellectually retarded** and couldn't close the gap between themselves and average children. However, the Skeels and Dye and the Skeels studies show how it is possible to **reverse** the effects of early privation after the age of two, as well as showing the long-term effects of privation.
- These findings suggest that it is **intellectual stimulation** that is crucial for intellectual development, rather than mothering (as claimed by Spitz, Goldfarb and Bowlby). Poor and unstimulating environments are associated with mental subnormality and retarded linguistic development.
- While privation can have harmful long-term effects, this doesn't necessarily mean they are not **reversible**. For example, Harlow found that providing 'therapist monkeys' could reverse the effects of early isolation in rhesus monkeys.
- Kagan and Klein's study of a Guatemalan Indian society found that, despite being largely isolated for their first year, receiving very little human contact or stimulation, and appearing to be mentally retarded, children form attachments, play and explore just like non-deprived children after being allowed out of their huts.
- According to Clarke and Clarke, the effects of

early privation are much more easily reversible than studies like that of Dennis suggest. Tizard, and Tizard and Hodges studied children who, on leaving care between the ages of two and seven, were either adopted or returned to their own families. While as a group the ex-institution children had no more problems than a comparison non-institutionalised group as reported by parents, teachers saw them as attention-seeking, restless, disobedient and having poor peer relationships.

- Hodges and Tizard reported that, at age 16, the family relationships of most of the adopted children seemed good, while those of the children returned to their biological families were still poor. However, **outside** the family, both the adopted and returned children were more often oriented towards adult affection and approval than a comparison group and were still more likely to have difficulties in peer relationships.
- Other adoption studies, such as those of Triseliotis and Kadushin, show that the outcome for late-adopted children is much better than might be expected given their early history of neglect and multiple changes of foster parents.
- Quinton and Rutter compared the mothering skills of a group of women brought up in care and a group of non-institutionalised mothers. Although the former as a group were less sensitive, supportive and warm, there was also considerable variability **within** the mothers brought up in care. This variability could be explained by examining the **developmental pathways** that led individual mothers from childhood experience to adult behaviour, so that similar adverse experience in childhood can give rise to multiple outcomes.
- A number of studies of **extreme** early privation, such as those of Koluchova (P.M./J.M./L.H.) and Skuse (Mary and Louise), show that the effects **can** be reversed. Some of them, such as Koluchova's study of the identical twin boys, highlight the importance of having somebody – not necessarily a mother-figure – with whom it is possible to form an emotional bond.
- According to Skuse, victims of extreme privation at first typically display motor retardation, absent or very basic vocal and symbolic language, grossly retarded perceptuomotor skills, poor emotional expression, lack of attachment behaviour and social withdrawal. Language is the most vulnerable cognitive faculty and was profoundly retarded at first in all the cases studied, even when other features of mental development were unaffected.
- Studies of extreme privation suggest that early experience is not, after all, of overriding importance for later growth. Some children are more resilient than others, and there is no inevitable or straightforward cause-and-effect connection.
- If recovery of normal ability in a particular faculty is going to happen, rapid progress is the rule. However, Skuse's study of Mary and Louise also shows that further progress can be made several years after discovery, even in cases where the obstacles were thought to be genetic or congenital. In the absence of such abnormalities, victims of extreme privation have an excellent prognosis.

CHILD REARING

Introduction and overview

Advice for parents on the ways in which to rear their children is big business. According to one estimate, nearly five million 'how to parent' books are sold every year in the United States alone. Perhaps the first psychologist to offer advice on raising children was the eminent behaviourist John B. Watson whose book *Psychological Care of Infant and Child* (1928) has been described as 'an odd mix of scientific fact and unscientific speculation' (Hassett and White, 1989). Watson adopted a no-nonsense approach to child rearing because of his belief that giving children too much love would make them 'totally unable to cope with the world in which they must live'. For Watson (1928):

> 'Treat [children] as though they were young adults. Dress them, bathe them with care and circumspection. Let your behaviour always be objective and kindly firm. Never hug and kiss them, never let them sit on your lap. If you must, kiss them once on the forehead when they say good night.'

Numerous other parenting guides followed Watson's book, perhaps the most famous being Dr Benjamin Spock's (1946) book *Baby and Child Care* which has sold an astonishing 40 million copies since its publication and is now in its seventh edition. The book began with the words: 'Trust yourself. You know more than you think you do.' Amongst other things, Spock advised parents to feed their babies on demand and avoid physically admonishing their children. Twenty years after his book was published, Spock was publicly blamed for the 'permissive society' of the 'swinging sixties' (Wilson, 1996). (See Figure 3.1.)

There has been a considerable amount of research devoted to identifying the major styles of parenting and their effects on children's development. Our aim in this chapter is to look at some of the social and cultural variations in child rearing, to consider research into culturally specific aspects of child rearing, and to examine cross-cultural studies of child-rearing styles.

Dimensions of child rearing

It is generally agreed that parental approaches to child rearing can be classified according to two main dimensions. These are *emotional responsiveness* and *control/demandingness*. Emotional responsiveness ranges from responding to children with warmth, love and affection to responding to them in cold and rejecting ways. According to Sears et al. (1957), 'warm' parents behave in ways which communicate their happiness at having children and their enjoyment in being with them. Such parents show great affection towards their children by hugging and kissing them, and frequently smiling at them. 'Cold' parents, by contrast, have few affectionate feelings towards their children and tend not to enjoy being with them. Such parents are likely to complain about their children's behaviour, and attribute such behaviour to 'naughtiness' or the child having 'a mind of its own'. Not surprisingly, the evidence indicates that children of warm parents differ from children of cold parents on a number of important measures. For example, they display fewer behavioural problems and are more likely to develop values which are similar to those of their parents (Martin, 1975).

The control/demandingness dimension describes the extent to which parents are restrictive with respect to their children's behaviour. Sears et al. (1957) showed that parents who are extremely restrictive (and might be described as showing *authoritarian power restriction*) impose many rules on their children's behaviour and watch them very closely. Parents who are extremely permissive impose few, if any, rules and supervise their children less closely. As a group, extremely permissive parents show little concern over their children's

Figure 3.1 The cover of what is, arguably, the most famous and influential guide to parenting ever written

cleanliness (and such parents might be described as *indifferent and neglecting*). It is important to note that the two dimensions described above are held to be *independent* of one another. What this means is that parents who are warm may be restrictive *or* permissive, as can parents who are cold.

Diana Baumrind's model of child rearing

For the last 30 years or so, Diana Baumrind (1967, 1991) has conducted research into specific styles of parenting. By observing the ways in which parents interacted with their three- and four-year-old children, and by interviewing these parents, Baumrind was able to identify three child-rearing styles which she called *permissive*, *authoritarian*, and *authoritative*. The differences between these specific styles are shown in Box 3.1.

Box 3.1 Baumrind's three styles of child rearing

In Baumrind's (1967) original research, four dimensions of child rearing were identified (cf. the dimensions we identified earlier on). *Control* refers to attempts by the parents to shape and modify their children's expressions of dependent, aggressive and playful behaviour. *Demands for maturity* refers to the pressures parents place on their children to perform up to their ability. *Clarity of communication* is the seeking-out of children's opinions and using reason when demanding compliance from them. *Nurturance* refers to the expressions of warmth towards children and pride in their accomplishments.

The permissive style: These parents make few demands on their children and are reluctant to punish their children's inappropriate behaviour. There is little attempt to 'control' the children but rather a 'hands-off' policy is adopted. The permissiveness shown by the parents may stem from their indifference or preoccupation with other functions. However, permissive parents hope that giving children their freedom will encourage the development of self-reliance and initiative.

The authoritarian style: These parents rely on strictly enforced rules to make children adhere to their standards. Authoritarian parents tend to be autocratic and leave little room for the discussion of alternative points of view. Punishment is often used to ensure compliance. The parents show minimal warmth, nurturance or communication towards their children.

The authoritative style: These parents also have definite standards/rules that their children are expected to meet. However, the children are usually asked for their opinion during discussion and rule-making sessions. Children are encouraged to think independently and acquire a sense that their views are valuable, although at the same time they are made aware of the parents' expected standards.

(adapted from Crooks and Stein, 1991)

Baumrind found that children of permissive, authoritarian and authoritative parents differed in terms of a cluster of traits she called *instrumental competence.* Instrumental competence is made up of 'social responsibility', 'independence', 'achievement orientation' and 'vitality'. According to Baumrind (1971), children of authoritative parents score highest on all four of the measures that comprise instrumental competence. Thus, they tend to be co-operative, friendly, successful, achievement oriented, independent and self-assertive in their dealings with peers and teachers. Children of authoritarian parents, by contrast, tend to be withdrawn, low in vitality, shy, dependent and tense around their peers. Children of permissive parents were quite confident and self-reliant as compared with children of authoritarian parents. On other measures of instrumental competence, however, their scores tended to be low.

Baumrind's research also showed that there were sex differences with respect to parenting style and instrumental competence. The main differences are summarised in Box 3.2.

Box 3.2 Child-rearing styles, instrumental competence and sex differences

The permissive style: Both boys and girls show low social competencies. However, whilst girls' cognitive competencies are low, cognitive competencies in boys are very low.

The authoritarian style: Both boys and girls show average social competencies. However, boys' cognitive competencies are low whereas girls' cognitive competencies are average.

The authoritative style: Boys show high cognitive and social competencies. Girls, however, show very high cognitive and social competencies.

(adapted from Shaffer, 1985)

Later research (Baumrind, 1975) assessed the children in the original study when they were adolescents, and confirmed the original findings. Thus, parents who use an authoritative style have socially competent and mature children. On the basis of Baumrind's research, it is widely accepted that whilst the authoritarian and permissive styles are almost opposite to one another, neither is helpful in developing social and emotional competence in children. For some researchers, this is because neither style enables children to develop *internal standards.* In the case of children raised by authoritarian parents, the excessive control exerted by them may result in this failure. In the case of permissive parents, the failure to hold children responsible for the consequences of their actions may be at fault.

Baumrind's original categories were subsequently modified by Maccoby and Martin (1983), who devised a two-dimensional classification of child-rearing styles which provides a way of distinguishing the different contexts parents can create for their children's development (Moshman et al., 1987). Maccoby and Martin's classification is shown in Table 3.1.

Table 3.1 Maccoby and Martin's (1983) classification of child-rearing styles

	Parent-centred	*Child-centred*
Demanding	AUTHORITARIAN-AUTOCRATIC	AUTHORITATIVE-RECIPROCAL
Undemanding	INDIFFERENT-UNINVOLVED	INDULGENT-PERMISSIVE

(taken from Moshman et al., 1987)

The authoritarian-autocratic and authoritative-reciprocal categories correspond respectively to the authoritarian and authoritative styles described by Baumrind. The undemanding dimension corresponds to Baumrind's permissive style. As Table 3.1 shows, Maccoby and Martin identify two permissive styles, the *indifferent-uninvolved* and the *indulgent-permissive.* The indifferent-uninvolved style is one in which parents minimise the amount of contact they have with their children, and there are few or no rules for behaviour. Children raised in this way tend to feel unloved and engage in behaviours designed to get others to pay attention to them. In extreme cases, parental neglect can lead to malnutrition, illness or even death (Patterson, 1982). In general, children of indifferent-uninvolved parents are considerably less achievement-oriented than other children.

Like the indifferent-uninvolved style, the indulgent-permissive style is characterised by a lack of rules, and few restrictions are placed on children. However, rather than being parent-centred, this style is child-centred. Indulgent-permissive parents are responsive to their children, tolerant and reinforce desirable behaviour but rarely use punishment. Few demands are made on children for mature behaviour, and children are allowed to make their own decisions wherever possible.

THE BENEFITS OF THE AUTHORITATIVE STYLE

Exactly why the authoritative style is the most beneficial for children is not known, but by looking at this style in more detail, it may be possible to suggest some reasons. Box 3.3 shows the key elements of the authoritative style identified by Baumrind (1971).

Box 3.3 A more detailed look at the key elements of the authoritative style of child rearing

Expectations for mature behaviour: Authoritative parents set their children clear standards and do not reinforce immature behaviour.

Encouragement of individuality: The child's individuality is seen as being positive by authoritative parents and is supported by them.

Respect for children's rights: Authoritative parents recognise that their children have rights, and these rights (along with their own) are respected.

Firm enforcement of rules: Having established clear expectations for mature behaviour, authoritative parents use commands to action and enforce sanctions wherever necessary.

Two-way communication: Communication occurs from child to parent as well as from parent to child. Authoritative parents encourage verbal 'give-and-take' and are receptive to communication.

(based on Baumrind, 1971)

According to Baumrind (1983), one of the advantages of the authoritative style is that it gives children *control* over their lives. Those rules that have been established have been negotiated rather than merely imposed. Because authoritative parents tend to enforce rules with consistent, predictable discipline, their children are more likely to acquire a sense of control over the consequences of their actions. As well as control, authoritative parenting also promotes the development of self-esteem, a sense of autonomy, and nurtures skills in interpersonal relations (Durkin, 1995). Patterson (1982) has shown that elements of the authoritative style can be *taught* to parents, and that as parents learn these elements, more positive social skills are developed by their children.

Durkin (1995) has pointed out that the media can also be influential in promoting an authoritative style of child rearing, and research (e.g. Burman, 1994) has shown that parents are influenced by scientific theories of child development as presented in the media. As Durkin (1995) has remarked:

> 'Look at the noticeboard the next time you visit your general practitioner. Most likely you will see posters from parents' associations advising that "A child needs love. A child needs respect. A child needs choice. A child needs responsibility". You will not find the Authoritarian Aunties' proclamation "A child needs a good hiding" (and the Permissive Parents never get around to producing a poster at all).'

Of course, no parents fit perfectly into any of the styles of parenting identified by research, and most parents show some of the characteristics of all of the styles at one time or another. As a result, many parents find themselves 'in between' in their parenting rather than confined clearly within any one style (Moshman et al., 1987). A number of factors have been shown to have important effects on parenting style. As Scarr (1984) has commented, a child's biological organisation has much to do with the sort of parenting it receives. Thus, 'hot-headed' children are more likely to prompt aggression from their parents than 'level-headed' children (Olweus, 1980). Durkin (1995) identifies marital discord and parental personality as other factors influencing the parental style adopted. In Bronfenbrenner's (1979) view, perhaps the most critical factor may be the child's *perception* of the parenting style used. If children understand that their parents love them and are genuinely concerned about them, then even an extreme authoritarian style may not be completely negative.

We should also note that the vast majority of research into child-rearing styles is *correlational*. Although it is tempting to conclude that a particular style of parenting produces a particular type of child, correlational studies do not allow cause-and-effect relationships to be inferred. Whilst it may well be the case that an authoritative style causes children to be socially, emotionally and cognitively competent, other causal mechanisms may be responsible or operating simultaneously. For example, Lewis (1981) has suggested that children who are socially and emotionally well adjusted *elicit* an authoritative style from their parents.

According to Darling and Steinberg's (1993) *contextual model of parenting style*, it is necessary to distinguish parental *styles* from parental *practices*. Parental practices are things like helping with homework and can directly affect children's behaviour. Parental styles create a particular emotional climate and affect children indirectly by making practices more or less effective, and influence children's receptiveness to those practices. In turn, children's receptiveness influences parental practices (Tavris and Wade, 1995). Box 3.4 describes some recently reported research into the effects of different styles of parenting.

Box 3.4 Parental temperament and the 'terrible twos'

According to researchers at Pennsylvania State University, the temper tantrums of toddlers are caused by their parents' 'failure to show respect for the emerging autonomy of the child'. The research team, led by Jay Belsky, discovered that children's temperament at a very early age was *not* correlated with the likelihood of them turning into a 'terrible two'. Rather, the temperament of their parents, and their attitude to discipline, was a much more important predictor.

The researchers found that parents who reported financial difficulties and a high level of occupational stress were much more likely to have children experiencing the 'terrible twos', and that such parents tended to use an authoritarian style of parenting. Parents who adopted what Belsky terms a *control-with-guidance* approach showed respect for their children's emerging autonomy and recognised them as individuals with a will, desires and needs.

Belsky and his colleagues also suggest that once the 'terrible two' emerges, he or she is likely to become a 'terrible' three, four and five. According to Belsky, the evidence suggests that 'those children having more difficulty at three years are much more likely to have such problems as they get into elementary school as well'.

(adapted from Matthews, 1996)

Enforcing restrictions

Psychologists have identified three methods of discipline used by parents to enforce restrictions on their children. These are *induction*, *love-withdrawal* and *power assertion*. Of the three, the evidence (e.g. Staub, 1979) suggests that inductive methods are the most effective. These are methods which try to give children knowledge that will enable them to behave in an appropriate way in other situations. The most widely used inductive technique is 'reasoning' with the child, that is, explaining to him or her why one behaviour is good and appropriate whilst another is bad and inappropriate.

Love-withdrawal uses the explicit or implicit message that 'if you don't behave in this way, I won't love you any more'. On some occasions, for example, parents ignore or isolate their children when they have misbehaved. On other occasions, they express great disappointment in their children.

Power assertion involves coercing children to behave in the desired way by overpowering and intimidating them. Parents who use power assertion believe strongly in the use of tangible rewards and punishments, and tend to yell at their children rather than reason with them.

Rewarding children for behaving in an appropriate way is generally more effective than punishing them for behaving in an inappropriate way. Unlike induction, which can foster the development of *empathy*, it is debatable as to whether punishment can achieve this. Krebs and Blackman (1988) have identified four general problems with the use of punishment. First, the punishing agent (the parent) presents an aggressive model to the child. Second, the negative feelings elicited by the punishment become associated with the surrounding cues. This makes it less likely that the child will turn to the parent in times of conflict or doubt. Third, punishing a child may teach the child what not to do, but it does not teach positive alternatives. Fourth, frequent punishment may make the child insecure about him or herself and erode the sense of autonomy and self-esteem.

Should parents hit their children? was the title of an article written by the eminent child psychologist Rosemary Leach (1993). Leach points out that in a number of countries, physical punishment is banned in educational and other care institutions (Britain is one such country). In certain other countries (including Sweden, Denmark and Austria), the use of physical punishment by parents has also been outlawed. Under current British law, parents are allowed to use 'reasonable chastisement' to discipline a child. An 1860 court case (Regina v. Hopley) concerned a boy who was beaten to death by his teacher. The judge, Chief Justice Cockburn, ruled that: 'By the law of England, a parent . . . may for the purpose of correcting what evil is in the child, inflict moderate and reasonable corporal punishment' (although what constitutes 'reasonable corporal punishment' is unclear: see below).

Leach argues that 'popular ideas' about psychology and punishment are usually seriously mistaken, the consequence of this being that parents are encouraged to see any aversive result of a child's action as a punishment, whether or not it reduces the likelihood of that action being repeated. For Leach, the 'pseudo-scientific' approach used in many popular books and magazines:

> 'lends credence to "common-sense" parental statements such as "If he gets a slap every time he does it, he'll soon learn not to" '.

There is, however, some evidence to suggest that punishment *can* be effective, at least in the situation in which it is applied. To be effective in *suppressing* behaviour, it must be emphatic and adminstered immediately after the inappropriate behaviour (Aronfreed, 1976). Also, Martin (1975) has shown that punishment is effective when the child perceives it to be judiciously applied and when the person administering the punishment is seen as being warm and loving. Despite this evidence, Leach (1993) argues powerfully that physical punishment is unlikely to be effective in helping parents to shape their children's behaviour as they themselves wish, or in building the self-discipline society requires of all socialised citizens.

For Leach, the use of physical punishment:

> 'frequently provokes or exacerbates behaviours parents and others wish to minimise, may be harmful to children in a number of ways, and increases their vulnerability to physical abuse. Literature from psychology and related professions provides clear evidence, and suggests some explanations, for the inter-generational continuance of physical punishment. It suggests that, despite evidence of the greater effectiveness of non-punitive disciplinary methods, the use – and abuse – of parental physical punishment is unlikely to end without external intervention such as legal change'.

Box 3.5 describes a case which is interesting in this respect.

Box 3.5 The case of Anne Davis

In July 1993, Anne Davis appealed against Sutton Borough Council's decision to remove her from its register of child-minders for refusing to undertake *not* to smack children in her care. Council policy insists that child-minders must promise not to use corporal punishment and cites the Department of Health guidance published with the 1989 Children Act.

One psychologist who spoke in support of Davis's appeal was Professor Richard Lynn, who suggested that 'for some children, physical discipline is an important part of [the morality] process. From time to time, the most effective way of controlling a child is a light smack'. Lynn informed the court that 'children whose minders and parents did not use any physical punishment were less likely to learn about what behaviour was "socially acceptable" '.

Davis was given further support by another 'expert witness', Lynn Burrows, a writer on child care, who claimed that 'young children particularly understand a smack better than verbal reasoning and were happier with it'. Miss Anne Foreman, the mother of one of the children minded by Davis, agreed that Davis should be allowed to smack her child when she felt it necessary. She said 'I believe that if a child is disciplined well in the early years, he makes a good adult'.

Sutton magistrates subsequently ruled in Davis's favour, their judgement being that 'there is nothing to prevent a parent using lawful chastisement on their child and this includes appropriate smacking. Therefore, a parent must have the right to arrange with another to use this. The chosen person can be a child-minder'. However, according to Allan Levy, QC, who investigated the 'pin-down' regime in Staffordshire children's homes, 'there is a strong argument that now we have ratified the United Nations Convention on the Rights of the Child, article nine imposes on the Government a duty to prevent any kind of punishment'.

In March 1994, the High Court ruled that magistrates were within their rights to overturn Sutton Borough Council's decision not to register Davis as a child-minder. Davis is currently a member of the pressure group *Parents for Discipline*.

(taken from McIlveen et al., 1994)

Even more recent than the Davis case is that of an unnamed 11-year-old boy who has launched a case in the European Court of Human Rights against the British Government. The boy's claim is that the Government failed in its duty to protect him from 'inhuman and degrading treatment' at the hands of his stepfather, who punished his misdemeanours by hitting him with a garden cane (McCartney, 1996). The case has yet to be heard, but it could result in the European Court laying down parameters for the circumstances in which corporal punishment would be permitted (Dyer, 1996).

MATT
EURO COURT
'There, that's the midwife who smacked me'

Figure 3.2 Children are asserting their rights at an increasingly early age! (© Telegraph Group Limited, London, 1996)

Although any such ruling would not be directly enforceable in Britain, the Government would be expected to bring the law into line to comply with its obligations under Article 3 of the European Human Rights Convention, which prohibits inhuman or degrading treatment or punishment. At the time of writing, the British Government has declared its intention to defend parents' right to smack their children, and has no plans to change domestic law (Muir et al., 1996).

The effect of parenting styles on the development of children's intelligence

As we saw in the previous chapter, in some cases babies are reared in unresponsive and unstimulating environments. In the worst of these environments, nothing the children do has any effect on what happens to them. Many babies reared in such environments are generally passive and apathetic because they stop trying to affect anything in their environments. Responsive environments, by contrast, are those in which the individual learns that events in the environment are contingent on his or her behaviour.

A large number of studies have shown that the early home environment and parenting styles can have an effect on IQ. For example, Rathus (1990) reports that high levels of maternal restrictiveness and punishment at age two are correlated with lower IQ scores later on in life. Good parent-child relationships and maternal encouragement of independence, however, have been shown to correlate positively with later IQ scores (McGowan and Johnson, 1984). Box 3.6 summarises some other findings concerning the relationship between parenting styles and IQ.

Box 3.6 Parental styles and IQ

Higher IQ in children has been linked to:

- the provision by parents of appropriate play material (Elardo et al., 1975)
- active parental involvement with the child (Bradley and Caldwell, 1976)
- the extent of home organisation and safety (Bradley and Caldwell, 1984)
- emotionally and verbally responsive mothers (Gottfried, 1984)

As Box 3.6 shows, child-rearing styles which are stimulating are clearly tied to the development of measured intelligence. The lower IQs of some children have been explained in terms of thwarted curiosity, an under-developed attention span, and a general mistrust of adults (Morris, 1988). However, Whitehurst et al. (1988) have shown that the parenting skills beneficial to children can be taught and can produce significant gains at least as far as language and vocabulary skills are concerned. We will discuss this issue further in Chapter 6.

Cross-cultural studies of child rearing

Berry et al. (1992) have identified two main approaches to the cross-cultural study of child-rearing practices. These are *archival studies* and *field studies*. A large number of archival studies have drawn on *ethnographic reports*, that is, reports of studies in which the investigator has become a member of the society that is being investigated. These reports are contained in the *Human Relations Area Files* (or HRAF).

ARCHIVAL STUDIES

The HRAF are based on Murdock's (1975) *Outline of World Cultures* and Murdock et al.'s (1971) *Outline of Cultural Material.* Murdock's (1975) publication identifies a large number of societies, data about which can be used to look for similarities and differences between cultures. Murdock et al.'s publication identifies 79 categories that are considered to be a universal set of concepts to be found in all cultural groups. Barry (1980) has arranged the original 79 categories into eight broader categories. For researchers interested in child rearing, two of these categories (*Individual and family activities* and *Sex and the lifecycle*) are the most important.

The HRAF have been used *holoculturally*, that is, to find correlations between cultural variables across cultures. As far as child rearing is concerned, the HRAF have been used to identify the major dimensions of *variation* in such practices as used in different cultures. As Berry et al. (1992) have noted:

> 'this archival approach allows us to examine child-rearing practices ... in the context of other variables ... that have also been included in the archives; we are thus able to examine how child-rearing fits into ... other features of the group's circumstances'.

In an early study using the HRAF, Whiting and Child (1953) argued that child rearing is identical the world over 'in that it is found always to be concerned with certain universal problems of behaviour'. However, Whiting and Child also argued that in other respects, child-rearing practices differ from one society to another. According to Barry et al. (1959), there are six central dimensions of child rearing which are common to all societies. These are shown in Box 3.7.

Box 3.7 The six central dimensions of child rearing identified by Barry et al. (1959) and believed to be common to all societies

1 Obedience training: The degree to which children are trained to obey adults.

2 Responsibility training: The degree to which children are trained to take responsibility for subsistence or household tasks.

3 Nurturance training: The degree to which children are trained to care for and help younger siblings and other dependent people.

4 Achievement training: The degree to which children are trained to strive towards standards of excellence in performance.

5 Self-reliance training: The degree to which children are trained to take care of themselves and to be independent of assistance from others in supplying their needs or wants.

6 General independence training: The degree to which children are trained (beyond self-reliance as defined above) toward freedom from control, domination and supervision.

(taken from Berry et al., 1992)

Using various techniques, Barry and his colleagues argued that the six dimensions could be essentially reduced to a single dimension which had *pressure towards compliance* (combining training for responsibility and obedience) at one end and *pressure towards assertion* (combining training for achievement, self-reliance and independence) at the other. Different societies could be placed at different positions along this dimension. The researchers also claimed that across *all* societies, girls were more socialised for 'compliance' and boys for 'assertion', and that the magnitude of these differences is linked to a society's *economic mode of subsistence.*

Societies which are pastoral or agricultural ('high food accumulating societies') showed greater 'pressure towards compliance' than hunter-and-gatherer societies ('low food accumulating societies'). However, the claims made by Barry et al. have been disputed. In a re-analysis of the HRAF data, Hendrix (1985), for example, has claimed that there are no sex differences in terms of the ways in which different societies socialise males and females, and that whilst attempts to correlate socialisation with economic mode of subsistence are 'more-or-less accurate', the conclusions drawn by Barry and his colleagues 'were oversimplified (and) somewhat misleading'.

Berry et al. (1992) have suggested that Hendrix is almost certainly wrong in his claims. According to them, the data actually show males to be more assertive, achievement oriented and dominant. Females tend to be socially responsive, passive and submissive, although we should note that Berry and his colleagues acknowledge that their interpretation 'risks oversimplification'.

FIELD STUDIES

Field studies of child rearing began with Whiting's (1963) 'Six cultures' project. The cultural groups studied in the project were the Ilocos (Philippines), Guisii (Kenya), Mixtecan (Mexico), Rajput (India), Taira (Japan) and 'Orchard Town' (United States). Using data derived from interviews with mothers in each of these cultural groups, Minturn and Lambert (1964) found that generally there was greater variation in child-rearing practices *within* cultures than *between* cultures. Some subsequent research studies have supported Minturn and Lambert's findings. In a study of 11 national populations, Lambert et al. (1979) showed that whilst there were variations in child-rearing practices, these were more due to individual and class differences than to cultural differences.

This finding is clearly different from Barry et al.'s finding that different cultures could be placed at different points on a single dimension of child rearing. For Berry et al. (1992):

'There is thus a major inconsistency in the literature: the studies employing ratings from archives have revealed a great deal of variation across cultures in child rearing, while those using direct field observations ... tend to find little. Since the archival indices of child rearing fit into a plausible pattern of relationship with other cultural and ecological variables, it is difficult to dismiss them as invalid. Similarly, the field studies provide compelling evidence that also needs to be taken seriously. This discrepancy clearly sets the stage for future research on these topics.'

Conclusions

Research has shown that there are a number of child-rearing styles used by parents. Styles using too much power or too little power do not seem to be as effective as the style which exercises neither too much nor too little power. Some research into child rearing in non-Western cultures has shown that there are cross-cultural variations in child-rearing practices. Other research has failed to find such variations and indicates that there are greater differences within cultures than between them.

Summary

- Advice on 'how to parent' is big business. According to John B. Watson, probably the first psychologist to offer such advice, giving children too much love would make them unable to cope with the world; they should be treated as though they were young adults, with a minimum of physical affection. Probably the most famous of all parenting guides is Dr Benjamin Spock's *Baby and Child Care*.

- Psychologists generally agree that child rearing can be classified in terms of two **independent** dimensions, i.e. **emotional responsiveness** and **control/demandingness**.
- Emotional responsiveness ranges from warmth, love and affection to coldness and rejection. 'Warm' parents communicate their happiness at having children and their enjoyment in being with them, while 'cold' parents tend to complain about their children's behaviour. Children of 'warm' parents display fewer behavioural problems and their values become more similar to their parents' compared with children of 'cold' parents.
- Control/demandingness ranges from extremely restrictive (**authoritarian power restriction**), whereby the parents impose many rules and supervise their children very closely, to extremely permissive (**indifferent and neglecting**), whereby parents impose few, if any, rules, supervise them less closely and show little concern over their children's cleanliness.
- Baumrind identified four dimensions of child rearing (**control, demands for maturity**, **clarity of communication** and **nurturance**) and three child-rearing styles: **permissive**, **authoritarian** and **authoritative**.
- **Permissive** parents, who may be indifferent or preoccupied with other things, make few demands on their children and are reluctant to punish them for inappropriate behaviour. A 'hands-off' policy is adopted in the hope that giving children their freedom will encourage self-reliance and initiative.
- **Authoritarian** parents rely on strictly enforced rules to make children adhere to their standards. They tend to be autocratic, leaving little room for the discussion of alternative points of view, show little warmth, nurturance or communication with their children and use punishment to ensure obedience.
- **Authoritative** parents have definite standards and rules that they expect their children to meet, but children are usually asked for their opinion during discussion and rule-making sessions and are encouraged to think independently and acquire a sense that their views are valued.
- According to Baumrind, children of parents using different child-rearing styles differ in terms of their **instrumental competence** (social responsibility, independence, achievement orientation and vitality). Children of authoritative parents score highest on all four measures, those of authoritarian parents tend to score lowest, while those of permissive parents were quite confident and self-reliant but score low on other measures. Baumrind also found sex differences in instrumental competence related to different styles.
- These early findings were confirmed when the children had reached adolescence. Consequently, it is widely accepted that neither the permissive nor the authoritarian styles helps to develop social or emotional competence in children. One possible reason for this is that neither style enables children to develop **internal standards**, due to either excessive control (authoritarian) or failure to hold children responsible for their actions (permissive).
- Maccoby and Martin modified Baumrind's original categories to produce a two-dimensional classification of child-rearing styles. The two dimensions are **demanding/undemanding** and **parent-centred/child-centred**.
- The undemanding dimension corresponds to Baumrind's permissive style. Maccoby and Martin identify two permissive styles. In the **indifferent-uninvolved** there is minimal parental contact with the children and few or no rules for behaviour. The **indulgent-permissive** style also involves a lack of rules, with few restrictions placed on children, but it is child-centred. Parents are tolerant and responsive towards their children, reinforcing desirable behaviour but rarely using punishment.
- What makes the authoritative style the most beneficial to children are parental expectations for mature behaviour, the encouragement of individuality, respect for children's rights, the firm enforcement of rules and the encouragement of two-way communication. It also gives children control over their lives.
- The authoritative style also aids the development of interpersonal skills. Elements of the style can be taught to parents, and as parents learn them, so their children develop more positive social skills. The media help to promote the authoritative style, and there is evidence that parents are influenced by scientific theories of child rearing as presented in the media.
- Most parents show some of the characteristics of all the styles at one time or another, making it difficult to categorise them. Parenting style is influenced by the child's biological organisation, marital discord and parental personality.
- According to Bronfenbrenner, perhaps the most crucial factor is the child's **perception** of the par-

enting style: even the most extreme authoritarian style may not be completely negative if children believe that their parents love them and are genuinely concerned about them.

- Most of the evidence is **correlational**, so we cannot be sure that a particular style produces a particular type of child. For example, socially and emotionally well-adjusted children may **elicit** an authoritative style from their parents.
- According to Darling and Steinberg's **contextual model of parenting style**, we should distinguish between parental **styles** and **practices**. Parental styles create a particular emotional climate and affect children indirectly by making practices (which can have a direct influence) more or less effective and influencing children's receptiveness to them. Children's receptiveness can also influence parental practices.
- Recent research by Belsky suggests that toddlers' temper tantrums are caused by their parents' failure to show respect for the child's emerging autonomy (**control-with-guidance**). 'Terrible twos' were much more likely to have parents with financial difficulties and high levels of occupational stress, and who tended to use an authoritarian style. A 'terrible two' is also likely to become a 'terrible' three, four and five.
- **Induction**, **love-withdrawal** and **power assertion** are three methods used by parents to **enforce restrictions** on their children. Most effective are inductive methods, in which children are given knowledge that will help them to behave appropriately in other situations.
- Love-withdrawal may involve ignoring or isolating the child or expressing disappointment. Power assertion involves coercing children by overpowering or intimidating them, as well as using tangible rewards and punishments.
- Rewarding children for appropriate behaviour is generally more effective than punishing inappropriate behaviour. The punisher presents an aggressive model to the child, and the negative feelings elicited become associated with the surrounding cues, making it less likely that the child will turn to the parent at times of conflict or uncertainty. Also, punishment cannot teach the child about appropriate behaviour and may erode his or her sense of autonomy, self-esteem and security.
- According to Leach, several countries, including Britain, have banned physical punishment in educational and other care institutions; others have outlawed its use by parents. The 'pseudo-scientific' approach taken by many popular books and magazines gives credibility to 'common-sense' parental statements about the effects of punishment.
- Punishment can effectively **suppress** inappropriate behaviour. However, it is unlikely to be effective in helping parents to shape their children's behaviour as they would like or in the self-disciplined way required by society.
- According to Leach, physical punishment can be harmful to children, making them more vulnerable to physical abuse. There is also evidence that punishment persists across generations, and it is unlikely to end without legal intervention. However, the British Government intends to defend parents' right to smack their children.
- Babies brought up in extremely unresponsive and unstimulating environments are generally passive and apathetic. Many studies have shown that high levels of maternal restrictiveness and punishment at age two are correlated with lower IQ scores later on in life, while having an emotionally and verbally responsive mother correlated with higher IQ scores.
- The lower IQs of some children have been explained in terms of thwarted curiosity, underdeveloped attention span and a general mistrust of adults. But it has been shown that parenting skills can be taught, producing significant benefits in their children, at least with regard to language and vocabulary.
- According to Berry et al., **archival studies** and **field studies** are the two main approaches to the **cross-cultural study** of child rearing. Many archival studies draw on **ethnographic reports**, which are contained in the **Human Relations Area File** (HRAF), which are themselves based on publications by Murdock.
- Murdock et al.'s *Outline of Cultural Material* identifies 79 categories believed to be a universal set of concepts found in all cultural groups. Barry has re-arranged these into eight broader categories.
- The HRAF have been used **holoculturally**, i.e. to find correlations between variables across cultures. They have been used to identify the major dimensions of **variation** in child-rearing practices as used in different cultures. This archival approach allows child rearing to be examined in the context of other cultural variables.
- In an early study, Whiting and Child concluded that child rearing is identical the world over, in that it is always concerned with certain universal problems of behaviour. But they also argued that in other respects, practices vary between cultures.
- According to Barry et al., there are six central

dimensions of child rearing common to all societies: **obedience training**, **responsibility training**, **nurturance training**, **achievement training**, **self-reliance training** and **general independence training**.

- These six dimensions could be reduced to a single dimension with **pressure towards compliance** at one end and **pressure towards assertion** at the other. Different societies could be placed at different positions along this dimension.
- Barry et al. also argued that across all societies, girls were more socialised for compliance and boys for assertion; the size of such differences is linked to a society's **economic mode of existence**. These claims have been disputed by Hendrix. However, according to Berry et al., males are clearly more assertive, achievement-oriented and dominant, and females more socially responsive, passive and submissive.
- Field studies of child rearing began with Whiting's 'Six cultures' project. Based on interviews with mothers, Minturn and Lambert found that generally there was greater variation **within** than **between** cultures. Subsequent research has supported this conclusion: differences that are found may be due more to individual and class than cultural differences.
- The findings of archival and field studies tend to be inconsistent, with the former showing a great deal of variation and the latter very little. According to Berry et al., both sets of findings need to be taken seriously and further research is clearly needed.

PART 2
Cognitive development

PIAGET'S THEORY OF COGNITIVE DEVELOPMENT

Introduction and overview

According to Meadows (1993, 1995), cognitive development is concerned with the study of 'the child as thinker'. Psychologists differ in terms of their images of what children are like. Information-processing theorists, for example, see children as being manipulators of symbols. 'Vygotskyans' (after the Russian psychologist Lev Vygotsky), by contrast, see children as participants in an interactive process by which socially and culturally determined knowledge and understanding become individualised. However, of all the theories of cognitive development that have been advanced, none has received as much attention as the cognitive-developmental theory proposed by Jean Piaget, for whom children's behaviour can be seen in terms of *adaptation to the environment.*

Our aim in this chapter is to describe and evaluate Piaget's theory of cognitive development. Although once regarded as the major framework for understanding cognitive development, Piaget's theory has been subject to a number of criticisms. Despite this, it continues to be a vital source of influence and inspiration within both psychology and education. Because of this, we feel justified in affording Piaget's theory of cognitive development a chapter to itself. In the following chapter we will consider the application of the theory to education, and some alternative theories of cognitive development and their application to education. We begin this chapter by briefly reviewing the various theories of cognitive development that have been proposed.

Theories of cognitive development: a brief review

Like other sciences, psychology is a discipline in which theories compete for acceptance as explanations of particular phenomena. In the case of cognitive development, a large number of theories have been advanced. The earliest theory of cognitive development, and the focus of this chapter, is that offered by Jean Piaget. One of the first to respond critically to Piaget's ideas was Lev Vygotsky who, during the period 1924–1934, outlined an approach to cognitive development which many see as being the most powerful alternative to Piaget and which we will consider in the next chapter.

As well as Vygotsky, early challenges to Piaget were made by B.F. Skinner (e.g. 1969), a *behaviourist psychologist,* and Jerome Bruner (e.g. 1963). Bruner is often referred to as an *interventionist psychologist* because of his belief that cognitive development could be accelerated by 'challenging' children to reach as high a level of academic performance as possible (Sutherland, 1992). We shall have more to say about this and Bruner's theory of cognitive development in Chapters 5 and 6. More recent challenges to Piaget have come from *constructivists* (e.g. Ausubel, 1968), *information-processing theorists* (e.g. Sternberg, 1986), *domain-specific theorists* (e.g. Carey, 1988), *structuralists* (e.g. Keil, 1986) and *meta-cognitive theorists* (e.g. Karmiloff-Smith, 1986). The views of information-processing theorists will, like the alternative theories offered by Vygotsky and Bruner, be considered in the next chapter.

Although it is clear from this brief review that there are many theories of cognitive development other than Piaget's, there are those who 'have remained loyal to the founding father' (Sutherland, 1992). These include *fundamentalist Piagetians* (e.g. Smith, 1982), *neo-Piagetians* (e.g. Pascual-Leone, 1976; Case, 1985) and the *post-Piagetians* (e.g. Peel, 1972). Although the terms 'neo-' and 'post-' are treated synonymously by some researchers, Sutherland (1992) has argued that it is possible to distinguish between them. Indeed, according to Sutherland, it is even possible to identify a distinct school of *American post-Piagetians* (e.g. Feldman, 1986) whose stance differs somewhat from the perspective of their European counterparts!

Jean Piaget's theory of cognitive development

Jean Piaget has been one of the most influential figures in psychology's history. Piaget was interested in the ways in which children's cognitive capacities develop, and his theory of cognitive development focuses on the organisation of intelligence and how it changes as children grow. Piaget is known as the founder of *genetic epistemology*, that is, the study of the development of knowledge. Based originally on observations of his own three children, Piaget concluded that younger children were not just *quantitatively* different from older children in terms of their intelligence, but they also thought in *qualitatively* different ways. Put another way, young children differ from older children in *kind* as well as *degree*.

Piaget believed that cognitive development occurred through the interaction between innate capacities and environmental events, and progressed through a series of *hierarchical stages*. These stages are held to be *invariant*, that is, all children pass through them in the same sequence without skipping any or, except in the case of brain damage, regressing to earlier ones. The stages are also held to be *universal*, that is, the same for all people irrespective of their culture. Underlying the changes that occur are certain *functional invariants* or fundamental aspects of the developmental process which remain the same and work in the same way through the various stages. Before we can understand these unchanging features of development (of which *assimilation*, *accommodation* and *equilibration* are of particular importance), we need to look at what it is that actually does change. The two principal *cognitive structures* subject to change are *schemas* (or *schemata*) and *concepts*.

SCHEMAS (OR SCHEMATA) AND CONCEPTS

A *schema* (or *scheme*) can be thought of as the basic building block or unit of intelligent behaviour. Piaget conceived of a schema as a mental structure which organises our past experiences and provides a way of understanding future experiences. Life begins with simple schemas which are largely confined to inbuilt reflexes (such as sucking and grasping) that operate independently of other reflexes and are activated only when certain objects are present. As we grow, so our schemas become increasingly complex, so that by adulthood we have very many schemas. Piaget sees the acquisition of knowledge of the environment as occurring through the development of *concepts* or rules that describe the properties of events and their relation with other concepts (Carlson, 1988).

ASSIMILATION, ACCOMMODATION AND EQUILIBRATION

Assimilation is the process by which we incorporate new information into our existing schemas. For example, babies will reflexively suck from a nipple and use this behaviour to suck from other objects such as a finger. Assimilation leads to *accommodation* as the infant learns about the properties of the object. So, in order to suck from a bottle or drink from a cup, the initial sucking reflex must be *modified* to enable drinking to take place from other vessels. When a child is able to deal with most, if not all, new experiences by assimilating them, it is in a state of *equilibrium*. This state is brought about by *equilibration* or the process of seeking 'mental balance'. However, if existing schemas are inadequate to cope with new situations, the less comfortable state of *cognitive disequilibrium* occurs. In order to restore equilibrium, *accommodation* must take place and the existing schema must be 'stretched' in order to take in (or 'accommodate') new information. The necessary and complementary processes of assimilation and accommodation constitute the fundamental process of *adaptation*.

Piaget's four stages of cognitive development

The four stages of cognitive development identified by Piaget and the approximate ages at which they begin and end are shown in Table 4.1.

Table 4.1 Piaget's four stages of cognitive development

Stage	*Approximate age*
Sensorimotor	Birth to two years
Preoperational	Two to seven years
Concrete operational	Seven to 11 years
Formal operational	11 years onwards

Each stage represents a stage in the development of intelligence (hence *sensorimotor intelligence*, *preoperational intelligence* and so on) and the stages are really a way of summarising the various schemas a child has at a particular time. The ages given in Table 4.1 are approximate because children move through the stages at different rates due to differences in both the environment and their biological maturation. Nor, we should note, do children move from one stage to another 'overnight'. Instead, they pass through *transitional periods* in which their thinking is a mixture of two stages.

We should also note that the concept of 'stages' in development is often taken to mean that development is *discontinuous*. For Piaget, development is a gradual and *continuous* process of change. However, later stages build on earlier ones (which is why the sequence is invariant). The passage from one stage to the next occurs through *cognitive disequilibrium*, which we described earlier. In order to achieve equilibrium, the child is 'forced' to higher levels of intellectual understanding (Krebs and Blackman, 1988).

THE SENSORIMOTOR STAGE

The sensorimotor stage lasts for approximately the first two years of life. During this stage, infants learn about the world primarily through their senses and discover things by sensing ('sensori-') and doing ('motor'). On the basis of observations of his own children, Piaget (1952) divided the sensorimotor stage into six sub-stages. These, and the 'milestones' associated with them, are summarised in Box 4.1.

Box 4.1 The six sub-stages of the sensorimotor stage

Sub-stage 1 (Exercising reflexes; birth to one month): Reflexes are practised until they function smoothly. The infant has no intentionality and no understanding of an object.

Sub-stage 2 (Primary circular reactions; one to four months): Reflexes are extended to new objects and the infant coordinates simple schemas (such as grasping and looking). Behaviours that cause specific events are repeated. The infant looks where an object disappears (for a few moments).

Sub-stage 3 (Secondary circular reactions; four to ten months): The infant achieves fluid coordination of all senses, and is able to anticipate events and results of actions. A partially hidden object can be found and, in the last months of this sub-stage, the infant achieves *object permanence* (but see main text).

Sub-stage 4 (The coordination of secondary circular reactions; ten to 12 months): The infant represents objects in its mind and demonstrates the beginning of symbolic behaviour and memory. A goal can be decided on and then acted on to be achieved. A completely hidden object can be found.

Sub-stage 5 (Tertiary circular reactions; 12 to 18 months): The infant searches for novelty in the environment and uses several interchangeable schemas to achieve goals. Experiments are conducted to see what will happen. An object hidden under one of several covers can be found.

Sub-stage 6 (Invention of new means through mental combinations; 18 to 24 months): The infant thinks about a problem before acting, and thoughts begin to dominate actions. Objects can be mentally manipulated to reach goals. An object placed in a container and then hidden can be found.

(based on Tomlinson–Keasey, 1985, and Krebs and Blackman, 1988)

Piaget saw the infant's physical exploration of the environment as being cognitively productive, the frequent interaction with objects ultimately leading to the development of *object permanence.* As Box 4.1 shows, Piaget discovered that in sub-stage 2, an infant will look where an object disappears for a few moments, but will not search for it. If the object does not reappear the infant appears to lose interest. Piaget called this *passive exploration,* because the infant expects the object to reappear but does not actively search for it (if it is 'out of sight', it is 'out of mind': see Figure 4.1).

In sub-stage 3, an infant will reach for an object that is partially hidden, suggesting that it realises that the rest of it is attached to the part that is showing. However, if the object is *completely hidden,* infants make no attempt to retrieve it. In sub-stage 4, object permanence has developed and the infant realises that objects removed from sight still exist, and so a hidden object will be searched for ('out of sight' is no longer 'out of mind': see Figure 4.2). Although the infant will retrieve a hidden object, its behavioural schemas for dealing with such objects are not yet fully developed. So, if the infant is allowed to retrieve an object hidden in the same place on several occasions, it will persist in looking for the object in that place even when it is hidden in a new place.

This phenomenon has disappeared in sub-stage 5, as a result of the infant's progressively more sophisticated understanding of the physical properties of objects. Even so, object permanence is not yet fully developed. For example, suppose an infant sees an object placed in a matchbox, and the matchbox is then put under a pillow. When the infant isn't looking, the object is removed from the matchbox and left under the pillow.

Figure 4.1 If an object is made to disappear from an infant's sight, the infant appears to lose interest in it and does not actively search for it

If the matchbox is given to the infant, it will open it expecting to find the object. On finding no object, the infant will *not* look under the pillow. This is because it

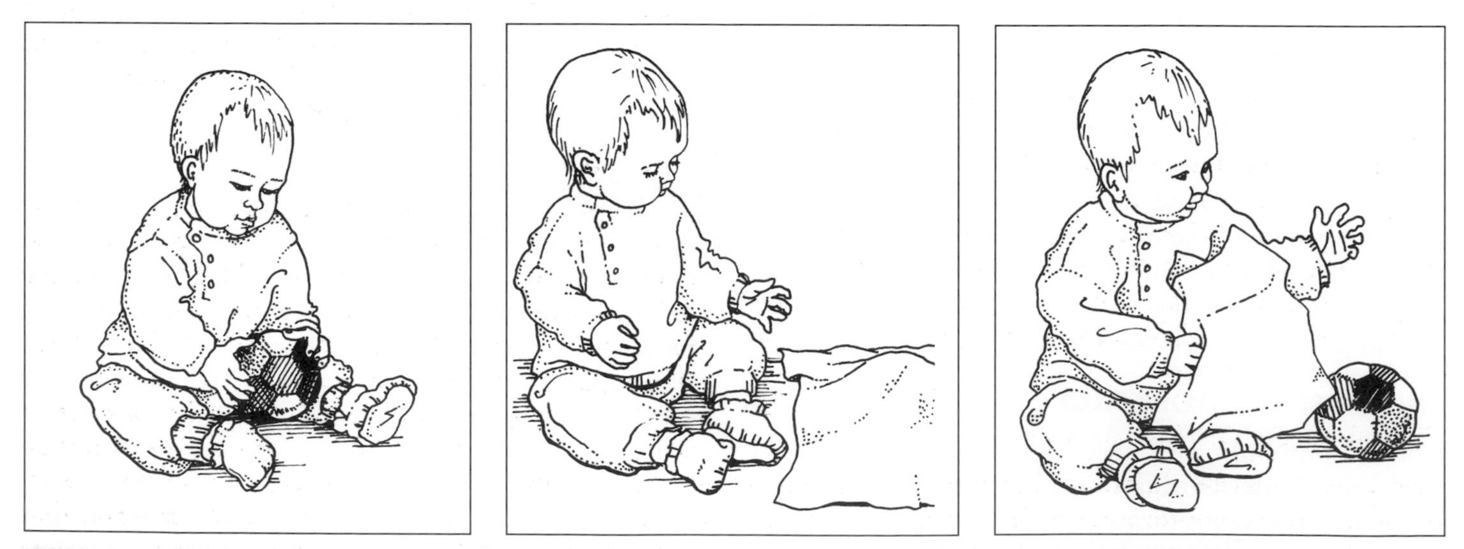

Figure 4.2 Whilst a six-month-old child will not search for an object that has been removed from its sight, an eight-month-old child will, because it has developed object permanence

cannot take into account the possibility that something might have happened that it has not actually seen, a phenomenon termed the *failure to infer invisible displacements*. Once the infant can infer 'invisible displacements' (in sub-stage 6), the development of object permanence is complete.

The emergence of object permanence occurs simultaneously with the emergence of a *fear of strangers* (which we described in Chapter 1). Note that if handed over to a stranger at eight or nine months of age, infants will cry and reach for their familiar caregivers. It is likely that, by the age of eight months, the infant has schemas for familiar faces, and faces that cannot be assimilated into these schemas result in distress (Kagan, 1984).

As well as object permanence, other cognitive structures have developed by the end of the sensorimotor stage. *Self-recognition*, the ability to name the self correctly in a mirror, is evident (Bertenthal and Fischer, 1978), as is *symbolic thought*. This is the capacity to construct a mental representation of an object (a symbol) and deal with it as though it were the object (Crider et al., 1989). *Language*, designating words for objects, is one example of symbolic thought.

By the end of the sensorimotor stage, schemas are 'interiorised' such that insightful solutions to problems can be found. For example, in order to open a door, an infant might need to put a cup down. After looking at the door and then the cup, the infant 'realises', through a mental image of the door opening, that the cup is in the way. So, the infant moves the cup to a safer place before opening the door.

Two other manifestations of the general symbolic function are *deferred imitation* and *representational* (or *make-believe*) play. Deferred imitation is the ability to imitate or reproduce something that has been seen or heard but is no longer present (Meltzoff and Moore, 1983). This indicates an important advance in the capacity to *remember*. Representational play involves using one object as though it were another. Like deferred imitation, this ability depends on the infant's growing ability to form mental images of things and people in their absence.

THE PREOPERATIONAL STAGE

Probably the main difference between the preoperational and sensorimotor stage is the continued development and use of internal images, symbols and language, which is especially important for the child's developing sense of self-awareness. At the same time, the child's world is still fundamentally absolute, and things are very much as they seem. As a result, the child tends to be influenced by how things look rather than by logical principles or operations (hence the term preoperational). Piaget subdivided the preoperational stage into the *preconceptual sub-stage* (two to four years) and the *intuitive sub-stage* (four to seven years). The absolute nature of the preconceptual child's thinking makes it difficult for it to understand relative terms such as 'bigger' or 'stronger' and things tend to be 'biggest' or just 'big'. The intuitive child does have this ability but, as we will now see, is still limited in terms of its ability to think logically.

Seriation and artificialism

Two characteristics of preoperational thought are lack of *seriation* and *artificialism*. In seriation, the preconceptual child has difficulty arranging objects on the basis of a particular dimension, such as increasing height (Piaget and Szeminska, 1952). Artificialism is the belief that environmental features have been designed and constructed by people. For example, the question 'What makes it rain?' might elicit the answer 'Someone emptying a watering can'. The question 'Why is the sky blue?' might produce the answer 'Somebody painted it'.

Transductive reasoning and animism

Transductive reasoning involves drawing an inference about the relationship between two things based on a single attribute. If both cats and dogs have four legs, then cats must be dogs. This sort of reasoning can lead to *animism*, that is, the belief that inanimate objects have life and mental processes. So, because the sun appears to follow us when we walk, it must be alive and the same as people (Piaget, 1973).

Centration

This is focusing on a single perceptual quality and the inability to take into account more than one perceptual factor at a time. A preconceptual child asked to divide apples into those that are 'big and red' and those that are 'small and green' will either put all the red (or green) apples together irrespective of their size or will put all the big (or small) apples together irrespective of their colour. Until the child can *decentre*, it will not be able to classify things in a logical or systematic way. Centration is also illustrated by *syncretic thought*, that is, the tendency to link neighbouring objects or events on the basis of what *individual instances* have in common. By the age of five, however, most children are able to select examples of things and say what they have in common. Centration is also associated with the inability to conserve (see below).

Egocentrism

According to Piaget, preoperational children are *egocentric*, that is, they see the world from their own standpoint and cannot appreciate that other people might see things differently. Put another way, the child cannot put itself 'in other people's shoes' in order to realise that other people do not know or perceive everything the child knows or perceives. Consider the following example (taken from Phillips, 1969) of a conversation between the experimenter and a four-year-old boy:

Experimenter: 'Do you have a brother?'

Child: 'Yes'

Experimenter: 'What's his name?'

Child: 'Jim'

Experimenter: 'Does Jim have a brother?'

Child: 'No.'

Similarly, if asked 'Why is grass green?', an egocentric child might reply 'Because it's my favourite colour'. One of the most famous examples of apparent egocentrism is Piaget and Inhelder's (1956) 'Swiss mountain scene' test. This is described in Box 4.2.

Box 4.2 The 'Swiss mountain scene' test of egocentrism

The three papier-mâché model mountains (see Figure 4.3) are of different colours. One has snow on the top, one has a house on the top, and one has a red cross on the top. The child is allowed to walk round and explore the model. Then the child is seated on one side and a doll is placed at some *different* location. The child is shown ten pictures of different views of the mountains and asked to choose the one that represents how the doll sees them.

Four-year-olds were completely unaware of perspectives different from their own and always chose a picture which matched their view of the model. Six-year-olds showed some awareness, but often chose the wrong picture. Only seven- and eight-year-olds consistently chose the picture that represented the doll's view. According to Piaget, children below the age of seven are bound by the *egocentric illusion*. They fail to understand that what they see is relative to their own position and instead take it to represent 'the world as it really is'.

Conservation

As we noted earlier, linked to centration is *conservation*, the understanding that any quantity (such as number, volume, length and weight) can remain the same despite physical changes in the arrangement of an object or objects. Piaget believed that preoperational

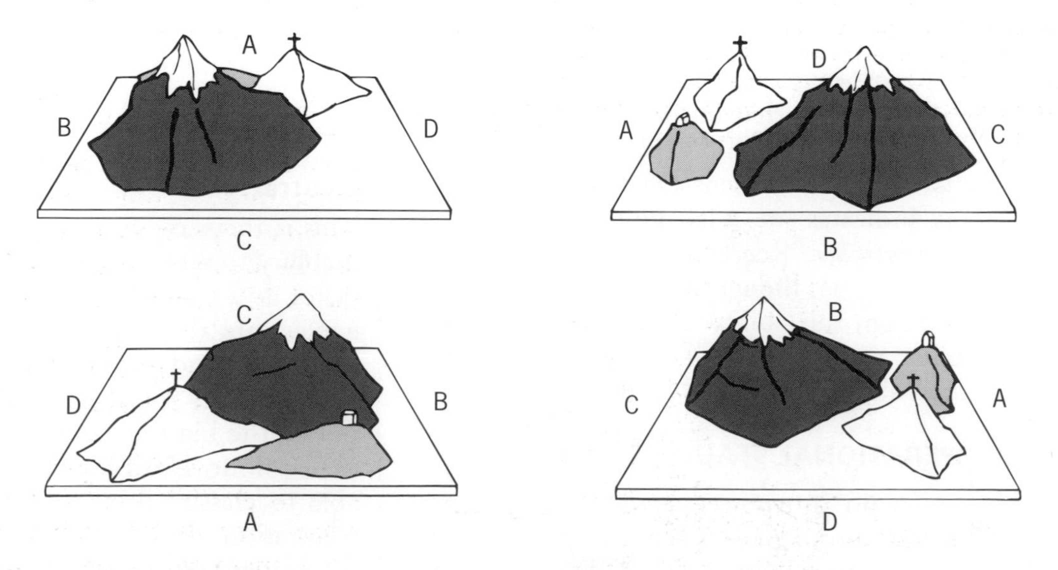

Figure 4.3 Piaget and Inhelder's three-mountain scene, seen from four different sides (from Gross, 1996, and based on Smith and Cowie, 1991)

FIGURE 4.4 Piaget's test for the conservation of liquid quantity

The child is shown two identical beakers and agrees that they contain the same amount of liquid

The contents of one of the beakers is then poured into another beaker which is taller but narrower

Although the child has seen the liquid being poured and agrees that none has been added or spilled in the process (Piaget calls this 'identity'), when asked if one beaker contains more or if the two have identical quantities, the preoperational child typically says that the taller beaker contains more

children could not conserve because their thinking is dominated by the perceptual appearance of things. Figure 4.4 shows Piaget's test for the conservation of *liquid quantity*, while Box 4.3 (overleaf) describes tests for the conservation of number, length and substance or quantity.

Piaget saw the child's inability to conserve as another example of centration. In the case of liquid quantity, for example, the child centres on just one dimension of the beaker, usually its height, and fails to take width into account. Only in the concrete operational stage does the child understand that 'getting taller' and 'getting narrower' tend to cancel each other out, an understanding Piaget calls *compensation*. If the contents of the taller beaker are poured back into the shorter one, the child will again say that the two shorter beakers contain the same amount. What it cannot seem to do is perform the operation mentally – it cannot show *reversibility*, the understanding that every action has a logical opposite and that what can be done can be undone *without any gain or loss*.

Concrete operational stage

In this stage, the child becomes capable of logical thought, but only in the presence of actual and observable objects. Thus, the mental operation can only be performed in the presence of actual objects, and the child must be looking at or manipulating those objects. The concrete operational stage is characterised by the ability to conserve and the related phenomena of reversibility and classification. For example, the child can recognise that dogs and cats are both animals and in this respect are the same.

Further examples of the child's ability to decentre include its being able to appreciate that objects can belong to more than one class (as in the case of Andrew being Bob's brother *and* Charlie's best friend). The concrete operational stage also heralds a significant decline in egocentrism (and the growing relativism of the child's viewpoint), the onset of seriation (learning how to order things) and reciprocity of relationships (such as knowing that adding one to three produces the same amount as taking one from five).

We should, however, note that some types of conservation are mastered before others, and that the order in which they appear tends to be invariant. Liquid quantity is mastered by age six to seven, substance/quantity and length by age seven to eight, weight by age eight to

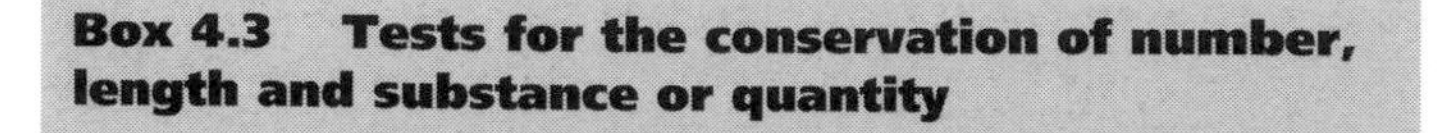

Box 4.3 Tests for the conservation of number, length and substance or quantity

Conservation of number
Two rows of counters are placed in one-to-one correspondence. The child agrees that the two rows contain an equal number of counters.

One of the rows is then elongated (or contracted). The child is asked whether each row still has the same number of counters.

Conservation of length
Two sticks are aligned in front of the child, who agrees that they are both the same length.

One of the sticks is moved to the right (or left). The child is asked whether they are still the same length.

Conservation of substance or quantity
The experimenter presents two identical Plasticine balls. The child agrees that there is the same amount in each.

The shape of one of the balls is changed, and the child is asked whether there is still the same amount in each.

(based on LeFrancois, 1986)

ten and volume by age 11 to 12. Piaget called the step-by-step acquisition of new operations *décalage* (displacement or 'slips in level of performance'). In the case of conservation, décalage is *horizontal* because there are inconsistencies within the same kind of ability or operation (a seven-year-old child can conserve number but not weight, for example). *Vertical* décalage refers to inconsistencies between different abilities or operations. For example, a child may have mastered all kinds of classification, but not all kinds of conservation.

One remaining problem for the concrete operational child is *transitivity* tasks. For example, if told that 'Alan is taller than Bob, and Bob is taller than Charlie' and asked whether Alan or Charlie is taller, children younger than 11 are unable to solve this problem entirely in their heads. The concrete operational child is usually limited to solving such problems using real (or concrete) objects (such as dolls). Despite these limitations, however, concrete operational children are becoming increasingly intellectually sophisticated and enjoy jokes that enable them to utilise abilities such as conservation, as shown by their appreciation of the following: Mr Jones went into a restaurant and ordered a whole pizza for his dinner. When the waiter asked if he wanted it cut into six or eight pieces, Mr Jones said 'Oh, you'd better make it six, I could never eat eight pieces!' (McGhee, 1976).

The formal operational stage

While the concrete operational child is still concerned with manipulating *things* (even if this is done in the mind), the formal operational thinker can manipulate *ideas or propositions* and can reason solely on the basis of verbal statements (these are called 'first order' and 'second order' operations respectively). 'Formal' refers to the ability to follow the form of an argument without reference to its particular content. In transitivity problems, for example, 'If A is taller than B, and B is taller than C, then A is taller than C' is a form of argument such that the conclusion is logically true and will always be true, regardless of what A, B and C might refer to.

The formal operational thinker, then, uses an essentially adult form of logical and symbolic representation. Those in this stage can also think *hypothetically*, that is, they can think about what could be as well as what actually is. To use Cowan's (1978) phrase, formal operational thinkers can 'discover the world of the hypothetical'. For example, Dworetzky (1981) notes that if formal operational thinkers are asked what it would be like if people had tails, they might say 'Dogs would know when you were happy' or 'Lovers could hold their tails in secret under the table'. Concrete operational thinkers might tell you 'not to be so silly' or say where on the body the tail might be, showing their dependence on what has actually been seen. The ability to imagine and discuss things that have never been encountered is evidence of the continued decentration that occurs beyond concrete combinations: formal operational thinkers display *hypothetico-deductive reasoning.*

One example of formal operational thinking is seen in Archimedes' law of floating bodies. If an object's density (defined as its weight divided by its volume) is less than that of water, the object will float. To decide if an object will float, the concept of both weight and volume must be understood. Both of these require operations, and these operations must be placed in a logical relationship to each other so that the density of the object relative to the density of water can be determined (Krebs and Blackman, 1988). By relating these operations in a logical way, the formal operational thinker is doing what Piaget calls *operating on operations.*

Another example of formal operational thinking was provided by Inhelder and Piaget (1958). They gave adolescents five containers filled with clear liquid. Four of these were 'test chemicals' and one an 'indicator'. When the proper combination of one or more test chemicals was added to the indicator, it turned yellow. The problem was to find this proper combination. Preoperational children simply mix the chemicals randomly, and concrete operational children, although more systematic, generally fail to test all possible combinations. Only formal operational thinkers consider all alternatives and systematically vary one factor at a time. Also, they often write down all the results and try to draw general conclusions about each chemical.

An evaluation of Piaget's theory of cognitive development

Piaget's theory has had an enormous impact on the way in which developmental psychologists have attempted to understand cognitive development. Despite its unmatched influence, however, Piaget's theory has received much criticism. As Flavell (1982) has remarked:

> 'Like all theories of great reach and significance . . . it has problems that gradually come to light as years and years of thinking and research get done on it. Thus, some of us now think that the theory may in varying degrees be unclear, incorrect and incomplete'.

Some of these problems are considered below.

OBJECT PERMANENCE

Piaget's claims about the sensorimotor stage have been criticised in both general and particular terms (e.g. Mandler, 1990). Piaget's claims about object permanence have received much attention. Bower and Wishart (1972), for example, found that the way in which an object is made to disappear influences the infant's response. If the infant is looking at an object and reaching for it and the lights are turned off, it will continue to search for up to one and a half minutes (as filmed with special cameras). This suggests that it *does* remember the object is there (so 'out of sight' is not 'out of mind': see page 42). Other research (e.g. Bower, 1977; Baillargeon, 1987) has shown that object permanence can occur as early as three and a half months of age and that it is *not* necessary for a baby younger than six months to see all of an object in order to respond to it.

CENTRATION

One way to study centration (and classification) is through *class inclusion tasks.* For example, suppose a preoperational child is presented with several wooden beads, mostly brown but a few white. If asked 'Are they all wooden?', the child will respond correctly. If asked 'Are there more brown or more white beads?', the child will again respond correctly. However, if asked 'Are there more brown beads or more beads?', the child will say there are more brown beads. According to Piaget, the child fails to understand the relationship between the whole (the class of wooden beads) and the parts (the classes of brown and white beads). These are referred to as the *superordinate* and the *subordinate* classes respectively. The child is still influenced by what it perceives. It can see the brown beads, which are more numerous than the white, in a more immediate and direct way than the wooden beads as a whole (despite being able to answer the first question correctly).

Piaget argued that this was another example of the inability to decentre. However, Donaldson (1978), for example, has asked if the difficulty the child experiences is to do with what is expected of it and how the task is presented. Donaldson describes a study with six-year-old children using four toy cows, of which three were black and one white. The cows were laid on their sides and the children told they were 'sleeping'. Of those asked 'Are there more black cows or more cows?', 25 per cent answered correctly. However, of those asked 'Are there more black cows or more *sleeping* cows?', 48 per cent answered correctly.

Similarly, Gelman (1978) has argued that the word 'more' has a different meaning for children and adults. Adults use 'more' to mean 'containing a greater number'. For children, however, 'more' refers to the general concept of larger, longer, occupying more space and so on. In one experiment (Hodkin, 1981), children were shown two rows of sweets as in Figure 4.5.

When asked if there were more Smarties or more sweets, the children replied that there were 'more Smarties'. However, when asked if there were 'more Smarties or more *of all of the sweets*, children replied that there were more of all of the sweets showing that they could understand class inclusion.

EGOCENTRISM

Piaget's views about the egocentrism of children younger than seven have also been challenged. For example, Gelman (1979) has shown that four-year-old children do adjust their explanations of things to make them clearer to a listener who is blindfold. If the children were entirely egocentric, such a finding would not be expected. Nor would we expect four-year-olds to use simpler forms of speech when talking to two-year-olds, yet this is what they do (Gelman, 1979). We would, however, expect egocentric children to choose toys *they* liked for their mothers' birthday. Marvin (1975) has shown that this is not the case, and at least some four-year-olds choose presents appropriate for their mothers.

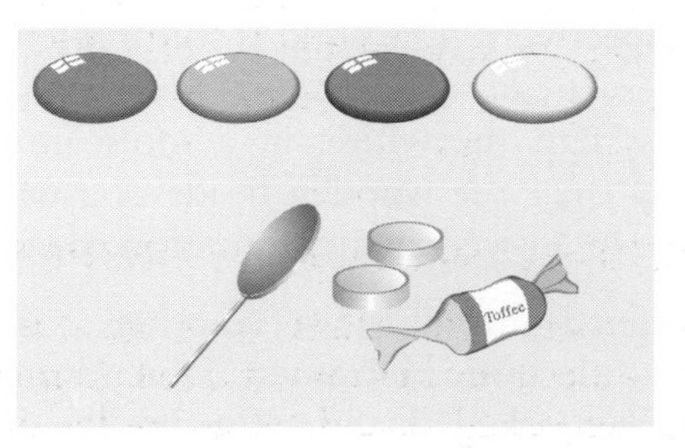

Top row = Smarties
Bottom row = Other kinds of sweets

Figure 4.5 Stimuli used in Hodkin's (1981) experiment

The 'Swiss mountain scene' test (see Box 4.2 and Figure 4.3) has also been challenged for being an unusually difficult way of presenting a problem to a young child. Research conducted by Borke (1975) and Hughes (cited in Donaldson, 1978) has shown that when the task is presented in a context that is meaningful to the child and makes what Donaldson calls 'human sense', even children as young as three and a half can appreciate the world as another person sees it.

CONSERVATION

The ability to conserve also seems to occur earlier than Piaget believed. Rose and Blank (1974), for example, showed that when the *pre-transformation* question (that is, the question asked before the contents of one beaker (say) are poured into another) was dropped from the procedure, then six-year-olds often succeeded on the conservation of number task and, importantly, made fewer errors on the standard version of the task when tested a week later. These findings were replicated by Samuel and Bryant (1984) who also showed that dropping the pre-transformation task resulted in liquid quantity and substance being conserved by preoperational children. According to Donaldson (1978), the standard version of the task unwittingly 'forces' children to produce the wrong answer against their better judgement by the mere fact that the same question is asked twice, before *and* after the transformation. In Donaldson's view, the children reason along the lines of: 'if the experimenter moves the row of counters (say) together, this must be happening for a reason. Something has happened, but I'm not sure what, so I'll give a different answer'. On this explanation, contextual cues may override purely linguistic ones.

Other research has shown that children's responses on conservation tasks depend on *who makes the transformation.* According to Piaget, it should not matter who, in the case of the conservation of number, rearranges the counters/Smarties or how this happens. Yet when 'Naughty Teddy', a glove puppet, causes the transformation 'accidentally', preoperational children can conserve number and length (McGarrigle and Donaldson, 1974; Light et al., 1979). This is also the case when the transformation is made by a *person* other than the experimenter (Hargreaves et al., 1982; Light, 1986). Of course, accidental transformations (by glove puppets or humans) could result in children being led into unwittingly making the correct judgement just as much as deliberate transformations could lead to the *incorrect* judgement being unwittingly made. Put another way, Piaget's original procedure might convey the implicit message 'take note of the transformation because it is relevant' whilst studies using accidental transformations might convey the message 'ignore the transformation, it makes no difference'. It follows that if some change actually takes place, the implicit message to ignore the transformation would make children give an incorrect answer. The standard Piagetian task involves an irrelevant perceptual change (nothing is added or taken away), but where some actual perceptual change occurs, children tested under the accidental/incidental transformation condition should do worse than those tested in the standard way. This outcome has been obtained in several studies (e.g. Light and Gilmour, 1983; Moore and Frye, 1986).

Like criticisms of other Piagetian tasks, the actual words used in the procedure may make a difference. For example, when the child is asked 'which contains more or do they both contain the same amount?' following the transformation in the liquid quantity task, the meaning the child attaches to 'more' may influence its judgement (cf. Gelman, 1979; see page 48). According to Bruner et al. (1966), some children use the words 'more' or 'less' when referring to height and length, so in their own terms on the conservation of liquid quantity task, they might be quite correct in saying that the taller beaker has 'more' in it. As Dworetzky (1981) has noted, when a child asks for 'more milk', it observes the level in the glass rise, and there may be other similar examples which explain why 'more' is understood as 'tall' or 'taller'.

Piaget believed that the attainment of a new stage arises from a major reorganisation of mental operations rather than the acquisition of new skills. For Piaget, attempts to teach children to conserve should, therefore, be unsuccessful. Smedslund (1961) showed that whilst children *could* be taught to behave as though they could conserve, they did not actually understand what conservation means. Other researchers (e.g. Botvin and Murray, 1975) dispute this. They argue that when non-conservers are placed with a group of conservers and listen to the reasoning the conservers give for their responses, understanding can occur.

The evidence in this regard is mixed, but for at least some researchers there are sufficient data to support the view that training *does* produce improvements in performance which can be considerable, long-lasting and pervasive. In general, special training techniques may speed children's understanding of conservation but only if they have reached the necessary stage of development. As Krebs and Blackman (1988) have noted, such training appears at most:

> 'to move children through a period of formation and into the period of attainment more quickly than they would otherwise progress'.

METHODOLOGICAL CRITICISMS

Piaget's observation of individual children, often his own, falls short of the controlled methodology characteristic of experimental psychology. Piaget's use of particular observations to demonstrate general points is also unscientific (Brainerd, 1978). In defence of Piaget, though, both Ginsberg (1981) and Dasen (1994) see Piaget's methods as being a superior way to explore the subtleties of a child's capabilities, since his procedures are tailored to an individual child's requirements.

THE AMBIGUITY OF CONCEPTS

According to Yussen and Santrock (1982):

> 'the most interesting concepts in the theory – assimilation, accommodation and equilibration – which are used to explain how progress is made in development are tricky to pin down operationally, despite their theoretical glitter. Despite work over the years to flesh out these concepts and anchor them in concrete procedures, not much progress has been made'.

For Yussen and Santrock (and others), Piagetian concepts are too loosely defined to be of any practical use.

THE VALIDITY OF STAGES

According to Horn (1976), children *can* reach later stages without having gone through earlier ones (as is the case in physical development when some children walk without ever having crawled). Whether the concept of 'stages' is valid or not is hotly disputed and has both its supporters (e.g. Flavell, 1971) and opponents (e.g. Sternberg, 1990).

THE CULTURAL UNIVERSALITY OF THE STAGES

Although some researchers have accepted that the stages are valid, they have questioned their cultural universality, suggesting that there are differences between cultures in the rates of development in the various cognitive domains. There is evidence to suggest that the development of the cerebral hemispheres tends to overlap with the timing of Piaget's originally proposed stages (Thatcher et al., 1978). For Dasen (1994):

'the *deep* structures, the basic cognitive processes, are indeed universal, while at the *surface* level, the way these basic processes are brought to bear on specific contents, in specific contexts, is influenced by culture. Universality and cultural diversity are not opposites, but are complementary aspects of all human behaviour and development'.

THE ROLE OF SOCIAL FACTORS IN COGNITIVE DEVELOPMENT

According to Meadows (1995), Piaget excluded the contribution of other people to children's cognitive development with his implied view that children are largely independent and isolated as far as their construction of knowledge and understanding of the physical world is concerned. The social nature of knowledge and thought has been investigated by others interested in cognitive development, including Jerome Bruner and Lev Vygotsky. Their views are examined in the next chapter.

THE PERMANENCE OF CONSERVATION AND THE ATTAINMENT OF FORMAL OPERATIONAL THOUGHT

Bower (1976) has argued that children appear to master and then lose the ability to conserve weight. This is illustrated by the concrete operational thinker's failure to realise that a pound of lead weighs the same as a pound of feathers. According to Bower, a stable understanding of this concept is not reached until the age of 13.

Some researchers (e.g. White and Ferstenberg, 1978; Dasen, 1994) have argued that only one-third of adolescents and adults actually reach the formal operational stage, and that in some cultures where it is reached, it is not the typical mode of thought. Conversely, other researchers (e.g. Riegel, 1976; Labouvie-Vief, 1980) have argued that some people reach stages *beyond* the formal operational stage. The ability to understand the nature of formal operational thinking (as shown by Piaget) is held to go beyond formal operational thought!

Conclusions

Although subject to much criticism, Piaget's theory of cognitive development continues to attract much interest. For Campbell (1996):

'the treatment of Piaget's work in Britain has been disgraceful. Convenient opinions of that work are casually constructed from reading a page of one Piaget book, or worse, from second-hand accounts. These opinions lead to crude experiments to refute them, and complaisant editors publish yet another paper proving a toy version of 'Piaget's theory' wrong'.

We hope our coverage of Piaget's theory of cognitive development has been balanced and fair.

Summary

- According to Meadows, cognitive development looks at 'the child as thinker'. While information-process theorists see children as symbol manipulators, those who subscribe to Vygotsky's theory see children as participants in an interactive process by which socially and culturally determined knowledge and understanding become individualised.
- Most attention has been focused on Piaget's cognitive developmental theory, according to which behaviour is seen as **adaptation to the environment**. Although much criticised from a number of perspectives, including Skinner's behaviourism, Vygotsky, and Bruner's **interventionist psychology**, Piaget's theory continues to be influential, within both psychology and education.
- More recent challenges to Piaget have come from **information-processing theorists**, **domain-specific theorists** and **meta-cognitive theorists**.
- Those theorists who have remained 'loyal' to Piaget include **fundamentalist Piagetians**, **neo-Piagetians** and **post-Piagetians**. According to Sutherland, it is possible to identify a distinct school of **American post-Piagetians** who differ from their European counterparts.
- Piaget's theory of cognitive development focuses on the organisation of intelligence and how it changes as children grow. He is the founder of **genetic epistemology**. He argued that younger

children's intelligence is both **quantitatively** (different in **degree**) and **qualitatively** (different in **kind**) different from that of older children.

- Cognitive development occurs through the interaction between innate capacities and environmental events, and progresses through a series of **hierarchical stages** which are **invariant** and **universal**. Underlying the changes that occur are certain **functional invariants**, the most important being **assimilation, accommodation** (which together constitute **adaptation**) and **equilibration**. The two major **cognitive structures** that change are **schemas/schemata** and **concepts**.
- A **schema/scheme** can be thought of as the basic building block or unit of intelligent behaviour. Our first schemas consist mainly of inborn reflexes which operate independently of each other. As we develop, our schemas become increasingly complex. Knowledge of the environment occurs through development of **concepts** or rules which describe the properties of events and their relationship to other concepts.
- **Assimilation** involves incorporating new information into our existing schemas, as in the baby's sucking reflex. **Accommodation** occurs when the baby **modifies** its sucking so that it is able to drink from a bottle or cup. When a child is able to deal with most or all new experiences by assimilating them, it is in a state of **equilibrium** (brought about by **equilibration**). When this is not the case, **cognitive disequilibrium** occurs, making accommodation necessary in order to restore equilibrium; this is the process by which the child moves through the developmental stages.
- Piaget's four stages of cognitive development are **sensorimotor** (birth to two years), **preoperational** (two to seven years), **concrete operational** (seven to 11 years) and **formal operational** (11 years onwards). Each stage represents a stage in the development of intelligence and is a way of summarising the various schemas present at a particular time. Children move through the stages at different rates, and all pass through **transitional periods**.
- While 'stage' often implies that development is **discontinuous**, Piaget saw it as a gradual or **continuous** process of change, although later stages build on earlier ones.
- During the **sensorimotor stage**, infants discover things primarily through sensing ('sensori-') and doing ('motor'). Frequent interaction with objects ultimately leads to **object permanence**, which develops throughout six sub-stages: 1) **Exercising reflexes** (birth to one month); 2) **Primary circular reactions** (one to four months); 3) **Secondary circular reactions** (four to ten months); 4) **Co-ordination of secondary circular reactions** (ten to 12 months); 5) **Tertiary circular reactions** (12 to 18 months); 6) **Invention of new means through mental combinations** (18 to 24 months). Object permanence is fully developed when the child can **infer invisible displacements**.
- The emergence of object permanence occurs simultaneously with that of a **fear of strangers**. By eight to nine months, the infant probably has schemas for familiar faces, and faces that cannot be assimilated result in distress.
- By the end of the sensorimotor stage, **self-recognition** and **symbolic thought** (one example of which is **language**) have emerged. Schemas are now 'interiorised', allowing insightful solutions to problems. **Deferred imitation** indicates an important advance in the child's capacity to **remember**, and **representational** and **make-believe play**, like deferred imitation, depend on the growing ability to form mental images of people or things in their absence.
- During the **preoperational stage**, the use of internal images, symbols and language continue to develop. But the child's world is still fundamentally absolute: things are very much as they **seem**, and logical principles and operations have little influence on the child. While this is more pronounced in the **preconceptual sub-stage** (two to four years), where the child cannot understand relative terms, the child in the **intuitive sub-stage** (four to seven years) is still limited in its ability to think logically.
- The preoperational child has difficulty in **seriation** tasks and also displays **artificialism, transductive reasoning** and **animism**. **Centration** involves focusing on a single perceptual quality (e.g. colour) to the exclusion of others (e.g. size). To be able to classify things in a logical or systematic way, the child must be able to **decentre**. Centration is also illustrated by **syncretic thought** and by the inability to conserve.
- Preoperational children are also **egocentric**. Their inability to put themselves in 'other people's shoes' prevents them from understanding that others may not know or perceive everything they themselves know or perceive.
- Egocentrism was tested by Piaget and Inhelder using the 'Swiss mountain scene' test, in which the child is asked to choose the picture, from a set of ten taken from different locations around the

model, that represents how a doll sees it, placed at a different location from the child. Only seven- and eight-year-olds consistently chose the correct picture; younger children are bound by the **egocentric illusion**.

- According to Piaget, preoperational children cannot **conserve** because their thinking is dominated by how things look and is another example of centration. In the case of **liquid quantity**, for instance, the child fails to understand **compensation**, such that the taller beaker is also narrower, the two dimensions cancelling each other out. Hence the child says the taller beaker contains more liquid, despite agreeing that none has been added or spilled (**identity**).
- Also required for conservation is **reversibility**, mentally pouring the liquid from the taller beaker back into the shorter one; the preoperational child fails to understand that every action has a logical opposite and that what can be done can be undone **without any gain or loss**.
- During the **concrete operational stage**, the child becomes capable of logical thought, but the mental operation can only be performed in the presence of actual or observable objects. The child can now conserve and in other ways decentre, such as appreciating that objects can belong to more than one class. There is also a significant decline in egocentrism, the onset of seriation and reciprocity of relationships.
- Some types of conservation appear before others in an invariant order. This step-by-step acquisition of conservation is an example of **horizontal décalage**. A child who has mastered all kinds of classification but not all kinds of conservation is displaying **vertical décalage**.
- The **formal operational** thinker can manipulate ideas and propositions and can reason solely on the basis of verbal statements ('second order' operations), whereas the concrete operational child can only manipulate **things**, even if this is done mentally ('first order' operations). 'Formal' refers to the ability to follow the form of an argument regardless of the particular content.
- Formal operational thinkers can also think **hypothetically** (what **could** be, as well as what **actually is**). This is evidence of the continued decentration and is called **hypothetico-deductive reasoning**.
- One example of formal operational thinking is seen in Archimedes' law of floating bodies. To decide if an object will float, the concepts of both weight and volume must be understood, and the operations involved must be related to each other in a logical way (**operating on operations**). Inhelder and Piaget tested formal operational thought by presenting a task involving five clear liquids, such that when combined in a particular way, the liquid would turn yellow. Only formal operational thinkers systematically consider all alternatives by varying one factor at a time.
- Piaget's theory has received considerable criticism. As far as **object permanence** is concerned, Bower and Wishart found that the **way** an object is made to disappear influences the infant's response, so that 'out of sight' does not always mean 'out of mind'. Other research has shown that object permanence can occur as early as three and a half months and that it is not necessary for a baby below six months to see the whole object in order to respond to it.
- Piaget tested centration and classification through **class inclusion tasks**, such as the wooden beads task. He claimed that the preoperational child fails to understand the relationship between the whole (the **superordinate class**) and the parts (the **subordinate classes**). But according to Donaldson, the child may have difficulty knowing what's expected of it, and using the '**sleeping cows**' alternative, six-year-olds performed very much better.
- Gelman argues that the word 'more' has a different meaning for children and adults. This can explain the usual 'failure' of preoperational children on class inclusion tasks. It is also relevant to understanding performance on **conservation** tasks: some children might take 'more'/'less' to refer to height/length, so that in their own terms they are correct to say the taller beaker has 'more' in it.
- Gelman has also shown that four-year-olds adjust their explanations to make them clearer to a **blindfolded** listener and use **simpler** forms of speech when addressing two-year-olds. Neither of these findings would be expected based on Piaget's views about the **egocentrism** of children below seven.
- The 'Swiss mountain scene' has been criticised for being too difficult for a young child. Borke and Hughes have shown that even three and a half-year-olds can take another person's viewpoint if the task is presented in a way that makes 'human sense' to the child.
- Rose and Blank showed that when the **pre-transformation** question in a **conservation** of number task is dropped, six-year-olds often succeeded and made fewer errors on the standard version of the task a week later. Samuel and Bryant repli-

cated these findings, testing conservation of number, liquid quantity and substance.

- According to Donaldson, the standard version of the conservation task unwittingly makes children give the wrong answer against their better judgement. While for Piaget it is irrelevant **who** makes the transformation or how it happens, the 'Naughty Teddy' experimental procedure shows that it does matter.
- Accidental transformations (as in the 'Naughty Teddy' procedure) could unwittingly lead children into making the correct judgement, since it might convey a message to ignore the transformation as it makes no difference. Several studies have shown that where some actual change occurs, children tested under the accidental or incidental condition do worse than those tested in the standard way.
- According to Piaget, the attainment of a new stage is due to a major reorganisation of mental operations, rather than to the acquisition of new skills. It follows that trying to teach children to conserve will fail. Although the evidence is mixed, at least some researchers believe that training **does** produce long-lasting and pervasive improvements in performance, but only if they have reached the necessary stage of development.
- Piaget's observation of individual children has been criticised as falling short of the controlled methodology of experimental psychology, but Ginsberg and Dasen both praise Piaget's methods for their ability to explore the subtleties of children's thinking.
- Yussen and Santrock criticise the concepts of assimilation, accommodation and equilibration for being difficult to pin down operationally. They and other researchers see Piagetian concepts as too loosely defined to be of any practical value.
- Horn believes that children **can** 'skip' stages, and there is heated debate over the validity of the concept of 'stage'. Even if it is valid, there is the further issue of the **cultural universality** of the stages. In support of Piaget, Dasen argues that the **deep** structures (the basic cognitive processes) are universal. But he also argues that how these basic processes are brought to bear on specific contents (at the **surface** level) is influenced by culture and so is culturally diverse.
- According to Meadows, Piaget excluded the contribution of other people to children's cognitive development, seeing them as largely independent and isolated in their construction of knowledge of the physical world. By contrast, Vygotsky and Bruner especially have stressed the social nature of knowledge and thought.
- Bower has argued that children seem to acquire and then lose the ability to conserve weight. Others have argued that only a third of adolescents and adults actually attain the formal operational stage, and in some cultures, it is not the typical mode of thought. Still others believe that some people reach stages **beyond** formal operations.

SOME ALTERNATIVE THEORIES OF COGNITIVE DEVELOPMENT AND THEIR APPLICATION TO EDUCATION

Introduction and overview

According to Dasen (1994) and Durkin (1995), the challenges to Piaget's theory of cognitive development have been so strong that there are few 'orthodox' Piagetians left, and even fewer who subscribe to 'stage' theories of cognitive development. Although this view may be challenged, there are, as we mentioned in the previous chapter, several alternatives to Piaget's theory. This chapter has two aims. The first is to consider the alternatives proposed by Lev Vygotsky, Jerome Bruner and the information-processing theorists. The second is to look at some of the ways in which these various alternatives have been applied to education. We will begin this chapter, however, by briefly considering some of the ways in which Piaget's theory of cognitive development can be applied to education.

Applying Piaget's theory to education

As Ginsberg (1981) has pointed out, Piaget did not actually advocate a 'theory of instruction'. However, it has been proposed that there are three main implications for education of Piaget's theory of cognitive development (Brainerd, 1983). These are not explicit recommendations, but rather ways in which educationalists and others have attempted to make Piaget's theory relevant to pre-school and primary education in particular. The three implications are *the concept of readiness, the curriculum* (that is, what should be taught) and *teaching methods* (the ways in which the curriculum should be taught).

As far as the concept of readiness is concerned, much of what was said in the previous chapter about limits set on learning by the child's current stage of development relates to the concept of readiness. The apparent success of some attempts to train certain concepts (such as conservation: see page 49) suggests that this is not a particularly helpful concept. With respect to the curriculum, appropriate concepts to teach would include logic (such as transitive inference), maths (numbers), science (conservation) and space (Euclidean geometry). Whatever the concepts chosen, the teaching materials should be made up of concrete objects of some sort that can be easily manipulated by the child.

Some researchers (such as Ginsberg, 1981) have, however, argued that attempting to base a curriculum on the teaching of Piagetian stages is an unfortunate misapplication of Piaget's theory. A much more useful approach would be to *modify* the curriculum in line with what is known about the various Piagetian stages, without placing undue emphasis on them and without allowing them to limit approaches to teaching. Piaget's theory seems to suggest that there are definite sequences in which concepts should be taught. As we saw in the previous chapter (see page 45), the conservation of substance/quantity precedes the conservation of weight, and the conservation of weight precedes the conservation of volume. But as Elkind (1976) has pointed out, many traditional schools do *not* base their teaching on this or other sequences of development.

Central to Piagetian views of the educational process is the idea of *active self-discovery* (or *discovery learning*). From a Piagetian perspective, children learn from actions rather than from passive observation. As far as teaching methods are concerned, Smith and Cowie (1991) have argued that teachers must recognise that each child needs to construct knowledge for itself, and that deeper understanding is the product of active learning. The role of the teacher in the Piagetian classroom is described in Box 5.1.

Box 5.1 The role of the teacher in the Piagetian classroom

- It is essential for teachers to assess very carefully each individual child's current stage of cognitive development (this relates to the concept of readiness). The child can then be set tasks which are tailored to its needs and so are *intrinsically motivating*.
- Teachers must provide children with learning opportunities that enable them to advance to the next developmental step. This is achieved by creating *disequilibrium* (see page 40). Rather than providing the appropriate materials and allowing children to 'get on with it', teachers should create a proper balance between actively guiding and directing children's thinking patterns and providing opportunities for them to explore by themselves (Thomas, 1985).
- Teachers should be concerned with the process of learning rather than its end product. This involves encouraging children to ask questions, experiment, explore and so on. During this, teachers should look for the reasoning behind children's answers, particularly when they make mistakes.
- Another role of the teacher is to encourage children to learn from each other. Hearing other (and often conflicting) views can help to break down egocentrism (see page 44). As well as having a cognitive value, peer interaction has a *social value*. As a result, small-group activity is as important as individual work.
- Teachers are the guides in the child's process of discovery, and the curriculum should be adapted to each child's individual needs and their intellectual level (Smith and Cowie, 1991).

Figure 5.1 In the traditional classroom (top), the teacher is at the centre of the learning process, imparting ready-made ('academic/school') knowledge. By contrast, in the Piagetian classroom the child actively discovers knowledge for itself, often through interaction with other children in small groups (bottom)

Vygotsky's theory of cognitive development

One of the first to respond critically to Piaget's views on cognitive development was Lev Vygotsky, a Russian, who some consider to be one of the greatest psychologists of all time (Sternberg, 1990). From 1924 until his untimely death from tuberculosis in 1934, Vygotsky outlined a major alternative to Piaget's theorywhich appeared in work published in the former Soviet Union in the 1920s and 1930s, but was not translated into English until the early 1960s (e.g. Vygotsky, 1962).

Vygotsky believed that a child's cognitive development cannot be seen as occurring in a social vacuum. In Vygotsky's view, our ability to think and reason by

ourselves and for ourselves (what he terms *inner speech* or *verbal thought*) is the result of a fundamentally social process. At birth, we are social beings who are capable of interacting with others, but able to do little either practically or intellectually by or for ourselves. Gradually, however, we move towards self-sufficiency and independence, and by participating in social activities, our capabilities become transformed. For Vygotsky, cognitive development involves an active internalisation of problem-solving processes that takes place as a result of mutual interaction between children and those with whom they have regular social contact (initially the parents, but later friends and classmates).

Vygotsky's process of internalisation is the reverse of how Piaget (at least initially) saw things. As Rogoff (1990) has noted, Piaget's idea of 'the child as a *scientist*' is replaced by the idea of 'the child as an *apprentice*', who acquires the knowledge and skills of a culture through graded collaboration with those who already possess such knowledge and skills. According to Vygotsky (1981):

> 'Any function in the child's cultural development appears twice, or on two planes. First it appears on the social plane, and then on the psychological plane.'

An example of this is the gesture of pointing. Initially, when a baby points, the gesture is nothing more than an unsuccessful attempt to grasp something beyond its reach. When the mother sees the baby pointing, she takes it as an 'indicatory gesture' that the baby wants something, and so she comes to its aid probably making the gesture herself. Gradually, the baby comes to use the gesture deliberately. The 'reaching' becomes reduced to movements which could not themselves achieve the desired object even if it were in reach and is accompanied by cries, looks at the mother and eventually words. The gesture is now directed towards the mother (it has become a gesture 'for others') rather than toward the object (it is no longer a gesture 'in itself') (Meadows, 1995).

SCAFFOLDING AND THE ZONE OF PROXIMAL DEVELOPMENT

We noted earlier on that Vygotsky sees children as 'apprentices' who acquire knowledge and skills through those who already possess such knowledge and skills. Wood et al. (1976) introduced the term *scaffolding* to refer to the role played by adults, teachers and so on by which children acquire their knowledge and skills. As a task becomes more familiar to the child and more within its competence, so those who provide the scaffold can leave more and more for the child to do until it can perform the task successfully. In this way, the developing thinker does not have to create cognition 'from scratch' (as Piaget's 'child as a scientist' image implies) because there are others available who have already 'served' their own apprenticeship when they were children.

The internalised cognitive skills remain social in two senses. First, as mature learners we can 'scaffold' ourselves through difficult tasks by 'instructing ourselves' as others once scaffolded our earlier attempts. Second, for most people the only skills practised to a high level of competence are those that their culture offers: cognitive potential may be universal, but cognitive expertise is culturally determined. As Meadows (1995) notes:

> 'Culturally given ways of thinking, remembering, categorising, reading and so forth build on and may supersede the biologically based ways we begin with.'

Meadows (1995) has also pointed out that since the 1980s, research has stressed the role of social interaction in language development, especially the facilitating effects of the use of child-contingent language by adults talking with children. This 'fit' betwen adult and child language closely resembles the concept of 'scaffolding' we have been describing.

In an investigation of 'scaffolding', Wood et al. (1976) found that on a construction task with four- and five-year-olds, different mothers used instructional strategies of varying levels of specificity. These ranged from general verbal encouragement to direct demonstration of a relevant action. No single strategy guaranteed learning, but the most efficient maternal instructors were those who combined general and specific interventions according to the child's progress.

The most useful help, according to Bruner (1983), is that which adapts itself to the learner's successes and failures. An example of this would be initially using a general instruction until the child runs into difficulties. At this point, a more specific instruction or demonstration is given. This style allows the child considerable autonomy, but also provides carefully planned guidance at the boundaries of its abilities, or what Vygotsky terms the child's *zone of proximal development*. According to Vygotsky (1978), the zone of proximal development (or ZPD) defines those functions that have not yet matured but are in the process of maturation, functions that will mature tomorrow but are currently in an embryonic state. These functions could be termed the 'buds' or 'flowers' of development rather than the 'fruits' of development. The actual developmental level characterises mental development retrospectively, while the ZPD characterises mental development prospectively. We shall explore the concept of the ZPD further in the following section, which considers some of the ways in which Vygotsky's theory has been applied to education.

Applying Vygotsky's theory to education

Vygotsky defines intelligence as the capacity to learn from instruction. Rather than teachers playing an enabling role (a Piagetian-influenced educational ideology), Vygotsky sees teachers occupying a *didactic role.* What this means is that teachers should *guide* pupils in paying attention, concentrating and learning effectively (Sutherland, 1992). By doing this, teachers *scaffold* children to competence.

The introduction of the National Curriculum and national testing at various ages has returned Britain to the 'teacher-centred' or 'traditional' approach to the education of young children. Whilst this approach was dominant up to the 1960s, it was 'revolutionised' by the Piagetian-influenced 'child-centred' or 'progressive' approach. The return to the traditional approach is consistent with Vygotsky's views on the role of teachers. However, Vygotsky did not:

> 'advocate mechanical formal teaching where children go through the motions of sitting at desks and passing exams that are meaningless to them . . . On the contrary, Vygotsky stressed intellectual development rather than procedural learning' (Sutherland, 1992).

Some approaches to education (such as that advocated by behaviourists) see teachers as having a rigid control over children's learning. For Vygotsky, such approaches are mistaken and, as with Piaget, teachers' control over the *activities* of children is seen as being most important. Vygotsky's approach to education is one in which teachers extend and challenge children to go beyond where they would otherwise have been.

Earlier we described Vygotsky's concept of the zone of proximal development (ZPD). Box 5.2 below shows how the concept of the ZPD can be applied to education.

Box 5.2 Applying the concept of the ZPD to education

Suppose that a child is currently functioning at level 'x' in terms of his or her attainment. Through innate/environmental means, the child has the potential to reach level 'x + 1'. As shown below, the area between 'x' and 'x + 1' is the child's ZPD. Note that the ZPD may be different for individual children, and that children with large ZPDs will have a greater capacity to be helped than children with small ZPDs. Irrespective of the size of the ZPD, Vygotsky saw the teacher as being responsible for giving children the cues they need or taking them through a series of steps towards the solution of a problem.

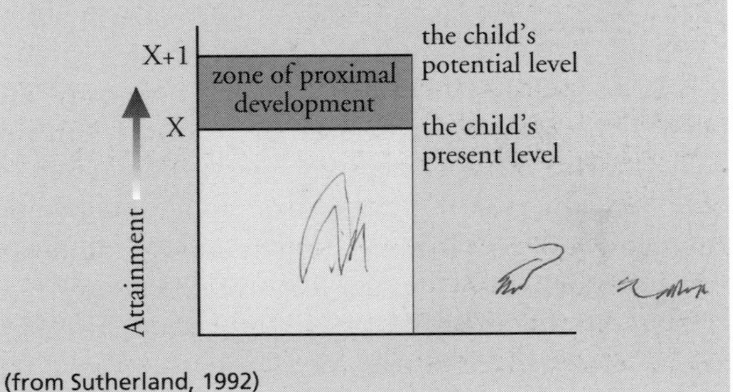

(from Sutherland, 1992)

Along with other perspectives on education (such as 'constructivist' perspectives), Vygotsky also believed in what is known as *collaborative learning.* As well as being helped by teachers, Vygotsky also saw more advanced children as being important in helping less advanced children. As Foot and Cheyne (1995) have observed:

> 'The child takes on or 'internalises' the communicative procedures that he or she experiences when interacting with a peer, and in the process enriches his or her own intellectual capacity'.

The use of the peer group for teaching was for a long time used as a basis of Marxist education in the former Soviet Union. Sutherland (1992) has this to say:

> 'The socialist rationale was one of all children working for the general good rather than the capitalist one of each child trying to get out of school as much benefit as (she or he) can without putting anything back into it. The brighter child is

helping society by helping the less able one since the latter . . . will be more of an asset to society as a literate than as an illiterate adult'.

This approach is supported by a number of other perspectives that are not necessarily Marxist in their approach (the 'constructivists' mentioned above are an example), especially with mixed-ability groups in which the more able pupil can act as what Sutherland (1992) has termed a 'substitute teacher'. Foot (1994) has argued that whilst much of the research into collaborative learning has been undertaken with young children, there is a growing body of literature which suggests that the use of group work and collaborative learning can also be effective in adult and higher education.

For Vygotsky, then, there is much educational value in the use of direct teaching, but with the child as an active learner. This view is shared by a number of researchers who see the social situation and influences, such as children's construction of their own concepts, as being of particular importance. For example, using techniques derived from Vygotsky's work, Shayer (cited in Sylva, 1996) has shown that specially designed material for the teaching of science can increase 'learning ability' (gains on tests of psychological functioning) as well as educational test scores and Standardised Attainment Tests (SATs). Moreover, such improvement also appears to generalise to performance in English and mathematics (see also the work of Adey et al., 1989, described on page 60).

Bruner's theory of cognitive development

Like Vygotsky, Bruner was amongst the first to offer criticisms of Piaget's theory. Bruner was strongly influenced by Vygotsky (the concept of 'scaffolding' being an example). However, despite his criticisms of Piaget's perspective, Bruner also shares some of Piaget's basic beliefs. For example, like Piaget, Bruner sees children as being born with a biological organisation that helps them to understand their world, and believes that their underlying cognitive structure matures over time enabling them to think about and organise the world in an increasingly complex way. Bruner also agreed that children are actively curious and explorative, capable of adapting to their environment through interacting with it. Abstract knowledge grows out of action, and competence in any area of knowledge is rooted in active experience and concrete mental operations.

Bruner's main disagreements with Piaget derive from certain shared beliefs with Vygotsky. In particular, Bruner stressed the role of language and interpersonal communication and the need for active involvement by expert adults (or more knowledgeable peers) in helping the child to develop as a thinker and problem-solver. As well as language playing a crucial part in the scaffolding process, instruction is seen as being important both in naturalistic settings and in educational ones. We will discuss language and instruction further in the following section.

BRUNER'S THREE MODES OF REPRESENTATION

Unlike Piaget's theory, Bruner's (1966) theory is not about stages of development as such. Rather, it is about ways or *modes* of representing the world, that is, forms that our knowledge and understanding can take. As a result, Bruner's theory is concerned with knowledge in general as well as with cognitive growth. The three modes of representation described by Bruner are the *enactive*, *iconic* and *symbolic* and they develop in this order in the child.

The enactive mode

The enactive mode corresponds to Piaget's sensorimotor stage of development. Initially, says Bruner, babies represent the world through actions, and any knowledge they have is based on what they have experienced through their own behaviour. Past events are represented through appropriate motor responses. Many of our motor schemas, such as those for riding a bicycle and tying knots, are represented 'in our muscles' or as 'motor memories'. Even when we have the use of language, it is often extremely difficult for us to describe only in words how we carry out certain behaviours. Through repeated encounters with the regularities of the environment (that is, recurrent events and conditions), we build up virtually automatic patterns of motor activity which are 'run off' as units in the appropriate situation. Like Piaget, Bruner sees the onset of object permanence (see page 42) as a major qualitative change in young children's cognitive development.

The iconic mode

An icon is an image, and this form of representation involves building up mental images of things we have experienced. Such images are normally composite, that is, made up of a number of past encounters with similar objects or situations. This mode, therefore, corresponds to the last six months of the sensorimotor stage (where schemas become interiorised) and the whole of the preoperational stage, where the child is 'at the mercy' of what it perceives in drawing intuitive conclusions about the nature of reality (things are as they look).

The symbolic mode

Bruner's main interest was in the transition from the iconic to the symbolic mode. Like Piaget, Bruner agrees that a very important cognitive change occurs at around the age of six or seven. Although Piaget describes this change as the start of logical operations (albeit tied to concrete reality), Bruner sees it as the appearance of the symbolic mode, with language coming into its own as an influence on thought. For Bruner (1957), the child is now freed from the immediate context and is beginning to be able to 'go beyond the information given'. The transition from the iconic to symbolic modes was demonstrated by Bruner and Kenney (1966). Their experiment is described in Box 5.3.

Box 5.3 Bruner and Kenney's (1966) experiment

Nine plastic glasses were arranged on a 3 × 3 matrix as shown in (a) below:

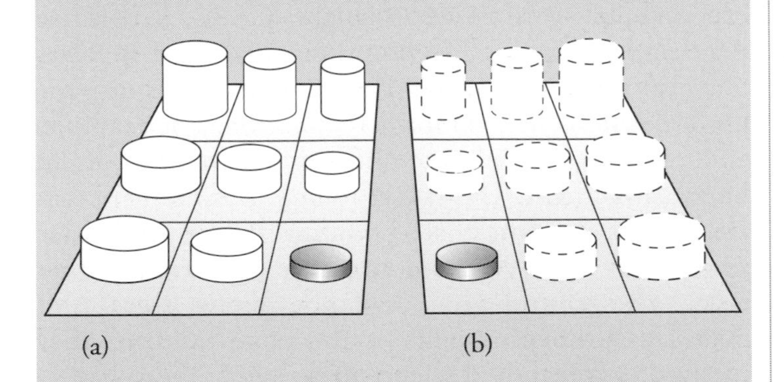

Three- to seven-year-olds who were familiar with the way in which the glasses were arranged were given a *reproduction task* and a *transposition task*. On the reproduction task, the glasses were 'scrambled' and the children were asked to put them back the way they had seen them before. On the transposition task, the glasses were removed from the matrix and the glass which had been in the bottom right-hand square was placed in the bottom left-hand square, and so on, until the glasses appeared as shown in (b). The task was to rebuild the matrix in the transposed manner.

Bruner and Kenney found that children could generally reproduce the matrix earlier than they could transpose it. The reproduction task involves the iconic mode, and 60 per cent of the five-year-olds, 72 per cent of the six-year-olds and 80 per cent of the seven-year-olds were successful in the task. The transposition task involves the symbolic mode, and none of the five-year-olds, 27 per cent of the six-year-olds and 79 per cent of the seven-year-olds were successful at the task.

These findings indicate that the five-year-olds were dominated by the visual image of the original matrix, whilst the six- and seven-year-olds were able to translate their visual information into the symbolic mode. They relied upon verbal rules to guide them, such as 'It gets fatter going one way and taller going another'. Thus, a child using images but not symbols can reproduce but not restructure.

LANGUAGE AND COGNITIVE DEVELOPMENT

The major difference between Bruner and Piaget concerns the role that language plays in cognitive development. Bruner believes that the leap from the iconic to the symbolic mode is due to the development of language. Piaget, by contrast, believes that the development of logical thought is due to the acquisition of operations – language is not the cause of cognitive development, but is a tool to be used in the course of operational thinking. For Bruner, language and logical thinking are inseparable, and without language human thought would be limited to what could be learned through actions or images. For Piaget, language merely reflects and builds on cognitive structures which have already developed through interaction with the environment.

One implication of Bruner's belief is that it should be possible to speed up cognitive development by training children in the use of symbols. For Piaget, such training should have no effect. There are several studies which are relevant in this regard. In one, Bruner et al.

(1966) gave four- to seven-year-olds the standard Piagetian test for the conservation of liquid quantity. The results showed that nearly all of the four- to five-year-olds failed to conserve, as did about half of the six- to seven-year-olds.

The children were then shown two standard beakers and a third which was much wider. The beakers were then screened, so that when the contents of one of the standard beakers was poured into the wider one, only the tops of the beakers (but not the level of liquid) could be seen. When asked which contained the most liquid, almost all five- to seven-year-olds answered correctly, as did about half of the four-year-olds. However, when the screen was removed, all of the four-year-olds reverted to the answer they had given before the screening took place.

The other children, however, stuck to the answer they had given when the screen was in place. The children were then given the standard Piagetian test of conservation using two beakers and a third taller one. Bruner et al. found that the four-year-olds were unaffected by having seen the beakers screened and failed to show conservation. However, the five-year-olds' success rate at conserving rose from 20 per cent to 70 per cent. For the six to seven-year-olds, the success rate rose from 50 per cent to 90 per cent.

Bruner and his colleagues argued that activating the children's speech (symbolic mode), by having them 'say' their judgement when the screen was covering the liquid levels, prevented those aged five and over (who normally fail to conserve on the standard Piagetian task) from being dominated by the iconic mode. The four-year-olds, however, were clearly not ready to benefit from the symbolic training and, to a degree, this finding supports Piaget's view that mental structures must have already developed before training can help. Nonetheless, the fact that the five-year-olds did benefit is contrary to what Piaget would predict, and so Bruner too is supported to some extent by the data.

Sinclair-de-Zwart (1969) has also shown that unless children understand the concepts of conservation, teaching them relevant words like 'as much as' and 'the same' has little effect on their ability to conserve. As far as formal operational thought is concerned, Piaget takes the view that while language may be necessary, it is not sufficient. Indeed, for Piaget, the language of the formal operational thinker does not seem to differ significantly from what it was at some earlier stage.

Applying Bruner's theory to education

Bruner's view that cognitive development can be significantly speeded up underlies his belief that teachers should try to find ways of stimulating children (particularly those from deprived backgrounds). As Sutherland (1992) has observed:

> 'Bruner's case for acceleration seems worth examining, particularly at a time when there is a special concern for below-average pupils. One reason for the introduction of the National Curriculum is to improve standards of attainment among the bottom 40 per cent of the school population. How can teachers reach the targets set by the government without some form of acceleration of the slow learner? Are the most able pupils being fully stretched in comprehensive schools, particularly in mixed-ability classes? Should they be accelerated on to the next stage?'

Attempts to accelerate development in science education have been reported by Adey et al. (1989). In their study, experimental and control groups were established in various comprehensive schools. The experimental groups were taught CASE (Cognitive Acceleration Science Education) material. This involves practical problems that, in Piagetian terms, require the use of formal schemata for their solution. For example, children are given tubes of different lengths and told to blow across them. The task is to determine which variable affects the note that is produced. The knowledge acquired is then expected to be transferred to other tasks. The control group did not receive the CASE material. Although taught by the same teachers, they received only standard science material.

Using the onset of formal operational thinking (as measured by standard Piagetian reasoning tests) as the criterion for cognitive understanding, the researchers found that after three years, the boys (but not the girls) were significantly better on the tests than the boys and girls in the control group. However, this effect was confined to those in Year 8. Year 7 pupils did not appear to benefit from the CASE material. These data suggest that specially designed material may produce accelerated learning at least with some children (those who are 'ready' to be accelerated) in at least one subject (science) (cf. Shayer's research described on page 58).

Another of Bruner's concepts which is directly relevant to education is that of the *spiral curriculum*, according to which the principles of a subject come to be understood at increasingly more complex levels of difficulty. Like Vygotsky, Bruner was unhappy with Piaget's concept of 'readiness' and proposed a much more active policy of intervention, based on his belief that:

> 'any subject can be taught effectively in some intellectually honest form to any child at any stage of development' (Bruner, 1963).

Bruner believed that educators should provide learners with the means of grasping the structure of a discipline, that is, the underlying principles and concepts, rather than just mastering factual information. This enables learners to go beyond the information they have been given and develop ideas of their own. As Smith and Cowie (1991) have noted, teachers also need to encourage learners to make links and understand the relationships within and between subjects (cf. Adey et al.'s (1989) research described above). Box 5.4 shows one way in which the spiral curriculum can be applied to the topic of volume.

Box 5.4 Applying the spiral curriculum to the topic of volume

The Baby: Volume can be introduced at the sensorimotor level by providing the baby with the opportunity to play with water in buckets (e.g. at the beach).

The pre-schooler: The topic can be re-introduced when the child is in Piaget's preoperational stage by giving the child buckets of water to play with. At the same time, words like 'bucket' and 'more' can be introduced, and intuitive concepts like 'more water' (when water is poured into the bucket) and 'less water' (when it is poured out) encouraged. This enables the child to develop preconcepts and then intuitive concepts.

The junior schooler: The child can be re-exposed to the topic in a variety of settings. Specific use of the word 'volume' is introduced and, through the use of planned activities and spontaneous behaviour by the child, conservation should be achieved along with a concrete operational understanding of 'volume'.

The secondary schooler: The topic is returned to and the child, now at Piaget's formal operational stage, is taught in abstract and symbolic terms, with formulae concerning volume being required to be learnt without 'concrete props'.

(adapted from Sutherland, 1992)

In Bruner's view, the role of the teacher is as an 'interventionist' (a view shared with Vygotsky) who is obliged 'to make demands on their pupils' (Sutherland, 1992). Cultural tools are also seen as being of vital importance, ranging from pencils to computers. Unlike Vygotsky, whose approach is essentially teacher-centred with direct instruction, Bruner favours a child-centred approach.

Information-processing theories of cognitive development

Information-processing (IP) theories of cognitive development focus on the process of cognition and the kinds of information children are capable of acquiring from the environment and what they are capable of doing with it (Krebs and Blackman, 1988). Information-processing theorists such as Sternberg (1990) share Piaget's view in assuming that there are psychological structures in people's minds that explain their behaviour and which are essentially independent of the individual's social relationships, social practices and cultural environment (Meadows, 1995).

The central metaphor underlying the IP approach to cognitive development is the computer. Like computers, children receive information (the 'input') from the environment, store, retrieve and manipulate it, and then respond behaviourally (the 'output'). In order to study the ways in which children's 'mental programs' develop and their strategies for processing information, IP theorists use *task analysis*. This approach argues that if we are going to understand why children cannot solve problems that adults can, it is necessary to understand the component steps involved in a particular task. For example, consider the question 'If Ann is not as bad as Betty, and Betty is not as bad as Carol, who is the best?' Oakhill (1984) has suggested that there are five crucial elements necessary to solve this problem.

First, the child must perceive and encode the important premisses of the question which involves attending to it. Second, the premisses must be stored in working memory. Third, the premisses must be combined in memory to form an integrated representation. Fourth, the question must be encoded. Fifth, the representation of the premisses must be scanned to answer the question or formulate a conclusion about it.

IP theorists argue that children fail to answer correctly questions such as the one above because of, amongst other things, errors in encoding the problem, being unable to hold information in memory for long enough, or because holding it in memory may interfere with the performance of other tasks (Trabasso, 1977). For example, in an experiment conducted by Maccoby and Hagen (1965), children aged six to 12 were shown pictures of various objects and told to remember only the colour of the picture's background, the picture itself being immaterial. The results showed that the ability to perform this task successfully increased with age, with 12-year-olds being able to accurately recall twice as many background colours as six-year-olds. However, when the children were later asked to remember the objects in the pictures (and ignore the colour of the background), the six-year-olds were more successful. This study shows how *selective attention* develops through childhood and how it is necessary for solving problems. Presumably, the six-year-olds performed better on the object recognition task because they were able to focus their attention according to the *original* task demands (Rathus, 1990).

One neo-Piagetian approach to cognitive development which is couched in information-processing terms is that of Pascual-Leone (e.g. 1980) and Case (e.g. 1985). According to these researchers, children do not use just one cognitive strategy in solving Piagetian tasks (as Piaget believed), but rather they employ several strategies, the number required being correlated with a problem's difficulty. Like Oakhill (1984), Pascual-Leone and Case also see working memory as storing the information necessary to solve problems. The amount of space in memory necessary to solve a problem is also correlated with the problem's complexity and, as the child develops, so space available in memory increases. Pascual-Leone and Case also believe that certain strategies become *automatic* with practice and so require less space in memory. An adult, for example, would instantly 'see' that (10 + 6) − (10 + 6) equals zero. A child, however, would require time to solve this problem, since each component of it must be stored in memory before a solution can be reached.

Applying information-processing theories to education

The application of information-processing theories to education has received support from many quarters (e.g. Papert, 1980). One of the strengths of the IP approach is the emphasis it places on the role played by memory and the limited capacity of young children to process information. As we have seen, this approach explains why younger children are poorer at tasks such as memorising and reading. As well as memory being important in the child's ability to operate effectively, knowledge also has a considerable influence on learning, and the more a child knows about a situation, the more successful he or she will be at dealing with it. As Sutherland (1992) has noted:

> 'Since knowledge is generally contained within language, the skill of storing knowledge in some valid linguistic form (whether this be oral memory or written) is a vital prerequisite of successful IP performance. One of the teacher's main roles is to help children find strategies for reducing their memory load – for instance to write down a list of the facts they need to solve a maths problem.'

Van Lehn (1983), for example, has shown that whilst young children can add numbers together when two digits are involved (e.g. 22 + 56), they make errors when three digits are used. For example, faced with the problem:

231 +
42

young children tend to either ignore the third column and arrive at 73 as the answer, or they muddle up the hundreds and tens columns to produce an answer of 673. Van Lehn uses the term *repair* to refer to the process by which addition involving three digits can be successfully achieved. This process implies a teacher-led approach to teaching mathematics. However, IP theories also see *metacognition* (or making children aware of their own learning) as playing a vital role. Kail and

Nippold (1984) have shown that as well as having greater information-processing capabilities, older children have a greater *insight* into how they process information. Davis (1984) argues that because of this, the information-processing approach should not imply 'passive' learning. Rather, children should be encouraged to (a) test hypotheses by, in the case of mathematics, checking their answers, and (b) use visual imagery to apply these answers to real-life situations.

Conclusions

This chapter has looked at some of the alternatives to Piaget's theory of cognitive development and has explored some of the ways in which they can be applied to education. Theories of cognitive development clearly have a role to play in education but, as Berveridge (cited in Sylva, 1996) has pointed out:

> 'Policy makers are moving quickly towards . . . the "commodification of education". This is the process by which "goods" called school learning are "produced" by teachers and others in such a way as to maximise their value to society and minimise the cost to taxpayers. Politicians and some practitioners are turning away from subtle theories of school learning and teaching in favour of a brutish instrumentalism centred on narrow educational attainment (grades) and records of school discipline'.

Summary

- Although Piaget did not actually advocate a 'theory of instruction', his theory of cognitive development has three main implications for education: **the concept of readiness**, **the curriculum** and **teaching methods**. These are not explicit recommendations, but ways in which educationalists and others have tried to make Piaget's theory relevant to pre-school and primary education in particular.
- The concept of readiness is related to the view that there are limits set on learning by the child's current stage of development. But the apparent success of some attempts to train certain concepts (such as conservation) suggests that this concept is not especially helpful. Appropriate concepts to teach (curriculum) would include logic/maths/science/space. Teaching materials should comprise concrete objects that the child can easily manipulate.
- Instead of basing a curriculum on Piagetian stages, a more useful approach might be to **modify** the curriculum in line with them, so that they don't limit teaching possibilities. Since different types of conservation appear at different times, Piaget's theory implies that there are definite sequences for teaching certain concepts. But many traditional schools do *not* base their teaching on this or other developmental sequences.
- Central to Piagetian views of the educational process is **active self-discovery/discovery learning**. Teachers must recognise that each child needs to construct knowledge for itself and that deeper understanding is produced by active learning. They must assess each individual child's current stage of cognitive development in order to set tasks that are **intrinsically motivating** and provide learning opportunities that create **disequilibrium**.
- Teachers should also be concerned with the learning process itself, encouraging children to ask questions, experiment and explore, and looking for the reasoning behind children's answers, especially their mistakes. Small-group activity can not only help break down egocentrism but also has a **social value**.
- According to Vygotsky, a child's cognitive development does not take place in a social vacuum: our ability to think and reason by and for ourselves (**inner speech/verbal thought**) is the result of a fundamentally social process, whereby the initially helpless baby actively internalises problem-solving processes through interaction with parents.
- While Piaget saw the child as a **scientist**, Vygotsky's child **apprentice** acquires the knowledge and skills of its culture through graded collaboration with those who already possess them. Any function in the child's cultural development appears twice, first on the social plane, then on the psychological plane. This is illustrated by the gesture of pointing.
- The role played by knowledgeable and skilled adults which allows the child apprentice to acquire knowledge and skills is called **scaffolding**

(Wood et al.). As the child becomes more familiar and competent with a task, so adults and teachers can leave more for the child to do on its own. Learning from others who have already served their own apprenticeship means that the child does not have to create cognition 'from scratch'.

- As mature learners, we can 'scaffold' ourselves through difficult tasks by instructing ourselves and, for most people, the only highly practised skills are those offered by their culture: while cognitive potential may be universal, cognitive expertise is culturally determined.
- Wood et al.'s study of scaffolding found that different mothers used instructional strategies of varying levels of specificity when their four- to five-year-olds worked on a construction task. While no single strategy guaranteed learning, the most efficient instructors were those who combined general and specific interventions according to the child's progress.
- According to Bruner, the most useful help adapts itself to the learner's successes and failures, as in initially using a general instruction until the child experiences difficulties, when a more specific instruction or demonstration is given. This relates to Vygotsky's **zone of proximal development** (ZPD), which defines those functions that are in the process of maturing and which characterises mental development prospectively. The size of the ZPD may differ for individual children, so that those with a larger ZPD have a greater capacity to be helped, but the teacher's role remains the same, i.e. to give children the cues they need and take them through the steps required to solve a problem.
- For Vygotsky, intelligence is the capacity to learn from instruction. He sees teachers as occupying a **didactic role**, **guiding** pupils in paying attention, concentrating and learning effectively and in this way **scaffolding** children to competence. However, this does not mean mechanical or formal teaching in order to pass exams as in the 'traditional approach'; he stressed intellectual development rather than procedural learning.
- With the introduction of the National Curriculum and national testing, the 'teacher-centred' or 'traditional' approach to the education of young children has returned to Britain. This had been revolutionised by the Piagetian-influenced 'child-centred' or 'progressive approach' starting in the 1960s.
- Vygotsky also believed in **collaborative learning**, whereby more advanced children ('substitute teachers') help other, less advanced ones. While much of the research into collaborative learning has involved mixed-ability groups of young children, there is growing evidence of its effectiveness in adult and higher education.
- Several researchers who stress the importance of the social situation and influences share Vygotsky's belief in the value of direct teaching combined with the child as an active learner. Shayer, for example, has shown that specially designed material for the teaching of science can increase 'learning ability' and performance on educational tests and Standardised Attainment Tests (SATs). Such improvement also generalises to performance in English and Maths.
- **Bruner** was strongly influenced by Vygotsky and also critical of Piaget's theory. But he shares with Piaget the belief that children are born with a biological organisation and that their underlying cognitive structure matures over time enabling them to think about and organise the world in an increasingly complex way. They also both saw the child as actively curious and explorative, capable of adapting to the environment through interacting with it. Abstract knowledge and competence grow out of active experience and concrete mental operations.
- Like Vygotsky, and unlike Piaget, Bruner stressed the role of language and interpersonal communication and the need for active involvement by expert adults and more advanced peers in helping the child to develop its thinking and problem-solving.
- Bruner's theory of cognitive development is not a stage theory, but identifies three **modes of representation**: **enactive**, **iconic** and **symbolic** which develop in this order.
- The **enactive mode** (corresponding to Piaget's sensorimotor stage) involves representing the world through actions and motor responses ('motor memories').
- The **iconic mode** (corresponding to the last six months of the sensorimotor stage and the whole preoperational stage) involves building up, usually composite, mental images of things we have experienced.
- The transition from the iconic to the **symbolic mode** occurs at about six or seven and involves language coming into its own as an influence on thought. This frees the child from the immediate context and allows it to 'go beyond the information given'.
- Bruner believes that the leap from the iconic to the symbolic mode is due to the development of language: without language, human thought

would be limited to what could be learned through actions or images. By contrast, Piaget believes that logical thought reflects the acquisition of cognitive structures which have already developed through interaction with the environment, and language is merely a tool used in operational thinking.

- Bruner's position implies that it should be possible to speed up cognitive development by training children to use symbols; for Piaget, this should not be possible. Bruner et al.'s study of conservation of liquid quantity, in which different-sized beakers were screened (providing symbolic training), offers support for both views.
- Sinclair-de-Zwart has shown that teaching children words relevant to conservation has little effect unless they understand the underlying concepts, thus supporting Piaget. Piaget argues that, while language may be necessary for formal operations, it is not sufficient and it is not very different from what it was at an earlier stage.
- Bruner believes that teachers should try to find ways of stimulating children, especially those from deprived backgrounds. This is a current concern in Britain for below-average pupils, and the National Curriculum was introduced partly to improve standards of attainment among the bottom 40 per cent of the school population.
- According to Bruner's **spiral curriculum** concept, the principles of a subject come to be understood at increasingly complex levels of difficulty.
- Like Vygotsky, Bruner proposed a much more active policy of intervention than Piaget's concept of 'readiness' implied, believing that educators should help learners grasp a discipline's underlying principles and concepts, so that they can go beyond the (factual) information they have been given and develop their own ideas. They both see the teacher as an 'interventionist', but while Vygotsky's approach is teacher-centred with direct instruction, Bruner's is more child-centred.
- **Information-processing (IP) theories** of cognitive development focus on the process of cognition and the kinds of information children are capable of acquiring from the environment and what they are able to do with it. Sternberg shares Piaget's belief in mental structures that explain people's behaviour and which are largely independent of their social relationships, social practices and cultural environment.
- The underlying metaphor in the IP approach is the computer, which receives information ('input'), stores, retrieves and manipulates it, and responds behaviourally ('output'). **Task analysis** is used to study how children's 'mental programs' and their strategies for processing information develop.
- Maccoby and Hagen's experiment with 6- to 12-year-olds found that the ability to remember the colour of a picture's **background** (while ignoring the objects shown) increased with age. But when they were later asked to remember the **objects** in the picture (ignoring the background colour), the youngest children were more successful. This shows how **selective attention** develops through childhood, and its necessity for problem-solving.
- According to Pascual-Leone and Case, children do not use just one cognitive strategy in solving Piagetian tasks (as Piaget believed) but several, depending on the problem's difficulty. They see working memory as storing the information necessary to solve a problem, the amount of space needed again depending on the problem's difficulty; as the child develops, so available memory space increases. With practice, certain strategies become **automatic**, so requiring less memory space.
- The IP approach, by emphasising the role of memory and the limited capacity of young children to process information, can explain why they are poorer at tasks involving memorising and reading. Knowledge also has a major influence on learning, and the skill of storing knowledge in some linguistic form is a vital prerequisite of successful IP performance. Teachers have a crucial role to play in helping children to find strategies for reducing memory load.
- IP theorists see **metacognition** as playing a vital role: not only do older children have greater information-processing abilities, but they also have greater **insight** into how they do it. The IP approach implies active learning, whereby children should be encouraged to test hypotheses by checking their answers and to use visual imagery to apply these answers to real-life situations.
- While theories of cognitive development clearly have a role to play in education, Beveridge argues that policy makers are moving quickly towards the 'commodification of education', whereby school learning is turned into 'goods' which are 'produced' by teachers. Theories of learning and teaching are being abandoned for a concern with grades and records of school discipline.

THE DEVELOPMENT OF MEASURED INTELLIGENCE

Introduction and overview

As Carlson (1988) has noted, both biological (or genetic) and environmental factors occurring before or after birth can influence the development of measured intelligence. Pre-natal influences affect *potential* intelligence by affecting the development of the brain. Genetic influences may be *hereditary* (as in the case of the inherited metabolic disorder *phenylketonuria*) or *non-hereditary* (as in *Down's syndrome*, which is caused by the presence of an extra twenty-first chromosome). A large number of pre-natal environmental factors are known to have harmful effects on development. These include maternal malnourishment, diseases (such as *maternal rubella*), toxic agents (such as lead and mercury), drugs (cigarettes, alcohol and so on), irradiation (X-rays), maternal stress during pregnancy and maternal age.

Our aim in this chapter is to consider the claims made by psychologists about the influence that genetic and environmental factors can have on the development of measured intelligence. We will begin by looking at the evidence for the view that differences between people in terms of measured intelligence are largely determined by genetic factors. Then, we will look at the evidence concerning the influence of post-natal environmental factors on the development of measured intelligence. In the last part of this chapter, we will examine the interaction between genetic and environmental factors in the development of measured intelligence.

Genetic influences on the development of measured intelligence

In a study carried out in 1940, R.C. Tryon attempted to show that the ability to learn mazes could be bred into rats. Tryon's rats were divided into two groups: those who were good at finding their way through mazes (the *maze-bright rats*) and those who were not so good (*the maze-dull rats*). The 'dull' and 'bright' rats were placed in separate but identical pens (in order to control for the effects of the environment) and left free to breed. Within a few generations, the 'maze-dull' offspring made many more mistakes in learning a maze than did their 'maze-bright' counterparts. As Morris (1988) has noted, although Tryon could not explain *how* maze-learning ability was transmitted, his study appeared to demonstrate that a specific ability can be passed down from one generation of rats to another.

Clearly, there are dangers in generalising the findings concerning maze-learning ability in rats to the complex cognitive abilities evident in humans, and the influence of genetic factors on the development of measured intelligence in humans cannot (for ethical, legal and practical reasons) be studied in the laboratory through selective breeding (Rathus, 1990). However, there are ways in which the influence of heredity on the development of intelligence as measured by IQ tests can be investigated.

STUDIES OF THE STABILITY OF IQ

Since the genetic inheritance of each of us is a constant, then if measured intelligence is largely determined by genetic factors there should be a high degree of continuity in IQ throughout an individual's life-span

(McGurk, 1975). IQ is not normally used as a measure of intelligence below the age of two. Instead, a *developmental quotient* (DQ) is used. This assesses a child's rate of development compared with the 'average' child of the same age (e.g. Bayley, 1969). The younger a child is when given a developmental test, the lower is the correlation between its DQ and later performance on IQ tests. Once IQ is measurable, it becomes a better predictor of adult IQ.

Yet whilst a large number of studies have shown that there is little fluctuation in IQ over time, there are many fluctuations in the short term, and these are often related to disturbing factors in an individual's life. Although the *stability coefficients* reported by some researchers (e.g. Honzik et al., 1948) are impressive, they are based on large numbers of people and tend to obscure individual differences. The stability coefficients reported by other researchers have been less than impressive. For example, McCall et al. (1973) found that in 140 middle-class children, the average IQ change between two and a half and 17 years of age was 28 points. The most 'stable' children changed an average of ten points, whilst 15 per cent of children shifted 50 points or more in either direction. One of the children's IQ increased by 74 points! Even in studies where the correlation between IQ at different ages is *statistically significant*, the stability coefficients are low and suggest greater fluctuation in scores than a simple genetic theory predicts (but see Rebok (1987) for an alternative perspective).

FAMILY RESEMBLANCE STUDIES

Another way of investigating the influence of genetic factors on the development of measured intelligence is to use family resemblance studies. These examine the correlation in intelligence test scores among people who vary in genetic similarity. If genetic factors do influence intelligence test performance, then the closer the genetic relationship between two people, the greater should be the correspondence (or *concordance*) between them with respect to measured intelligence.

Monozygotic (MZ) or identical twins are unique in having exactly the same genetic inheritance, since they develop from the same single fertilised egg. *Dizygotic* (DZ) or non-identical twins, by contrast, develop from two eggs and are no more alike than ordinary siblings. Whereas MZ twins share all of their genes, DZ twins share only about 50 per cent of theirs. If genes have any influence on the development of measured intelligence, then identical twins should show the *greatest* correspondence in terms of their intelligence test performance. Any difference between them would have to be attributed to environmental or experiential influences. Because of their uniqueness, identical twins have been of considerable interest to psychologists investigating the development of measured intelligence. A large number of studies (e.g. Erlenmeyer-Kimling and Jarvik, 1963; Bouchard and McGue, 1981; Wilson, 1983) have shown that the closer the genetic similarity between people, the more strongly correlated are their IQs. Table 6.1 (overleaf) presents a summary of Bouchard and McGue's world-wide literature review of 111 studies reporting IQ correlations between people of varying genetic similarity.

As Table 6.1 shows, the closer the genetic relationship between two individuals, the stronger the correlation between their IQ scores. So, the correlation between cousins (who share roughly 12.5 per cent of their genes) is weaker than that for parents and their offspring (who share roughly 50 per cent of their genes). The correlation between the IQ scores of unrelated people who are reared separately is zero, a finding which is not surprising given that such people share neither heredity nor environment. The strongest correlation of all, however, is for MZ twins. At first sight, these data suggest that heredity makes a strong contribution to a person's performance on an intelligence test. However, it is also true to say that as the genetic similarity between people increases, so their environments become more similar (parents and offspring usually live in the same household, whereas unrelated people usually do not).

Studies of separated twins

One way of overcoming this problem has been to compare the IQs of identical twins *reared together* in the same environment with those raised *separately* in different environments. As we can see from Table 6.1, the evidence suggests that identical twins reared together show a greater similarity in IQ scores than identical twins reared separately. However, the fact that identical twins reared separately are still more similar than DZ twins of the same sex reared together suggests that a strong genetic influence is at work (Bouchard et al., 1990). The data obtained from studies of separated identical twins has, however, been criticised (e.g. Kamin, 1974). Box 6.1 summarises the important criticisms that have been made.

	0.0 0.10 0.20 0.30 0.40 0.50 0.60 0.70 0.80 0.90 1.00	No. of correlations	No. of pairings	Median correlation	Weighted average
Monozygotic twins reared together		34	4672	0.85	0.86
Monozygotic twins reared apart		3	65	0.67	0.72
Midparent–midoffspring reared together		3	410	0.73	0.72
Midparent–offspring reared together		8	992	0.475	0.50
Dizygotic twins reared together		41	5546	0.58	0.60
Siblings reared together		69	26 473	0.45	0.47
Siblings reared apart		2	203	0.24	0.24
Single parent–offspring reared together		32	8433	0.385	0.42
Single parent–offspring reared apart		4	814	0.22	0.22
Half-siblings		2	200	0.35	0.31
Cousins		4	1176	0.145	0.15
Non-biological sibling pairs (adopted/natural pairings)		5	345	0.29	0.29
Non-biological sibling pairs (adopted/adopted pairings)		6	369	0.31	0.34
Adopting midparent–offspring		6	758	0.19	0.24
Adopting parent–offspring		6	1397	0.18	0.19
Assortative mating		16	3817	0.365	0.33
	0.0 0.10 0.20 0.30 0.40 0.50 0.60 0.70 0.80 0.90 1.00				

Table 6.1 Familial correlations for IQ. The vertical bar on each distribution indicates the median correlation. The arrow indicates the correlation predicted by a simple polygenic model (i.e. the view that many pairs of genes are involved in the inheritance of intelligence) (from Gross, 1996, and based on Bouchard and McGue, 1981)

Box 6.1 Criticisms of twin studies

- 'Separated' twins often turn out not to have been reared separately at all. In several of the studies used as support for genetic influences on the development of measured intelligence (e.g. Shields, 1962; Juel-Nielsen, 1965), some of the twins were raised in related branches of the parents' families, attended the same school and/or played together (Farber, 1981; Horgan, 1993). When these twins are excluded from analysis in Shields' study, for example, the correlation decreases from 0.77 to 0.51. Moreover, even if the twins are separated at birth, they have shared the same environment of the mother's womb for nine months. Their identical *pre-natal* experiences may account for the observed similarities in IQ.
- When twins do have to be separated, the agencies responsible for placing them will try to match the respective families as closely as possible. This might account for much of the similarity found between them. When the environments are substantially different, there are marked differences in IQ between the twins (see, for example, Newman et al., 1937).
- Experimenter and participant bias may also play an important role. In Newman et al.'s and Shields' studies, the experimenters *knew* which twins were identical and which had been separated. Participants in Bouchard et al.'s studies were recruited by means of media appeals and 'self-referrals'. Kaprio (cited in Horgan, 1993) has claimed that Bouchard et al.'s studies have tended to attract people who enjoy publicity and, as a result, they are an atypical sample.
- Different tests have been used to measure intelligence in the various studies. This makes comparisons between studies difficult. Moreover, some of the tests used were inappropriate and/or not standardised on certain groups.
- The most widely quoted and best-known studies of identical twins are those reported by Sir Cyril Burt (e.g. 1966) who found high correlations between the IQs of 53 pairs of twins supposedly reared in very different environments. After noticing several peculiarities in Burt's procedures and data, Kamin (1974) and Gillie (1976) questioned the genuineness of Burt's research. Even Burt's most loyal

Figure 6.1 Barbara Herbert and Daphne Goodship, one of the pairs of (English) separated identical twins reunited through their participation in the Minnesota Twin Study

supporters have conceded that at least some of his data were fabricated (e.g. Hearnshaw, 1979).

The various problems with twin studies undoubtedly led to an *overestimation* of the influence of heredity. However, methodological improvements have led to correlations being reported that are still impressive and, for Plomin and DeFries (1980):

'implicate genes as the major systematic force influencing the development of individual differences in IQ'.

One of the major ongoing studies into the influence of heredity on the development of measured intelligence is that directed by Thomas Bouchard at the University of Minnesota. Separated and non-separated twins are given comprehensive psychological and medical tests and answer some 15,000 questions! The data indicate that for some abilities (such as verbal ability), the correlations between MZ twins reared apart are very high, suggesting a strong genetic influence. However, for other abilities (such as memory), the correlations are low or, in the case of spatial ability, inconsistent (Thompson et al., 1991).

Adoption studies

Further support for the view that individual differences in IQ test scores are influenced by genetic factors comes from studies of adopted children. These children share half their genes but none of their environment with their biological parents, and they share at least some of their environment but none of their genes with their adoptive parents. One research methodology involves comparing the IQs of children adopted in infancy with those of their adoptive and biological parents. Support for the influence of genetic factors would be obtained if the correlation between the IQ scores of the adopted children and their biological parents was stronger than that between the adopted children and their adoptive parents.

This is exactly what some studies have shown (e.g. Plomin et al., 1988). Munsinger (1975), for example, found that the average correlation between adopted children and their biological parents was 0.48, a figure higher than the 0.19 value obtained for adopted children and their adoptive parents. Also, by the end of adolescence, the IQ scores of adoptive children are correlated only weakly with their adoptive siblings who share the same environment but are biologically unrelated (Plomin, 1988).

One of the problems with adoption studies is the difficulty in assessing the amount of similarity between the environments of the biological and adoptive parents. There is evidence to suggest that when the environments of the biological and adoptive parents are very different (as when children of poor, under-educated parents are adopted into families of high socio-economic status), substantial increases in IQ scores can be observed. For example, Scarr and Weinberg (1976) carried out a 'transracial' study of 101 white families, above average in intelligence, income and social class, who adopted black children. If genetics were the only factor influencing the development of measured intelligence, then the average IQ of the adopted children would have been expected to be more or less the same as before they were adopted. In fact, their average IQ was 106 following adoption, a figure higher than the average of 90 before adoption. This finding has been replicated in several other studies. For example, Schiff et al. (1978) studied a group of economically deprived French mothers who had given up one baby for adoption whilst retaining at least one other child. The average IQ of the children adopted into middle-class homes was 110, whilst the average IQ of the siblings that remained with the biological mother was 95. Similarly, in another French study Capron and Duyme (1989) found that adoptees raised by parents of high socio-economic status were around 12 IQ points higher than adoptees raised by parents of low socio-economic status, irrespective of their biological background.

Scarr and Weinberg's (1976) data also indicated that children adopted early in life (within their first year) have higher IQs than those adopted later. What the evidence seems to suggest, then, is that when adoptive homes provide a superior intellectual climate, they can have a substantial effect on the development of measured intelligence. However, when the economic status of the biological and adoptive parents is roughly equal, the IQs of adopted children tend to be much more similar to those of the biological parents than the adoptive parents (Scarr and Weinberg, 1978). We will now explore the role played by the environment in more detail.

Environmental influences on the development of measured intelligence

Supporters of the view that the environment influences the development of measured intelligence do not deny that genetic factors play a role. In their view, however, the development of measured intelligence can be strongly influenced by a whole range of environmental factors. As we noted at the beginning of this chapter, such influences can occur before or after birth. Here, we will look at those influences occurring after birth.

DATA FROM NON-HUMAN ANIMAL STUDIES

We have already referred to Tryon's (1940) findings concerning 'maze-bright' and 'maze-dull' rats (see page 66) which seemed to suggest that genetic factors can influence maze learning. A later study conducted by Cooper and Zubek (1958) mixed groups of 'bright' and 'dull' rats in either absolutely plain or stimulating environments (the latter containing, for example, toys, activity wheels and a ladder). The results showed that there were no differences between the 'bright' and 'dull' rats raised in the plain environment, indicating that the inherited abilities of the 'bright' rats had failed to develop. In the case of the rats raised in the stimulating environments, there were also no differences between the 'dull' and 'bright' rats, suggesting that the genetically dull rats had 'made up' (through experience) the differences they lacked in heredity compared with their 'bright' counterparts. Moreover, the rats raised in the stimulating environment had heavier brains than those raised in the plain environment, irrespective of whether they were 'maze dull' or 'maze bright'.

Other researchers (e.g. Wallace, 1974; Greenough and Black, 1992) have shown that rats raised in enriched conditions develop more regions for synaptic connections, and thicker and heavier cortexes than rats raised in deprived conditions. Along with Cooper and Zubek's findings, these findings suggest that (at least in rats) the environment can have a direct impact on the brain, which is, of course, the biological basis for intelligence.

DATA FROM STUDIES OF HUMANS

In humans, research has uncovered a variety of environmental influences on the development of measured intelligence. For example, Stock and Smythe (1963) found that infants who suffered *extreme malnutrition* during infancy averaged 20 IQ points lower than similar children with adequate diets. Such a finding is not unexpected, but research also indicates that the surroundings in which humans are raised and many other factors are as important to our intellectual development as diet. Some of the known post-natal environmental influences are described in Box 6.2.

Box 6.2 Some known post-natal environmental influences on the development of measured intelligence

Environmental 'insults', illness and disease: Lead from lead-based paint chips peeling from walls is just one environmental toxin that is associated with reduced IQ (Needleman et al., 1990). Anoxia (lack of oxygen) at birth, head trauma and various childhood illnesses (such as encephalitis) can cause brain damage and lower potential intelligence. In later life, brain damage from strokes, metabolic disturbances, infections of the brain, and diseases such as Alzheimer's disease can all adversely affect measured intelligence.

Family size and birth order: According to Zajonc and Markus (1975):

> 'Intelligence declines with family size; the fewer children in your family, the smarter you are likely to be. Intelligence also declines with birth order; the fewer older brothers or sisters you have, the brighter you are likely to be'.

One large-scale study of 200,000 children from large Israeli families (Davis et al., 1977) has supported Zajonc and Markus's claim at least up to the seventh child. At this point, the trend reverses itself, so that the tenth-born child has a higher IQ than the ninth-born, who in turn has a higher IQ than the eighth-born. One potential explanation for the birth-order/family-size effect is that each new-born that enters a family lowers the 'intellectual environment' because the intellectual capacity of the parents needs to be spread among a larger number of children. Alternatively, it could be that the mother's uterus is less conducive to optimal pre-natal growth for later than for earlier pregnancies, and this affects IQ (Crooks and Stein, 1991). The difficulty with both of these explanations, of course, is that neither can account for the trend reported by Davis after the seventh child.

Coaching: Coaching involves specific instruction and practice in taking intelligence tests in order to promote higher scores. The evidence suggests that whilst short-term coaching may increase a person's IQ score, the increase is seldom great. Additionally, the higher IQ scores produced by coaching do not seem to produce any improvement in underlying mental abilities (Linn, 1982).

The IQ testing situation: Zigler et al. (1982) have shown that by doing nothing more than making testing conditions optimal for all children, IQ test scores can increase by about six points.

Stressful family circumstances: Sameroff and Seifer's (1989) *Rochester Longitudinal Study* indicates that intellectual competence and general adjustment are correlated with a variety of 'family risk factors' including low parental work skills and a father who does not live with the family. Children with no risk factors score more than 30 points higher on IQ tests than children with seven or eight risk factors.

Child-rearing styles: As we saw in Chapter 3, the ways in which parents interact with their children and the stimulation they provide are correlated with the development of measured intelligence.

(based on Morris, 1988, Wade and Tavris, 1993, and Zimbardo and Weber, 1994)

ENVIRONMENTAL ENRICHMENT STUDIES

In Chapter 2, we described the research conducted by Skeels (1966) into the effects of removing children from orphanages into more stimulating environments. As we noted, 20 years after Skeels and Dye (1939) had originally studied the children, most of them raised by foster mothers had shown significant improvements in their measured intelligence, whereas those raised in the orphanage had dropped out from high school, or were still institutionalised or not self-supporting.

Other studies of children raised in orphanages have also shown that environmental enrichment can have beneficial effects. For example, Hunt (1982) studied 11 children living in an Iranian orphanage. The typical child could not sit up unassisted at age two or walk at age four. The children were emotionally retarded and were passive and unresponsive to the environment. Hunt began a programme of 'tutored human enrichment' in which, for example, the caregivers were trained to play vocal games with the infants. All 11 infants showed a marked acceleration in the acquisition of language skills and generally began to behave in ways typical of children raised in a natural home environment.

In the early 1960s, Hunt's *Intelligence and Experience* (1961) and Bloom's *Stability and Change in Human Characteristics* (1964) argued that intelligence was not a fixed attribute but depended on, and could be increased by, experience. These books led to the United States government initiating a number of *intervention programmes* based on the assumption that intelligence could be increased through special training.

In 1965, *Operation Headstart* began. This was an ambitious compensatory programme designed to give culturally disadvantaged pre-school children enriched opportunities in early life. Operation Headstart began as an eight-week summer programme and shortly afterwards became a full year's pre-school project. In 1967, two additional *Follow Through* programmes were initiated, in an attempt to involve parents and members of the wider community (see, for example, Ryan, 1974). Early findings indicated that there were significant short-term gains for the children, and this generated a great deal of optimism among those connected with Operation Headstart. However, when the IQ gains did occur, they were short-lived. The gains disappeared within a couple of years, and the educational improvement shown by the children was minimal.

A similar project to Operation Headstart had been initiated by Rick Heber in the *Milwaukee Project* which began in 1961. Heber and his colleagues worked with 40 poor, mostly black families, among whom the average IQ score was 75. Twenty of the women (the 'experimental group') were given job training and sent to school. The other twenty (the 'control group') received no job training or special education. The findings initially showed that the children of parents in the 'experimental group' had an average IQ score of 126, a score which was 51 points higher than the average obtained by their mothers. The average score of the 'control group' children was 94, a figure also higher than their mothers' average score.

As with the Headstart programme, however, the IQ gains diminished over time. Moreover, the academic benefits enjoyed by the children were very modest, in that whilst the experimental group did have better reading scores than the controls, there was little difference between them in mathematics, in which both groups performed poorly. Like Operation Headstart, the Milwaukee project showed that vigorous and relatively prolonged intervention can make a difference to the cognitive performance of severely disadvantaged children. However, much of the gain is lost in the years following the end of the programme, at the time of starting school (Rutter and Rutter, 1992). Figure 6.2 illustrates this.

Operation Headstart in particular has been subject to a number of criticisms. Hunt (1969), for example, has claimed that the programme was inappropriate to the needs of the children and did not provide them with the skills they had failed to develop at home during their first four years, and which are developed by most middle-class children. Headstart has also been criticised for its emphasis on changes in IQ as an outcome measure in evaluating its effectiveness. Critics such as Weinberg (1989) have argued that measures which reflect social competence, adaptability and emotional health are much better criteria of success.

It seems, though, that the criticisms were premature, and several reviews of studies looking at the long-term effects of Operation Headstart have concluded that the programme has brought about lasting changes in children's cognitive abilities (Brown and Grotberg, 1981), with the greatest gains being shown by children whose IQ scores were initially the lowest. Additionally, Collins (1983) has suggested that there is a *sleeper effect* at work in that the impact of intervention programmes is cumulative, as shown in Box 6.3.

Box 6.3 Collins' conclusions about intervention programmes

Compared with non-participants, participants in intervention programmes:

- tend to score somewhat higher on tests of reading, language and maths, and this 'achievement gap' tends to widen between the ages of six and 14;
- are more likely to meet the school's basic requirements, that is, they are less likely to be assigned to special education/remedial classes, to repeat a year in the same grade or to drop out of high school;
- are more likely to want to succeed academically;
- have mothers who are more satisfied with their children's school performance and hold higher occupational aspirations for their children.

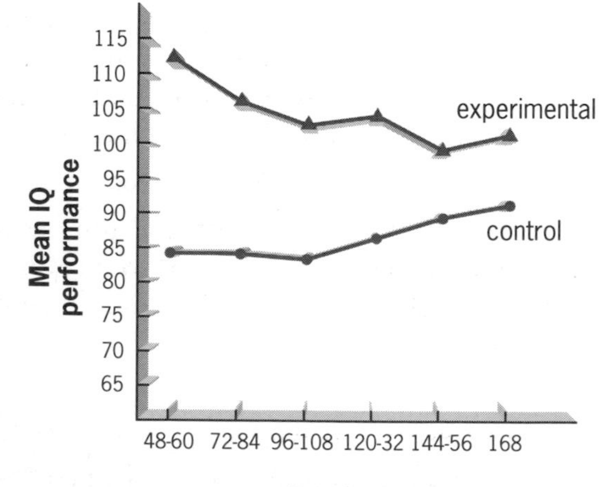

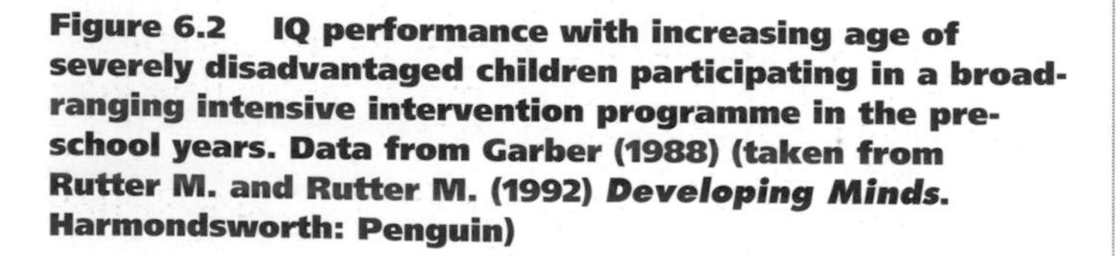
Figure 6.2 IQ performance with increasing age of severely disadvantaged children participating in a broad-ranging intensive intervention programme in the pre-school years. Data from Garber (1988) (taken from Rutter M. and Rutter M. (1992) *Developing Minds*. Harmondsworth: Penguin)

The gains in IQ, which lasted for up to four years after the programme ended, were *not* sustained, and by age 11 to 12 there were no differences between those who had participated and those who had not. However, the *academic benefits* were long lasting. Garber (1988) reports the reverse result in the Milwaukee programme, although as Figure 6.2 shows, the IQ gains declined over time.

Other intervention studies, such as Schweinhart and Weikart's (1980) Perry Pre-school programme in Ypsilanti, Michigan, have also provided evidence that cognitive abilities can be enhanced through extensive training. However, for some researchers (e.g. Hobbs and Robinson, 1982), there has been an overemphasis on the early childhood period. In their view, intervention can be effective *at any time* during the life-span, particularly as regards problem-solving skills and abstract thinking. This was certainly the view of the Venezuelan government who, in 1978, appointed Louis Alberto Machado as Minister of State for the Development of Intelligence. Machado invited a team from Harvard University to develop a programme called 'Project Intelligence', and Venezuelans were taught modules on 'The Foundations of Reasoning', 'Problem Solving' and 'Inventive Thinking'. However, in 1982 a change of government resulted in the project being abandoned even though encouraging results had been obtained (Barber, 1996).

Although many methodological criticisms of the various intervention and enrichment studies have been made, it seems clear that they can have beneficial effects and indicate that the environment does have an important influence on the development of measured intelligence, at least in those children who have been subjected to poor environmental circumstances. According to Scarr (1984), such programmes have less impact on children raised in 'normal' environments. We will discuss Scarr's view in more detail in the following section.

Hothousing

According to Scarr (1984):

> 'Parents who are very concerned about providing special educational lessons for their babies are wasting their time'.

Whether it is possible and, indeed, desirable to accelerate development in children is currently the subject of much debate. For some psychologists (including Scarr), development is largely a matter of maturation. Others believe that whilst accelerated progress can occur in some areas, other skills (such as language) are essentially pre-programmed and not much affected by early experience (Howe, 1995). Howe (1990) and Howe and Griffey (1994) have reviewed the evidence concerning the possibility of early acceleration. In their view, the evidence suggests that efforts to help babies gain basic skills (such as running and jumping) earlier than usual can have a beneficial effect. Even language development can be accelerated such that at 24 months of age, children given special graduated language programmes were as linguistically capable as typical 32-month-old children. Beneficial effects have also been found in terms of pronoun and plural use and, in general, children given the special programmes are well ahead of those not given such programmes (Howe, 1995).

Although Howe and Griffey's review suggests that the effects of accelerated progress appear to be long-lasting, researchers have cautioned against generalising about the effects of providing children with enriched environments. White (1971), for example, showed that infants in enriched visual surroundings (a highly colourful mobile suspended over their cribs) were advanced in some respects but *delayed* in others. A similar conclusion was reached by Cratty (1970) whose studies of perceptual and motor development in children indicate that acceleration in one area of development can have a 'blunting' effect on development in other areas.

Concern about the negative effects of accelerated learning has been expressed in other forms too. Parents who are determined to make their child into a genius or prodigy can pressurise it with their high expectations and by sending it to one of many organisations set up to serve 'gifted children' (and note that there is no convincing evidence that such organisations are actually effective: Llewellyn Smith, 1996). Also, children who experience intensive *hothousing regimes* may miss other experiences which, whilst not necessarily 'educational', are important for healthy development (Howe, 1995). A child who can successfully complete a university degree in mathematics before the age of 14 clearly has developed a useful skill. But if that same child has never heard of Oasis or seen *EastEnders*, he or she might not develop important social skills (such as the ability to make friends) because of an inability to join in 'normal' children's conversations.

Howe and Griffey (1994) have suggested a number of ways in which children can be encouraged to learn that avoid the potential problems described above. Some of these are shown in Box 6.4.

Box 6.4 Encouraging learning

- Learning should be informal and take place in the context of game or play activities.
- Parents should never persist in encouraging learning when the child demonstrates a lack of interest or reluctance.
- Children's efforts should never be criticised or

the child made aware that parents are disappointed with the progress being made.

- Parents should make sure that there are times when the child has their full attention.
- Children should share in their parents' everyday activities and be included in their daily life as much as is reasonably possible.
- Children should be talked to, not talked at. Parents should create opportunities when they and their children can respond to one another.
- Parents should try to see things from the child's perspective, and act as 'guides' rather than 'teachers'.
- Parents should be serious about directing their child towards experiences that provide opportunities for learning and discovering.

(adapted from Howe, 1995)

The interaction between genetic and environmental factors

On the basis of the research we have described, it is clear that both genetic and environmental factors can influence the development of measured intelligence. For most psychologists, measured intelligence can be attributed to an *interaction* between genetic and environmental factors. As Weinberg (1989) has noted:

> 'Genes do not fix behaviour. Rather, they establish a range of possible reactions to the range of possible experiences that environments can provide. Environments can also affect whether the full range of gene reactivity is expressed. Thus, how people behave or what their measured IQs turn out to be or how quickly they learn, depends on the nature of their environments and on their genetic endowments bestowed at conception'.

Researchers have attempted to determine the *relative contributions* made by genetic and environmental factors. The term *heritability* is used by behaviour geneticists to refer to the mathematical estimate of how much variability in a particular trait is a result of genetic variability (Carlson, 1988). Something like eye colour, for example, is affected almost entirely by heredity and little, if at all, by environmental factors. As a result, we

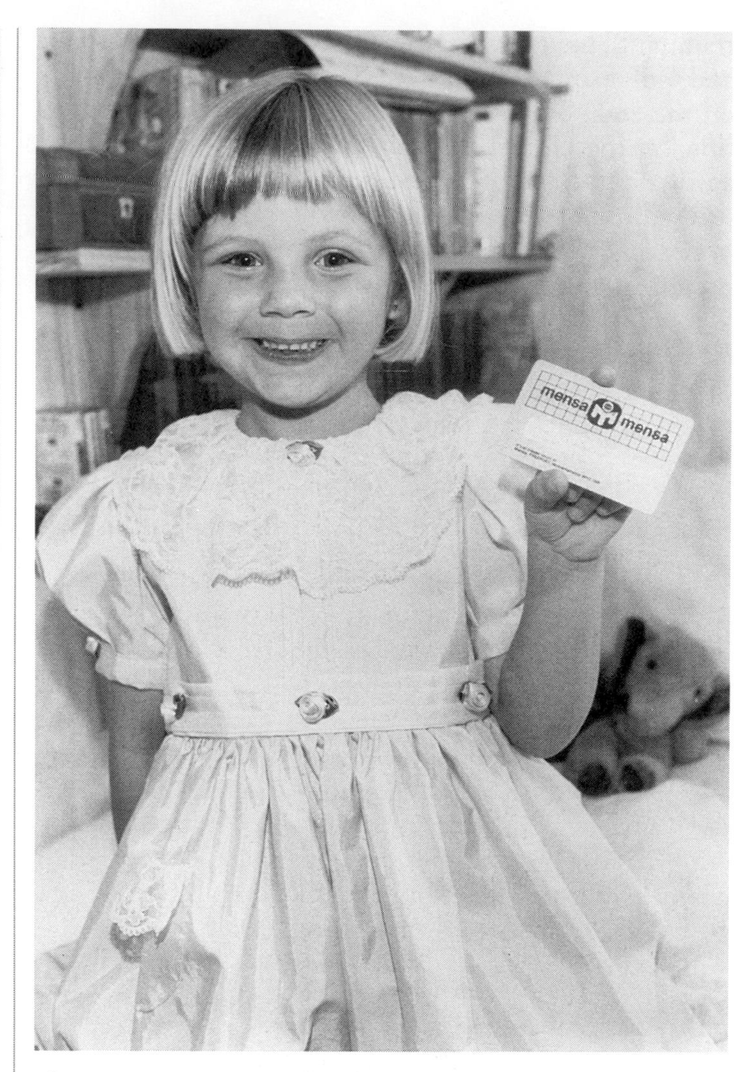

Figure 6.3 Lucinda Cash-Gibson, one of the youngest members of MENSA, the high-IQ society. Aged four when the photograph was taken, her IQ was a staggering 161

can say that the heritability of eye colour is close to 100 per cent.

Early assessments of the extent to which the variation in IQ scores can be attributed to genetic factors suggested a heritability estimate of 80 per cent (Jensen, 1969), but more recent assessments put the estimate at around 50 to 60 per cent (Bouchard and Segal, 1988). However, to say that the heritability of measured intelligence is 50 to 60 per cent does *not* mean that 50 to 60 per cent of measured intelligence is determined by genetic factors. This is because heritability estimates apply only to a particular population or group of people and not to a single individual. So, of the variation in intelligence test scores *within a group of people*, about 50 to 60 per cent (if Bouchard and Segal's estimate is correct) can be attributed to genetic factors. However, this statement must be qualified because the heritability of any trait depends on the *context* in which it is being studied. Thus, a trait that is highly heritable is not necessarily fixed at birth and impossible to change.

Lewontin (1976), for example, asks us to consider ten tomato plants grown in poor soil. Their different heights will be the result of genetic factors. If the same ten plants were grown in fertile soil, differences in height would again be the result of genetic factors. However, the difference in the average height of the plants grown in poor and fertile soil is due to the environmental differences of the soils. So, even when the heritability of a trait is high *within* a particular group, differences in that trait *between* groups may have environmental causes (Myers, 1990). This is illustrated in Figure 6.4.

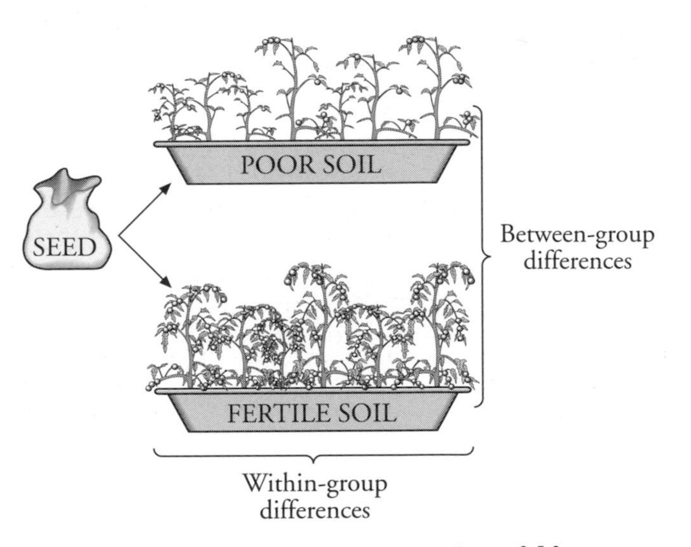

Figure 6.4 Although we can account for *within-group differences* in terms of genetic factors, *between-group differences* may be caused by environmental factors (i.e. poor/fertile soil)

Genetic and environmental factors, then, can never be isolated from one another. For this reason, it is logically absurd to ask how much of an individual's measured intelligence is *determined* by genetic factors and how much by environmental factors, since the answer will depend on the group that is studied and the environment in which they were raised. Bear this in mind as you read Box 6.5.

Box 6.5 X factor is 'key to intelligence'

Bright men may owe their brain power to genes they inherit from their mothers. If a man wants to have smart children, his best bet may be to marry a clever woman, for it seems that several genes which determine intelligence appear located on the X chromosome, as Professor Gillian Turner writes in the latest issue of *The Lancet*.

'These genes are distributed along the whole length of the X chromosome and, presumably, code for various anatomical or functional parts of the neural substratum of intelligence', Professor Turner says. Women have two X chromosomes. Men have one. A woman 'may be driven to mate by her partner's physique, but the brightness of her children lies mainly within her', she says. Deleterious mutations in 'intelligence genes' on an X chromosome will tend to have more effect in a man, explaining why men suffer mental retardation more often. This is because a woman inherits two X chromosomes, one from her father and one from her mother. Therefore, if she inherits a mutant gene on an X chromosome from one parent, there is a good chance she will inherit a normal gene on the X chromosome from the other parent, which will dilute the mutant's impact.

A man, on the other hand, has only one X chromosome inherited from his mother. It is paired with the much smaller Y chromosome from his father. As the Y chromosome is so small, it does not have a gene to match every gene found on the X chromosome. Therefore, in a man a mutant gene on the X chromosome is likely to be the only such gene and, unopposed, will have its full effect. If, however, a mutation is one that increases intelligence, then its full effect will be seen in men, while in women the benefit would be less pronounced. This may explain why some men are extraordinarily intelligent, Professor Turner says.

(adapted from Highfield, 1996)

Conclusions

Both genetic and environmental factors can influence the development of measured intelligence. These factors are intertwined, not separate. In order for measured intelligence to develop to its full potential, people should be provided with an optimal environment, whatever their heredity may be.

Summary

- Both biological/genetic and environmental factors, both pre- and post-natal, can influence the development of measured intelligence. Pre-natal influences affect **potential** intelligence by affecting brain development. Genetic influences may be **hereditary** (as in **phenylketonuria**) or **non-hereditary** (as in **Down's syndrome**). Pre-natal environmental factors that are known to have harmful effects on development include maternal malnourishment, stress, diseases, toxic agents, drugs, irradiation and maternal age.
- An early demonstration of the influence of **genetic** factors was Tryon's study of the ability of rats to run a maze involving **maze-bright** and **maze-dull** rats. However, we cannot generalise from Tryon's results with rats to complex human cognitive abilities, and there are ethical, legal and practical barriers to selectively breeding human beings in order to study the influence of heredity on measured intelligence.
- One way of investigating the influence of heredity on measured intelligence is to study the **stability of IQ**. Since an individual's genetic inheritance is a constant, if IQ is largely determined by genetic factors, then it should remain stable throughout the individual's life-span.
- Below the age of two, a **developmental quotient** (DQ) is used as a measure of intelligence (rather than IQ). The younger the child when tested, the lower the correlation between its DQ and its later IQ test performance; after age two, IQ becomes a better predictor of adult IQ.
- Although several studies have shown little fluctuation in IQ over time (i.e. high **stability coefficients**), there are many short-term fluctuations, often reflecting disturbing life experiences. High stability coefficients are also based on large numbers of people, thus obscuring sometimes very large individual differences. Even where the stability coefficients are **statistically significant**, they are low and suggest greater fluctuation in scores than a simple genetic theory predicts.
- **Family resemblance studies** involve examining the correlations in IQ among people who vary in genetic similarity. If genetic factors influence IQ test performance, then the closer the genetic relationship between two people, the greater the correspondence or **concordance** between their measured intelligence.
- **Monozygotic** (MZ) twins have all their genes in common, while **dizygotic** (DZ) twins share only about half theirs and are no more alike than ordinary brothers or sisters. If genes influence the development of measured intelligence, then MZ twins should show the **greatest** correspondence; any difference between them is attributable to environmental or experiential influences.
- Bouchard and McGue's review of 111 studies concluded that the correlations between cousins is weaker than that for parents and their offspring, while that for unrelated people reared separately is zero. All these findings are consistent with the genetic theory, as is the finding that the strongest correlation of all is for MZ twins.
- However, as the genetic similarity between people increases, so does the similarity of their environments. A way of overcoming this problem is to compare the IQs of MZ twins **reared together** with those raised **separately**. Although MZs reared together are more alike than those reared separately, Bouchard and McGue also found that MZs reared separately are still more similar than DZs of the same sex reared together, suggesting a strong genetic influence.
- However, a number of serious criticisms have been made of studies of separated MZs. The twins often turn out not to have been truly separated at all. Even if they are truly separated at birth, their identical **pre-natal** environment of the mother's womb may account for their similar IQs.
- When twins are separated, they are placed in families that are as similar as possible; when their environments are very different, there are marked differences in their IQs. There is also experimenter and participant bias, as when the experimenters know which twins are identical and which had been separated, and where twins are recruited via media appeals or 'self-referrals'.
- Different studies have used different IQ tests, making comparisons difficult, and some of the tests were either inappropriate and/or not standardised on certain groups. Kamin and Gillie questioned the authenticity of Burt's research, the most widely quoted and best-known studies of separated twins, and even some of his supporters concede that he invented at least some of his data.
- Despite the **overestimation** of the influence of heredity resulting from flawed twin studies, methodological improvements have produced correlations that still implicate genes as the major influence on individual differences in IQ. The

ongoing, comprehensive Minnesota twin study indicates that for verbal ability the correlations among separated MZs are very high, while for memory they are low and for spatial ability inconsistent.

- Further support for the influence of genetic factors comes from **adoption studies**. When the IQs of children adopted in infancy are correlated with those of their adoptive parents and biological parents, the former are found to be far lower than the latter, supporting the view that genetic factors play a major role. Also, by the end of adolescence, there is only a weak correlation between the IQ scores of adoptive children and their adoptive siblings.
- When the economic status of the biological and adoptive parents is roughly equal, biological factors seem to be more influential. However, when children from poor or undereducated parents are adopted into high socio-economic families, substantial gains in IQ can occur, as in Scarr and Weinberg's 'transracial' study. Also, children adopted within their first year have higher IQs than those adopted later.
- Scarr and Weinberg's findings in the USA have been replicated by two French studies (Schiff et al., and Capron and Duyme).
- While not denying the role of genetic factors, supporters of the environmentalist position argue that the development of measured intelligence can be strongly influenced by **environmental factors**. Cooper and Zubek's study of rats found no differences between 'bright'/'dull' groups, either when raised in a plain or in a stimulating environment. Those raised in a stimulating environment, both bright and dull, also had heavier brains.
- Other research has shown that rats raised in enriched conditions develop more regions for synaptic connections and thicker, heavier cortexes than those raised in deprived conditions. At least in rats, it seems that the environment can have a direct impact on the brain, which is the biological basis for intelligence.
- As far as **human studies** are concerned, research has revealed a variety of post-natal environmental influences on the development of measured intelligence. Infants suffering **extreme malnutrition** have much lower IQs than similar children with adequate diets. **Environmental 'insults', illness** and **disease** can all cause brain damage and lower potential intelligence.
- **Family size** is also related to intelligence, such that the more children, the lower the intelligence. Also, intelligence declines with **birth order**, at least up to the seventh child, after which the trend reverses itself.
- **Coaching** in taking intelligence tests may be effective in the short term, but the increase is usually small and does not produce any improvement in underlying mental abilities. Merely making the **IQ testing situation** optimal for all children can increase scores. Intellectual competence and general adjustment are correlated with various 'family risk factors' and **stressful family circumstances**. **Child-rearing styles** are also correlated with the development of measured intelligence.
- Skeels' 20-year follow-up of children removed from orphanages and raised in more stimulating environments (originally studied by Skeels and Dye) found that they were still significantly superior in their measured intelligence (as well as educationally and socially) than those who stayed behind.
- McVicker Hunt began a programme of 'tutored human enrichment' in Iranian orphanages with children who were physically and emotionally retarded. All 11 children showed a marked acceleration in language development and generally began to behave much more like children raised in a natural home environment.
- Hunt and Bloom in the early 1960s argued that intelligence was not a fixed attribute but depended on and could be increased by experience. These arguments led to the setting up of a number of **intervention programmes** by the US government, starting with **Operation Headstart**.
- Headstart began as an eight-week summer programme, then became a full year's pre-school project. Then two **Follow Through** programmes began, aimed at involving parents and the wider community. Early findings indicated significant short-term IQ gains, but these were short-lived and disappeared within two years; the educational improvement was minimal.
- Initial results of the **Milwaukee Project** showed that children whose mothers were given job training and sent to school had an average IQ way above their mothers', while that of children whose mothers were not was far lower, but still higher than their mothers'. But, as with Headstart, these gains diminished over time and the educational benefits were very modest.
- Hunt criticised Headstart for not catering appropriately for the needs of the children involved and providing the skills they had failed to develop at home by the age of four. It also overemphasised changes in IQ as a measure of effectiveness, at the

expense of criteria such as social competence, adaptability and emotional health.

- However, studies of the long-term effects of Headstart have concluded that it has lasting cognitive benefits, especially for those children whose IQ scores are initially the lowest. There is also a **sleeper effect** at work.
- However, the IQ gains, unlike the **academic benefits**, were not sustained. The reverse was found in the Milwaukee programme, although the IQ gains declined over time.
- Other intervention studies, such as the Perry Preschool programme in Ypsilanti, have also shown that cognitive abilities can be enhanced. Hobbs and Robinson believe there has been an overemphasis on early childhood: intervention can be effective **at any time** during the life-span, particularly with problem-solving skills and abstract thinking.
- According to Scarr, intervention and enrichment programmes have less impact on children raised in 'normal' environments compared with those raised in poor environments: development is largely a matter of maturation, and attempts to accelerate development (**hothousing**) are a waste of time.
- According to Howe, and Howe and Griffey, attempts to help babies acquire basic motor skills earlier than usual can be beneficial, and even language development can be accelerated by special graduated language-programmes. While these effects appear to be long-lasting, we should not generalise from them, as demonstrated by White's finding that infants exposed to enriched visual surroundings were advanced in some respects but **delayed** in others. Similarly, Cratty found that acceleration in one area of perceptual or motor development can have a 'blunting' effect on others.
- Parents determined to make their child a genius or prodigy can pressurise it with their high expectations. Those exposed to **hothousing regimes** may miss other experiences that are important for healthy development, such as friendships with other children and the ability to join in 'normal' conversations.
- For most psychologists, the development of measured intelligence is due to an **interaction** between genetic and environmental factors. Genes do not fix behaviour but establish a range of possible reactions to environmental experiences. Environments can also affect whether the full range of gene reactivity is expressed.
- Researchers have tried to determine the **relative contributions** made by genetic and environmental factors. **Heritability** refers to the mathematical estimate of how much variability in a particular trait is due to genetic variability **within a particular population or group of people** (not within a single individual). In the case of IQ scores, Jensen's early heritability estimate of 80 per cent has been modified more recently to 50 to 60 per cent (Bouchard and Segal).
- The heritability of a trait depends on the **context** in which it is studied, so that a highly heritable trait is not necessarily fixed at birth or impossible to change. Lewontin's example of tomato plants grown in **poor** or **fertile** soil demonstrates that even when the heritability of a trait is high **within** a particular group, differences in that trait **between** groups may have environmental causes.
- Because genetic and environmental factors cannot be isolated from each other, it is logically absurd to ask how much of an individual's measured intelligence is **determined** by each kind of factor.

PART 3

Social behaviour and diversity in development

THEORIES OF MORAL DEVELOPMENT

Introduction and overview

At birth, humans are *amoral*, that is, we do not possess any system of personal values and judgements about either what is fundamentally right or wrong, or about our obligations to behave in ways that do not interfere with other people's rights. By the time we are adults, though, most of us possess *morality*. Psychologists are not interested in morality as such. Rather, it is the *process* by which morality is acquired that has been the focus of attention. The progression from amoral to moral has attracted much psychological interest and theories of moral development have been advanced from a number of distinct theoretical camps. These include the psychoanalytic account offered by Freud (1924), accounts based on learning (e.g. Eysenck, 1964) and social learning theories (Aronfreed, 1976), evolutionary-based explanations (Alexander, 1985) and cognitive-developmental approaches (e.g. Piaget, 1932; Kohlberg, 1963).

Our aim in this chapter is to critically consider some of the theories that have been advanced. We begin by looking at Freud's psychoanalytic theory and, after that, we examine the contribution made by social learning theory. Our major concern, however, is with the cognitive-developmental theories proposed by Jean Piaget and Lawrence Kohlberg, and the evidence on which these theories are based.

Freud's psychoanalytic theory of moral development

Sigmund Freud saw life as being a continual conflict between the sexual and aggressive instincts he believed all of us possess, and society's constraints on our behaviour. Freud believed that a part of personality called the *ego* developed in us in order to negotiate compromises between such instincts and constraints. However, this part of personality is concerned with *practical* rather than moral compromises, and so a person with a particularly 'strong' ego might still behave immorally if he or she felt that such behaviour would be undetected and go unpunished.

For Freud, morality is rooted in the *superego*, a part of the personality that punishes us (in the form of *guilt*) when society's standards are violated, and rewards us (in the form of enhanced *self-esteem*) when these standards are upheld. The terms *conscience* and *ego-ideal* are used to describe the punishing and rewarding aspects of the superego respectively, and according to Freud these are held to be acquired by the age of five or six.

Freud's explanation of the mechanism by which the superego is acquired is an elaborate one. When we are young, the people who make judgements about our

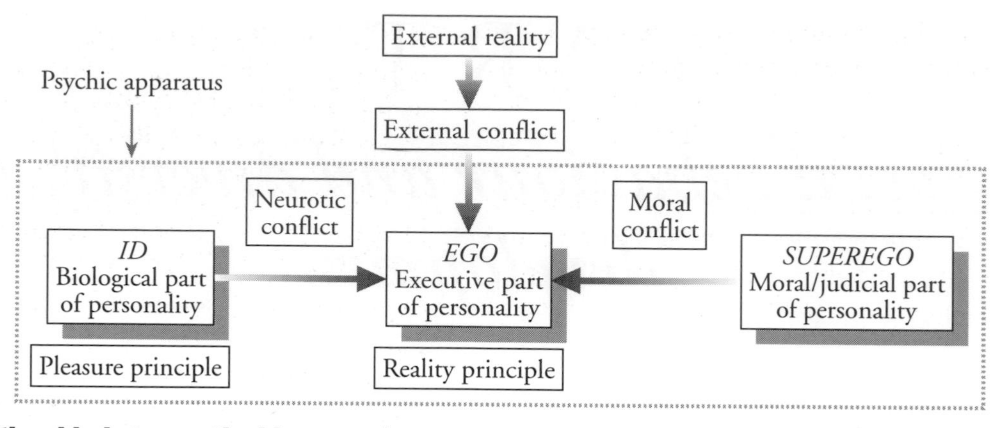

Figure 7.1 The relationship between the id, ego and superego

behaviour, and punish or reward it accordingly, are our *parents*. Freud believed that during development, we experience what he called the *Oedipus complex*. This term was originally used by Freud to refer to the experience of boys, the term *Electra complex* being used to refer to the equivalent experience of girls. However, Freud mostly used the terms 'male and female Oedipus complex'. Briefly, in boys this is a conflict in which the young male wishes to possess his mother sexually and perceives his father as a rival in love. In girls, there is a sexual desire for the father and resentment of the mother. Once the conflict has been resolved, by *identification* with the parent of the same sex, we internalise (or *introject*) the image of that parent into our ego and this becomes the superego. According to Freud (1933):

> 'This new psychical agency (the superego) continues to carry on the functions which have hitherto been performed by people in the external world: it observes the ego, gives it orders, judges it and threatens it with punishment, exactly like the parents whose place it has taken'.

Freud (1924) saw the *fear of castration* as being a very powerful motive for boys identifying with their fathers. As he noted, however:

> 'the fear of castration being thus excluded in a little girl, a powerful motive also drops out for the setting up of a superego'.

Although Freud's logic about the strength of identification between girls and their mothers and hence the development of the superego has been questioned (e.g. Kohlberg, 1969), Freud maintained that women would have weaker superegos than men. There is, however, little evidence that males are morally superior to females. Indeed, in a review of studies testing this hypothesis, Hoffman (1975) concluded that there are no overall gender differences in at least some aspects of morality and where there are (as in the case of resisting temptation), women behave with *greater* morality.

There are several reasons for doubting the usefulness of Freud's theory of moral development. First, and as we will see later on in this chapter, Kohlberg (1969) and others (e.g. Hoffman, 1976) have argued persuasively that moral development is a *gradual* process which begins in childhood and extends into adulthood, rather than something which comes into existence at around the age of five or six. Second, the Freudian view of an *internalised* conscience implies that moral behaviour should be consistent across *different situations*: if our moral behaviour is determined by an unchanging part of personality, moral behaviour should not depend on the details of the moral situation. The evidence does not support such an inference. For example, Hartshorne and May (1930) showed that when 11- to 14-year-olds were given the opportunity to cheat, lie and steal under conditions in which they were confident of not being found out, behaviour was highly inconsistent. So, a child who cheated on an arithmetic test, say, would not necessarily cheat on a spelling test. This suggests that children do not have a uniform, generalised code of morals. Rather, the situation can be important in determining the morality of behaviour, a phenomenon that has been termed the *doctrine of specificity*. In Freud's defence, however, we should note that reanalyses of Hartshorne and May's data have shown a small but significant tendency for moral behaviour on one test to be correlated with moral behaviour on another. Such reanalyses lend *some* degree of support to Freud's view that personality, in the form of a person's strength of conscience, is involved in moral behaviour.

It is also the case that children today are exposed to moral influences which extend much more beyond the family than was true in Freud's time. For example, there is greater exposure to moral influences through the mass media (e.g. television) than there was when Freud was formulating his theory. Also, the influence of the family was much greater than it is now, and today's children are probably more exposed to influences from teachers and peers than was true in Freud's time.

A social learning theory account of moral development

Orthodox learning theorists argue that moral behaviours are acquired through the processes of classical and operant conditioning. One reason we resist temptation, they argue, is because we have been *reinforced* for so doing and *punished* whenever we have transgressed (Aronfreed, 1963). Whilst social learning theorists accept that much moral behaviour is acquired through conditioning, they emphasise the importance of *modelling* (or *observational learning*) and see the *cognitive factors* intervening between a stimulus (such as seeing a wallet on the floor) and a response (taking the money from it) as being of crucial importance.

Bandura (1977) argues that the development of self-control is strongly influenced by *models*, or people children closely observe. Self-control is also influenced by patterns of direct reinforcement children encounter, that is, the disciplinary measures used by adults. Whilst it is not necessary for us to know a model personally, research suggests that there are several aspects of their specific behaviour that make them more likely to be imitated. Box 7.1 summarises some of the more important aspects.

Box 7.1 Factors influencing the likelihood of a model being imitated

- *Appropriateness*: The more appropriate or fitting a behaviour is seen as being, the more likely it is to be imitated. Bandura et al. (1961), for example, showed that children were more likely to imitate aggressive males than aggressive females because in our culture at least, aggression is more acceptable in men than women.

- *Relevance and similarity*: The more relevance a behaviour has, the more likely it is to be imitated. In Bandura et al.'s (1961) experiment, boys were more likely to imitate an aggressive male than were girls. The greater relevance to the boys lies in their perception of similarity between themselves and the model. Perception of similarity is based on gender identity (see Chapter 8).

- *Consistency*: One of the most consistent characteristics of human behaviour is its inconsistency! Children tend to imitate adults in a rather 'literal' way. If adults behave in a way which is inconsistent with how they say they'll behave, children typically imitate the inconsistency.

Mischel (1973) has argued that people develop *self-regulatory systems and plans.* These are self-imposed standards or rules which we use to regulate our own behaviour. Rather than seeing reinforcement and punishment as always being *external* (as when children are directly rewarded or punished), social learning theorists argue for *internal* sources of reinforcement. Like psychoanalytic theorists, social learning theorists see children as eventually no longer needing an external agency (parents and other adults) to administer rewards and punishments: children can reward themselves through feelings of pride (a *rewarding reaction*) and punish themselves through guilt (a *punishing reaction*) by thoughts of doing wrong or the intention to do wrong.

Self-reinforcement and self-punishment (social learning theory's equivalent of psychoanalytic theory's superego: see above) are acquired through observation and imitation of the parents' rewards and punishments. Behaviour which was previously rewarded or punished by parents can be reinforced or punished by the child's own *imitative self-approval* or *disapproval.* For social learning theorists, then, children who model the behaviour of an adult construct an *internal image* of the behaviour. This 'image' then serves as a guide for performing that type of behaviour in the future.

Support for a social learning theory perspective on moral behaviour comes from findings reported by Hoffman (1970) who showed that excessive use of power-assertive techniques of punishment (such as physical punishment, withdrawal of privileges, or the threat of either) by parents was associated with low levels of moral development. Reasoning or explaining, by

Figure 7.2 This father is modelling behaviour which his daughters are learning spontaneously, i.e. observing his behaviour is the crucial factor, rather than being directly reinforced for 'doing the dishes'

contrast, was correlated with high levels of moral development. According to social learning theorists, parents who explain why particular behaviours are wrong induce children to understand the principles of moral behaviour rather than learning how to avoid punishment or maximise reward (see Chapter 3, page 29).

Although social learning theory has been a popular alternative to Freud's psychoanalytic theory, critics argue that it says nothing about *moral progress.* Social learning theorists accept that children learn more as they get older and so in that sense become 'more' moral. However, they do not see development as having certain laws of its own. Rather than changes being qualitative (with children changing in similar ways as they get older), social learning theorists view such changes as being quantitative. Additionally, social learning theory does not appear to offer an adequate explanation of *how* children develop internal moral standards, that is, it does not explain where the standards that parents attempt to instil in children originate from. Finally, social learning theory has difficulty in explaining why some people who become moral leaders (such as Gandhi and Martin Luther King) *defy* the traditional moral and legal standards of their countries.

The weaknesses of both psychoanalytic and social learning approaches to moral development have been addressed by other theories of moral development. It is to two of these that we now turn.

Cognitive-developmental theories of moral development

JEAN PIAGET'S THEORY OF MORAL DEVELOPMENT

According to cognitive-developmental theorists it is the reasons that *underlie* a behaviour, rather than the behaviour itself, which make it right or wrong. In *The Moral Judgement of the Child*, Piaget (1932) argued that morality developed gradually during childhood and adolescence and that children passed through *stages* of moral development which are *qualitatively* different (that is, different in kind). In order to discover how moral knowledge and understanding change with age, Piaget began his research by looking at children's ideas about the rules of the game of marbles, because he believed that the essence of morality lies in rules and that marbles is a game in which children create and enforce their own rules free from the influence of adult teaching. By studying the acquisition of moral knowledge in games, Piaget felt he could discover how children's moral knowledge in general develops. As he noted:

> 'Children's games constitute the most admirable social institutions. The game of marbles, for instance, as played by boys, contains an extremely complex system of rules, that is to say, a code of laws, a jurisprudence of its own . . . All morality consists in a system of rules, and the essence of all morality is to be sought after in the respect which the individual acquires for these rules.'

By pretending he did not know the rules, Piaget asked children to explain them to him and, during the course of a game, to tell him who made the rules, where they came from, and whether they could be changed. He found that children aged between five and nine or ten tended to believe that the rules had always existed in their present form and that they had been put in place by older children, adults or even God. Moreover, the rules were seen as sacred and could not be changed in any way (a so-called *external law*). However, Piaget also found that even though children held these beliefs, they unashamedly broke the rules to suit themselves and saw nothing contradictory in the idea of both players winning the game.

Children aged ten and above understood that the rules were invented by children themselves and that they could be changed, although such changes could only be made if all players agreed, the function of rules being to prevent quarrelling and ensure fair play. These children adhered rigidly to the rules and were able to discuss the finer points and implications of any changes that were made. Piaget called this moral orientation towards cooperation with peers *mutual respect*, to distinguish it from the *unilateral respect* shown by younger children and their morality oriented towards the authority of adults.

As well as watching children play marbles, Piaget explored their ideas about morality by telling them pairs of stories about (hypothetical) children who had told lies, stolen or broken something. Two of these pairs of stories are shown in Box 7.2.

Box 7.2 Examples of pairs of stories used by Piaget

Example 1a

A little boy called John was in his room. He was called to dinner and went into the dining room. Behind the door there was a chair and on the chair there was a tray with 15 cups on it. John couldn't have known that the chair was behind the door, and as he entered the dining room, the door knocked against the tray and the tray fell on the floor, breaking all of the cups.

Example 1b

One day, a little boy called Henry tried to get some jam out of a cupboard when his mother was out. He climbed onto a chair and stretched out his arm. The jam was too high up, and he couldn't reach it. But while he was trying to get it, he knocked over a cup. The cup fell down and broke.

Example 2a

A little girl called Marie wanted to give her

Figure 7.3 Mahatma Gandhi, Mother Teresa and Martin Luther King, moral leaders who *defied* their countries' traditional moral and legal standards, in pursuit of humanistic causes. They seem to be guided by *universal ethical principles* (Kohlberg's stage 6 – see page 88)

mother a nice surprise and so she cut out a piece of sewing for her. But she didn't know how to use the scissors properly and she cut a big hole in her dress.

Example 2b
A little girl called Margaret went and took her mother's scissors one day when her mother was out. She played with them for a bit and then, as she didn't know how to use them properly, she made a hole in her dress.

Piaget asked children who they believed was the naughtier and who should be punished more. Rather than looking at the answers themselves, Piaget was more interested in the *reasons* the children gave for their answers. He found that whilst children aged between five and nine or ten were able to distinguish an intentional act from an unintentional one, they tended to base their judgement on the severity of the outcome or the sheer amount of damage done. In the example shown in Box 7.2, then, John and Marie were typically judged to be naughtier. Piaget called this type of judgement *objective* or *external responsibility.*

By contrast, children aged ten or above judged Henry and Margaret to be naughtier because they were both doing something they shouldn't have been doing. Although the damage caused by Henry and Margaret was not deliberate, older children saw the motive or intention behind an act as being important in determining naughtiness. Piaget called this *internal responsibility.* As far as punishment was concerned, Piaget discovered that younger children believed that people who were naughty should pay for their crimes and, generally, the greater the suffering the better, even though the form of punishment might be quite arbitrary. Such *expiatory* (or 'paying the penalty for') *punishment* is seen as being decreed by authority and accepted as just because of its source, which Piaget called *moral realism.* Thus, when a child in a class does not admit to a misdeed and the rest of the class do not identify the offender, young children see *collective punishment* (punishment for all) as being acceptable.

Piaget also found that younger children often construe a misfortune which befalls a peson who has behaved naughtily as a punishment for the misdeed, a phenomenon he called *immanent justice.* For example, a child who lied but was not found out and later fell and broke an arm was seen as being punished for the lie. For Piaget, younger children believe that God (or an equivalent force) is in league with those in authority to ensure that 'the guilty will always be caught in the end'.

When older children were asked about punishment, Piaget found that they saw it as bringing home to the guilty person the nature of the offence and as a deterrent to behaving wrongly in the future. They also believed that punishing innocent people for the misdeeds of only one was immoral and that 'the punishment should fit the crime'. So, if one child stole another's sweets, the *principle of reciprocity* should apply, and the offender must be deprived of his or her own sweets or punished in some other appropriate way. (Note that at least part of the philosophy of *community service* applies the principle of reciprocity, as when a footballer who assaults a spectator, say, is required to spend time working with young footballers.) Unlike young children, who display moral realism, older children display *moral relativism* in which justice is no longer tied to authority, there is less belief in immanent justice, and collective punishment is seen as wrong.

Piaget called the morality of younger children *heteronomous* or 'being subject to another's laws or rules'. Older children have *autonomous morality* or the *morality of cooperation*, and see rules and regulations as being the product of social agreements rather than sacred and unchangeable laws. Piaget believed that the change from heteronomous to autonomous occurred because of the shift from egocentric to operational thought (see Chapter 4). This occurs around the age of seven and enables children to see things from other people's perspectives. This suggests that cognitive development is necessary for moral development, but since the latter lags at least two years behind the former, it cannot be sufficient for it. In Piaget's view, two other factors are important. One is the freedom from unilateral respect (the child's unconditional and absolute obedience of parents and other adults) and adult constraint to mutual respect within the peer group, where disagreements and disputes between equals have to be negotiated, resolved and a compromise reached. The other factor is the increasing sophistication of the child's understanding of the world as reflected by its grasps of concepts such as reciprocity.

An evaluation of Piaget's theory of moral development

Piaget's theory has been supported by a number of studies conducted by researchers other than himself (e.g. Kruger, 1992), and by cross-cultural studies which

Figure 7.4 Eric Cantona, whose infamous attack on a Crystal Palace supporter resulted in punishment by both the football authorities and the police. His *community service* took the form of working with young footballers in and around Manchester

suggest that the shift from heteronomous to autonomous morality occurs around the age of nine or ten (see Gross, 1996). However, the theory has also been subject to criticism. For example, Wright (1971) has argued that Piaget's theory really intends to explain how *practical morality* develops, that is, how we conceive those situations in which we are actively involved and which demand a moral response or decision. However, Wright points out that Piaget's evidence was derived from samples of children's *theoretical morality*, that is, how their own and others' real and hypothetical moral problems are thought about when they are not immediately or directly involved.

Piaget believed that practical and theoretical morality were related by *conscious realisation*. For Piaget, theoretical morality is the conscious realisation of the moral principles on which we actually operate. Put another way, Piaget felt that we can already do things by the time we come to think about and reflect on them (as is the case with children's language, in which children learn to talk using the rules of grammar long before they realise that there are such things as grammatical rules: Gross, 1996). So, there will always be a delay before developmental change at the practical level is registered at the theoretical level, which implies that theoretical morality is shaped by practical morality rather than the other way round. As Wright (1971) has argued, adult theorising (or tuition) may help theoretical morality catch up with practical morality, but it cannot affect it.

Additionally, Piaget believed that popular girls' games (such as hopscotch) were so simple compared with the most popular game among boys (marbles) that they did not warrant investigation. Whilst Piaget believed that girls *eventually* achieve similar moral levels to boys, he saw girls as being less concerned with *legal elaborations*. This apparent gender bias in Piaget's theory has also been identified in connection with Kohlberg's theory of moral development which we will consider shortly.

Empirically, research has shown that children's understanding of *intention* is much more complex than Piaget believed, and that children are able to bring this understanding to bear on moral decision-making, something Piaget would have seen as being impossible. As Durkin (1995) has remarked, research suggests that the pre-school child is *not* amoral. Some of the findings that support Durkin's claim are shown in Box 7.3.

Box 7.3 Some experimental challenges to Piaget's theory of moral development

• In a study conducted by Constanzo et al. (1973), six-, eight- and ten-year-old children read stories about a boy who emptied his box of toys onto the floor so that he could either sort them out (good motive/intention) or make a mess (bad motive/intention). When his mother, who was unaware of his intentions, entered the room, she either approved or disapproved of his behaviour (a measure of the consequences of his actions). Consistent with Piaget's earlier findings, only six-year-olds judged him as being naughty, regardless of his actual intentions, when his mother *disapproved*. However, when she approved, the older children *and* the six-year-olds were just as likely to judge him according to his intentions.

Figure 7.5 According to Piaget, popular girls' games, such as hopscotch, are so simple compared with marbles, the most popular game among boys, that they do not warrant investigation. He believed that the rules of marbles could be used to study morality, since all morality consists of a system of rules

There are a number of plausible explanations for the six-year-olds' judgements (see, for example, Karniol, 1978), but the fact that the judgement of the youngest children was no different from that of the older children is difficult for Piaget's theory to explain.

- Nelson (1980) has argued that Piaget's stories make the consequences of a behaviour explicit rather than the intentions behind it. When three-year-olds see people bringing about negative consequences, they assume that the intentions are negative. However, when information about intentions is made explicit, even three-year-olds can make judgements about those intentions, regardless of the behaviour's consequences. This suggests that three-year-olds are *less proficient* than older children at discriminating intentions from consequences and in using these separate pieces of information to make moral judgements.

- Armsby (1971) has shown that depending on the extent and nature of the damage that is described to them, six-year-olds *are* capable of judging that a small amount of deliberate damage is naughtier than a large amount of accidental damage. In Armby's study, 60 per cent of six-year-olds (as compared with 90 per cent of ten-year-olds) judged the deliberate breaking of a cup as being more deserving of punishment than accidental damage to a television set. This suggests that at least some six-year-olds are capable of understanding intention in the sense of 'deliberate naughtiness'.

- Information-processing theorists (e.g. Gelman and Baillargeon, 1983) argue that aspects of development which Piaget believed to be a result of an increasing capacity for the complexity and quality of thought are actually a result of an increasing capacity for the storage and retrieval of information. Recall from Box 7.2 the stories of John and Henry. Most five-year-olds say that John is naughtier because he broke more cups than Henry. For Piaget, this is because five-year-olds focus on the amount of damage done instead of the wrongdoer's intentions. However, Gelman and Baillargeon argue that children make such judgements because, although they can remember who broke more cups, *they cannot remember all the other details of the stories*. When an effort is made to ensure that all details of the stories are remembered, five-year-olds frequently *do* consider intentions as well as the amount of damage.

LAWRENCE KOHLBERG'S THEORY OF MORAL DEVELOPMENT

Whilst Piaget's theory continues to attract research interest, the theory that has had the most impact on the study of moral development is that advanced by Lawrence Kohlberg. Kohlberg argued that the only way to find underlying consistencies and developmental trends in people's behaviour was by studying the philosophy, logic or reasoning behind their thinking (Piaget's theoretical morality) and behaviour (Piaget's practical morality). Like Piaget, Kohlberg believed that morality developed gradually during childhood and adolescence and that children passed through stages of moral development. However, his method of studying moral development was quite different.

Kohlberg (1963) created a number of *moral dilemmas* (ten in all) that typically involved a choice between two alternatives, both of which would be considered to be generally unacceptable by society. Box 7.4 illustrates one of the most famous of these dilemmas and the questions asked by Kohlberg.

Box 7.4 An example of a moral dilemma

In Europe, a woman was near death from a special kind of cancer. There was one drug that the doctors thought might save her. It was a form of radium that a druggist in the same town had recently discovered. The drug was expensive to make, but the druggist was charging ten times what the drug cost him to make. He paid $400 for the radium and charged $4000 for a small dose of the drug. The sick woman's husband, Heinz, went to everyone he knew to borrow the money, but he could only get together about $2000, which is half of what the drug cost. He told the druggist that his wife was dying and asked him to sell it cheaper or let him pay later. But the druggist said, 'No, I discovered the drug and I'm going to make money from it.' So Heinz gets desperate and considers breaking into the man's store to steal the drug for his wife.

1 Should Heinz steal the drug?
  a) Why or why not?
2 If Heinz doesn't love his wife, should he steal the drug for her?
  a) Why or why not?
3 Suppose the person dying is not his wife but a stranger. Should Heinz steal the drug for the stranger?
  a) Why or why not?
4 (If you favour stealing the drug for a stranger.) Suppose it's a pet animal he loves. Should Heinz steal to save the pet animal?
  a) Why or why not?
5 Is it important for people to do everything they can to save another's life?
  a) Why or why not?
6 Is it against the law for Heinz to steal? Does that make it morally wrong?
  a) Why or why not?
7 Should people try to do everything they can to obey the law?
  a) Why or why not?
  b) How does this apply to what Heinz should do?

(taken from Kohlberg, 1984)

Like Piaget, Kohlberg was not so much interested in the specific things that are considered to be right or wrong; rather, he was more interested in the ways in which thinking about right and wrong changes with age. For example, irrespective of our age, most of us would say that it is wrong to break society's laws. Our *reasons* for upholding the law, however, as well as our views about whether there are circumstances in which breaking the law can be justified, might change as we develop. In the case of Heinz, then, Kohlberg was interested in why people believed Heinz should act in a particular way rather than whether he should or should not steal the drug.

Kohlberg (1963) presented his moral dilemmas to 58 males aged between seven and 17. Based on the reasoning offered by his sample, Kohlberg concluded that there were six qualitatively different ways of viewing moral issues. Because these types of moral reasoning differed in complexity, with more complex types being used by older children, Kohlberg argued that they could be seen as *stages* in the development of morality which approximated to Piaget's stages of cognitive development (see Chapter 4). Kohlberg argued that the six stages spanned three basic *levels* of moral reasoning. Between four and ten years of age, we have a *pre-conventional morality* in which our reasoning has a self-serving function such that actions serve the function of avoiding punishment (in Stage 1) and obtaining rewards (in Stage 2). At the pre-conventional level, then, we do not have a personal code of morality, but rather morality is shaped by the standards of adults and the consequences of following or breaking their rules.

In late childhood or early adulthood, our sense of right and wrong matures to the level of *conventional morality*, and we begin to internalise the moral standards of valued adult role models. In Stage 3, our desire to help others and gain their approval guides our morality, whilst in Stage 4, morality is guided by the desire to maintain social order. People who can reason in the abstract way of Piaget's formal operational thought (see Chapter 4, page 46) may progress to the level of *post-conventional morality*. Although this can occur at any time during adolescence, Kohlberg (1975) believed that only about ten per cent of adults progress beyond Stage 4, and that most of those who do, do so in adulthood. Other research (e.g. Colby et al., 1983) puts the figure at 15 per cent.

Stage 5 affirms the values society agrees on such as individual rights, the need for democratically determined rules, and *reciprocity* (or *mutual action*). In Stage 6, people are guided by *universal ethical principles* in which they do what they believe to be right as a matter of conscience, even if such behaviour conflicts with society's rules. Box 7.5 illustrates the six stages proposed by Kohlberg and gives examples of moral reasoning favouring or opposing Heinz's behaviour as described in Box 7.4.

Box 7.5 Kohlberg's three levels and six stages of moral development

LEVEL 1: PRE-CONVENTIONAL MORALITY

Stage 1 (Punishment and obedience orientation): What is right and wrong is determined by what is punishable and what is not. If stealing is wrong, it is because authority figures say so and will punish such behaviour. Moral behaviour is essentially the avoidance of punishment.

Heinz *should* steal the drug because if he lets his wife die, he would get into trouble.

Heinz *should not* steal the drug because he would get caught and sent to jail.

Stage 2 (Instrumental relativist orientation): What is right and wrong is determined by what brings rewards and what people want. Other people's needs and wants are important, but only in a reciprocal sense ('if you scratch my back, I'll scratch yours').

Heinz *should* steal the drug because his wife needs it to live and he needs her companionship.

Heinz *should not* steal the drug because he might get caught and his wife would probably die before he got out of prison, so it wouldn't do much good.

LEVEL 2: CONVENTIONAL MORALITY

Stage 3 (Interpersonal concordance or 'good boy–nice girl' orientation): Moral behaviour is whatever pleases and helps others and doing what they approve of. Being moral is 'being a good person in your own eyes and the eyes of others'. What the majority thinks is right by definition.

Heinz *should* steal the drug because society expects a loving husband to help his wife regardless of the consequences.

Heinz *should not* steal the drug because he will bring dishonour on his family and they will be ashamed of him.

Stage 4 (Maintaining the social order orientation): Being good means doing one's duty – showing respect for authority and maintaining the social order for its own sake. Concern for the common good goes beyond the Stage 3 concern for one's family: society protects the rights of individuals, so society must be protected by the individual. Laws are unquestionably accepted and obeyed.

Heinz *should* steal the drug because if people like the druggist are allowed to get away with being greedy and selfish, society would eventually break down.

Heinz *should not* steal the drug because if people are allowed to take the law into their own hands, regardless of how justified an act might be, the social order would soon break down.

LEVEL 3: POST-CONVENTIONAL MORALITY

Stage 5 (Social contract-legalistic orientation): Since laws are established by mutual agreement, they can be changed by the same democratic process. Although laws and rules should be respected, since they protect individual rights as well as those of society as a whole, individual rights can sometimes supersede these laws if they become destructive or restrictive. Life is more 'sacred' than any legal principle, and so the law should not be obeyed at all costs.

Heinz *should* steal the drug because the law is not set up to deal with circumstances in which obeying it would cost a human life.

Heinz *should not* steal the drug because even though he couldn't be blamed if he did steal it, even such extreme circumstances do not justify a person taking the law into his own hands. The ends do not always justify the means.

Stage 6 (Universal ethical principles orientation): The ultimate judge of what is moral is a person's own conscience operating in accordance with certain universal principles. Society's rules are arbitrary and they may be broken when they conflict with universal moral principles.

Heinz *should* steal the drug because when a choice must be made betwen disobeying a law and saving a life, one must act in accordance with the higher principle of preserving and respecting life.

Heinz *should not* steal the drug because he must consider other people who need it just as much as his wife. By stealing the drug he would be acting in accordance with his own particular feelings with utter disregard for the values of all the lives involved.

(based on Rest, 1983, Crooks and Stein, 1991, and Gross, 1996)

Kohlberg tested his idea that moral development occurred in stages by following up his original sample to see if those who were initially at a low stage had advanced to a higher one. Since the original study, Kohlberg's sample has been tested every two to five years. Based on findings reported by Colby et al. (1983), which suggest that 'moral progression' does occur, Kohlberg argued that the first five stages of moral reasoning were *universal* and that all people pass through them in an *invariant sequence*. So, irrespective of our culture, we all start with a Stage 1 orientation to morality, we cannot 'skip' a stage and, whilst we might become 'fixated' in one stage, we never *regress* to an earlier one (except in unusual circumstances such as when the brain is damaged). Additionally, Kohlberg argued that the changes do not occur 'overnight' and that whilst the ideas we express about morality stem from the particular stage we are in, we may express ideas from stages below or above a particular stage.

Both Piaget and Kohlberg see cognitive development as being necessary but not sufficient for moral development, that is, cognitive development sets a limit on the maturity of moral reasoning with the latter usually lagging behind the former. Furthermore, just because a person is capable of formal operational thought and capable of conventional and post-conventional moral reasoning, there is no *guarantee* that he or she will behave more morally, even though the evidence suggests this tends to be the case (Lerner and Shea, 1982). Because formal operational thought is achieved by a comparatively small proportion of people, it is hardly surprising that the percentage of people attaining the highest level of moral reasoning is so small (cf. Colby et al., 1983; see above). The relationship between Kohlberg's and Piaget's stages of moral development and Piaget's stages of cognitive development is shown in Table 7.1 (overleaf).

Kohlberg's theory has received support from several quarters. For example, Smetena (1990) has shown that when factors like education and social class are controlled for, juvenile delinquents are more likely to show lower levels of moral reasoning than non-delinquents of the same ages. As we have seen, in Stage 2, right and wrong are seen in terms of satisfying personal needs. According to Thornton and Reid (1982), this stage of reasoning is also characteristic of adults who engage in robbery and other 'instrumental' crimes. A 20-year longitudinal study conducted by Rest (1983) of men from adolescence to their mid-30s has shown that stages of moral development do seem to occur in the order described by Kohlberg, although such change is *gradual* with, on average, the sample changing less than two stages. Finally, from 45 studies conducted in 27 different cultures, Snarey (1987) has concluded that the data 'provide striking support for the universality of Kohlberg's first four stages'.

Not surprisingly, Kohlberg's theory has also been subjected to considerable evaluation. Box 7.6 summarises some of the major theoretical, methodological and empirical issues that researchers have raised. The reader is directed to Gross (1996) for a detailed discussion of other issues, such as Einsenberg's (1986) research into *pro-social moral reasoning*.

Box 7.6 Some concerns about Kohlberg's theory of moral development

- Whilst at least some of Kohlberg's stages may be universal, it has been claimed that his theory is biased towards *Western* cultures. As we saw, Stage 6 reasoning is based on supposedly 'universal' ethical principles. Whilst the principles of justice, equality, integrity and reverence for life may be relevant to a culture that idealises them, they are *not* universally held (Shweder, 1991; Eckensberger, 1994). Moreover, some societies have developed moral principles that are not covered by Kohlberg's theory. Amongst Papua New Guineans, for example, a *principle of collective moral responsibility* exists (Snarey, 1987). One aspect of this principle says that Heinz should steal the drug because all resources should be available to the community at large.

- Gilligan (1982) has argued that because Kohlberg's theory was based on his study of males, his stages are based on a male definition of morality. Gilligan sees men and women as having different ideas about what constitutes morality. Whilst men's morality is based on abstract principles of law and justice, women's is based on principles of compassion and care. As a result, women are rated as being at the conventional level whilst men are at the post-conventional level. Rather than one type of moral reasoning being *better* than another, Gilligan argues that the woman's social perspective is a different view which *complements* male notions of morality. More recent research, however, suggests that when the domain of moral reasoning is restricted to one of *common interest*, men and women produce very similar types of moral reasoning. According to Clopton and Sorell (1993), gender differences in moral reasoning are due to *situational differences* rather than stable gender differences, and women and men are likely to use similar forms of reasoning when faced with similar moral problems.
- Kohlberg has been almost exclusively concerned with moral *thinking*, and his dilemmas assess only 'storybook morality', that is, the way people reason about relatively unusual hypothetical dilemmas. Gibbs and Schnell (1985) have argued that moral reasoning and moral behaviour do not necessarily go together. Whilst moral reasoning may determine moral talk, 'talk is cheap' (Blasi, 1980), and what we say and what we do when faced with a moral dilemma often differ, particularly when we find ourselves under strong social pressure (Rosenhan, 1973). As Mischel and Mischel (1976) have noted, moral development research should really look at what people do rather than what they say they would do.
- Rest and Thoma (1986) have noted that Kohlberg's study began in the 1950s in the USA. The original participants have lived through the civil rights movement, Vietnam, Watergate and the women's movement. The judgements of these participants are unlikely to be the same as those who grew up with the depression, World War II and the Cold War. Nor are they

Table 7.1 The relationship between Kohlberg's and Piaget's stages of moral development and Piaget's stages of cognitive development

Kohlberg's levels of moral development	Age group included within Kohlberg's developmental levels	Corresponding stage of moral development (Piaget)	Corresponding stage of cognitive development (Piaget)
1 Pre-conventional (Stages 1 and 2)	Most nine-year-olds and below. Some over nine	Heteronomous (five to nine or ten)	Preoperational (two to seven)
2 Conventional (Stages 3 and 4)	Most adolescents and adults	Heteronomous (e.g. respect for the law and authority figures) plus autonomous (e.g. taking intentions into account)	Concrete operational (seven to 11)
3 Post-conventional (Stages 5 and 6)	Ten to 15 per cent of adults, not before mid-30s	Autonomous (ten and above)	Formal operational (11 and above)

(taken from Gross, 1996)

likely to be the same as those who grow up in the next 20 to 30 years.

- Sobesky (1983) has suggested that Kohlberg's dilemmas are unfamiliar to most people asked to consider them, and that more mature reasoning might be shown if the dilemmas were about relevant, real-life, day-to-day experiences. They are also hypothetical and do not involve any serious personal consequences. Sobesky gave people Heinz's dilemma with the consequence of him being sent to prison because he would definitely be caught. Sobesky found that when asked to imagine themselves in Heinz's position, people were less likely to advocate stealing *and* their levels of moral reasoning were lower.
- Shweder et al. (1987) have suggested that the higher stages in Kohlberg's theory are associated with education and verbal ability, which should not necessarily be prerequisites for moral judgement. As Coles (1986) has remarked, it is 'possible to get all As and flunk life'. The evidence suggests that 'college-educated' people give higher level and more mature explanations of moral decisions than people not educated at college. The former may not be more moral than the latter, but might be more verbally sophisticated. Additionally, Shweder (1991) has argued that post-conventional morality may not necessarily be preferable to conventional morality. Even Kohlberg (1978) has acknowledged that there may not be a separate sixth stage and Schweder argues that because most people do not reach Stages 5 and 6, education programmes designed to take people to these stages could be catastrophic if most people chose to act according to individual moral principles which had little regard for society's rules.

Conclusions

Several theories of moral development have been proposed. In this chapter, psychoanalytic, social learning and cognitive-developmental theories have been described and evaluated. The psychoanalytic and social learning theories see morality as being imposed on people by parents and other socialising agents. Cognitive-developmental theories concentrate on the structures of reasoning that underlie behaviour and assume that moral reasoning develops through qualitatively different stages.

Summary

- Human beings at birth are **amoral**, but by the time we are adults, most of us possess **morality**. Psychologists are mainly interested in the **process** by which morality is acquired. Theories of development from amoral to moral include Freud's psychoanalytic account, accounts based on learning theories and social learning theories, evolutionary-based explanations and the cognitive-developmental theories of Piaget and Kohlberg.
- According to Freud, the function of the **ego** is to negotiate compromises between our sexual and aggressive instincts and society's restrictions on our behaviour, which are in continual conflict. The ego is concerned with **practical** rather than moral compromises.
- Morality is rooted in the **superego**, acquired by age five or six. It comprises **conscience**, which punishes us (in the form of **guilt**) when society's standards are violated, and **ego-ideal**, which rewards us (in the form of enhanced **self-esteem**) when they are upheld.
- All children experience the **Oedipus complex** (in the case of girls, originally called the **Electra complex**), in which boys wish to possess their mother sexually and see their father as a rival, and girls sexually desire their father and resent their mother.
- The conflict is resolved through **identification** with the same-sex parent, whereby the child **introjects** that parent's image into its ego, forming the superego, which takes over the parental role of punisher within the child's psyche.
- While the **fear of castration** is a very powerful motive for boys identifying with their fathers, this motive is missing in girls, making their identification with their mothers weaker and, hence, giving them weaker superegos. However, there is little evidence that males are morally superior.

- An important criticism of Freud's theory is that moral development is a much more **gradual** process than he claimed, extending into adulthood. Also, his view of an **internalised** conscience implies the consistency of moral behaviour across **different situations**, but the evidence presents a different picture, in which children do not have a generalised code of morals and the situation can influence moral behaviour (the **doctrine of specificity**).
- Children today are exposed to many more moral influences, such as the mass media, teachers and peers, than was true in Freud's time; also, the family was much more of an influence then than it is now.
- According to orthodox learning theorists, we resist temptation because we have been **reinforced** for doing so and **punished** for transgressing. While **social learning theorists** accept that much moral behaviour is acquired through classical or operant conditioning, they emphasise the importance of **modelling** or **observational learning** and see the **cognitive factors** intervening between a stimulus and a response as crucial.
- According to Bandura, the development of self-control is strongly influenced by **models**, as well as by patterns of direct reinforcement and adults' disciplinary measures. Models are more likely to be imitated the more **appropriate** their behaviour and the greater the **relevance** of their behaviour, based on perceived **similarity**. **Consistency** is another model characteristic influencing the likelihood of imitation.
- According to Mischel, people develop **self-regulatory systems and plans**. These self-imposed standards and rules represent **internal** sources of reinforcement, whereby children eventually no longer need an **external** agent of reinforcement or punishment but can reward themselves through pride (a **rewarding reaction**) or punish themselves through guilt (a **punishing reaction**).
- Self-reinforcement and self-punishment are social learning theory's equivalent of Freud's superego. They are acquired through observation and imitation of the parents' rewards (**imitative self-approval**) and punishments (**imitative self-disapproval**). Children construct an **internal image** of adults' behaviour which serves as a guide for future performance of that type of behaviour.
- Hoffman's findings that parents' excessive use of power-assertive techniques of punishment was associated with low levels of moral development in the child supports the social learning theory perspective. By contrast, parents who use reasoning and explaining tend to have children with higher levels of moral development.
- One limitation of social learning theory is its failure to deal with **moral progress**. Although it recognises that children learn more as they get older and become 'more' moral (quantitative changes), it does not see development as having its own laws or involving qualitative changes. It also has difficulty explaining why some moral leaders **defy** their country's traditional moral or legal standards.
- **Cognitive-developmental theorists** see the reasons that **underlie** a behaviour as what make it right or wrong. According to Piaget, morality develops gradually during childhood and adolescence, the individual passing through **stages** which are **qualitatively** different. He began by studying children's ideas about the rules of marbles, since the essence of morality lies in rules, and marbles is not influenced by adult teaching.
- Children aged five to nine or ten told Piaget that the rules of marbles had always existed in their present form and had been put in place by older children, adults or even God. They were seen as sacred and unchangeable (an **external law**), yet children broke the rules to suit themselves. They showed **unilateral respect**.
- Children aged ten and above understood that the rules, designed to prevent argument and ensure fair play, were made by children themselves and could be changed if all players agreed. They stuck rigidly to the rules, discussing the finer points and implications of any changes made. They showed **mutual respect**.
- Piaget also explored children's ideas about morality by telling them pairs of stories about (hypothetical) children, such as John and Henry/Marie and Margaret. He asked them who was the naughtier and who should be punished more. Although children aged between five and nine or ten could distinguish intentional from unintentional acts, the **reasons** for their judgements related to the severity of the outcome and amount of damage done: the greater the damage, the naughtier the child (**objective/external responsibility**).
- Ten-year-olds and above made judgements based on the motive or intention behind the act: even if the child was not deliberately causing damage, it was naughtier if the act occurred while doing something it wasn't meant to do (**internal responsibility**).
- Younger children believe that people should pay

[Figur]e 8.1 Renee Richards, formerly known as Richard [Rask]in, one of the world's best-known transsexuals. Born [as] Richard had his sex reassigned through surgery [and s]he continued her tennis career as a woman

[...]al differences between males and females which [...] reflect gender roles (see below).

[...]term *sex typing* refers to our discovery that we are [...] or female (that is, our acquisition of a sex or gen[der i]dentity) and our learning of the behaviours appro[priat]e to our gender (that is, adopting an appropriate [gender ro]le). Sex typing begins early in Western culture, [with] parents often dressing their new-born baby in blue [if it i]s a boy and pink if it is a girl. As Condry and Ross, [(198]5) have noted, even in the earliest days of infancy, [our g]ender influences how people react to us. Indeed, [the fi]rst question asked by friends and relatives of par[ents] with a new-born baby is 'Boy or girl?' (Intons[-Peter]son and Reddel, 1984). By the age of three or four, most children have some knowledge about their gender. They know, for example, that boys become men and girls become women, and that some games are played by boys and others by girls. A permanent gender identity is usually acquired by the age of five, and children know that a girl is a girl even if she can climb a tree (Zimbardo and Weber, 1994).

Gender stereotypes and gender differences

Research conducted by Williams and Best (1994) suggests that there is a high degree of agreement across the 30 countries studied by them regarding the characteristics associated with each gender group. For example, male-associated terms included 'aggressive', 'determined' and 'sharp-witted' whilst female-associated terms included 'cautious', 'emotional' and 'warm'. Williams and Best also found systematic *cultural variations*, with stereotypes being related to several variables including socio-economic development, education and religion.

As far as *actual* differences are concerned, several reviews have found that many stereotypes about males and females actually have little empirical support. Box 8.1 summarises some of the findings that have been reported.

Box 8.1 Some findings relating to gender differences

Aggression: According to Maccoby and Jacklin (1974) and Weisfeld (1994), boys are more verbally and physically aggressive than girls, a difference which shows itself as soon as social play begins (around two and a half years). Whilst both sexes become less aggressive with age, boys and men remain more aggressive throughout development. However, these findings have been challenged (Durkin, 1995). For example, some studies have shown that women sometimes score higher for certain kinds of indirect non-physical aggression, whilst others have found no differences at all between the sexes (e.g. Campbell and Muncer, 1994).

Verbal ability: From pre-school to adolescence, the sexes are very similar with respect to verbal ability. At age 11, however, Maccoby and Jacklin

for their crimes and, generally, the greater the suffering the better (**expiatory punishment**). This is decreed by authority and accepted as just because of its source (**moral realism**). They also believe in **immanent justice**.

- For older children, punishment is designed to make the guilty person aware of the nature of the offence and to discourage future offences. The punishment should fit the crime, so that the **principle of reciprocity** should apply. Older children display **moral relativism**, and belief in immanent justice is much reduced.
- Piaget called the morality of younger children **heteronomous**, while that of older children is **autonomous**, showing **morality of co-operation**. The change occurs due to the shift from egocentric to operational thought at about seven, suggesting that cognitive development is necessary but not sufficient for moral development. Also needed are freedom from unilateral respect and adult constraint to mutual respect within the peer group, and the ability to grasp concepts such as reciprocity.
- Several studies have found support for Piaget's theory, including cross-cultural studies which suggest that the shift from heteronomous to autonomous morality occurs at about age nine or ten. However, Wright has argued that while Piaget's theory is meant to explain the development of **practical morality**, his evidence was derived from samples of children's **theoretical morality**.
- For Piaget, theoretical morality is the **conscious realisation** of the moral principles on which we actually operate (practical morality); the former will always lag behind the latter, implying that theoretical morality is shaped by practical morality. While adult theorising and tuition may help theoretical morality catch up, they cannot affect it.
- Children's understanding of **intention** is much more complex than Piaget believed, and this understanding influences their moral decision-making. The pre-schooler is **not** amoral.
- Armsby found that, depending on the extent and nature of the damage, six-year-olds **are** capable of judging that a small amount of deliberate damage (such as breaking a cup) is naughtier than a large amount of deliberate damage (such as damaging a TV set).
- According to Nelson, Piaget's stories emphasise the consequences compared with the actor's intentions. While three-year-olds infer negative intentions from behaviour that has negative consequences, when information about intentions is made explicit, they are able to make judgements about these intentions regardless of the consequences. They may only be **less proficient** than older children at discriminating intentions from consequences and using these separate pieces of information to make moral judgements.
- According to information processing theorists, aspects of development which Piaget attributed to the increasing complexity and quality of thought are actually a result of an increasing capacity for the storage and retrieval of information. Gelman and Baillargeon argue that most five-year-olds judge John (who broke more cups) to be naughtier than Henry because, although they can remember who broke more cups, they cannot remember all the other details of the stories. Intentions can be taken into account by encouraging them to remember all the details.
- **Kohlberg's** is the most influential theory of moral development. He agreed with Piaget that there are stages of moral development but, unlike Piaget, he created ten **moral dilemmas**, typically involving a choice between two socially unacceptable alternatives, as in the case of Heinz.
- Like Piaget, Kohlberg was more interested in how thinking about right and wrong changes with age. While most people would see breaking the law as wrong, their **reasons** for upholding the law, and views regarding the circumstances in which breaking it can be justified, might change as we develop.
- Based on the responses of 58 males aged seven to 17 to his dilemmas, Kohlberg identified six qualitatively different ways of viewing moral issues, increasing in complexity with age, i.e. **stages** in moral development. The stages span three basic **levels** of moral reasoning: **pre-conventional morality** (four to ten) **conventional morality** (late childhood to early adulthood) and **post-conventional morality** (about 10 to 15 per cent of adults).
- In pre-conventional morality, reasoning has a self-serving function: actions serve to avoid punishment (Stage 1/**Punishment and obedience orientation**) and obtain rewards (Stage 2/**Instrumental relativist orientation**). There is no personal code of morality: morality is shaped by the standards of adults and the consequences of breaking their rules. In conventional morality, we begin to internalise the moral standards of valued adult role-models: morality is guided by desire to help others and gain their approval (Stage 3/**Interpersonal concordance/'good**

boy–nice girl' orientation), then to maintain social order (Stage 4/**Maintaining the social order orientation**).

- Post-conventional morality depends on the development of formal operational thought. Stage 5 (**Social contract-legalistic orientation**) affirms social values such as individual rights and the need for democratically determined rules. In Stage 6 (**Universal ethical principles orientation**), people are guided by **universal ethical principles**, i.e. doing what we believe to be right as a matter of conscience, even if this conflicts with society's rules.
- Kohlberg concluded that the first five stages are **universal** and occur in an **invariant sequence**, and while we might become 'fixated' in one stage, we never **regress** to an earlier one. The changes are gradual.
- Both Piaget and Kohlberg see cognitive development as necessary but not sufficient for moral development, with the latter usually lagging behind the former. Even if someone is capable of conventional or post-conventional moral reasoning, there is no **guarantee** that he or she will behave more morally.
- In support of Kohlberg, Smetena found that juvenile delinquents are more likely to show lower levels of moral reasoning than non-delinquents of the same age. Thornton and Reid have shown that Stage 2 reasoning is also characteristic of adults who engage in robbery and other 'instrumental' crimes.
- Rest's 20-year longitudinal study of men from adolescence to their mid-30s confirmed the sequence of the stages. Snarey's review of 45 studies in 27 countries concluded that support for the universality of the first four stages is striking.
- Nevertheless, it has been claimed that Kohlberg's theory is biased towards **Western** cultures. According to Schweder and Eckensberger, ethical principles such as justice, equality, integrity and reverence for life are **not** universally held. Conversely, some societies (e.g. Papua New Guinea) have developed moral principles not covered by Kohlberg's theory (e.g. **principle of collective moral responsibility**).
- According to Gilligan, Kohlberg's stages are based on a male definition of morality, namely one that stresses abstract principles of law and justice. By contrast, women's definition is based on principles of compassion and care. Consequently, women are rated as being at the conventional level while men are at the post-conventional level. These two moralities are different but **complementary**.
- Clopton and Sorell believe that gender differences are due to **situational differences** and the nature of the moral problem they are faced with, rather than to stable gender differences.
- Kohlberg has been concerned almost exclusively with moral **thinking**: his dilemmas assess only how people reason about relatively unusual hypothetical dilemmas ('storybook morality'). But moral reasoning and moral behaviour do not necessarily go together.
- Kohlberg's study began in the 1950s in the USA, with the original participants living through the civil rights movement, Vietnam, Watergate and the women's movement. Their moral judgements are unlikely to be the same as either earlier or later generations.
- According to Sobesky, Kohlberg's dilemmas are unfamiliar to most participants: more mature reasoning might be shown if the dilemmas dealt with relevant, real-life, everyday experiences. When people were asked to imagine themselves in Heinz's position of being caught and sent to prison, they were less likely to advocate stealing **and** they showed lower levels of reasoning.
- Shweder et al. suggest that the higher stages of moral reasoning are associated with education and verbal ability: while college-educated people give higher-level and more mature explanations of moral decisions, this may only be because they are more verbally sophisticated, not more moral.

8 THE DEVELOPMENT OF GENDER

Introduction and overview

Every known culture distinguishes between male and female, a distinction which is accompanied by a widely held belief that males and females are substantially different in terms of their psychological make-up and behaviour. The characteristics and behaviours held to be typical of males and females in particular cultures are called *stereotypes* and the study of psychological sex differences is really an attempt to see how accurate these stereotypes are.

Research interest in sex differences has a chequered history, waning with the advent of behaviourism and then rising again in the 1970s, largely as a result of the work of feminist psychologists. Although there are many feminist interpretations of sex differences, they tend to share the belief that social, political, economic and cultural factors are fundamental in determining *gender*, that is, our awareness and understanding of the differences that distinguish males from females. This view is in stark contrast to the belief held by sociobiologists and evolutionary psychologists, who argue that sex differences are 'natural' in that they have evolved as a part of the more general adaptation of the human species to its environment.

As well as feminist and sociobiological interpretations of gender, which adopt diametrically opposed views regarding the nature-nurture or heredity-environment debate, several other theoretical accounts have been advanced. These include biological approaches, biosocial theory, psychoanalytic theory, social learning theory, cognitive-developmental theory and gender schema theory. Our aim in this chapter is to consider all of these theoretical accounts of gender and gender differences. To make this task easier, we shall begin by defining some of the basic terms that are used in this area of research, and which we need to understand in order to evaluate the different theories.

The 'vocabulary' of gender

Feminist psychologists such as Unger guish between *sex* and *gender*. Our sex biological fact about us, such as a pa make-up and reproductive anatomy a The terms 'male' and 'female' are describe our sex, although as we shall s is actually more complex than this. Ou trast, is what culture makes out of the biological sex. It is, therefore, the soci social interpretation of sex.

Our *sexual identity* is an alternative wa our biological status as male or female to our gender is *gender identity*, our ourselves (and others) as male or fem and so on. Although sexual and gen respond for most of us, this is not t *sexualism*. A transsexual is a person w anatomically male or female, genui believes that he or she is a member of As a result, the transsexual's biological fundamentally inconsistent with his o tity.

Gender role (or *sex role*, as it is often the behaviours, attitudes, values, b which a particular society either exp siders appropriate to males and fema their biological sex. To be *masculin* male to conform to the male gender *nine* requires a female to conform to role.

All societies have carefully defin although as we shall see, societies do the roles they prescribe for men an (or *sex*) *stereotypes* are, as we mention tion to this chapter, widely held be for their crimes and, generally, the greater the suffering the better (**expiatory punishment**). This is decreed by authority and accepted as just because of its source (**moral realism**). They also believe in **immanent justice**.

- For older children, punishment is designed to make the guilty person aware of the nature of the offence and to discourage future offences. The punishment should fit the crime, so that the **principle of reciprocity** should apply. Older children display **moral relativism**, and belief in immanent justice is much reduced.
- Piaget called the morality of younger children **heteronomous**, while that of older children is **autonomous**, showing **morality of co-operation**. The change occurs due to the shift from egocentric to operational thought at about seven, suggesting that cognitive development is necessary but not sufficient for moral development. Also needed are freedom from unilateral respect and adult constraint to mutual respect within the peer group, and the ability to grasp concepts such as reciprocity.
- Several studies have found support for Piaget's theory, including cross-cultural studies which suggest that the shift from heteronomous to autonomous morality occurs at about age nine or ten. However, Wright has argued that while Piaget's theory is meant to explain the development of **practical morality**, his evidence was derived from samples of children's **theoretical morality**.
- For Piaget, theoretical morality is the **conscious realisation** of the moral principles on which we actually operate (practical morality); the former will always lag behind the latter, implying that theoretical morality is shaped by practical morality. While adult theorising and tuition may help theoretical morality catch up, they cannot affect it.
- Children's understanding of **intention** is much more complex than Piaget believed, and this understanding influences their moral decision-making. The pre-schooler is **not** amoral.
- Armsby found that, depending on the extent and nature of the damage, six-year-olds **are** capable of judging that a small amount of deliberate damage (such as breaking a cup) is naughtier than a large amount of deliberate damage (such as damaging a TV set).
- According to Nelson, Piaget's stories emphasise the consequences compared with the actor's intentions. While three-year-olds infer negative intentions from behaviour that has negative consequences, when information about intentions is made explicit, they are able to make judgements about these intentions regardless of the consequences. They may only be **less proficient** than older children at discriminating intentions from consequences and using these separate pieces of information to make moral judgements.
- According to information processing theorists, aspects of development which Piaget attributed to the increasing complexity and quality of thought are actually a result of an increasing capacity for the storage and retrieval of information. Gelman and Baillargeon argue that most five-year-olds judge John (who broke more cups) to be naughtier than Henry because, although they can remember who broke more cups, they cannot remember all the other details of the stories. Intentions can be taken into account by encouraging them to remember all the details.
- **Kohlberg's** is the most influential theory of moral development. He agreed with Piaget that there are stages of moral development but, unlike Piaget, he created ten **moral dilemmas**, typically involving a choice between two socially unacceptable alternatives, as in the case of Heinz.
- Like Piaget, Kohlberg was more interested in how thinking about right and wrong changes with age. While most people would see breaking the law as wrong, their **reasons** for upholding the law, and views regarding the circumstances in which breaking it can be justified, might change as we develop.
- Based on the responses of 58 males aged seven to 17 to his dilemmas, Kohlberg identified six qualitatively different ways of viewing moral issues, increasing in complexity with age, i.e. **stages** in moral development. The stages span three basic **levels** of moral reasoning: **pre-conventional morality** (four to ten) **conventional morality** (late childhood to early adulthood) and **post-conventional morality** (about 10 to 15 per cent of adults).
- In pre-conventional morality, reasoning has a self-serving function: actions serve to avoid punishment (Stage 1/**Punishment and obedience orientation**) and obtain rewards (Stage 2/**Instrumental relativist orientation**). There is no personal code of morality: morality is shaped by the standards of adults and the consequences of breaking their rules. In conventional morality, we begin to internalise the moral standards of valued adult role-models: morality is guided by desire to help others and gain their approval (Stage 3/**Interpersonal concordance/'good**

boy–nice girl' orientation), then to maintain social order (Stage 4/**Maintaining the social order orientation**).

- Post-conventional morality depends on the development of formal operational thought. Stage 5 (**Social contract-legalistic orientation**) affirms social values such as individual rights and the need for democratically determined rules. In Stage 6 (**Universal ethical principles orientation**), people are guided by **universal ethical principles**, i.e. doing what we believe to be right as a matter of conscience, even if this conflicts with society's rules.
- Kohlberg concluded that the first five stages are **universal** and occur in an **invariant sequence**, and while we might become 'fixated' in one stage, we never **regress** to an earlier one. The changes are gradual.
- Both Piaget and Kohlberg see cognitive development as necessary but not sufficient for moral development, with the latter usually lagging behind the former. Even if someone is capable of conventional or post-conventional moral reasoning, there is no **guarantee** that he or she will behave more morally.
- In support of Kohlberg, Smetena found that juvenile delinquents are more likely to show lower levels of moral reasoning than non-delinquents of the same age. Thornton and Reid have shown that Stage 2 reasoning is also characteristic of adults who engage in robbery and other 'instrumental' crimes.
- Rest's 20-year longitudinal study of men from adolescence to their mid-30s confirmed the sequence of the stages. Snarey's review of 45 studies in 27 countries concluded that support for the universality of the first four stages is striking.
- Nevertheless, it has been claimed that Kohlberg's theory is biased towards **Western** cultures. According to Schweder and Eckensberger, ethical principles such as justice, equality, integrity and reverence for life are **not** universally held. Conversely, some societies (e.g. Papua New Guinea) have developed moral principles not covered by Kohlberg's theory (e.g. **principle of collective moral responsibility**).
- According to Gilligan, Kohlberg's stages are based on a male definition of morality, namely one that stresses abstract principles of law and justice. By contrast, women's definition is based on principles of compassion and care. Consequently, women are rated as being at the conventional level while men are at the post-conventional level. These two moralities are different but **complementary**.
- Clopton and Sorell believe that gender differences are due to **situational differences** and the nature of the moral problem they are faced with, rather than to stable gender differences.
- Kohlberg has been concerned almost exclusively with moral **thinking**: his dilemmas assess only how people reason about relatively unusual hypothetical dilemmas ('storybook morality'). But moral reasoning and moral behaviour do not necessarily go together.
- Kohlberg's study began in the 1950s in the USA, with the original participants living through the civil rights movement, Vietnam, Watergate and the women's movement. Their moral judgements are unlikely to be the same as either earlier or later generations.
- According to Sobesky, Kohlberg's dilemmas are unfamiliar to most participants: more mature reasoning might be shown if the dilemmas dealt with relevant, real-life, everyday experiences. When people were asked to imagine themselves in Heinz's position of being caught and sent to prison, they were less likely to advocate stealing **and** they showed lower levels of reasoning.
- Shweder et al. suggest that the higher stages of moral reasoning are associated with education and verbal ability: while college-educated people give higher-level and more mature explanations of moral decisions, this may only be because they are more verbally sophisticated, not more moral.

THE DEVELOPMENT OF GENDER

Introduction and overview

Every known culture distinguishes between male and female, a distinction which is accompanied by a widely held belief that males and females are substantially different in terms of their psychological make-up and behaviour. The characteristics and behaviours held to be typical of males and females in particular cultures are called *stereotypes* and the study of psychological sex differences is really an attempt to see how accurate these stereotypes are.

Research interest in sex differences has a chequered history, waning with the advent of behaviourism and then rising again in the 1970s, largely as a result of the work of feminist psychologists. Although there are many feminist interpretations of sex differences, they tend to share the belief that social, political, economic and cultural factors are fundamental in determining *gender*, that is, our awareness and understanding of the differences that distinguish males from females. This view is in stark contrast to the belief held by sociobiologists and evolutionary psychologists, who argue that sex differences are 'natural' in that they have evolved as a part of the more general adaptation of the human species to its environment.

As well as feminist and sociobiological interpretations of gender, which adopt diametrically opposed views regarding the nature-nurture or heredity-environment debate, several other theoretical accounts have been advanced. These include biological approaches, biosocial theory, psychoanalytic theory, social learning theory, cognitive-developmental theory and gender schema theory. Our aim in this chapter is to consider all of these theoretical accounts of gender and gender differences. To make this task easier, we shall begin by defining some of the basic terms that are used in this area of research, and which we need to understand in order to evaluate the different theories.

The 'vocabulary' of sex and gender

Feminist psychologists such as Unger (1979) distinguish between *sex* and *gender*. Our sex refers to some biological fact about us, such as a particular genetic make-up and reproductive anatomy and functioning. The terms 'male' and 'female' are usually used to describe our sex, although as we shall see, the situation is actually more complex than this. Our *gender*, by contrast, is what culture makes out of the 'raw material' of biological sex. It is, therefore, the social equivalent or social interpretation of sex.

Our *sexual identity* is an alternative way of referring to our biological status as male or female. Corresponding to our gender is *gender identity*, our classification of ourselves (and others) as male or female, boy or girl, and so on. Although sexual and gender identity correspond for most of us, this is not the case in *transsexualism*. A transsexual is a person who, whilst being anatomically male or female, genuinely and firmly believes that he or she is a member of the opposite sex. As a result, the transsexual's biological sexual identity is fundamentally inconsistent with his or her gender identity.

Gender role (or *sex role*, as it is often termed) refers to the behaviours, attitudes, values, beliefs and so on which a particular society either expects from or considers appropriate to males and females on the basis of their biological sex. To be *masculine*, then, requires a male to conform to the male gender role. To be *feminine* requires a female to conform to the female gender role.

All societies have carefully defined gender roles, although as we shall see, societies do differ in terms of the roles they prescribe for men and women. *Gender* (or *sex*) *stereotypes* are, as we mentioned in the introduction to this chapter, widely held beliefs about psycho-

Figure 8.1 Renee Richards, formerly known as Richard Raskin, one of the world's best-known transsexuals. Born male, Richard had his sex reassigned through surgery and she continued her tennis career as a woman

logical differences between males and females which often reflect gender roles (see below).

The term *sex typing* refers to our discovery that we are male or female (that is, our acquisition of a sex or gender identity) and our learning of the behaviours appropriate to our gender (that is, adopting an appropriate *sex role*). Sex typing begins early in Western culture, with parents often dressing their new-born baby in blue if it is a boy and pink if it is a girl. As Condry and Ross, (1985) have noted, even in the earliest days of infancy, our gender influences how people react to us. Indeed, the first question asked by friends and relatives of parents with a new-born baby is 'Boy or girl?' (Intons-Peterson and Reddel, 1984). By the age of three or four, most children have some knowledge about their gender. They know, for example, that boys become men and girls become women, and that some games are played by boys and others by girls. A permanent gender identity is usually acquired by the age of five, and children know that a girl is a girl even if she can climb a tree (Zimbardo and Weber, 1994).

Gender stereotypes and gender differences

Research conducted by Williams and Best (1994) suggests that there is a high degree of agreement across the 30 countries studied by them regarding the characteristics associated with each gender group. For example, male-associated terms included 'aggressive', 'determined' and 'sharp-witted' whilst female-associated terms included 'cautious', 'emotional' and 'warm'. Williams and Best also found systematic *cultural variations*, with stereotypes being related to several variables including socio-economic development, education and religion.

As far as *actual* differences are concerned, several reviews have found that many stereotypes about males and females actually have little empirical support. Box 8.1 summarises some of the findings that have been reported.

Box 8.1 Some findings relating to gender differences

Aggression: According to Maccoby and Jacklin (1974) and Weisfeld (1994), boys are more verbally and physically aggressive than girls, a difference which shows itself as soon as social play begins (around two and a half years). Whilst both sexes become less aggressive with age, boys and men remain more aggressive throughout development. However, these findings have been challenged (Durkin, 1995). For example, some studies have shown that women sometimes score higher for certain kinds of indirect non-physical aggression, whilst others have found no differences at all between the sexes (e.g. Campbell and Muncer, 1994).

Verbal ability: From pre-school to adolescence, the sexes are very similar with respect to verbal ability. At age 11, however, Maccoby and Jacklin suggest that females become superior and this superiority increases during adolescence and possibly beyond. Again, though, there is evidence to suggest that any difference that does exist is actually so small as to be negligible (Hyde and Linn, 1988).

Spatial ability: Maccoby and Jacklin found that males' ability to perceive figures or objects in space and establish their relationship to each other was consistently better than that of females in adolescence and adulthood. Durkin (1995) disagrees and argues that whilst there is some male superiority on some spatial tasks, *within-sex* variability is large. Moreover, when between-sex differences are found, they are usually small.

Mathematical ability: According to Maccoby and Jacklin, mathematical skills increase faster in boys, beginning around the age of 12 or 13. According to Hyde et al. (1990), there are significant differences between the sexes, but these are in the reverse direction to the stereotype.

(adapted from Durkin, 1995)

Durkin (1995) suggests that:

> 'The overwhelming conclusion to be drawn from the literature on sex differences is that it is highly controversial'.

Certainly, the data reported are open to several types of interpretation. For example, a statistically significant difference does not imply a large behavioural difference. Rather, what determines a significant result is the *consistency* of the differences between groups, such that if all the girls in a school (say) scored 0.5 per cent higher than all the boys on the same test, a small but highly significant result would be produced (Edley and Wetherell, 1995).

Eagly (1983), however, has argued that in at least some cases a significant difference does reflect a sizeable difference between the sexes. By combining the results of several different but comparable studies (a technique known as *meta-analysis*), substantial differences between the sexes do emerge on some measures. According to Eagly, research has actually tended to *conceal* rather than *reveal* sex differences, and such differences are mainly confirmed by the available research, although the differences within each gender are, as we noted earlier, at least as great as the differences between them (Maccoby, 1980).

Biology and sexual identity

Biologically, sex is not a unidimensional variable, and attempts to identify the biological factors that can influence gender identity have yielded at least five biological categories. These are shown in Box 8.2.

Box 8.2 Five categories of biological sex

Chromosomal sex: Normal females inherit two X chromosomes, one from each parent (XX). Normal males inherit one X chromosome from the mother and one Y chromosome from the father (XY). Research suggests that two chromosomes are needed for the complete development of both internal and external female structures, and that the Y chromosome must be present for the complete development of male internal and external structures (Page et al., 1987). If the Y chromosome is absent, female external genitals develop. A gene on the Y chromosome called TDF (*testis-determining factor*) appears to be responsible for testis formation and male development (Hodgkin, 1988).

Gonadal sex: This refers to the sexual or reproductive organs (ovaries in females and testes in males). According to Amice et al. (1989), *H-Y antigen*, controlled by genes on the Y chromosome, causes embryonic gonads to be transformed to testes. If H-Y antigen is not present, gonadal tissue develops into ovaries.

Hormonal sex: When the gonads are transformed to testes or ovaries, genetic influences cease and biological sex determination is controlled by *sex hormones*. The male sex hormones are called *androgens*, the most important of which is *testosterone* (secreted by the testes). The ovaries secrete two distinct types of female hormone. These are *oestrogen* and *progesterone*. Both males and females produce androgens and oestrogens, but males usually produce more androgens and females more oestrogens.

Sex of the internal reproductive structures: The Wolffian ducts in males and the Mullerian ducts in females are the embryonic forerunners of the internal reproductive structures. In males these are the prostate gland, sperm ducts, seminal vesicles and testes. In females, the structures are the fallopian tubes, womb and ovaries.

Sex of the external genitals: In males, the external genitalia are the penis and scrotum. In females, they are the outer lips of the vagina (*labia majora*). Testosterone influences, in a male direction, both the internal and external structures of chromosomal males. If testosterone is absent, female structures develop (see text).

The categories identified in Box 8.2 are usually highly correlated so that a person tends to be male (or female) in all respects. The categories also tend to be correlated with non-biological aspects of sex, including the sex to which the baby is assigned at birth, how the child is brought up, gender identity, gender-role identity and so on. Either pre- or post-natally, however, certain disorders occur which lead to an inconsistency or low correlation between the categories. These disorders can tell us a great deal about the development of gender identity, gender role and gender-role identity.

People with such disorders are called either *true hermaphrodites* or *pseudohermaphrodites*. True hermaphrodites have either simultaneously or sequentially functioning organs of both sexes. They are very rare and their external organs are often a mixture of male and female structures. Pseudohermaphrodites are more common. Although they too possess ambiguous internal and external reproductive structures they, unlike true hermaphrodites, are born with *gonads* that match their chromosomal sex.

In *androgen insensitivity syndrome* (AIS) (which is also known as *testicular feminising syndrome*), a chromosomally normal (XY) male develops testes that produce normal levels of pre-natal androgens. A defect caused by a recessive gene, however, results in the body cells being insensitive to the action of androgens. The consequence of this is that pre-natal development is *feminised*. There is no development of the internal reproductive structures of either sex and the external genitals fail to differentiate into a penis and scrotum. The testes, which normally descend from inside the abdomen to the scrotum towards the end of pregnancy, remain in the abdomen, and at birth the individual has normal-looking female external genitals and a shallow vagina. At puberty, breast development occurs (as a result of the action of oestrogen) but the individual does not develop pubic hair and fails to menstruate (because of the absence of a womb). Often, AIS is discovered when a supposed hernia (or lump in the abdomen) turns out to be a testis. The testes are usually surgically removed because of the likelihood that they will become malignant. Because of the presence of a very shallow (or 'blind') vagina, little or no surgery is needed for the adoption of a female appearance.

Another example of pseudohermaphroditism occurs with *fetally androgenised females*. In so-called *adrenogenital syndrome*, a chromosomally normal (XX) female is exposed to an excessive amount of androgens or androgen-like substances during the critical period of prenatal sexual differentiation. This can happen either internally (or *endogenously*), as when the mother's adrenal glands are excessively active during pregnancy, or it can happen externally (or *exogenously)*, as when the mother takes artificial hormones (such as *progestin*) in an attempt to prevent miscarriage. Irrespective of its cause, adrenogenital syndrome results in the female's internal reproductive structures being apparently unaffected (and such individuals are often fertile), while the external structures resemble those of a male infant. For example, an enlarged clitoris appears to be a penis, and the fusing of the labia gives the appearance of a scrotum (see Figure 8.2). Until recently, sex at birth was assigned on the basis of inspection of the genitalia, so that two individuals with equivalent ambiguities might have been classified differently. More recently, information about the structure of the gonads and the chromosomal make-up of the individual has been acquired so that females with the syndrome are usually raised as females. A relatively small amount of cosmetic surgery is all that is required to bring the external appearance into line with other aspects of the individual's sexual identity.

One final example of pseudohermaphroditism occurs with *DHT-deficient males*. Pre-natally, testosterone is converted into *dihydrotestosterone* (DHT). This hormone is necessary for the normal development of male external genitals. As a result of a genetic disorder, this conversion occasionally fails to take place. Although the internal structures develop normally, the testicles are undescended at birth, the stunted penis resembles a clitoris, and a partially formed vagina and incompletely formed scrotum (resembling labia) are present. These males are usually incorrectly identified as females and raised as girls. However, at puberty the undescended testicles begin to produce testosterone with the result that the voice deepens, the clitoris-like organ enlarges and becomes a penis, and the testes finally descend (Imperato-McGinley et al., 1979).

Given that genetic and hormonal differences are

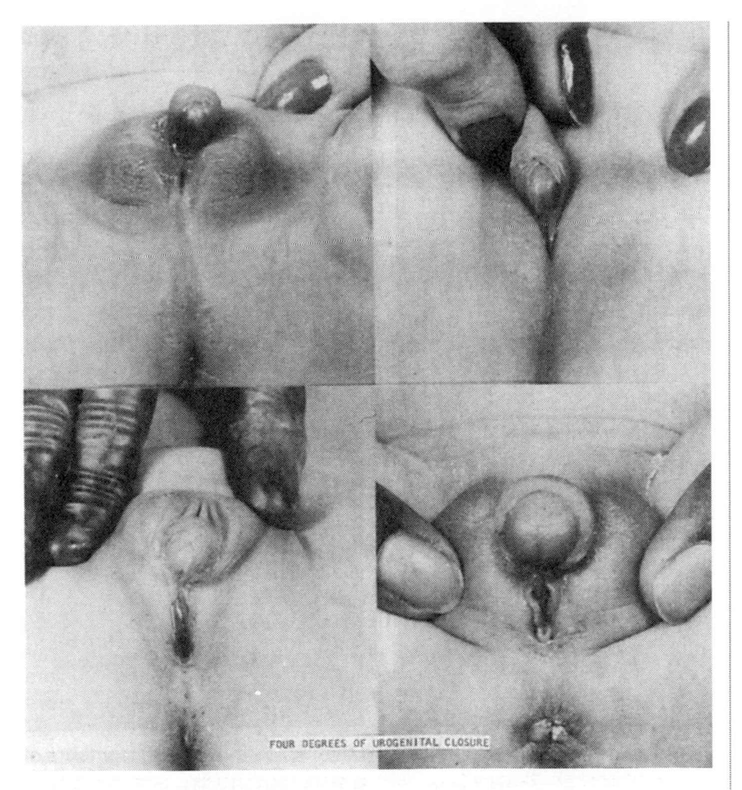

Figure 8.2 Ambiguous appearance at birth of the genitalia of individuals with the adrenogenital syndrome (XX, but with excessive androgen during pre-natal differentiation) (from Money and Ehrhardt, 1972)

responsible for a number of sex-linked characteristics present either at birth or shortly thereafter, supporters of a biological approach argue that males and females are *biologically programmed* for certain kinds of activities that are compatible with male and female roles. Imperato-McGinley et al.'s study of DHT-deficient males is certainly supportive of this. Of the 18 boys they studied, all but two responded to the marked biological changes in their bodies by adopting the male gender-role of their Dominican cultures, despite being raised as females. Of the two that did not, one acknowledged that he was a male but continued to dress as a female, whilst the other maintained a female gender-identity, married and underwent a sex-change operation.

The fact that the majority of the DHT-deficient males could easily assume male roles suggests that their testosterone had pre-programmed masculinity into their brains. The view that male and female brains are structually different has been advanced by a number of researchers (e.g. Dorner, 1976; Geschwind and Behan, 1984; Thompson, 1985). Dorner (1976), for example, found that destruction of a small part of the hypothalamus in the rat resulted in new-born males behaving as though they were female (and, for Dorner, as though they were *homosexual*). However, evidence from studies of humans tends not to support the claim that the brains of males and females are different. Consider, for example, the case of Daphne Went, a woman with testosterone insensitivity. Although chromosomally a male, her external appearance is female. She is married, has adopted two children and leads an active and successful life as a woman (Goldwyn, 1979).

In terms of functional differences in the brains of males and females, however, there is some evidence of sex differences in *hemispheric specialisation.* For example, Bryden and Saxby (1985) have shown that when males perform spatial tasks, there is greater electrical activity in the right hemisphere. In women, both hemispheres are activated. According to McGlone (1980), the right hemisphere is generally the dominant one in men, whilst the left is generally dominant in women. Researchers who argue for the existence of sex differences (see Box 8.1) would use this to explain those studies which have found that men are generally superior at spatial and mathematical tasks whilst women are generally superior at verbal tasks.

Although emerging evidence indicates that the corpus callosum is 'dimorphic', such that in women it is larger overall and longer towards the back of the brain, Kimura (1992) has cautioned against accepting this evidence uncritically. For example, it has been assumed that the larger the corpus callosum, the greater the number of fibres connecting the hemispheres and the more efficient the communication between them. However, Kimura notes that it has not been clearly established that it is the number of fibres which is the crucial male-female difference, and that sex differences in cognitive functioning have yet to be related to the size of the corpus callosum.

Biosocial theory of gender

According to Edley and Wetherell (1995), to ask the question 'What is the biological basis of masculinity (or femininity)?' is to pose a false question. In their view:

> 'It requires us to separate what cannot be separated: men (and women) are the product of a complex system of factors and forces which combine in a variety of ways to produce a whole range of different masculinities (and femininities)'.

The biosocial theory of gender identity, as its name suggests, takes social factors into account in relation to biological ones. More specifically, the theory focuses on how babies of different temperaments contribute to their own development by influencing how others treat them.

According to biosocial theory, then, it is the *interaction* between biological and social factors that is important rather than the influence of biology directly. Certainly, adults prefer to spend time with babies who respond to them in 'rewarding' ways, and 'demanding' babies tend to receive more attention from adults than 'passive' babies. As far as other people are concerned, the baby's sex is just as important as its temperament. For example, the 'baby X' experiments conducted by Smith and Lloyd (1978) involved dressing babies in unisex snowsuits and giving them names which were sometimes in line with their true gender and sometimes not. When adults played with them, they treated the babies according to the gender they believed them to be. The 'baby X' experiments indicate that a person's (perceived) biological make-up becomes part of his or her social environment through the process of others' reactions to it. According to Money and Ehrhardt (1972), 'anatomy is destiny', by which they mean that how an infant is labelled sexually determines how it is raised or socialised. In turn, this determines the child's gender identity, and from this follow its gender role, gender-role identity and sexual orientation.

Based on their study of girls with adrenogenital syndrome who were raised as boys and, before the age of three, had their genitals surgically corrected and were reared as girls, Money and Ehrhardt (1972) claim that it is possible to change the sex of rearing without any undue psychological harm being done. Beyond a 'critical' or 'sensitive period' of about two and a half to three years for the development of gender identity, however, being reassigned to the opposite sex can cause extreme psychological disturbance. Money and Ehrhardt's study of ten people with testicular feminising syndrome (genetic males who are reared as females because of their external appearance), showed there was a strong preference for the female role, which also supports the view that sex of rearing is more important than biological sex.

Diamond (1978) has suggested that just because some people appear, at least from Money and Ehrhardt's research, to be flexible in their psychosexual identity does not in itself disprove that 'built-in biases' still have to be overcome. The participants in Money and Ehrhardt's research are clearly an atypical sample, and there is no evidence to indicate that people in general are as flexible in their psychosexual orientation and identity. Money (1974), however, has reported a case in which, as a result of an accident during a circumcision, one of a pair of twins lost his penis. This 'penectomised' boy was raised as a girl and, at 17 months, 'he' was castrated (the androgen-secreting testes were removed), oestrogen was given, and a vaginal canal constructed. At age four, the child preferred dresses to trousers, took pride in 'his' long hair, and was cleaner than 'his' brother. He also sat whilst urinating, in the usual female fashion, and was modest about exposing 'his genitals'. At age nine, although 'he' had been the dominant twin since birth, 'he' expressed this by being a 'fussy little mother' to 'his' brother. The brother continued to play the traditional protective male role. This finding seems to support the view that gender identity (and gender role) is *learned* (a view we will further consider later on in this chapter).

The reversal of original sexual assignment is possible if it takes place early enough and is consistent in all respects, which includes the external genitalia conforming well enough to the new sex. However, castration and the use of oestrogen clearly contributed to the ease of reassignment and probably also account for the unaffected twin being taller. Significantly, Diamond (1982) found that when the 'girl' had reached her teens she was an unhappy adolescent, with few friends, uncertain about 'her' gender, and maintaining that boys 'had a better life'. She also looked rather masculine. For Diamond, these findings indicated that biology had ultimately proven irrepressible.

Sociobiological theory

Sociobiologists (evolutionary theorists) argue that our gender has gradually evolved over the course of human development as part of our broader adaptation to the environment (Lumsden and Wilson, 1983). According to Wilson (1978) and Hoyenga and Hoyenga (1979), males and females have developed different roles as a function of their respective contributions to reproduction and domestic labour. The relatively greater physical strength, lung capacity and so on of males make them better suited to hunting and defending territory and family. The childbearing and milk-producing capacities of females, however, make them ideally suited to childcare and other nurturant roles.

This relates to *parental investment theory* (e.g. Kenrick, 1994) which argues that females invest considerably more in reproduction than do males. Society came to be organised in sexually exclusive domestic partnerships as a way of meeting the female's needs for protection and the male's need for preventing his mate from mating with other males. The consequence of this was the evolution of different courtship displays and roles (such as 'playing hard to get') which are still evident in many Western and other cultures. According to Buss (1994), what females universally find attractive in males are the characteristics associated with the provision of resources. Men, by contrast, see physical beauty as being of most importance.

The sociobiological approach has been criticised on a number of grounds. For example, Sayers (1982) has argued that dominance patterns are not, as sociobiological approaches assume, equated with greater aggression. In humans, at least, dominance often relates to status seeking, which implies the role of culturally determined values. Sociobiological approaches to sex differences are also difficult to test. We have only incomplete knowledge about the ways in which our ancestors adapted to their environments, and so our guesses about which characteristics were adaptive and why differences between the sexes evolved are 'educated guesses' at best (Krebs and Blackman, 1988).

Freud's psychoanalytic theory

Freud's theory of gender identity is related to his explanation of the development of *conscience* (see Chapter 7). As we noted on page 80, Freud believed that children aged between three and five develop sexual desires for their opposite-sex parent. Up until the resolution of the Oedipus complex, gender identity is held to be flexible. Resolution of the Oedipus complex occurs through *identification* with the parent of the same sex, and the child adopts the attitudinal and behavioural characteristics of that parent. By resolving the complex, boys develop a sense of conscience by *introjecting* their version of their father's conscience into their ego. They also acquire their gender identity. Freud believed that girls did not resolve their complex as effectively as boys did. As a result, he saw the development of conscience as being weaker in girls than boys (a point we made also on page 80). As well as a weaker conscience, Freud also saw the development of gender identity as being weaker in girls than boys.

There are at least three reasons for doubting a Freudian interpretation of the development of gender identity. First, the evidence suggests that children of a particular age do *not* acquire gender identity in what Krebs and Blackman (1988) have termed 'one fell swoop'. Second, a number of studies have shown that children who grow up in 'atypical' families (e.g. single-parent or homosexual couples) are not adversely affected in terms of their gender identity (Golombok et al., 1983). Also, whilst identification might promote gender identity, the evidence suggests that children are aware of gender roles well before the age at which Freud believed their complexes are resolved. O'Brien et al. (1983), for example, found that boys prefer stereotypically masculine toys (such as trucks) and girls stereotypically feminine toys (such as dolls) *in infancy*. We should additionally note that, in terms of their activities, boys are more explorative and independent than girls even within their first year. Girls are relatively more restrained, dependent and quiet than boys in their first year of life (Goldberg and Lewis, 1969).

Social learning theory

According to social learning theory (SLT), one of the reasons girls and boys behave differently is because they learn to behave in different ways as a result of being *treated differently* by their parents and others. As we noted at the beginning of this chapter, in Western culture new-born boys are often dressed in blue and girls in pink. As we saw in the 'baby X' study (see above), when informed of a child's biological sex, parents and others often react to it according to their *gender-role expectations*. Thus, girls and boys are often given different toys, have their rooms decorated differently, and are even spoken about in different terms (Rubin et al., 1974). When girls play with soft toys and dolls, parents tend to react positively. When boys play with those toys, parents tend to react negatively (Fagot, 1978). The response from fathers to boys playing with such 'feminine' toys is more aggressive than from mothers (Lansky et al., 1961).

SLT also emphasises the role played by *observational*

Figure 8.3 Playing with dolls and displaying nurturant behaviour, and playing with guns and displaying assertive, even aggressive, behaviour, conform to female and male *gender role expectations/stereotypes* respectively. According to social learning theory, children receive parental reinforcement for displaying such gender-appropriate behaviour

learning and *reinforcement*. By observing others behave in particular ways and then imitating that behaviour, children receive reinforcement from 'significant others' (such as parents or teachers) for behaviours considered to be sex appropriate (Bandura, 1977). According to Block (1979), parents tend to give boys more positive reinforcement for behaviours that reflect independence, self-reliance and emotional control. Girls, however, tend to be reinforced for compliance, dependence, nurturance, empathy and the expression of emotion. Support for an SLT account has been derived from a number of studies. A selection of these are briefly described in Box 8.3.

Box 8.3 Findings supportive of SLT

- Sears et al. (1957) found that parents allowed more aggression to be expressed by boys in their relationships with other children, and that boys were allowed to express more aggression towards their parents than were girls. For some mothers, 'being a boy' meant being aggressive, and boys were often encouraged to fight back. According to Huston (1983), although parents believe they respond in the same way to aggressive acts committed by boys and girls, they actually intervene much more frequently and quickly when girls behave aggressively.
- Studies conducted by Bandura et al. (1961, 1963) found that boys were more likely to imitate aggressive male models than were girls (which was based on their perceived similarity and relevance: see Chapter 7, page 81). Additional research showed that children are more likely to imitate a same-sex model than an opposite-sex model, even if the behaviour is sex inappropriate.
- Although parents are important models, social learning theorists are also interested in the portrayal of males and females in the media. There is a large body of evidence to suggest that *gender-role stereotypes* (see page 95) are held by the media, as well as by parents and teachers (Wober et al., 1987). Moreover, Gunter (1986) has reviewed a number of studies which, taken together, suggest that children categorised as 'heavy' viewers of television hold stronger stereotyped beliefs than 'lighter' viewers.

Social learning theorists see the reinforcement of sex-typed behaviours as continuing throughout life rather than being confined to childhood. Block (1978), for example, found that parents of adolescents endorse different statements concerning the ways in which their sons and daughters are treated. For example, the statement 'I encourage my child always to do his/her best' tended to be endorsed for boys whereas the statement 'I encourage my child to keep control of his/her feelings at all times' tended to be endorsed for girls. Although the evidence for SLT appears impressive, the supportive studies we described in Box 8.3 have been challenged, as Box 8.4 shows.

Box 8.4 Findings not supportive of SLT

- According to Maccoby and Jacklin (1974), there are no consistent differences in the extent to which boys and girls are reinforced for aggressiveness or encouraged to be autonomous. Rather, there appears to be remarkable uniformity in the socialisation of the sexes. Maccoby and Jacklin's claim is supported by Lytton and Romney (1991) whose review of a large number of studies found very few sex differences in terms of parental warmth, overall amount of interaction, encouragement of achievement or dependency, restrictiveness and discipline, or clarity of communication.
- Although the research of Bandura and his colleagues is often cited, the evidence concerning imitation and modelling is actually inconclusive, and at least some studies have failed to find evidence that children are more likely to imitate same-sex models than opposite-sex models. Indeed, it has been found that children prefer to imitate behaviour that is appropriate to their own sex *regardless* of the sex of the model (Maccoby and Jacklin, 1974).
- The view that television can impact upon a passively receptive child audience with messages about sex-role stereotyping and mould young children's conceptions of gender is generally considered to be oversimplistic. For Gunter and McAleer (1990), children respond in a selective fashion to particular characters and events, and their perceptions, memories and understanding of what they have seen may often be mediated by the dispositions they bring along with them to the viewing situation. Whilst children categorised as 'heavy' viewers of television might hold stronger stereotyped beliefs than other children, no precise measures were taken of the programmes actually watched by them.

Whilst social reinforcement certainly does play a role in the sex-typing of young children, the evidence concerning modelling is less impressive. Thus, whilst modelling plays an important role in children's socialisation, they do not appear to show a consistent preference for the behaviour of their same-sex parent (Hetherington, 1967). Instead, they prefer to model the behaviour of those with whom they have most contact (and this is usually the mother). We should also note Smith and Daglish's (1977) finding that there is no significant correlation between the extent to which parents engage in sex-typed behaviours and the strength of sex-typing in their children.

Cognitive-developmental theory and gender-schematic processing theory

COGNITIVE-DEVELOPMENTAL THEORY

The cognitive-developmental approach (Kohlberg, 1969; Kohlberg and Ullian, 1974) emphasises the child's participation in developing both an understanding of gender and a sense of what behaviour is appropriate for each gender. According to this account, children's discovery that they are male or female *causes* them to identify with members of their own sex and not the other way round, as psychoanalytic and social learning theories suggest. Whilst rewards and punishments influence children's choices of the toys they play with and the activities they engage in, cognitive-developmental theory does not see these as mechanically strengthening stimulus-response connections. For cognitive-developmental theory, rewards provide children with *information* about when they are behaving in ways that other people deem appropriate.

According to cognitive-developmental theorists, young children acquire an understanding of the concepts *male* and *female* in three stages. These are described in Box 8.5.

Box 8.5 Stages in the development of gender identity according to cognitive-developmental theory

Stage 1: Gender labelling or basic gender identity
This stage occurs somewhere around the age of three (Ruble, 1984) and refers to the child's recognition that it is male or female. According to Kohlberg, knowing one's gender is an achievement that allows us to understand and categorise the world. However, Kohlberg felt that this knowledge is fragile, and that children do not yet realise that boys invariably become men and girls always become women.

Stage 2: Gender stability
By the age of four or five, most children acquire

gender stability and recognise that people retain their genders for a lifetime. However, there are still limitations, in that children rely on superficial signs (such as the length of a person's hair) to determine their gender (Marcus and Overton, 1978).

Stage 3: Gender constancy or consistency
At around the age of six or seven, children reach the stage of gender constancy and realise that gender is *immutable*. So, even if a woman has her hair cut very short, her gender remains constant. Gender constancy represents a kind of *conservation* (see Chapter 4) and, significantly, appears shortly after the child has mastered the conservation of quantity (Marcus and Overton, 1978).

Once children acquire a sense of gender constancy, they come to value the behaviours and attitudes associated with their sex. Cognitive-developmental theorists argue that only at this point do children identify with the adult figures who possess the qualities they see as being most central to their concepts of themselves as male or female (Perry and Bussey, 1979).

There is evidence to suggest that the concepts of gender identity, stability and constancy do occur in the order proposed by cognitive-developmental theory across a number of cultures (Munroe et al., 1984). Additionally, several experimental studies have lent support to the cognitive-developmental perspective. In one of these, Slaby and Frey (1975) divided two- to five-year-olds into 'high' and 'low' gender constancy. The children were then shown a silent film of adults

Figure 8.4 A woman with well-developed muscles (even if she is a Gladiator) might cause confusion in a child who has not yet achieved gender constancy/stability. Falcon's muscular frame (right) is likely to be more confusing than Wolf's long hair (left). Who's *your* favourite Gladiator?

simultaneously performing a series of simple activities. The screen was 'split', with males performing activities on one side and females performing activities on the other. Those children rated as being 'high' in gender constancy showed a marked same-sex bias, as measured by the amount of visual attention they gave to each side of the screen. This supports Kohlberg's belief that gender constancy is a *cause* of the imitation of same-sex models rather than an effect: children actively construct their gender-role knowledge through purposeful monitoring of the social environment.

One of the major problems for cognitive-developmental theory, though, is that it predicts there should be little or no expression of gender-appropriate behaviour *before* gender constancy is achieved. However, a large body of evidence indicates that, even in infancy, both sexes show a marked preference for stereotypical male and female toys (e.g. Huston, 1983). Whilst such children might have developed a sense of gender identity, they are, as far as cognitive-developmental theory is concerned, some years away from achieving gender stability and constancy (Fagot, 1985).

GENDER-SCHEMATIC PROCESSING THEORY

The possibility that gender identity alone can provide a child with sufficient motivation to assume sex-typed behaviour patterns has been addressed by gender-schematic processing theory (e.g. Bem, 1985; Martin, 1991). This approach has elements of both social learning theory and cognitive-developmental theory. Thus, like social learning theory, it suggests that children learn 'appropriate' patterns of behaviour by observation. However, and consistent with cognitive-developmental theory, children's active cognitive processing of information also contributes to their sex-typing.

As far as the strength-weakness dimension is concerned, for example, children learn that strength is linked to the male sex-role stereotype and weakness to the female stereotype, and that some dimensions (including strength-weakness) are more relevant to one gender (males) than the other (Rathus, 1990). So, a boy learns that the strength he displays in wrestling (say) affects the way others perceive him. Unless competing in some sporting activity, most girls do not see this dimension as being important. However, whilst boys are expected to compete in sports, girls are not, and so a girl is likely to find that her gentleness and neatness are more important in the eyes of others than her strength (Rathus, 1990).

According to gender-schematic processing theory, then, children learn to judge themselves according to the traits that are considered to be relevant to their genders. The consequence of this is that the self-concept becomes mixed with the gender schema of a particular culture, with the latter providing standards for comparison. The theory sees gender identity as being sufficient to produce 'sex-appropriate' behaviour. The labels 'boy' and 'girl', once understood, give children the basis for mixing their self-concepts with their society's gender schema. As Rathus (1990) notes, children with gender identity will actively seek information about the gender schema, and their self-esteem will soon become wrapped up in the ways in which they 'measure up' to their gender schema.

Conclusions

In this chapter, we have considered a wide variety of theories that try to account for the development of gender and psychological sex differences. While every known culture distinguishes between male and female, which is reflected in stereotypes regarding typical male/female characteristics and behaviour, we have seen that the evidence for the truth of such stereotypes is far from conclusive. As in other areas of psychology, no single theory on its own can adequately explain the complex process by which a person acquires his or her gender role, yet the theories discussed in this chapter have a contribution to make to our understanding of that process.

Summary

- Every known society distinguishes between male and female and sees them as having substantially different characteristics and behaviours, as reflected in **stereotypes**; the study of psychological sex differences is really an attempt to test the accuracy of these stereotypes.
- Feminist psychologists stress the influence of social, political, economic and cultural factors in

determining **gender**. This challenges the views of sociobiologists and evolutionary psychologists who argue that sex differences are 'natural', having evolved as part of the more general adaptation of the human species.

- Feminist psychologists distinguish between **sex**, or **sexual identity**, which refers to some aspect of our biological make-up as 'male' or 'female', and **gender**, which refers to the social equivalent and interpretation of sex. **Gender identity** refers to how we classify ourselves and others as male or female. While sexual and gender identity correspond for most people, an exception is the **transsexual**.
- **Gender/sex role** refers to the behaviours, attitudes, values and beliefs which a particular society expects from and considers appropriate to males or females: to be **masculine** or **feminine** requires a male or female to conform to the male or female gender role. Related to these are **gender** and **sex stereotypes**.
- **Sex-typing** refers to our discovery that we are male or female and our learning of an appropriate **sex role**.
- There appears to be a high degree of cross-cultural agreement regarding the characteristics associated with males and females, although there are also systematic **cultural variations** related to socio-economic development, education and religion.
- Several reviews have found that there is little empirical support for **actual** gender differences. While boys are more verbally and physically **aggressive** than girls from about two and a half years and the reduction of male aggression with age is less than that of females, some studies have shown that women can score higher for certain kinds of indirect or non-physical aggression or have failed to find any difference.
- Any superiority in females' **verbal ability** after age 11 may be only negligible. Similarly, although males' **spatial ability** has been shown to be consistently better during adolescence and adulthood, the differences are usually small and **within-sex** variability is large. Females sometimes show greater **mathematical ability** than males, in reverse direction to the stereotype.
- The sex-difference research is highly controversial and open to many interpretations. A statistically significant difference is a **consistent** difference and does not imply a large behavioural difference. However, the use of **meta-analysis** sometimes produces large differences on some measures.
- **Biologically**, sex refers to at least five categories: **chromosomal sex**, **gonadal sex**, **hormonal sex**, **sex of the internal reproductive structures** and **sex of the external genitalia**.
- Normal females inherit two X chromosomes and normal males inherit an X and a Y. Two chromosomes are needed for complete development of internal and external female structures, and the Y chromosome (which contains **testis-determining factor** or **TDF**) is needed for the complete development of male internal and external structures. **H-Y antigen**, controlled by genes on the Y chromosome, causes embryonic **gonads** to transform into testes; in its absence, gonadal tissue develops into ovaries.
- After development of testes or ovaries, **sex hormones** take over control of sexual development. The most important of the **androgens** (secreted by the testes) is **testosterone**; **oestrogen** and **progesterone** are secreted by the ovaries. While both males and females produce androgens and oestrogens, males usually produce more androgens and females more oestrogens.
- The Wolffian ducts are the embryonic forerunners of the prostate gland, sperm ducts, seminal vesicles and testes, while the Mullerian ducts become the fallopian tubes, womb and ovaries. The male external genitals are the **penis** and **scrotum**; in females they are the **labia majora**.
- The five biological categories are usually highly correlated with each other, as well as with non-biological factors such as sexual assignment at birth, sex of rearing and gender identity. In the case of **hermaphrodites** and **pseudohermaphrodites**, pre- and post-natal disorders have produced an inconsistency between these categories.
- **Androgen insensitivity syndrome** (AIS) or **testicular feminising syndrome** is caused by a recessive gene, resulting in a chromosomally normal male whose pre-natal development is **feminised**.
- **Adrenogenital syndrome** involves a **fetally androgenised female**: a chromosomally normal female is exposed to an excessive amount of androgens (either **endogenously** or **exogenously**) during the critical period of pre-natal sexual differentiation. Her internal reproductive structures are apparently unaffected, but her external appearance is that of a normal male.
- In **dihydrotestosterone (DHT)-deficient males**, chromosomally normal males fail to develop DHT needed for the normal development of the external genitals. While the internal structures develop normally, the testicles are undescended at birth

and the genitals resemble those of a female, resulting in the baby being identified and raised as a girl. At puberty, the testes descend and the clitoris-like organ grows into a penis.

- According to supporters of the biological approach, males and females are biologically programmed for certain kinds of activities compatible with gender roles. Of the 18 DHT-deficient males studied by Imperato-McGinley et al., 16 adopted the male gender role of their Dominican cultures, despite being raised as females, suggesting that testosterone had pre-programmed masculinity into their brains.
- Several researchers have claimed that male and female brains are structurally different. Dorner found that destruction of a small part of the newborn male rat's hypothalamus caused it to behave in a female or **homosexual** fashion. Human evidence, such as the case of Daphne Went, fails to support this claim.
- Studies of **hemispheric specialisation** are consistent with some of the findings regarding male/female differences in spatial, mathematical and verbal abilities.
- While there is emerging evidence that the corpus callosum is sexually 'dimorphic', there is no clear-cut evidence that the number of fibres is the crucial male/female difference or that sex differences in cognitive functioning are related to callosal size.
- **Biosocial theory** stresses the **interaction** of social and biological factors, rather than the influence of biology directly, specifically how babies of different temperaments contribute to their own development by influencing how others treat them.
- The 'baby X' experiments indicate that a person's (perceived) biological make-up (such as sex) becomes part of his or her social environment through how others react to it. The child's sex of rearing determines its gender identity, from which follows its gender role, gender-role identity and sexual orientation.
- Money and Ehrhardt's study of girls with adrenogenital syndrome who were raised as boys then reassigned as girls before age three, supports the claim that there is a 'critical' or 'sensitive' period for the development of gender identity. Their study of ten people with AIS raised as girls also supports the view that sex of rearing is more important than biological sex.
- Money and Ehrhardt's participants were clearly atypical: just because they seem to be flexible in their psychosexual identity does not mean that people in general are so flexible or that there is no 'in-built bias' to be overcome. However, Money's study of a 'penectomised' twin boy raised as a girl seems to support the claim that gender identity and gender role are **learned**, although 'her' development in adolescence led Diamond to conclude that biology had proved the more powerful influence.
- According to **sociobiologists**, our gender has evolved as part of human beings' broader adaptation to the environment, with males and females developing different roles as a function of their respective contributions to reproduction and domestic labour.
- According to **parental investment theory**, females invest considerably more in reproduction than do males. Sexually exclusive domestic partnerships meet the female's need for protection/male's need for preventing his mate from mating with other males. From this evolved different courtship displays and roles still evident in many Western and other cultures.
- According to Freud's **psychoanalytic theory**, gender identity is related to the development of **conscience**. Before the resolution of the Oedipus complex, gender identity is flexible, but **identification** with the same-sex parent involves adopting that parent's attitudes and behaviours. Boys' consciences develop through **introjecting** their version of their father's conscience into their ego, as does their gender identity. Girls do not resolve their Oedipus complex as effectively as do boys, resulting in a weaker conscience and gender identity.
- Critics of Freud argue that gender identity develops much more gradually than he claimed. Also, studies of children who grow up in 'atypical' families show that their gender identity is not adversely affected. Children are aware of gender roles well before age five or six, when the Oedipus complex is resolved. Boys and girls prefer stereotypically masculine or feminine toys **in infancy** and their activities are different within the first year.
- According to **social learning theory** (SLT), girls and boys learn to behave differently through being **treated differently** by parents and others. The 'baby X' experiment shows that others react to children according to their **gender-role expectations**.
- SLT also stresses the role of **observational learning** and **reinforcement**. Children are reinforced by 'significant others' for imitating sex appropriate behaviours, such as independence, self-

reliance and emotional control in boys and compliance, dependence, nurturance, empathy and expression of emotion in girls.

- In support of SLT, Sears et al. found that parents allowed boys to express more aggression in their relationships with other children and towards their parents than girls, and Huston found that they intervene more when girls behave aggressively, despite believing that they treat girls and boys alike.
- Bandura et al. found that boys were more likely to imitate aggressive male models than were girls (based on perceived similarity and relevance) and that children in general are more likely to imitate a same-sex model than an opposite-sex model, regardless of the behaviour's sex-appropriateness. But there is also some evidence that children are more likely to imitate behaviour that is appropriate to their own sex regardless of the sex of the model.
- According to Gunter, several studies together suggest that 'heavy' child viewers of television hold stronger **gender-role stereotypes** than 'lighter' viewers, consistent with Wober et al.'s finding that the media portray such stereotypes. However, this research is based on an oversimplistic view of the child as a passive recipient of media messages.
- Maccoby and Jacklin found that there are **no consistent** differences in the extent to which boys and girls are reinforced for aggressiveness and autonomy. Lytton and Romney also concluded that there is remarkable uniformity in socialisation of the sexes.
- While modelling plays an important role in young children's sex-typing, there is no consistent preference for the behaviour of their same-sex parent. Rather, they prefer to model the behaviour of those with whom they have the most contact (usually the mother).
- According to the **cognitive-developmental approach**, children's discovery that they are male or female **causes** them to identify with members of the same sex. Rewards and punishments do not mechanically strengthen stimulus-response connections but provide children with **information** about when they are behaving in appropriate ways.
- Cognitive-developmental theorists identify three stages in the child's understanding of **male** and **female**: **gender labelling** or **basic gender identity** (about age three), **gender stability** (four or five) and **gender constancy** or **consistency** (six to seven). Only after gender constancy is acquired do children identify with the adults who possess the qualities they see as being most central to their concepts of themselves as male or female.
- Cross-cultural evidence suggests that gender identity, stability and constancy do develop in that sequence. There is also experimental support, which backs up Kohlberg's claim that gender constancy **causes** imitation of same-sex models and that children actively construct their gender-role knowledge through purposely monitoring their social environment.
- The possibility that gender identity alone can provide a child with sufficient motivation to assume sex-typed behaviour has been addressed by **gender-schematic processing theory**. Like SLT, it suggests that children learn 'appropriate' behaviours through observation, but like cognitive-developmental theory, children's active information processing also contributes to their sex-typing.
- Children learn, for example, that strength and weakness is linked to the male and female sex-role stereotypes respectively. Also, while the strength–weakness dimension is more relevant to males than to females, a girl's gentleness and neatness are more important than her strength. So children learn to judge themselves according to the traits seen as relevant to their genders, resulting in a self-concept that is mixed with the gender schema of a particular culture.

THE DEVELOPMENT OF THE SELF

Introduction and overview

When we look in a mirror, we are both the person being looked at and the person doing the looking. When we think of the kind of person we are, or something we have done, we are both the person being thought about and the person doing the thinking. We use the personal pronoun 'me' to refer to ourselves as the *object* (what is being looked at or thought about) and 'I' to refer to ourselves as the *subject* (the person doing the looking or thinking).

Although non-human animals have consciousness in that they have sensations of hunger, thirst, pain and so on, only humans have *self-consciousness* in the sense that our same self can be both the subject and the object. Our aim in this chapter is to look at the development of the self-concept, that is, our perception of our own personality. After examining the various components of the self-concept, the chapter will focus on some of the theoretical approaches to the development of the self and the evidence on which these theories are based.

Components of the self-concept

According to Murphy (1947), the self is 'the individual as known to the individual'. The self-concept has three components: the *self-image*, *self-esteem* (or *self-regard*) and the *ideal-self*.

SELF-IMAGE

Our self-image is the way in which we describe ourselves, that is, the sort of person we think we are. One way of assessing people's self-image is to ask them to answer the question 'Who am I?' 20 times. Kuhn and McPartland (1954) found that this approach typically produces two main categories of answer relating to *social roles* and *personality traits*.

Social roles are usually quite objective aspects of our self-image (such as being a son, daughter, student and so on) which can be verified by others. Personality traits, by contrast, are more a matter of opinion and judgement, and what we think we are like may be different from how others see us. For example, we might think we are quite friendly, but others might see us as being quite cold or a little aloof. However, and as we will see, how others behave towards us has an important influence on our self-perception.

Social roles are one of several factors that have been identified as important in the development of the self-concept (Argyle, 1983). Kuhn (1960), for example, asked seven-year-old children and undergraduates to give 20 different answers to the question 'Who am I?' (cf. Kuhn and McPartland, 1954). On average, the children gave five answers relating to social roles whereas the undergraduates gave an average of ten. As we get older, we incorporate more and more roles into our self-image. This is not unexpected since, as we get older, we assume an increasing number and variety of roles. The pre-schooler is a son or a daughter, perhaps a brother or a sister, has other familial roles, and is also likely to be another child's friend. However, the number and range of roles are limited when compared with the older child or adult. As we grow up and venture into the 'big wide world', our duties, responsibilities and choices involve us in all kinds of roles and relationships with others.

As well as social roles and personality traits, we often make reference to our *body image*, *bodily self* or *bodily me*. This refers to our physical characteristics such as being tall, short, brown-haired and so on. Our 'bodily me' also includes bodily sensations (usually temporary states) such as pain, cold and hunger. A more permanent feature of our body image is concerned with what we count as part of our body (and so belonging to us). Allport (1955) gives two vivid examples of how intimate our bodily sense is, and just where we draw the boundaries between 'me' and 'not me'. These are shown in Box 9.1.

Box 9.1 Allport's examples of the boundaries between 'me' and 'not me'

- Imagine swallowing your saliva, or actually do this. Now imagine spitting it into a cup and drinking it. Clearly, once we have spat out our saliva, we have disowned it – it no longer belongs to us.
- Imagine sucking blood from a finger you have cut (something we do automatically when the cut is slight). Now imagine sucking the blood from a plaster on your finger. Again, once the blood has soaked into the plaster it has ceased to be part of ourselves.

The 'rule' concerning the boundaries between 'me' and 'not me' does not always apply, however. For example, we might feel that we have lost part of ourselves when our very long hair is cut short. Clearly, whenever our body changes in some way, so our body image changes. In extreme cases, as when a leg is amputated, we would expect a correspondingly dramatic change in body image which will sometimes be unfavourable and sometimes favourable.

As part of the normal process of maturation, all of us experience 'growth spurts', changes in height, weight and the general appearance and 'feel' of our body. Each time this happens, we have to make an adjustment to our body image. One fundamental aspect of our body image relates to our biological sex. *Gender* is the social interpretation of sex, which we discussed in the previous chapter. Other fundamental aspects of body image are the bodily changes involved in *puberty*. Puberty marks the onset of *adolescence*, and we shall look at some of the theories and research into personality change and social development in adolescence in the following chapter.

SELF-ESTEEM

Whilst our self-image is essentially *descriptive*, self-esteem (self-regard) is essentially *evaluative*. Coopersmith (1967) has defined self-esteem as 'a personal judgement of worthiness that is expressed in the attitudes the individual holds towards himself [or herself]'. Put another way, self-esteem is the extent to which we like and accept or approve of ourselves, and how worthwhile we think we are. How much we like or value ourselves can be an overall judgement or it can relate to specific aspects of our lives. For example, we might have a generally high opinion of ourselves yet not like certain aspects of our characteristics or attributes (as might be the case if we lacked assertiveness but wanted to be assertive). Alternatively, it might be impossible, or at least very difficult, to have high overall self-esteem if we are very badly disfigured or desperately shy. Our self-esteem can be regarded as how we evaluate our self-image, that is, how much we like the kind of person we think we are. Clearly, certain abilities (such as being good at sport) and characteristics (such as being attractive) have a greater value in society generally, and these are likely to influence our self-esteem accordingly. The value attached to abilities and characteristics will also depend on culture, gender, age, social background and so on.

In his book *Psychology of Human Conflict*, Guthrie (1938) tells of a dull and unattractive female student whose classmates decided to play a trick on her by pretending she was the most desirable girl in the college. Her classmates drew lots to decide who would take her out first, second and so on. By the fifth or sixth date, she was no longer regarded as dull and unattractive. By being treated as attractive she had, in a sense, *become* attractive (perhaps by wearing different clothes or smiling more), and her self-image had clearly changed. For the boys who dated her later, it was no longer a chore! Within a year, 'she had developed an easy manner and a confident assumption that she was popular' (Guthrie, 1938).

The *reaction of others* (another factor identified by Argyle as influencing the development of the self) is, as we shall see, stressed in the theories of self-development advanced by William James and C.H. Cooley. Also important in influencing the development of the self is *comparison with others*. Certain parts of our self-image and self-esteem are affected by how we compare with others. Indeed, there are certain parts of our self-image which only take on significance *through* comparison with others. For example, 'tall' and 'fat' are not *absolute* characteristics (like, say, blue-eyed) and we are only tall or fat *in comparison* with people who are taller or shorter or fatter or thinner than ourselves. This is true of many other characteristics, including intelligence. Parents and other adults often react to children by comparing them with their siblings or unrelated other children. If a child is told repeatedly that it is 'less clever' than its big sister, it will come to incorporate this as part of its self-image. As a result, the child will probably have lower self-esteem. This could adversely affect academic performance so that the child does not achieve in line with its true abilities. A child of above average intelligence who has grown up in the shadow of a brilliant brother or sister may be less successful academically than an average or even below-average child who has not had to face these unfavourable comparisons. According to Rosenberg (1965), adolescents with the highest self-esteem tend to be of higher social class, to have done better at school and to have been leaders in their clubs, all of which represent the basis for a favourable comparison between self and others.

IDEAL-SELF

Our self-esteem is also partly determined by how much our self-image differs from our ideal-self, the third component of the self-concept. As we have seen, our self-image is the kind of person we think we are. Our ideal-self (*ego-ideal* or *idealised self-image*) is the kind of person we would *like* to be. This can vary in both extent and degree. So, we might want to be different in certain aspects or we may want to be a totally different person (and might even wish we were someone else). One reason for wanting to be different might be a dissatisfaction with what we are like. Alternatively, we might basically like ourself and want to develop and extend along essentially the same lines. In general, the greater the gap between our self-image and our ideal-self, the lower is our self-esteem.

SELF-SCHEMATA

As well as representing and storing information about other people, we also represent and store information about ourselves, but in a more complex and varied way. This information constitutes the self-concept. We tend to have very clear self-schemata on some dimensions (including those that are important to us), but not on others. For example, if we think of ourselves as being athletic and being athletic is important to us, then we would be *self-schematic* on that dimension. Being athletic, then, would be part of our self-concept (Hogg and Vaughn, 1995).

Most people have a complex self-concept with many self-schemata. These include an array of 'possible selves', or future-oriented schemata of what we would like to be (our ideal-self). Visions of future possible selves may influence some of the decisions we make, such as our choice of career. The idea of multiple selves raises the question of whether any one self is actually more real or authentic than any other. As Hampson (1995) has noted, personality theorists typically assume that a person has a single, unitary self (and so the instructions on a personality questionnaire do not specify which self should be described). Social psychologists, however, recognise the possibility that the self refers to a complex set of perceptions, composed of a number of schemata relating both to what we *are* like and what we *could* be like.

How does the self-concept develop?

Lewis and Brooks-Gunn (1979) have argued that achieving identity, in the sense of acquiring a *self-schema* (or set of beliefs about the self) is one of the central developmental tasks of a social being. Identity development progresses through several levels of complexity and continues throughout the life-span. According to a number of psychologists (including Jean Piaget, see Chapter 4), new-born babies have no self-concept and cannot distinguish between 'me' and 'not me'. For Piaget (1952):

> 'When a baby discovers his own body – his fingers, feet, arms – he looks at them no differently than he regards other objects, without any idea that he himself is the one responsible for moving the particular objects that he is admiring ... To begin with, a baby has no sense of self at all'.

During its first few months, the baby gradually distinguishes itself from its environment and from other people, and related to this is a sense of continuity through time (the *existential self*). The baby's discovery that it can control things other than its hands and feet contributes to this development, as does its discovery that some things (such as its limbs) are always there whereas other things (such as its mother) are not. However, the infant's self-knowledge at this time is comparable to that of other species (such as monkeys). What makes our self-knowledge distinctive is becoming aware that we have it – we are conscious of our existence and uniqueness (Gross, 1996).

Maccoby (1980) has argued that there are at least two counts on which babies are able to distinguish between themselves and others. First, their own fingers hurt when they are bitten, but these sensations do not occur when they bite things like their rattle or mother. Second, and probably quite early in life, they begin to associate the feelings of their own body movements with the sight of their own limbs and the sounds of their own cries. These sense-impressions are bound together into a cluster that defines the bodily self, and so this is likely to be the first aspect of the self-concept to develop.

Other aspects of the self-concept develop by degrees, although clearly defined *stages* of development do not seem to exist. Whilst young children may know their own names and understand the limits of their own bodies, they may not yet be able to think about themselves as coherent entities. *Self-awareness* or *self-consciousness*, then, develops very gradually. In Piaget's view, an awareness of the self comes through the gradual process of adaptation to the environment (see Chapter 4). As the child explores objects and *accommodates* to them (resulting in new sensorimotor schemas), it simultaneously discovers aspects of itself. Trying to put a large block into the mouth and finding that it will not fit, for example, is a lesson in selfhood as well as a lesson about certain objects.

SELF-RECOGNITION

One way in which the bodily self's development has been studied is through *self-recognition*. This involves more than just a simple discrimination of bodily features. For example, to determine that the person in a photograph, video-recording or reflection in a mirror is ourself, we need to have a rudimentary knowledge of ourself as continuous through time (in the case of photographs or video recordings) and space (in the case of mirrors). We must also know what we look like (our particular features). Other kinds of recognition, such as our voice or feelings, are also possible, but only visual recognition has been studied extensively in both humans and non-humans.

The evidence suggests that at around six months of age, babies make deliberate repetitive movements in front of a mirror, apparently to explore the mirror's possibilities. They also look behind the mirror (Krebs and Blackman, 1988). Many non-humans (such as fish, birds and monkeys) react to their mirror images as though they were *other animals*, and they do not seem to recognise their own reflection at all. In the higher primates (chimpanzees and other great apes), however, self-recognition has been found. Box 9.2 illustrates this.

Box 9.2 Self-recognition in chimpanzees

When Gallup (1977) placed a full-length mirror on the wall of several pre-adolescent, wild-born chimps' cages, the animals acted as if their reflection was another chimp. However, although they initially threatened, vocalised or made conciliatory gestures, these behaviours had almost disappeared after three days. Then the chimps used the reflection to explore themselves. For example, they would pick up a piece of food and place it on their face, which could not be seen without the mirror.

After ten days with the mirror, the chimps were anaesthetised. Using odourless and non-irritating dye, a bright red spot was painted on the uppermost part of one eyebrow ridge and a second spot on the top of the opposite ear. After recovering from the anaesthetic, the chimps were returned to their cages. The mirror had been removed and Gallup observed the number of times they touched the painted parts of their body. When the mirror was put back in the cage, Gallup found that they explored the red spots 25 times more often than had been done without the mirror's presence.

The procedure was repeated with chimps who had *never* seen themselves in a mirror. They reacted to their mirror image as if it was another chimp, and did not touch the red spots. This suggests that the first group had learned to recognise themselves, a finding which supports the theories of Mead and Cooley which we will describe later on in this chapter. Other research has shown that lower primates (monkeys, gibbons and baboons) are unable to recognise their mirror image whether they are raised in isolation or normally.

A version of Gallup's technique has also been used with six- to 24-month-old humans. Whilst pretending to wipe the baby's face, its mother carefully applies a dot of rouge to its nose. After observing how many times the baby touches its nose, it is then placed in front of a mirror. Lewis and Brooks-Gunn (1979) found that touching did not occur before 15 months. However, between 15 and 18 months, five to 25 per cent of infants touched their noses, whilst between 18 and 20 months 75 per cent did. In order to use the mirror image to touch the dot, babies must have built up a schema of how their face should look in the mirror before they can notice the discrepancy caused by the dot. Since this does not appear to develop before about 18 months, the time when Piaget believes *object permanence* (see Chapter 4, page 42) is completed, it is likely that object permanence is a *necessary* condition for the development of self-recognition.

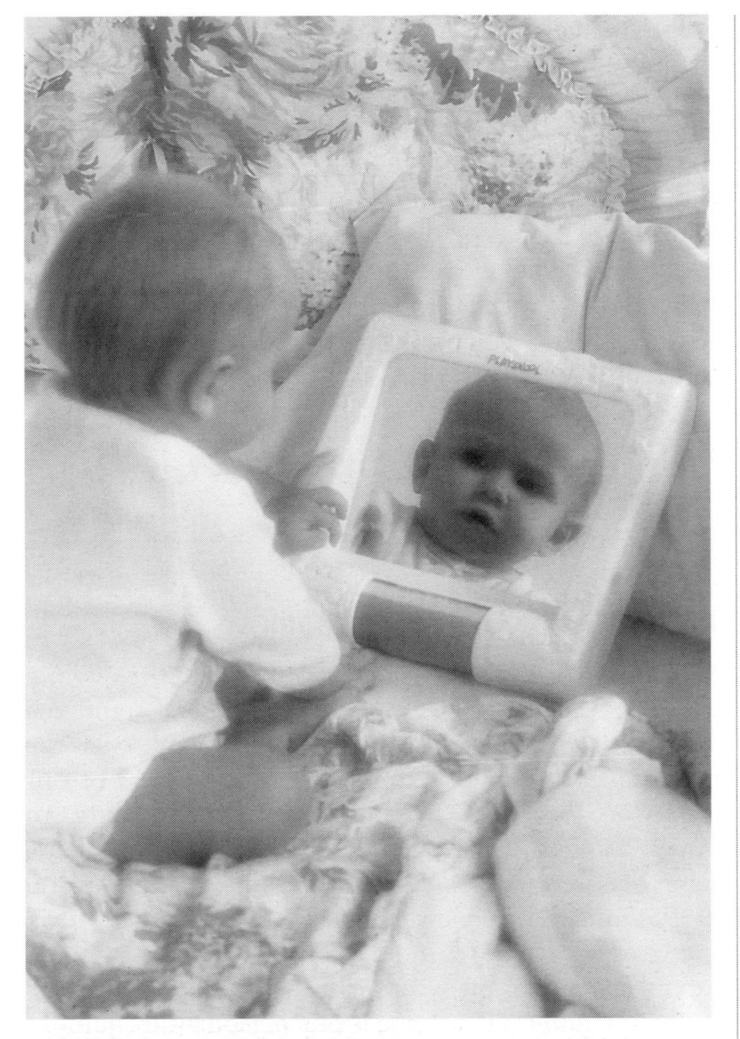

Figure 9.1 Self-recognition appears quite early in the development of self-awareness/self-consciousness. Human beings share this ability with chimpanzees and other great apes

SELF-DEFINITION

Language plays an important role in consolidating the early development of self-awareness by providing labels which permit distinctions to be made between self and non-self (such as 'I', 'you', 'me' and 'it'). These labels can then be used by infants to communicate notions of selfhood to others. An important label is a *name*. Parents choose names they like and sometimes name a child after, for example, a relative or famous person. Names are not neutral labels in terms of how people respond to them and what they associate with them, and there is a large body of evidence to suggest that names can be used as one basis for *social stereotyping*. Jahoda (1958) has described the naming practices of the Ashanti people of West Africa. Children born on different days of the week are given names accordingly, because the Ashanti believe that they have different personalities. Police records indicated that among juvenile delinquents, a very high proportion were born on a Wednesday (the day of the 'naturally aggressive' personality) whilst a very low proportion were born on a Monday (the day of the 'quiet and calm' personality). It seems reasonable to suggest that Ashanti boys are treated in a way which is consistent with the name given to them, and that as a result they 'become' what their names indicate they are 'really' like. This is known as a *self-fulfilling prophecy*. In English-speaking countries, some days of the week (such as Tuesday) and some months (such as April) are used as names, and they have associations which may influence others' reactions (as in the rhyme 'Monday's child is fair of face, Tuesday's child is full of grace . . .').

When children refer to themselves as 'I' or 'me' and others as 'you', they are reversing the labels that are normally used to refer to them by others. Also, of course, they hear others refer to themselves as 'I' and not as 'you', 'he' or 'she'. This is a problem of *shifting reference*. Despite this, most children do not invert 'I' and 'you', but two interesting exceptions to this are *autistic* and *blind* children, who often use 'I' for others and 'you' for the self (Gross, 1996).

THE PSYCHOLOGICAL SELF

What exactly do children mean when they refer to themselves as 'I' or 'me'? Are they referring to anything more than a physical entity enclosed by an envelope of skin? A study reported by Flavell et al. (1978) found that young children are aware that whilst people and dolls are alike in some ways (such as having hands and legs), they are different in others (such as dolls not being able to think about things). When asked to identify the location of the part of themselves that knows their name and thinks about things, some children gave a fairly clear localisation for the thinking self (namely 'in the head'). When looked directly in the eye and asked 'Can I see you thinking in there?' most children thought not.

These findings suggest that by the age of three and a half to four years, children have a rudimentary concept of a private thinking self that is not visible, even to someone looking directly into their eyes, and which can be distinguished from the bodily self, which they know is visible to others. By about the age of four, then, most children have begun to develop a *theory of*

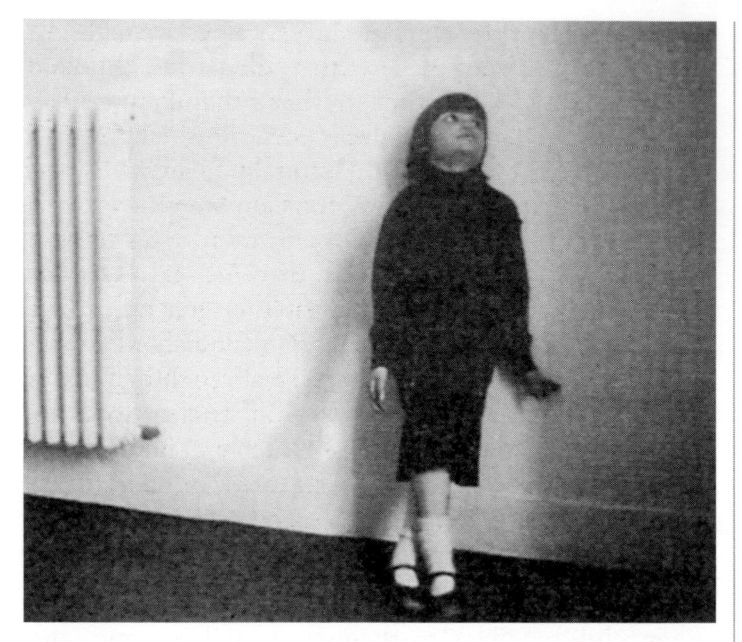

Figure 9.2 The self-absorption displayed by this autistic girl prevents her from developing a normal 'theory of mind'

mind, that is, an awareness that they and other people have mental processes (Shatz, 1994) that influence their behaviour. Our theory of mind is used to explain other people's behaviour and it helps in social interaction and interpersonal communication. Given its importance for social life, anyone who lacked a theory of mind (or whose theory was deficient in some way) would be seriously handicapped. This core inability to appreciate the mental states of others is called *mind-blindness* (Baron-Cohen, 1990). In all cases of *autism*, the child fails to develop normal social relationships and, according to Baron-Cohen (1995), this is an inevitable consequence of the absence of a theory of mind.

THE CATEGORICAL SELF

Parts of the central core of our self-image are *age* and *gender*. These represent two of the categories regarding the self which are also used to perceive and interpret the behaviour of others. Age is the first social category to be acquired, and this occurs even before a concept of number develops. For example, Lewis and Brooks-Gunn (1979) found that six- to 12-month-old infants can distinguish between photographs, slides and papier-mâché heads of adults and babies. By 12 months, they prefer interacting with strange babies to strange adults and, as soon as they have acquired labels like 'mummy' and 'daddy', they almost never make age-related mistakes.

Before the age of seven, children tend to define the self in physical terms (such as height, favourite activities and so on). Their inner psychological experiences and characteristics are not described as being distinct from overt behaviour and external, physical characteristics. Although there are important cultural differences in how the self-concept develops, between middle childhood and adolescence self-descriptions do include many more references to internal, psychological characteristics such as competencies, knowledge, emotions, values and personal traits (Damon and Hart, 1988).

Theoretical approaches to the self

JAMES'S AND COOLEY'S THEORIES

William James (1890) was the first to make the distinction between the *self-as-subject or knower* ('I') and the *self-as-known or object* ('me'). The 'I' represents the principal form of the self and lies at the centre of our state (or 'stream') of consciousness. According to James, the self is *multifaceted*, that is, we have as many selves as we have social relationships. As Hampson (1995) notes, this view is consistent with the widely shared view that we modify our behaviour to some extent depending on who we are with: different others bring out different aspects of our personalities. James's view of the self as multifaceted is also consistent with Goffman's (1959) account of *self-presentation*. For Goffman, self-presentation is the creation and maintenance of a public self. Using the theatre as an analogy, Goffman argues that each participant in a social interaction is engaged in a 'performance' designed as much for its effect on the 'audience' as it is for honest and open expression of the self. Indeed, according to this *dramaturgical approach*, personality is equated with the various roles a person plays in life. However, James's idea of multiple selves goes much further than this by suggesting that different personalities are constructed in the context of every relationship a person has (Hampson, 1995).

C.H. Cooley's (1902) *looking-glass self* theory holds that the self is reflected in the reactions of other people, who are the 'looking-glass' for oneself. For Cooley, in order to understand what we are like, we need to see how others see us, and this is how children gradually build up an impression of what they are like. What is reflected back to us are judgements and evaluations of our behaviour and appearance which produce some form of self-feeling (such as pride or shame). Consistent with James's idea of multiple selves, Cooley claims that the looking-glass is not a 'mere technical reflection' because it will differ depending on whose view we take. The individual and society are opposite sides of the same coin (Denzin, 1995).

MEAD AND SYMBOLIC INTERACTIONISM

A major theoretical approach to the self is *symbolic interactionism*, which is mainly associated with G.H. Mead (1934). Influenced by James and Cooley, Mead argued that people act towards things in terms of their meanings. As well as existing in a physical environment, we exist in a symbolic environment, such that the importance of a social interaction is derived from the meaning it holds for the participants. The 'interaction' refers specifically to the fact that people communicate with each other, and this provides opportunities for meanings to be learned. Because we share a common language and have the ability for symbolic thought, we can, at least in principle, look at the world from other perceivers' points of view and take their role. For Mead, this is essentially the process by which the self develops.

Mead argued that children initially think about their conduct as good or bad only as they react to their own acts in the remembered words of their parents. At this stage 'me' is a combination of the child's memory of its own actions and the kind of reaction they received. Later, in 'pretend play', children *role-take* and play 'mummies and daddies', 'doctors and nurses' and so on. This helps them to understand and incorporate adult attitudes and behaviour. The child is not merely imitating, but in Mead's (1934) words also 'calls out in himself the same response as he calls out in the other', that is, the child is being both him or herself *and* the parent. As the 'parent', the child is responding to him or herself as the child. So, when playing with a doll, the child: 'responds in tone of voice and attitude as (its) parents respond to (its) cries and chortles' (Mead, 1934). For Mead, play can be distinguished from games, which involve rules:

> 'The child must not only take the role of the other, as (it) does in play, but must assume the various roles of all the participants in the game accordingly'.

In this way, children acquire a variety of social viewpoints or 'perspectives' (mother, father, nurse, doctor and so on) which are then used to accompany, direct and evaluate their own behaviour. This is how the socialised part of the self (Mead's 'me') expands and develops. At first, these viewpoints are based upon specific adults. Over time, the child comes to react to itself and its behaviour from the viewpoint of a 'typical mother', a 'typical nurse' or 'people in general'. Mead called these 'the perspectives of the generalised other', and the incorporation of the generalised other marks the final qualitative change in the 'me' and provides the child with a self. Grammatically, our 'me' is third person (like 'she' or 'he'), and it is an image of the self seen from the perspective of a judgemental, non-participant observer. By its very nature, 'me' is social because it grows out of this role-playing whereby the child is being the other person.

Mead's theory turns those of James and Cooley on their heads. Mead does not see the self as mentalistic or something privately going on inside a person. Rather, like mind, the self is a cognitive process lodged in the ongoing social world. However, Mead did accept Cooley's view that the self and society are two terms in a reciprocal process of interaction (Denzin, 1995). Our knowledge of self and others develops simultaneously, both being dependent on social interaction, and the self and society represent a common whole with neither being able to exist without the other.

Mead sees people as organisms with a self and this converts us into special kinds of actors, transforms our relation to the world, and gives our actions a unique character. People are objects to themselves, that is, we can perceive ourselves, have conceptions about ourselves, communicate with ourselves and so on. We are, for Mead, capable of interacting with ourselves, and this *self-interaction* is a great influence on our transactions with the world in general and other people in particular. Self-interaction is a *reflexive* process, and is Mead's way of making the 'I'/'me' distinction. The experiencing 'I' cannot be an object and cannot itself be experienced, because it is the very act of experiencing. What we experience and interact with is our 'me'.

Language and the self

Many sociologists and psychologists have been influenced by Mead and see the role of language as fundamental to the construction and maintenance of the self. What we say about ourselves often depends on who is listening, and in selecting what to say and not to say, we are actively constructing a self in relation to the other person and constantly 'making a self'. As Petkova (1995) has commented, the self is not a static, internal entity, but a process that is constantly changing.

Harré (1985, 1989) has argued that our understanding and experience of ourselves as human beings (our subjective experience of selfhood) are laid down by the beliefs about a person that are implicit in our language. The structure of our language implies certain assumptions and beliefs about human nature, which we live out in our daily interactions with others. For example, the words 'I' and 'me' mislead us into believing that each of us is represented by a coherent, unified self which operates mechanisms and processes that are responsible for our actions. However, 'self', 'ego', 'mind' and so on do not refer to anything that exists objectively in the world. Rather they are *hypothetical constructs* which perform the very important function of helping us organise and structure our world (Burr, 1995).

Similarly, Potter and Wetherell (1987) have argued that the very experience of being a person, the kind of mental life one can have and perhaps even how we experience sensory information, are dependent on the particular representations of selfhood (the particular ways of accounting for and talking about ourselves) that are available to us in our culture. These 'stories' or accounts, whose meaning is shared by members of a culture, are called *discourses*. Since these discourses differ from culture to culture, it follows that members of different cultures will experience being 'selves' in different ways. The self-concept as a *cultural phenomenon* is discussed further in Box 9.3.

Box 9.3 The self-concept as a cultural phenomenon

In Maori culture, a person is invested with a particular kind of power (*mana*), given by the gods in accordance with his or her family status and birth circumstances. This is what enables a person to be effective, whether in battle or everyday dealings with others. However, this power is not a stable resource but can be increased or decreased by the person's day-to-day conduct. A person who forgot a ritual observance or committed some misdemeanour would have his or her power decreased. A person's social standing, successes and failures, and so on are seen as being dependent on external sources rather than internal states (such as personality or motivation). Indeed, *mana* is only one of the external forces which inhabit a person.

People living in such a culture would necessarily experience themselves quite differently from what we are used to in Western culture. Instead of representing themselves as the centre and origin of their actions, which is crucial to the Western concept of the self, the individual Maori does not own experiences such as the emotions of fear, anger, love and grief. Rather, 'they are visitations governed by the unseen world of powers and forces' (Potter and Wetherell, 1987).

According to Moscovici (1985), 'the individual' is the greatest invention of modern times. Only recently has the idea of the autonomous, self-regulating and free-standing individual become dominant. Smith and Bond (1993) argue that we need to distinguish between the *independent* and the *interdependent* self. The former is what is stressed in Western, individualist cultures and the latter by non-Western, collectivist cultures.

Another important theory of the self is the humanistic theory advanced by Carl Rogers, which is often discussed as a theory of personality or, more commonly, as part of the theory underlying his *client-centred therapy* (e.g. Rogers, 1951). Analysis of this can be found in Gross and McIlveen (1996).

Conclusions

The self-concept comprises self-image, self-esteem and ideal-self. The bodily self is the first aspect of self-image to develop, beginning in early infancy and, as we have seen, this is gradually followed by self-recognition, self-definition, the psychological self and the categorical self. Most major theories of self have stressed the influence of interaction with others, with Mead and Cooley in particular seeing self and society as two sides of the same coin. The nature of the self is also shaped by one's culture, with language playing a crucial role.

Summary

- Although non-human animals have consciousness, only humans have **self-consciousness**: the same self can be both **object ('me')** and **subject ('I')**.
- The self-concept consists of the **self-image**, **self-esteem** (**self-regard**) and **ideal-self** (**ego-ideal** or **idealised self-image**). Our self-image refers to how we **describe** ourselves and the sort of person we think we are. Kuhn and McPartland assessed the self-image by asking people 20 times 'Who am I?' Answers typically fall into two categories: **social roles** and **personality traits**.
- Social roles are usually quite objective aspects of our self-image, while personality traits are largely a matter of opinion or judgement. Social roles are important in the development of the self-concept. As we get older, we assume an increasing number and variety of roles, reflecting new duties, responsibilities and choices.
- Other aspects of self-image are **body image**, **bodily self** and **bodily me**. This includes our physical characteristics, bodily sensations and what we count as part of our body (and so belonging to us). The boundaries between 'me'/'not me' are sometimes quite easy to draw (as in Allport's saliva and blood examples), sometimes not. Whenever our body changes in some way, so does our body image.
- Our biological sex is a fundamental aspect of our body image. **Gender** is the social interpretation of sex. Another fundamental aspect of body image is the bodily changes involved in **puberty** which marks the onset of **adolescence**. Growth spurts and other changes in the general appearance and 'feel' of our body require a corresponding adjustment to our body image.
- Self-esteem is essentially **evaluative** and refers to how much we like, accept and approve of ourselves and how worthwhile we think we are. Certain abilities and characteristics have a greater value in society generally and will have a correspondingly greater influence on our self-esteem. Their value will also depend on culture, age, gender, social background, etc.
- Guthrie's account of a formerly unattractive female student whose classmates pretended that she was the most desirable girl in the college demonstrates how (the development of) self-esteem can be influenced by the **reaction of others**. Also important is **comparison with others**.
- A child who is repeatedly told that he or she is 'less clever' than an older sibling will come to incorporate this into his or her self-image, lowering self-esteem and adversely affecting academic performance. Rosenberg found that adolescents with the highest self-esteem tend to be those who compare most favourably with their peers.
- Self-esteem is also partly determined by how much our self-image differs from our ideal-self, the kind of person we would **like** to be. In general, the greater the gap between self-image and the ideal-self, the lower our self-esteem.
- We represent and store information about ourselves in a complex and varied way in the form of **self-schemata**, which constitute our self-concept. These tend to be very clear in relation to dimensions that are important to us, in which case we would be **self-schematic** on those dimensions.
- Most people's self-concept is complex with many self-schemata, including a variety of 'possible selves' and future-oriented schemata. The idea of multiple selves raises the question of whether there is a single real or unitary self, as typically assumed by personality theorists. Social psychologists recognise the possibility that the self refers to a complex set of schemata relating to both what we **are** like and what we **could** be like.
- According to Lewis and Brooks-Gunn, achieving identity and a **self-schema** is one of the central developmental tasks of a social being. Piaget and many other psychologists see the new-born baby as having no self-concept, unable to distinguish between 'me'/'not me'. Related to this is development of the **existential self** and the baby's discovery that it can control things besides its hands and feet. At this time, self-knowledge is comparable to that of monkeys: being aware of our existence and uniqueness is what makes human self-knowledge distinctive.
- According to Maccoby, babies are able to distinguish between themselves and others because their own fingers hurt when bitten and, from an early age, they begin to associate the feelings of their own body movements with the sight of their own limbs and sounds of their cries. These various sense impressions cluster to form the bodily self, probably the first aspect of the self-concept to develop.
- **Self-awareness** and **self-consciousness** develop very gradually. For Piaget, discovering aspects of the self occurs through the gradual process of adaptation to the environment, exploring and **accommodating** objects.

- The bodily self has been studied through (mainly visual) **self-recognition** which involves more than just a simple discrimination of bodily features. It also requires a basic knowledge of ourself as continuous through time and space.
- Many non-human species react to their mirror-images as though they were **other animals** and fail to recognise their own reflection at all. But chimps and other great apes, although not lower primates, do have self-recognition, as demonstrated by Gallup's study of chimps.
- Lewis and Brooks-Gunn used a version of Gallup's technique with six- to 24-month-old humans. Between 15 and 18 months, a small minority use their mirror reflection to touch the dot of rouge on their nose, while most do so between 18 and 20 months. They must have already built up a schema of how their face should look in the mirror before they can notice the discrepancy caused by the dot; this seems to require the development of **object permanence**.
- Language provides labels which permit distinctions to be made between self and non-self; these can then be used by infants to communicate notions of selfhood to others (**self-definition**). **Names** are important labels, which can form the basis of **social stereotyping**. This is well illustrated by the naming practices of the Ashanti people of West Africa, and can lead to a **self-fulfilling prophecy**.
- When children refer to themselves as 'I' or 'me' and to others as 'you', they are reversing the labels normally used by others to refer to them (**shifting reference**). Despite this, most children do not invert these labels, but interesting exceptions are **autistic** and **blind** children.
- Flavell et al.'s study found that by three and a half or four years, children have a rudimentary concept of a private thinking self or **psychological self**, distinct from the bodily self which they know others can see.
- By age four, children have begun to develop a **theory of mind**. Understanding that other people have mental processes is used to explain their behaviour, and this helps in social interaction and interpersonal communication. Failure to develop a (normal) theory of mind (**mind-blindess**) is seriously socially handicapping: **autistic** children's lack of a theory of mind inevitably prevents the development of normal social relationships.
- **Age** and **gender** form part of the central core of the self-concept (**categorical self**) and represent two central categories used to perceive and interpret other people's behaviour. Age is the first social category to be acquired, even before a number concept develops.
- Before age seven, children tend to define the self in physical terms. They do not describe their inner psychological experiences or characteristics as being distinct from overt behaviour and external, physical characteristics. Between middle childhood and adolescence, self-descriptions include many more references to internal psychological characteristics.
- William James first made the distinction between **self-as-subject/knower** ('I') and **self-as-known/object** ('me'), the former lying at the centre of the 'stream' of consciousness. The self is **multifaceted**, with as many selves as we have social relationships: different personalities are constructed in the context of every relationship an individual has.
- James's view of the self is consistent with the widely shared view that different others bring out different aspects of our personality, as well as with Goffman's account of **self-presentation**. According to the **dramaturgical approach**, personality is seen as the various roles a person plays in life.
- According to Cooley's **looking-glass self** theory, the self is reflected in others' reactions. Children gradually build up an impression of what they are like by seeing how others react to them. The looking glass will differ depending on whose view we take, consistent with James's belief in multiple selves. The individual and society are two sides of the same coin.
- **Symbolic interactionism** is mainly associated with G.H. Mead. Not only do we exist in a physical environment, we also exist in a symbolic one. It is the communication involved in interactions that provides opportunities for meanings to be learned. Sharing a common language and having the ability to see the world from others' points of view and take their role is the process by which the self develops.
- Initially, 'me' is a combination of the child's memory of its own actions and the kind of reaction it received, especially from its parents. Later, in 'pretend play', children **role-take**, which helps them to understand and incorporate adult attitudes and behaviour. The child is not merely imitating, but is being both him or herself **and** the parent or adult, responding to him or herself as the child. **Games** differ from play because they involve **rules**, whereby the child must assume the role of all the participants.
- Children acquire a variety of social viewpoints or

'perspectives' which are then used to accompany, direct and evaluate its own behaviour, expanding the 'me'. At first, these viewpoints are based on specific adults, but gradually these are replaced by 'the perspectives of the generalised other'. Incorporation of the generalised other marks the final qualitative change in the 'me'.

- While James and Cooley see the self as mentalistic, for Mead the self is a cognitive process located in the ongoing social world. But Mead agreed with Cooley that our knowledge of self and society develops simultaneously; both are dependent on social interaction, and they represent a common whole, so that one cannot exist without the other.
- Many sociologists and psychologists, influenced by Mead, see language as being fundamentally important in the construction and maintenance of the self. In selecting what to say to different listeners, we are actively constructing a self in relation to them.
- For Harré, our understanding of ourselves as human beings with subjective experience of selfhood is based in the beliefs about a person implicit in our language. 'I' and 'me' misleadingly imply that each of us is represented by a coherent and unified self which operates mechanisms and processes that determine our actions. But 'self', 'ego', etc. are only **hypothetical constructs** which help us organise and structure our world.
- According to Potter and Wetherell, the very experience of being a person depends on the particular 'stories', **discourses** and ways of talking about ourselves available in our culture and whose meaning is shared by other members of our culture. These differ from culture to culture, such that the self-concept is a **cultural phenomenon**.
- According to Moscovici, 'the individual' is the greatest invention of modern times. Smith and Bond distinguish between the **independent** and **interdependent** self: the former is what is stressed in Western, individualist cultures, the latter by non-Western, collectivist cultures.

PART 4
Adolescence, adulthood and old age

PERSONALITY CHANGE AND SOCIAL DEVELOPMENT IN ADOLESCENCE

Introduction and overview

The word 'adolescence' comes from the Latin *adolescere* meaning 'to grow into maturity'. As well as being a time of enormous physiological change, adolescence is also marked by changes in behaviour and expectations. Traditionally, adolescence has been regarded as a prelude to and preparation for adulthood, a transitional period of life between immaturity and maturity. Although there is no single initiation rite in our society that signals the passage into adulthood, there are a number of important 'marker' events, such as leaving school or college, obtaining a job, or moving out of the family home. In Western societies, adolescence typically spans the ages 12 to 20 which, by the standard of other cultures, is unusually long. Indeed, in some non-industrialised societies, adolescence is either virtually non-existent or simply a period of rapid physical changes leading to maturity.

Our aim in this chapter is to examine several theories and associated research studies into personality change and social development in adolescence. A large number of theoretical accounts of personality change and social development exist. In this chapter, we will concentrate on the theories advanced by G. Stanley Hall, Erik Erikson, James Marcia and John Coleman. We will also examine sociological (or social psychological) approaches to adolescence. Before examining the various theories, however, we will first look at the concept of adolescence.

The concept of adolescence

Adolescence is usually taken to begin at *puberty*, the period when sexual maturation begins. Physiologically, puberty begins when the seminal vesicles and prostate gland enlarge in males and the ovaries enlarge in females. Both males and females experience a rapid spurt of growth (the *adolescent growth spurt*), which may result in them growing five or six inches in a year. The developments of sexual maturity in boys and girls are called *secondary sex characteristics*. Male development is characterised by the growth of pubic and then chest and facial hair, and the production of sperm. The larynx (*Adam's apple*) becomes much larger in puberty, and the vocal cords it encases double in length. For some boys this change occurs abruptly and they have difficulty in controlling their vocal cords – their voices have 'broken'. In females, breast size increases, pubic hair grows, and menstruation begins. Figure 10.1 (overleaf) shows the usual sequence of development of secondary sex characteristics in males and females.

According to Chumlea (1982), puberty typically begins about two years later for boys than for girls. However, whilst 10 and 12 are the ages by which most girls and boys respectively have entered puberty, there are consid-

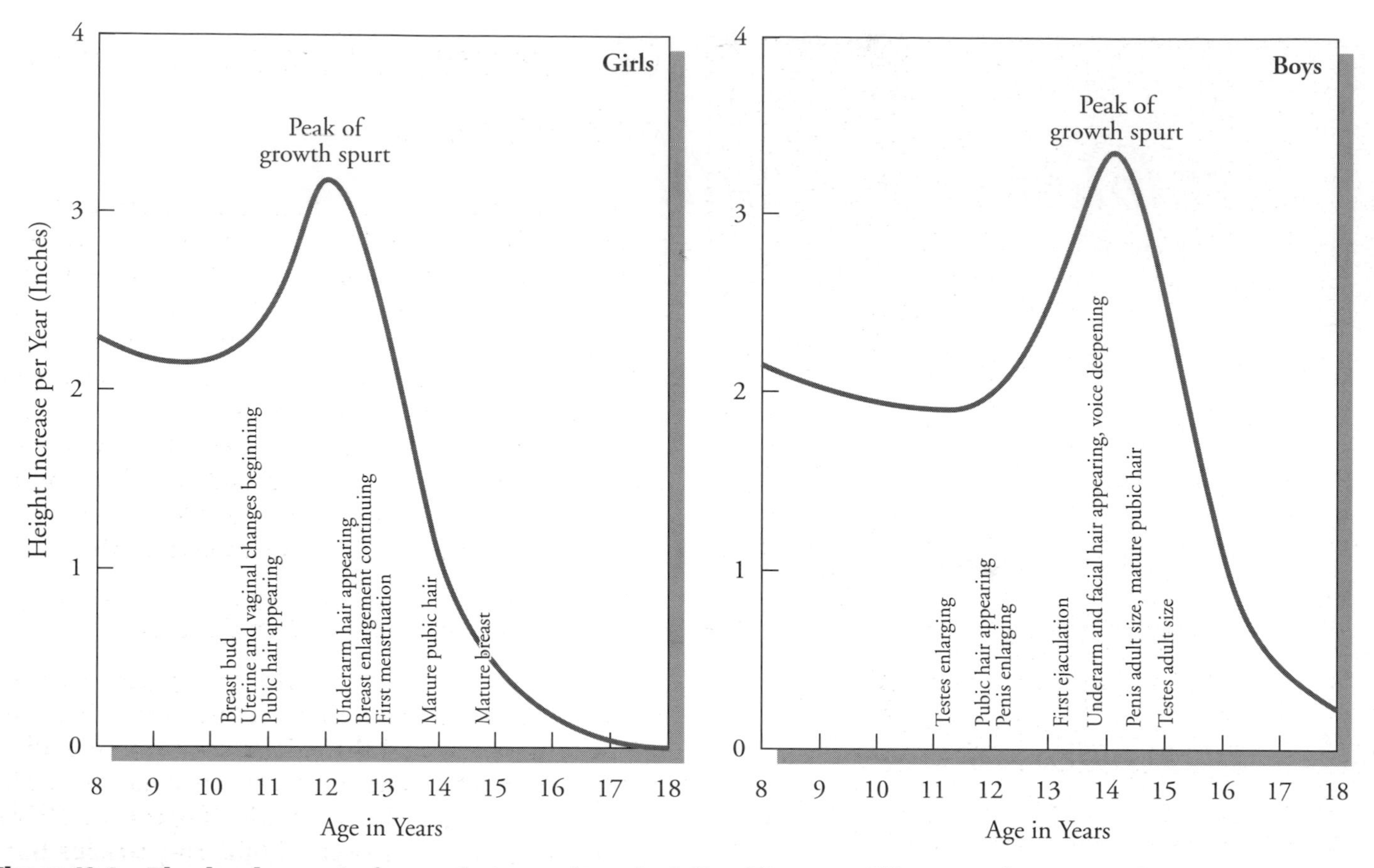

Figure 10.1 The development of secondary sex characteristics. The curved lines are the average increase in height from 8 to 18 years of age. The characteristics shown may occur earlier or later in a person's development but usually occur in the order shown (based on Tanner, 1978, and Tanner and Whitehouse, 1976)

erable individual differences. Faust (1977), for example, has reported that puberty begins as early as seven or eight in some girls and as late as 16 in others. Other research (e.g. Hamburg and Takanishi, 1989) has shown that there are also *secular growth trends*, that is, differences between *cultures* with respect to the age at which puberty begins. Hamburg and Takanishi have also shown that in some cultures the age at which puberty is entered has been *declining* over the last few decades. In those cultures where these changes have occurred, there have been improvements in nourishment and health care, and it is probable that these improvements are at least in part responsible for the observed secular growth trends.

The fact that there is considerable variation in the timing of the physical changes described above makes it difficult for us to define adolescence in terms of *chronological age* (such as 'the teenage years'). Indeed, for some researchers, adolescence is difficult to define because it is a stage in human development that has been *artificially created* by Western culture and is a recent 'invention' of Western capitalist society. For Coleman (1995), however, such a view is difficult to defend. For example, it has been argued that the concept of the 'rebellious teenager' is a relatively recent phenomenon, popularised in the 1950s through films such as *Rebel Without A Cause.* As Coleman notes, though, the 2000-year-old writings of the ancient Greek philosopher Plato illustrate how the young were seen as being the most likely to challenge the existing social order. Furthermore, research conducted by Montemayor (1983), in which parent-adolescent relationships from the 1920s to the 1980s were analysed, has shown that both the issues over which disagreement occurred and the overall levels of conflict were extremely similar.

Montemayor's research shows that adolescence has changed very little in the twentieth century despite the enormous social and economic changes that have occurred. Although the term 'teenager' came into existence only in 1953, adolescence has been in existence

Figure 10.2 1950s films such as *Rebel Without A Cause*, starring James Dean, have been seen as helping to create the concept of the 'rebellious teenager'. However, Plato was writing about youth's challenge to the existing social order more than 2000 years ago

for very much longer. It is probably true to say that adolescence has manifested itself differently according to culture and historical context. However, and as Coleman (1995) has noted, *some* form of transitional change is common to most societies, suggesting that adolescence is *not* an invention of Western capitalist society.

What researchers have termed the 'classical' view of adolescence is seen as having three main components, these being *storm and stress*, an *identity crisis* and the *generation gap*. Several theories of adolescence have, in various ways, contributed to this classical view. In the following sections we will critically consider some of these theories of personality change and social development in adolescence and the evidence relevant to the three main components.

G. Stanley Hall's theory of adolescence

Perhaps the earliest theory of adolescence was that proposed by G. Stanley Hall in his book *Adolescence* (which, since it was published in 1904, suggests that adolescence must have existed before then!: see above). Influenced by Darwin's evolutionary theory, Hall believed that each person's psychological development *recapitulates* (or recaptures) both the biological and cultural evolution of the human species. Hall saw adolescence as being a time of 'storm and stress' (or *Sturm und Drang*) which mirrored the volatile history of the human race over the last 2000 years, and in which:

> 'every step of the upward way is strewn with the wreckage of the body, mind, and morals'.

Certainly, there is some evidence to suggest that reactions are more *intense* during adolescence than any other period of life and that adolescence can be a 'difficult' phase, at least as far as parents are concerned. The National Children's Bureau study (Fogelman, 1976), for example, looked at over 14,000 16-year-olds born in a single week in 1958 in England, Scotland and Wales. The data indicated that parents most often described their adolescent children as solitary, irritable ('quick to fly off the handle') or 'fussy and overparticular'. Box 10.1 describes a novel approach to the study of adolescent reactions conducted by Csikszentmihalyi and Larson (1984).

Box 10.1 Csikszentmihalyi and Larson's (1984) study of adolescent reactions

The researchers asked 75 Chicago-area high-school students from diverse social and racial backgrounds to wear electronic pagers for a week. Every two hours, the pager signalled to the students who were instructed to write down a description of what they were doing and how they felt about it. At the end of the week, the students filled out questionnaires about both their general moods and their specific mood during particular activities. The results showed that about 40 per cent of waking time was spent pursuing leisure activities, such as socialising with friends, playing sport or just 'thinking'. For the other 60 per cent, the students spent their time roughly equally in 'maintenance activities' (such as commuting and eating) and 'productive activities' (such as studying and working).

What was particularly revealing, though, was the extreme swings of mood shown by the students. Consistent with the view that adolescents are 'moody', Csikszentmihalyi and Larson found that the students swung from extreme happiness to deep sadness (and vice versa) in less than an hour. For adults, such mood swings usually require several hours to reach the same emotional peaks and troughs.

Although adolescence can be a difficult time of life, there is little evidence to support Hall's contention that it is a period of storm and stress, and much to reject it. For example, Bandura and Walters (1959) found that amongst families of middle-class American adolescents, adolescence is no more stressful than childhood or adulthood. British research has reached the same conclusion. In one study, Rutter et al. (1976) found only small differences between the number of ten-year-olds (10.9 per cent), 14-year-olds (12.5 per cent) and adults (11.9 per cent) judged as having mental disorders. Moreover, a large proportion of 14-year-olds with disorders had had them since childhood. When difficulties did first appear during adolescence, they were mainly associated with stressful situations such as parents' marital discord.

Likewise, Siddique and D'Arcy (1984) found that over a third of adolescents reported no symptoms of psychological distress, and around 40 per cent reported only mild levels. So whilst adolescence may be a period of stress and turmoil for some, the evidence suggests that the vast majority adjust well to the transitional phase of adolescence. For Offer (1969), the reason for adolescent resilience is that the vast majority of adolescents possess an ego which is strong enough to withstand the pressures of that phase of life. Because they are in touch with their feelings and develop meaningful relationships with significant others, they do not experience the turmoil of the disturbed adolescent.

Erik Erikson's theory of adolescence

Along with Alfred Adler, Erik Erikson was one of the first to challenge the view that personality development stops in childhood. Erikson (e.g. 1963) believed that there was a fixed and pre-determined sequence of stages in human development. His *epigenetic principle* is based on embryology, which maintains that the entire pattern of development is governed by a genetic structure common to all humans in which genes dictate a timetable for the growth of each part of the unborn baby. According to Erikson, this principle applies to social and psychological growth, and he believed that it was human nature to pass through a genetically determined sequence of *psychosocial stages*.

Erikson saw the sequence of stages as being *universal*, that is, the same for all cultures. However, he also saw the social-cultural environment as having a significant influence on our dominant modes of acting and thinking. Based on observations of patients in his psychoanalytic practice, Erikson suggested that there were eight psychosocial stages through which people passed, each of which centres around a crisis involving a struggle between two conflicting personality outcomes. One of these outcomes is positive (or *adaptive*) whilst the other is negative (or *maladaptive*). Erikson did not, however, see these as either/or alternatives. Rather, he saw every personality as being some mixture of the two relative outcomes, with healthy development involving the adaptive outweighing the maladaptive. Table 10.1 identifies the eight psychosocial stages, the relevant personal and social relationships, the nature of the conflict, and the possible outcome.

As Table 10.1 shows, the major challenges of adolescence represent the fifth of Erikson's eight psychosocial changes, and the stage in which the individual must face the crisis of establishing a strong sense of personal identity. The dramatic onset of puberty, combined with more sophisticated intellectual abilities (see Chapter 4), results in adolescents becoming particularly concerned with finding their own personal places in adult society. It also results in a lengthy and sometimes painful process of assessing particular strengths and weaknesses so that realistic goals can be set.

Western societies, at least, see adolescence as a *moratorium*, an authorised delay of adulthood, which frees adolescents from most responsibilities and tries to help them make the difficult transition from childhood to adulthood. Although this can be helpful, it can also be extremely unhelpful. Thus, although adolescents may still be dependent on adults, they are expected to behave like adults in an independent and adult way. As Coleman (1995) has remarked, the question 'When do I become an adult?' elicits a response from a teacher

Table 10.1 Erik Erikson's eight psychosocial stages of development

Stage	Personal and social relationships	Crisis or conflict	Possible outcome
Birth to 1 year	Mother	Trust vs. mistrust	Trust and faith in others or a mistrust of people.
2 years	Parents	Autonomy vs. shame and doubt	Self-control and mastery or self-doubt and fearfulness.
3 to 5 years	Family	Initiative vs. guilt	Purpose and direction or a loss of self-esteem.
6 to 11 years	Neighbourhood and school	Industry vs. inferiority	Competence in social and intellectual pursuits or a failure to thrive and develop.
Adolescence	Peer groups and outgroups; models of leadership	Identity vs. role confusion	A sense of 'who one is' or prolonged uncertainty about one's role in life.
Early adulthood	Partners in friendship, sex, competition, cooperation	Intimacy vs. isolation	Formation of deep personal relationships or the failure to love others.
Middle age	Divided labour and shared household	Generativity vs. stagnation	Expansion of interests and caring for others or a turning inward toward one's own problems.
Old age	'Mankind', 'My kind'	Integrity vs. despair	Satisfaction with the triumphs and disappointments of life or a sense of unfulfilment and a fear of death.

(after Erikson, 1963)

which is different to that from a doctor, parent or police officer.

As well as having to deal with the question 'Who am I?', the adolescent must also deal with the question 'Who will I be?'. Erikson saw the creation of an adult personality as being accomplished mainly through choosing and developing a commitment to an occupation or role in life. The development of *ego identity*, that is, a firm sense of who one is and what one stands for, is positive (or adaptive) and can carry people through difficult times and colour their achievements. For some, however, the need to meet their potential and create the best possible life is contrasted with the concern to remain true to their ideals. When working with psychiatrically disturbed soldiers in World War II, Erikson coined the term *identity crisis* to describe the loss of personal identity which the stress of combat seemed to have caused. Some years later, he extended the use of what is now a familiar term to include 'severely conflicted young people whose sense of confusion is due . . . to a war within themselves'. The identity confusion, or failure to integrate perceptions of the self into a coherent whole, results in *role confusion*.

According to Erikson, role confusion can take several forms. Sometimes it is shown in an aimless drifting through a series of social and occupational roles. However, the consequences can be more severe, leading the adolescent into abnormal or delinquent behaviour (such as drug taking and even suicide). Erikson terms this type of role confusion *negative identity*, the choice of adolescents who, because they cannot resolve their identity crisis, adopt an extreme position that sets them aside from the crowd. For those with negative identity, the extreme position they adopt is preferable to the loneliness and isolation that come with the failure to achieve a distinct and more functional role in life. Box 10.2 illustrates the three other forms of role confusion identified by Erikson.

Box 10.2 Three other major forms of role confusion

Intimacy: This is a fear of commitment to, or involvement in, close relationships which arises out of a fear of losing one's own identity. The result of this may be stereotyped and formalised relationships or isolation.

Time perspective: This is the inability to plan for the future or retain any sense of time. It is associated with anxieties about change and becoming an adult.

Industry: This is a difficulty in channelling resources in a realistic way in work or study, both of which require commitment. As a defence, the adolescent may find it impossible to concentrate or become frenetically engaged in a single activity to the exclusion of all others.

Attempts to address Erikson's theory have typically used measures of the self-concept (especially self-esteem: see Chapter 9) as indicators of crisis. Some research (e.g. Simmons and Rosenberg, 1975) has shown that low self-esteem is more common during early adolescence than in either late childhood or later adolescence. The research reported by Simmons and Rosenberg has also revealed that this is more evident in girls than boys. However, in general, the evidence suggests that there is no increase in the disturbance of the self-image during early adolescence (e.g. Offer et al., 1988). For Coleman and Hendry (1990), such disturbance is more likely in early than late adolescence (especially around puberty), but only a very small proportion of the total adolescent population is likely to have a negative self-image or very low self-esteem.

Erikson's theory has also been criticised on the grounds that it is based on observations of a restricted group of people (largely middle-class, white males). Gilligan (1982) has argued that Erikson's theory must be seen in that context. As we saw in Chapter 7, Gilligan criticised Kohlberg for making generalisations about moral development based on a restricted group of people. She raises an identical charge against Erikson, whose theory she sees as being applicable only to males. Whilst it might be true that male adolescents want to forge a separate identity, Gilligan argues that females are more interested in developing warm and nurturing relationships and less interested in the idea of separateness. For Gilligan, Erikson (like Kohlberg) is guilty of advocating universal stages in the absence of supportive data.

James Marcia's theory of adolescence

In an extension of Erikson's work, James Marcia (e.g. 1980) has defined identity as:

'A self structure – an internal, self-constructed, dynamic organisation of drive, abilities, beliefs and individual history. The better developed this structure is, the more aware individuals appear to be of their own uniqueness and similarity to others and of their strengths and weaknesses in making their way in the world.'

Marcia identified four *statuses* of adolescent identity formation which characterise the search for identity. For Marcia, a mature identity can be achieved if an individual experiences several *crises* in exploring and choosing between life's alternatives, and finally arrives at a *commitment* or investment of the self in those choices. Marcia's four statuses and an example of how adolescents from each status might answer the question 'How willing do you think you'd be to give up going into an occupation if something better were to come along?' are illustrated in Box 10.3.

Box 10.3 Marcia's four statuses

Identity diffusion: The individual is in crisis and is unable to formulate clear self-definition, goals and commitments. Identity diffusion represents an inability to 'take hold' of some kind of adult identity.

Associated occupational commitment: 'Sounds like a good idea. I haven't thought about it, but I'll try everything once. I could switch just like that.' (snapping his fingers).

Identity foreclosure: The individual has avoided the uncertainties and anxieties of crisis by rapidly committing him or herself to safe and conventional goals without exploring the many options open to the self.

Associated occupational commitment: 'I doubt I'd be willing. I've always known what I wanted to do. My parents have agreed, and we're happy with it.'

Identity moratorium: Decisions about identity are postponed while the person tries out alternative identities without being committed to any particular one.

Associated occupational commitment: 'It's possible. I kind of like a couple of fields – and if something else was related, I'd want to think about it and get some information.'

Identity achievement: The individual has experienced a crisis but has emerged successfully with firm commitments, goals and ideology.

Associated occupational commitment: 'I've given it a lot of thought. If I could see that there might be something better, I'd consider it.'

(from Gross, 1996, and Sarafino and Armstrong, 1980)

According to Marcia, identity moratorium is a prerequisite for identity achievement. Beyond that, however, Marcia does not see the four statuses as being sequential, which means that they are not Eriksonian-type stages. However, there is evidence to suggest that, amongst 12- to 24-year-old men, the statuses *are* broadly age related. Meilman (1979), for example, has reported that younger men (aged 12 to 18 years) were more likely to experience diffusion or foreclosure, whereas older men were increasingly likely to be identity achievers. Meilman also found that irrespective of age, relatively few men were achieving moratorium, the peak of Marcia's statuses of adolescent identity formation. Since Marcia sees moratorium as the peak of crisis, Meilman's data cast doubt on the validity of the four statuses. Additionally, when applied to females, even Marcia (1980) accepts that his statuses work 'only more or less'. The view that the male experience is the standard, a criticism that Gilligan (1982) has made of Erikson (see above), would also seem to apply to Marcia.

A sociological (or social psychological) theory of adolescence

According to Coleman (1995), sociologists see *role change* as an integral feature of adolescent development. Things like changing school or college, leaving home and beginning a job all involve a new set of relationships producing different and often greater expectations. These expectations themselves demand a substantial reassessment of the self-concept and *speed up* the process of socialisation. Although it is possible to cope with this speeding up, some adolescents find it problematic because of the wide variety of competing socialisation agencies (such as the family, mass media and peer group) which often represent *conflicting* values and demands.

Sociologists also see socialisation as being dependent more on the adolescent's *own generation* than on the family or other social institutions, a phenomenon Marsland (1987) has called *auto-socialisation.* As Marsland has observed:

> 'The crucial meaning of youth is withdrawal from adult control and influence compared with childhood. Peer groups are the milieu into which young people withdraw . . . this withdrawal . . . is, within limits, legitimated by the adult world.'

What Marsland describes has been termed *the generation gap.* However, contrary to many reports (particularly in the mass media), there does not seem in general to be a large gap in the attitudes and beliefs between adolescents and their parents. For example, Bandura and Walters (1959) found that the typical American adolescent tended to accept most parental values quite freely and associated with other adolescents who shared such values. Other data, too, have indicated that the vast majority of parents and their 16-year-olds reported harmonious family relationships. In the National Children's Bureau study, for example, parents were given a list of issues on which it is commonly believed that they and their adolescent children disagree. As Tables 10.2 and 10.3 (overleaf) illustrate, parents saw their relationships with their adolescent children as being harmonious, a view which was confirmed by their children. The only major disagreements concerned appearance and evening activities. Data from other research (e.g. Lerner, 1975; Noller and Callan, 1990) have shown that music, fashion and sexual behaviour tend to be the issues on which a sizeable 'generation gap' appears.

Of course, it is almost inevitable that there is conflict between parents and their adolescent children. As Coleman (1995) has remarked, adolescents could not grow into adults unless they were able to test out the boundaries of authority, and they could not discover their beliefs unless given the opportunity to push hard against other people's beliefs. However, there is little evidence to support the extreme view that whatever generation gap exists leads to a 'war' between the generations or the formation of an adolescent sub-culture. For example, Offer et al. (1988) found that over 91 per cent of adolescents in nine different cultures (including Bangladesh, Turkey and Taiwan) denied holding grudges against their parents. A similar percentage rejected the idea that their parents were ashamed of them or would be disappointed in them in the future.

gramme *Men Behaving Badly* and Patsie and Eddy from *Absolutely Fabulous*. Real-life examples of 'Peter Pans' include Mick Jagger, Cliff Richard and Richard Branson.

According to psychotherapist Susie Orbach (cited in Beaumont, 1996), one of the problems created by adults who refuse to grow up is their own parenting. Unable to look up to figures of authority themselves, they feel a sense of loss and look to their own children for emotional sustenance in a curious role reversal.

Figure 11.1 Gary and Tony, the 'perpetual adolescents' in BBC TV's *Men Behaving Badly*

Levinson et al.'s 'Seasons of a Man's Life' approach to early and middle adulthood

One of the most systematic studies of personality and life changes in adulthood began in 1969, when Daniel Levinson and his colleagues interviewed 40 men aged between 35 and 45 from a variety of occupational backgrounds. Transcripts were made of the five to ten tape-recorded interviews that each participant gave over several months, producing more than 300 pages for each. Unlike Erikson, who saw successive stages of healthy development as requiring the resolution of specific personal and social crises, Levinson and his colleagues looked at how adulthood is actually *experienced*.

The findings of the study were reported in a book entitled *The Seasons of a Man's Life* (1978). In it, the researchers advanced a *life structure theory*, defining life structure as the underlying pattern or design of a person's life at any given time. Life structure allows us to 'see how the self is in the world and how the world is in the self', and is held to evolve through a series of *phases* or *periods* which give overall shape to the course of adult development. Figure 11.2 illustrates Levinson and his colleagues' model of adult development as a sequence of *eras* which overlap in the form of *cross-era transitions*. These last about five years, terminating the outgoing era and initiating the incoming one. The four eras are those of pre-adulthood (age 0–22), early adulthood (17–45), middle adulthood (40–65) and late adulthood (60 onwards).

The phases or periods alternate between those that are *stable* (or *structure-building*) and those that are *transitional* (or *structure-changing*). Although each of the phases involves biological, psychological and social adjustments, the family and work roles are seen as being central to the life structure at any time, and individual development is interwoven with changes in these roles.

Let us now look at the eras of early and middle adulthood.

THE ERA OF EARLY ADULTHOOD

Early adult transition is the period between 17 and 22

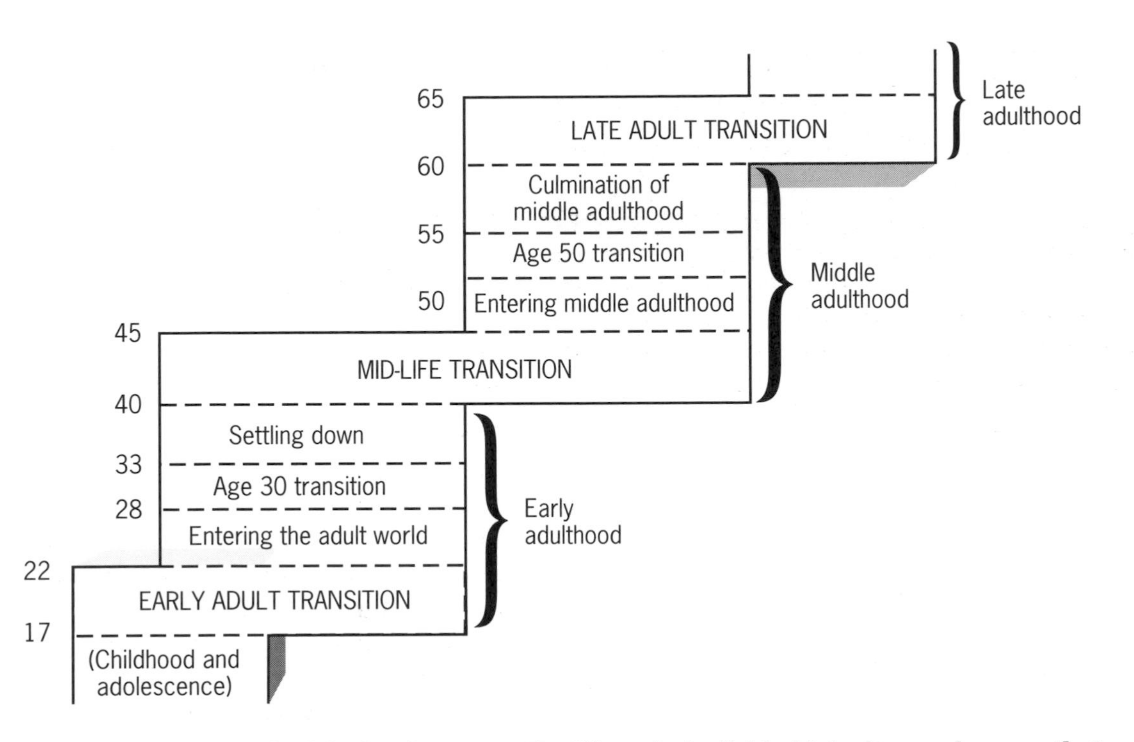

Figure 11.2 Levinson et al.'s model of adult development. The life-cycle is divided into four major eras that overlap in the form of cross-era transitions (from Gross, 1996)

and a developmental 'bridge' between adolescence and adulthood. Two key themes are *separation* and the formation of *attachments* to the adult world. Separation is *external*, in that it involves moving out of the family home, increasing financial independence, and entering more independent and responsible roles and living arrangements. It is also *internal* in that there is greater psychological distance from the family, less emotional dependence on the parents, and greater differentiation between the self and family. Although we separate from our parents, Levinson and his colleagues argue that we never complete the process and that it continues throughout life. Attachment involves exploring the world's possibilities, imagining ourselves as part of it, and identifying and establishing changes for living in the world before we become 'full members' of it.

Between the ages of 22 and 28, we *enter the adult world*. This is held to be the first *structure-building* (rather than *structure-changing*) phase and hence it is referred to as the *entry life structure for early adulthood*. Levinson et al. see this phase as one in which we try to fashion 'a provisional structure that provides a workable link between the valued self and adult society'. In the so-called *novice phase*, we try to define ourselves as adults and live with the initial choices we make concerning jobs, relationships, lifestyles and values. However, we need to create a balance between 'keeping our options open' (which allows us to explore possibilities without being committed to a given course) and 'putting down roots' (that is, creating a stable life structure).

Our decisions are made in the context of our *dreams*, that is, the 'vague sense' we have of ourselves in the adult world and what we want to do with our lives. We must overcome disappointments and setbacks, and learn to accept and profit from successes, so that the dream's 'thread' does not get lost in the course of 'moving up the ladder' and revising the life structure. To help us in our efforts at self-definition, we look to *mentors* – older and more experienced others – for guidance and direction. Mentors can take a *formal* role in guiding, teaching and helping novices to define their dreams. Alternatively, their role may be *informal*, providing an advisory and emotionally supportive function (as a parent does).

Levinson and his colleagues see the *age-30 transition* (28–33) as providing an opportunity to work on the flaws and limitations of the first life structure, and to create the basis for a more satisfactory structure that will complete the era of young adulthood. Most of the participants in Levinson et al.'s study experienced an *age-30 crisis* which involved stress, self-doubt, feelings that life was losing its 'provisional quality' and becoming more serious, and time pressure. Thus, the participants saw this as being the time for change, if change was needed. However, a minority of the participants experienced a 'smooth process of change', one which was crisis-free, satisfactory in terms of relationships with family and friends, and in which occupational pursuits progressed quickly.

The *settling down* (or *culminating life structure for early adulthood*: 33–40) phase represents consolidation of the second life structure. This involves a shift away from tentative choices regarding family and career towards a strong sense of commitment to a personal, familial and occupational future. A path for success in work and the roles of husband and father are mapped out and, instead of just beginning to find out what is important and what our opinions are, we see ourselves as responsible adults.

Levinson and his colleagues identify two sub-stages in the settling down stage. In the *early settling down* sub-stage (33–36), we try to establish a niche in society by 'digging in' and 'building a nest'. This contributes to the stability of a defined structure. In the *becoming one's own man* or *BOOM* sub-stage (36–40), we strive to advance and succeed in building a better life, improve and use our skills, be creative, and in general contribute to society. We want recognition and affirmation from society, but we also want to be self-sufficient and free of social pressure and control. Although a 'boy-man' conflict may be produced, this can represent a step forward. This sub-stage may also see us assume a *mentor role* for someone younger (see above).

THE ERA OF MIDDLE ADULTHOOD

The *mid-life transition* (40–45) involves terminating one life structure, initiating another, and continuing the process of individuation that was started during the *BOOM* sub-stage. This is a time of soul-searching, questioning and assessing the real meaning of the life structure's achievement. It is sometimes referred to as the *mid-life crisis*, although this term was not actually used by Levinson and his colleagues. For some people, the change is gradual and fairly painless. For others, however, it is full of uncertainties. As Levinson and his colleagues (1978) remarked:

> 'They question nearly every aspect of their lives and feel that they cannot go on as before. They will need several years to form a new path or modify the old one'.

The age-50 mid-life crisis stems from unconscious tensions between attachment and separation, the resurfacing of the need to be creative (which is often repressed in order to achieve a career), and retrospective comparisons between our 'dreams' and life's reality.

Most of the participants in Levinson et al.'s study had not reached the age of 45. After follow-up interviews two years after the study was concluded, some were chosen for more extensive study. However, the evidence for the remaining phases is much less detailed than that for the earlier ones. We shall therefore confine our consideration to the first structure-building phase of middle adulthood.

In *entering middle adulthood* (or *early life structure for middle adulthood*: 45–50), we have resolved (in a more-or-less satisfactory way) whether what we have committed ourselves to really is worthwhile, and we must again make choices regarding a new life structure. Sometimes these choices are defined by *marker events* such as divorce, illness, occupational change, or the death of a loved one. However, the choices may also be influenced by less obvious but significant changes such as shifts in the enthusiasm for work or in the quality of marriage. As before, the resulting life structure varies in how satisfying it is and how connected it is to the self. It may not be intrinsically happy and fulfilling. The restructuring consists of many steps and there may be setbacks in which options have to be abandoned (and we 'go back to the drawing board').

THE VALIDITY OF THE 'MID-LIFE CRISIS'

In the same way that the 'identity crisis' is part of the popular stereotype of adolescence, Levinson and his colleagues have helped to make the 'mid-life crisis' part of our common-sense understanding of adult development. Like Erikson, Levinson and his colleagues see crisis as *inevitable*. As they note:

> 'It is not possible to get through middle adulthood without having at least a moderate crisis in either the mid-life transition or the age-50 transition'.

They also see crisis as *necessary*. If we do not engage in soul searching, we will:

> 'pay the price in a later developmental crisis or in a progressive withering of the self and a life structure minimally connected to the self'.

The view that crisis is both inevitable and necessary (or *normative* to use Erikson's term) is controversial. All

Figure 11.3 The image of an older man's attraction to younger women is part of the popular concept of the 'mid-life crisis'. It is portrayed here by Woody Allen and Juliette Lewis in *Husbands and Wives*

people of all ages suffer occasional depression, self-doubt, sexual uncertainty and concerns about the future. Indeed, there appears to be an increasingly wide age range (and a growing number) of people who decide to make radical changes in their life-style, both earlier and later than predicted by Levinson et al.'s theory. Box 11.2 illustrates this.

Box 11.2 'Downshifting'

According to Tredre (1996), the concept of a mid-life crisis is too narrow in that traditionally, or stereotypically, it refers to someone in his or her late 40s, with grown-up children, who gives up a secure and well-paid 'respectable' career, and moves to a small market town or village in order to enjoy a less stressful, more peaceful and generally better quality of life. Tredre argues that we need to spread the net wider nowadays and think in terms of early-, mid- and late-life crises: people of all age groups and walks of life are 'feeling the itch'.

Downshifting refers to voluntarily opting out of a pressurised career and interminably long hours in the office, and often involves giving up an exceptionally well-paid job in a high-profile industry in the pursuit of a more fulfilling way of life. Tredre identifies a number of possible reasons for downshifting, including anti-urbanism (fuelled by concerns over urban pollution), crime and violence, and increasing job insecurity.

Penny Collie, 45, from London, was a high-flying executive, co-owner of a remainder book company, and a devotee of designer clothes and smart restaurants. In January 1996, however, after a long period of depression and frustration, she traded in her BMW for a Peugot 205 and resolved to make do on £10,000 a year. Although she has yet to decide exactly how she wants to lead her life, and faces the future with some unease, she believes she has made the right decision for her own peace of mind.

Consistent with the findings shown in Box 11.2, Durkin (1995) notes that a large proportion of middle-aged people actually feel *more* positive about this phase of life than earlier ones, with only 10 per cent reporting feeling as though they had experienced a crisis. For Durkin, the mid-life crisis is not as universal as Levinson and his colleagues suggest, and the time and extent to which we experience uncomfortable self-assessments are subject to variability as a function of

Figure 11.4 A dramatic illustration of 'downshifting'

several factors (such as our own personality). Although the evidence is sparse, Rutter and Rutter (1992) suggest that going through middle age in a relatively peaceful and untroubled way is actually a *favourable* indicator of future development, that is, a *lack* of emotional disturbance predicts better rather than poorer functioning in later life.

Two other components of the mid-life crisis are much less contentious. The first is a wide range of adaptations in the life pattern. Some of these stem from role changes that produce fairly drastic consequences, such as divorce, remarriage, a major occupational change, redundancy or serious illness. Others are more subtle, and include the ageing and likely death of parents, the new role of grandparent, and the sense of loss which sometimes occurs when all of the children have moved away from the family home (*empty-nest distress* – see Chapter 12, page 150). The impact of some of these life or marker events will be discussed in detail in the following chapter.

The second component of the mid-life crisis is the significant change in the *internal* aspects of our life structure which occurs regardless of external events. This involves reappraising our achievements and remaining ambitions, especially those to do with work and the relationship with our sexual partner. A fundamental development at this time is our realisation that the final authority for life rests with us. This relates to another theory of development in adulthood, advanced by Gould (1978, 1980), which is described later on in this chapter. Some writers (e.g. Sheehy, 1976) have suggested that men in their 40s begin to explore and develop their more 'feminine' selves (by becoming more nurturant, affiliative and intimate). Women, by contrast, discover their more 'masculine' selves (by becoming more action-oriented, assertive, and ambitious). The passing-by in *opposite directions* produces the pain and distress which is the 'mid-life crisis'. It has, however, been argued that the mid-life crisis is not a stage through which everyone *must* pass. Hopson and Scally (1980), for example, believe that the mid-life crisis can come from a number of sources, including the ineffective adjustment to the normal stresses of growth and transition in middle-age and the reaction of a particularly vulnerable person to these stresses. Since adult experience is diverse, researchers such as Hopson and Scally feel that terms like 'stages' and 'seasons' are inappropriate, and that *themes* is, perhaps, a better term to use.

According to Bee and Mitchell (1980), there are a large number of stressful biological, social and psychological life changes that are likely to happen together in any society. As a result, most people will experience a transition or crisis at roughly the same time in their lifecycle. People will differ in terms of how much stress can be tolerated before a 'crisis' is experienced, and in the way in which they will respond to it when it does occur. Personal growth may be one response, and changing the major 'external' aspects of our lives (by, for example, changing jobs, getting divorced and so on) another.

THE SEASONS OF A WOMAN'S LIFE

Although we have used the words 'our' and 'ourselves' as we outlined Levinson and his colleagues' theory, it should be noted that the research was carried out on men and *no* women were included in the sample. Similar research investigating women has found similarities with the findings reported by Levinson and his colleagues. However, men and women have been shown to differ in terms of their *dreams*. Levinson argues that a 'gender-splitting' phenomenon occurs in adult development. Men have a fairly unified vision of their future which tends to be focused on a career. Women, however, have 'dreams' which are more likely to be split between a career and marriage. This was certainly true of academics and business women, although the former were less ambitious and more likely to forego a career whereas the latter wanted to maintain their careers but at a reduced level. Only the *homemakers* had a unified dream, which was to be full-time wives and mothers (as their own mothers had been). Roberts and Newton (1987) saw the family as playing a 'supportive' role for men. Women's dreams were constructed around their relationship with the husband and family which subordinated their personal needs. So, part of *her* dream is *his* success. For Durkin (1995), this difference in women's and men's priorities may put women at greater risk:

> 'of disappointment and developmental tension as their investment in others' goals conflict with their personal needs'.

The age-30 transition is as important for women as men. The evidence suggests that women who give marriage and motherhood top priority in their 20s tend to develop more individualistic goals for their 30s. However, those who are career-oriented early on in adulthood tend to focus on marriage and family con-

Figure 11.5 An illustration of 'gender splitting' in a woman's *dream* compared with the unified *dream* of a man

cerns. Generally, the transitory instability of the early 30s lasts longer for women than for men, and 'settling down' is much less clear cut. Trying to integrate career and marriage/family responsibilities is very difficult for most women, who experience greater conflicts than their husbands are likely to do. A summary of research into the pattern of career development in women can be found in Gross (1996).

The validity of stage theories as explanations of adult development

As we have seen, Erikson's and Levinson's theories of adult development, and the personality changes that take place in adulthood, emphasise a 'ladder-like' progression through an inevitable and universal series of stages. Figure 11.6 (overleaf) shows a comparison of the developmental paths that Erikson and Levinson suggest everyone takes. The view that adult development is 'stage-like' has, however, been criticised (e.g. Rutter and Rutter, 1992) on the grounds that it underestimates the degree of *individual variability*. According to Craig (1992), many of the mainstream working-class population do *not* grow or change in systematic ways. Instead, they show many rapid fluctuations depending on things like a person's relationships, work demands and other life stresses that were taking place.

Stage theories also imply a *discontinuity* of development. However, for many psychologists there is also considerable *continuity* of personality during adult life. As Hopson and Scally (1980) have remarked, the popular stereotype sees middle adulthood as the time when a person is responsible, settled, contented and at the peak of achievement. People who find that they do not conform to this stereotype tend to blame themselves rather than seeing the stereotype as being wrong. Schlossberg et al. (1978) have suggested that we use some sort of *social clock* to judge whether we are 'on time' with respect to particular life events (such as getting married). If we are 'off time', either early or late, then we are *age deviant*. Like other types of deviancy, this can result in social penalties, such as amusement, pity or rejection.

Craig (1992) sees changes in adult thought, behaviour and personality as being less a result of chronological age or specific biological changes and more a result of personal, social and cultural events or forces. Because of the sheer diversity of experiences in an adult's life, Craig does not believe it is possible to describe major 'milestones' that will apply to nearly everyone. As Pearlin (1980) has put it:

> 'the variety is as rich as the historic conditions people have faced and the current circumstances they experience'.

Gould's theory of the evolution of adult consciousness

Whereas Levinson and his colleagues discussed adult development in terms of evolving life structures, Gould (1978, 1980) prefers to talk about the evolution of adult consciousness which occurs when 'we release ourselves from the constraints and ties of childhood

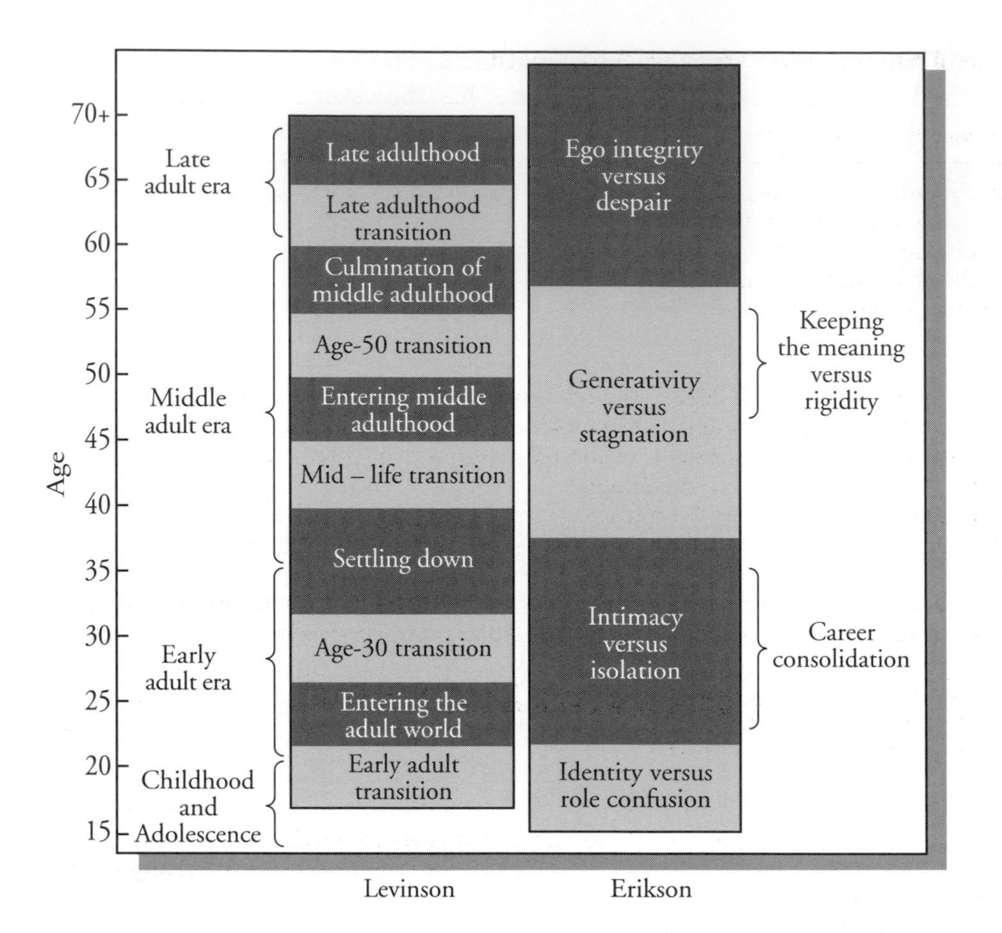

Figure 11.6 A comparison of Levinson et al.'s and Erikson's adult stages. Note how the former's are defined primarily by age and the latter's by crisis (from Santrock, 1986)

consciousness'. Gould sees the thrust of adult development as being towards the realisation and acceptance of ourselves as creators of our own lives, and away from the assumption that the rules and standards of childhood determine our destiny. Gould's theory is an extension of the Freudian idea of *separation anxiety*. According to Gould, we have to free ourselves of what he terms the *illusion of absolute safety*, an illusion which dominated our childhood. This involves *transformations*, that is, giving up the security of the past to form our own ideas. Gould argues that we have to replace the concept of parental dependency with a sense of *autonomy*, or owning ourselves. This, however, is no straightforward task because parental dependency and other beliefs are a normal feature of childhood. Indeed, without them childhood would be very difficult.

According to Gould we must give up the beliefs and assumptions we have about the self and the world if we are to grow up. Table 11.1 illustrates the major false assumptions and beliefs identified by Gould and the ages at which they are addressed.

As well as shedding childhood consciousness, Gould believes that our *sense of time* also changes. Up until the age of 18 or so, we feel both protected and constrained by our parents, and never quite believe that we will escape the 'family world'. Gould sees this as like being in a timeless capsule in which 'the future is a fantasy space that may possibly not exist'. However, we begin to glimpse an endless future and see an infinite amount of time ahead of us *provided* we are not suddenly snatched back into the restricted world of childhood.

In our 20s, we become confident about being separated from the family. However, to use Levinson's term, we have not yet formed an early-adult life structure. Gould (1980) puts it like this:

> 'Because of all the new decisions and novel experiences that come with setting up new adult enterprises, our time sense, when we're being successful, is one of movement along a chosen path that leads linearly to some obscure prize decades in the future. There is plenty of time, but we're still in a hurry once we've developed a clearer, often stereotyped, picture of where we want to be by then'.

Table 11.1 The major false beliefs and assumptions identified by Gould

AGE	FALSE ASSUMPTIONS AND THEIR COMPONENT PARTS
Late teens, early 20s	I will always belong to my parents and believe in their version of reality. (i) If I get any more independent, it'll be a disaster. (ii) I can only see the world through my parents' assumptions. (iii) Only they can guarantee my safety. (iv) They must be my only family. (v) I don't own my body.
20s. Apprenticeship period of life. We need to look outward and develop competency in roles outside the family	Doing it my own way with will power and perseverence will bring results, but when I am frustrated, confused, tired or unable, they will step in and show me the way. (i) Rewards will come automatically if we do what we are supposed to do. (ii) There is only one right way to do things. (iii) My loved ones are able to do for me what I haven't been able to do for myself. (iv) Rationality, commitment and effort will always prevail over all other forces.
Late 20s, early 30s. Return to inner selves, confronting parts suppressed. Disillusionment and confusion about what life is all about	Life is simple, not complicated. There are no significant unknown inner forces within me; there are no multiple coexisting, contradictory realities present in my life. (i) What I know intellectually, I know emotionally. (ii) I am not like my parents in ways I don't want to be. (iii) I can see the reality of those close to me quite clearly. (iv) Threats to my security aren't real.
35–50. Ending of illusion of absolute safety	There is no evil or death in the world. The demonic has been expelled. (i) My work (for men) or my relationship with men (for women) grant me immunity from death and anger. (ii) There is no life beyond the family. (iii) I am innocent.

(taken from Gross, 1992, and based on Sugarman, 1986, and Hayslip and Panek, 1989)

At the end of our 20s, our sense of time incorporates our adult past as well as future. The future is neither infinite nor linear, and we must choose between different options because there isn't time to take them all. From our mid-30s to mid-40s, we develop a sense of urgency that time is running out. We also have an awareness of our own mortality which, when attained, is never far from our consciousness. How we spend our time becomes a matter of great importance. Additionally, we begin to question whether our 'prize' (freedom from restrictions by those who have formed us – our parents) either exists or, if it does, whether it has been worth it (an idea similar to Levinson et al.'s 'dream').

Conclusions

This chapter has considered several theories that have been advanced to explain personality change in early and middle adulthood. The stage theory approach to adult development has been popular, although critics of it argue that such development does not occur in predictable and ordered ways. The debate over whether personality development in adulthood is characterised by stability or change has yet to be resolved, and if we are going to understand the complexity of development in adulthood, considerably more research is required.

Summary

- Until recently, psychologists showed little research interest in adulthood, the longest phase of the life-cycle. Early and young adulthood covers the years 20 to 40, while middle adulthood spans the years 40 to 60 or 65.
- In Erikson's psychosocial theory, early and young adulthood involves the establishment of **intimacy**, which is a criterion of having attained the psychosocial state of adulthood. **Identity** is a prerequisite for intimacy.
- Intimacy can be achieved through friendship as well as through a sexual relationship; identity becomes fully realised and consolidated through sharing oneself with another. Failure to achieve intimacy results in a sense of **isolation**, a sense of being alone without anyone to share with or care for.
- The central task of middle adulthood is the attainment of **generativity**. This is not confined to parents, but is shown by anyone actively concerned with making the world a better place for young people to live and work in.
- People who successfully achieve generativity establish clear guidelines for their lives and are usually productive and happy within this **directive framework**. Failure to achieve generativity results in **stagnation**, a preoccupation with one's personal needs and comforts.
- The sequence from identity to intimacy may no longer accurately reflect patterns of relationships, with adults tending to live together before marrying, so marrying later in life. Many people struggle with issues of identity **at the same time** as intimacy issues are being dealt with. There is additional evidence that females achieve intimacy **before** 'occupational identity'. According to Sangiuliano, most women submerge their identity into that of their partners and only search for a separate identity in mid-life.
- There is evidence that working-class men see early adulthood as a time for 'settling down', marriage, having a family and maintaining a steady job. By contrast, middle-class men and women see early adulthood as a time for exploration; marriage tends to occur later, and 'settling down' does not occur until after age 30.
- While Erikson's psychosocial stages were meant to be **universal**, he himself acknowledged that the sequence of stages is different for women, for whom identity and intimacy seem to be fused. The influence of both gender and social class suggests that it is almost impossible to describe universal stages of development for adults.
- According to Sheehy, while childhood is ending earlier, people, especially those from middle-class backgrounds, are prolonging their adolescence into their 30s.
- Levinson et al. were concerned with how adulthood is actually **experienced**. According to their **life-structure theory**, life structure evolves through a series of **phases** or **periods** which give overall shape to the course of adult development; these are either **stable** (**structure-building**) or **transitional** (**structure-changing**).
- Although each of the phases or periods involves biological, psychological and social adjustments, the family and work roles are seen as central to the life structure at any time.
- Adult development consists of a sequence of **eras**: pre-adulthood (0–22), early adulthood (17–45), middle adulthood (40–65) and late adulthood (60 onwards). These overlap in the form of **cross-era transitions**, each lasting about five years.
- **Early adult transition** (17–22) is a developmental bridge between adolescence and adulthood. It involves **separation**, which is both **external** and **internal**. It also involves **attachment** to the adult world.
- **Entry life structure for early adulthood** (22–28) is the first **structure-building** phase. In the **novice phase**, we try to define ourselves as adults in terms of job, relationships, lifestyles and values, but need to keep a balance between 'keeping our options open' and 'putting down roots'. Our choices are made in the context of our **dreams**, and we look to **mentors** to help us in the task of self-definition and definition of our dreams.
- The **age-30 transition** (28–33) provides an opportunity to correct the limitations of the first life structure and to create the basis for a more satisfactory one that will complete the era of young adulthood. Although most of Levinson et al.'s participants experienced an **age-30 crisis**, a minority experienced no crisis.
- The **culminating life structure for early adulthood/settling down** phase (33–40) represents a consolidation of the second life structure. Two sub-stages are **early settling down** (33–36) and **becoming one's own man** (**BOOM**) (36–40), which may involve a 'boy-man' conflict and the assumption of a **mentor role** for some younger adult.

- The **mid-life transition** (40–45) is a time of soul-searching, questioning and assessing the meaning of the life-structure achievement (**mid-life crisis**), one source of which is an unconscious tension between attachment and separation.
- In **early life structure for middle adulthood/ entering middle adulthood** (45–50), we must again make choices regarding a new life structure. These choices are sometimes defined by **marker events**, sometimes by changes in enthusiasm for work or the quality of marriage.
- Levinson et al. have helped to make the 'mid-life crisis' part of our common-sense understanding of adult development. They see crisis as both **inevitable** and **necessary** (i.e. **normative**).
- People of all ages suffer occasional depression, self-doubt, sexual uncertainty and concerns about the future. Indeed, there appears to be an increasingly wide age range and growing number of people who decide to make radical changes in their life-style (**downshifting**) both earlier and later than predicted by Levinson et al.
- According to Durkin, a large proportion of middle-aged people actually feel **more** positive about their life than earlier. The mid-life crisis is not as universal as Levinson et al. suggest; personality is one of several factors that can influence the time and extent of uncomfortable self-assessments. Rutter and Rutter believe that not experiencing mid-life crisis is a **favourable** indicator of future development.
- The mid-life crisis entails changes in the **internal** aspects of our life structure which occur regardless of external events: we reappraise our achievements and remaining ambitions and realise that the final authority for life rests with us. This relates to Gould's theory of adult development.
- One view of middle adulthood is that men begin to explore their more 'feminine' selves, while women discover their more 'masculine' selves. According to Sheehy, this passing-by in **opposite directions** produces the pain and distress of the mid-life crisis.
- The inevitability of the mid-life crisis has been questioned. For example, it may come from a variety of sources, including the ineffective adjustment of particularly vulnerable people to the normal stresses of growth and transition in middle-age. Hopson and Scally prefer **themes** to 'stages' or 'seasons', reflecting the diversity of adult experience.
- Research involving women has found similarities with Levinson et al.'s findings based on their all-male sample. However, there is a 'gender splitting' that occurs in relation to men's and women's **dreams**: men have a fairly unified, career-focused vision of their future, while women's dreams are split between career and marriage. Only **home-makers** have a unified dream.
- The age-30 transition generally lasts longer for women than for men, and 'settling down' is much less clear cut. Trying to integrate career and marriage and family responsibilities is very difficult for most women, who experience greater conflicts than do their husbands.
- The view that adult development is 'stage-like' has been criticised on the grounds that it underestimates **individual variability**. This may be related to social class, as shown by Fiske's findings that many mainstream working-class individuals do **not** develop systematically or in a 'ladder-like' progression.
- Stage theories also imply a **discontinuity** of development, while many psychologists stress the **continuity** of personality during adulthood. People who do not conform to the popular stereotype of middle adulthood tend to blame themselves; this relates to Schlossberg et al.'s concept of a **social clock** by which we judge whether we are 'on time' or **age deviant** with respect to particular life events.
- According to Craig, changes in adulthood are due more to personal, social and cultural events or forces than to chronological age or specific biological changes. The sheer diversity of adult experience makes it impossible to describe major 'milestones' that apply to everyone.
- According to Gould, the thrust of adult development is towards the realisation and acceptance of ourselves as creators of our own lives (adult consciousness), freeing ourselves of the **illusion of absolute safety**, along with other false assumptions, which dominated childhood consciousness. This involves difficult **transformations**, replacing the concept of parental dependency with a sense of **autonomy**.
- Gould also believes that adult development involves a change in our **sense of time**. By the end of our 20s, the future is seen as neither infinite nor linear, and we must make choices. From our mid-30s to mid-40s, we sense that time is running out and are aware of our mortality. We also begin to question whether freedom from our parents (our 'prize') exists or has been worth it.

THE IMPACT OF LIFE EVENTS IN ADULTHOOD

Introduction and overview

As we saw in the previous chapter (see page 139), the evidence concerning the predictability of changes in adult life (or what Levinson (1986) calls *psychobiosocial transitions*) is conflicting. According to Hetherington and Baltes (1988), there are three kinds of influence that can affect the way we develop in adulthood. So-called *normative age-graded influences* are those biological (such as the menopause) and social (such as marriage and retirement) changes that normally occur at fairly predictable ages. *Normative history-graded influences* are those historical events that affect whole generations or cohorts at about the same time (examples include wars, recessions and epidemics). *Non-normative influences* are those idiosyncratic transitions such as divorce, unemployment and illness.

Levinson (1986) has used the term *marker events* to refer to the age-graded and non-normative influences. Other researchers prefer the term *critical life events* to describe such influences (although we should note that it is perhaps more accurate to describe them as *processes* rather than events). Some of these life events tend to happen early in adulthood. Included here would be marriage and parenthood. Others occur much later in adulthood. Retirement, for example, can be seen as marking the entry into late adulthood. Yet others, such as bereavement and unemployment, can occur at any age. Studying the impact of events such as these is another way of looking at the ways in which we adjust to adulthood. Our aim in this chapter is to examine research findings concerning the impact of some of these life events.

Unemployment

Argyle (1989) has argued that unemployment produces both psychological and physical effects and that these take some time to emerge rather than occurring immediately after an individual has been made unemployed. One psychological effect is *depression*. As well as being more prevalent amongst the unemployed, the severity of the depression is strongly correlated with the *length* of unemployment. In the case of the long-term unemployed, a sense of *learned helplessness* (Seligman, 1975) develops. In this, the unemployed see themselves as being the main cause of their unemployment and think that nothing can be done to change the state of affairs. Along with other factors associated with unemployment, such as poverty and reduced social support, depression is one of the factors that contributes to *suicide*. Suicide is much more common among the unemployed than the employed.

Unemployment is also associated with a *loss of self-esteem* through ceasing to be the bread-winner and becoming a recipient of government benefits. The material hardships of low income bring a financial strain which is greatest when there are dependent children. Not surprisingly, financial problems are themselves a major source of emotional distress. Some other major sources of distress associated with unemployment are shown in Box 12.1.

Box 12.1 Some of the major sources of distress among the unemployed

Length of unemployment: The initial response to unemployment is *shock*, *anger* and *incomprehension*. This is followed by *optimism*, a feeling of being between jobs which is a kind of 'holiday' that is coupled with active job searching. As job searching fails, optimism is replaced by *pessimism*. Pessimism then gives way to *fatalism*, that is, hopelessness and apathy set in and job hunting is sometimes abandoned completely.

Commitment: Those who are most committed to their jobs are most distressed by unemployment.

This might explain why unemployment has a greater negative effect on middle-aged men than young people or married women (Warr, 1987).

Social support: The complex set of relationships we enjoy at work conveys identity and status which are both lost in unemployment. The unemployed typically withdraw from friendships, partly because they cannot afford to pay for drinks, entertainment and so on. Because the unemployed is a group to which a large number of people do not wish to belong, the bonds between the unemployed are weak. Social support, especially from the family, can act to 'buffer' these effects.

Level of activity: Those unemployed who have a structured or organised pattern of life (achieved by undertaking unpaid work, pursuing a hobby or keeping active in other ways) experience less distress than those who adapt by staying in bed, watching a lot of television and 'killing time'.

Perceived cause of unemployment: During periods of full employment, to be out of work was mainly due to personal incompetence. Being unemployed might be seen as a sign of failure. However, because unemployment is widespread and includes people from all sections of society, many of the unemployed feel less responsible for their plight and more accepting of it. For example, Warr (1984) has found that satisfaction with the self is greater among unemployed people when the local level of unemployment is high.

(as reported in Argyle, 1989)

Research into the links between mental health and unemployment is at least half a century old (see, for example, Beales and Lambert, 1934). As well as depression and a loss of self-esteem, mental states associated with unemployment include anxiety, negative affect, self-reported cognitive difficulties, worry about the future, demoralisation and resignation (Dooley and Prause, 1995). Fryer (1992, 1995) has reviewed the available evidence about the psychological effects of unemployment. Box 12.2 summarises Fryer's findings.

Box 12.2 Some of the effects of unemployment

- Unemployment *causes*, rather than results from, poor psychological health.
- The risk of a person's mental health deteriorating in at least some ways increases compared with an otherwise similar person who does not become unemployed.
- Unemployment puts at risk the mental health not only of unemployed people but also their spouses, children and members of the extended family.
- The implicit assumption that the transition from unemployment to re-employment is symmetrical to the transition from employment to unemployment is not fully warranted, since it is known that some of the effects of unemployment may persist into the period of re-employment.
- The anticipation of unemployment is at least as distressing as the experience of unemployment itself.
- Job insecurity is associated with experienced powerlessness and impaired mental health.
- Indicators of psychological stress are associated with measures of both subjective and objective financial stress.

(based on Fryer, 1992, 1995)

Although it is clear that unemployment is associated with impaired mental health, Argyle's claim that physical health suffers as a result of unemployment is not as strongly supported by the evidence. For example, a survey conducted by Warr (1984) showed that whilst 27 per cent of unemployed men said that their physical health had deteriorated, 11 per cent reported that it had *improved*, an improvement which was said to be due to less work strain and more relaxation and exercise. However, the negative effects that unemployment can have on physical health have been clearly illustrated by Moser et al. (1984). In a ten-year census study of British men who had lost their jobs in 1971, Moser et al. showed that the death rate was 36 per cent higher than for the whole population of males aged between 15 and 64. When social class and age were taken into account, the figure was 21 per cent. The data also indicated that the wives of unemployed men were 20 per cent more likely to die prematurely, a risk that was greater in the second half of the decade in which the study was conducted (cf. Fryer, 1992, 1995: see above).

Retirement

Unlike unemployment, which is a sudden and generally unanticipated loss of work, retirement is an anticipated loss of work which many of us experience without undue psychological upheaval (Raphael, 1984). For most of us, retirement is inevitable and often acceptable. However, it may be unacceptable to people when, for example, they see themselves as being 'too young' to stop work.

One consequence of retirement is the loss of everyday, ritualised patterns of behaviour which contribute to the very fabric of our existence. Whilst the early weeks of retirement may be celebrated, emptiness is experienced for a while following retirement. As the months go by, frustration and a sense of 'uselessness' set in and this may produce an angry and irritable response to the world (TV's Victor Meldrew might, perhaps, be a good illustration of this).

Figure 12.1 Victor Meldrew (star of BBC TV's *One Foot in the Grave*) seems to personify the sense of frustration and uselessness that often sets in, especially for men, after the 'honeymoon period' of retirement

Retirement also leads to change. For example, many couples must find themselves spending an increased amount of time together. Some people compound the negative aspects of retirement by moving to a new house, which involves loss of familiar surroundings, friendships and neighbourhood network. The transition from an economically productive role to one which is unproductive can also be a source of stress. All of these factors mean that psychological adjustment to retirement is necessary, and those who are able to develop a lifestyle that retains continuity with the past, and meets their long-term needs, adjust well.

According to Atchley (1982, 1985), retirement is a *process* and *social role* which unfolds through a series of six phases, each of which requires an adjustment to be made. The phases do not correspond with any particular chronological ages, occur in no fixed order, and not all of them are necessarily experienced by everyone. Atchley's six phases are shown in Box 12.3.

Box 12.3 The six phases in the process of retirement

1. **Pre-retirement phase:** (i) In the remote sub-phase, retirement is seen as in a reasonably distant future; (ii) the near sub-phase may be initiated by the retirement of older friends and colleagues and there may be much anxiety about how lifestyle will change, especially financially.
2. **Honeymoon phase** (immediate post-retirement): Typical euphoria, partly due to new-found freedom, often a busy period (which may be long or short).
3. **Disenchantment phase:** Involves a slowing down after the honeymoon phase, feelings of being let down and even depressed. The degree of disenchantment is related to declining health and finances. Eagerly anticipated post-retirement activities (e.g. travel) may have lost their original appeal. Disenchantment may be produced by unrealistic pre-retirement fantasies or inadequate anticipatory socialisation (i.e. preparation for retirement).
4. **Reorientation phase:** Time to develop a more realistic view of life alternatives. May involve exploring new avenues of involve-

ment, sometimes with the help of community groups (e.g. special voluntary or paid jobs for the retired); this helps to decrease feelings of role loss and is a means of achieving self-actualisation.

5 **Stability phase:** Involves the establishment of criteria for making choices, allowing the individual to deal with life in a fairly comfortable and orderly way. They know what's expected of them, what their strengths and weaknesses are, allowing mastery of the retirement role.

6 **Termination phase:** Usually illness and disability make housework and self-care difficult or impossible, leading to the assumption of a sick or disabled (as opposed to retirement) role.

(taken from Gross, 1996, and based on Atchley, 1982, and Atchley and Robinson, 1982)

People who retire *voluntarily* seem to have little or no difficulty in adjusting to retirement. However, those who retire because they have reached a compulsory age tend to be dissatisfied at first, although eventually they adapt. The least satisfied are those whose health is poor when they retire (and their poor health may even have caused their retirement), although it should be noted that health often improves following retirement.

Bromley (1988) believes that it is the transition between employment and retirement that causes adjustment problems. Those who are most satisfied in retirement tend to be scientists, writers and other academics, who simply carry on working with very little loss of continuity from very satisfying jobs. Those who discover satisfying leisure activities, which have at least some of the characteristics of work, also adjust well.

Some people decide to retire before their job requires them to. This means that retirement cannot be seen as a necessarily sudden and enforced dislocation of a working life, which inevitably causes feelings of rejection and leads to physical and psychological ill health. Even after 60 or 65, many people do not actively seek paid work, although the lower level of income in retirement constitutes a strong incentive to work. As far as women are concerned, as well as adjusting to their own retirement, they may also have to adjust to their husband's retirement or to widowhood. However, since home and family still occupy a major part of a working woman's time, it is possible they see retirement as less of a change in lifestyle than do men.

Figure 12.2 Marriage represents a very different type of major transition, depending, among other things, upon cultural background. The wedding ceremony shown here is the culmination of detailed and prolonged planning by the bride and groom's families, with the couple themselves having little choice or control

Clearly, retirement and unemployment are similar in some respects and different in others. According to Campbell (1981), retirement is an accepted and 'honourable' social status whereas unemployment is not. Moreover, retirement is seen as a proper reward for a hard life's work, whilst unemployment has the implication of failure, being unwanted and a 'scrounger' who is 'living on state charity'. Most men might see retirement as a rather benign condition of life, but being unemployed is a disturbing and often degrading experience.

Marriage and divorce

Since over 90 per cent of adults marry at least once, marriage is an example of a normative age-graded influence (see page 144). Marriage is an important transition for many young adults because it involves a lasting personal commitment to another person, financial responsibilities and, perhaps, family responsibilities. However, it cannot be the *same* type of transition for everyone. In some cultures, for example, people have little choice as to who their partner will be (as is the case in *arranged marriages*).

Marriage and preparation for marriage can be very stressful. In an early study, Davies (1956) identified psychological disorders occurring for the first time in those who were engaged to be married. Typically, these were anxiety and depression, which usually began in connection with an event that hinged on the marriage date (such as booking the reception). Since the disorders improved when the engagement was broken off or the marriage took place, Davies concluded that it was the *decision* to make the commitment that was important rather than the act of getting married itself.

Although there has been little systematic research, it seems that couples who live together (or *cohabit*) before marriage are actually *more* likely to divorce later, and be less satisfied with their marriage, than those who marry without having cohabitated. Also, about 40 per cent of couples who cohabit do not marry, a figure which is higher as compared with previous generations. Whilst this suggests that cohabitation may prevent some divorces, we should remember that cohabitees who do marry are more likely to divorce. Why is this? Bee (1994) argues that this is because people who choose to cohabit are *different* from those who choose not to. As a group, cohabitees seem to be more willing to flout tradition in many ways (such as being less religious and disagreeing that one should stay with a marriage partner no matter what). Those who do not cohabit include a large proportion of 'more traditional' people. The growing trend towards living together, without getting married, is shown in Figure 12.3.

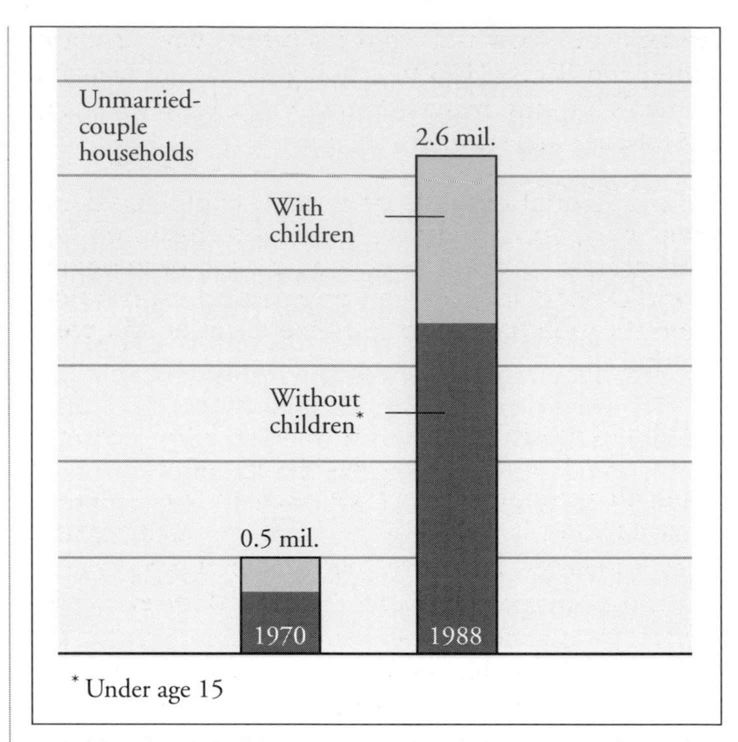

Figure 12.3 The growing trend towards living together, without getting married, both with and without children. The data are based on the US Census Bureau, which defines cohabitation as sharing the same residence (from *Newsweek*, 1990)

The view that mortality is affected by marital status was advanced as long ago as 1885 by William Farr, Superintendent of the Statistical Department of the Registrar General's Office for England (Cramer, 1995). Using the 1851 mortality rates for single, married and widowed women, Farr concluded that: 'Marriage is a healthy state. The single individual is more likely to be wrecked on his voyage than the lives joined together in matrimony' (reported in Humphreys, 1975). Farr also observed that the difference between the single and the married was more striking for men than for women. Contemporary research has generally confirmed Farr's conclusions. For example, Hu and Goldman (1990) have found that married people tend to live longer than unmarried people, and Cramer (1994) has shown that married people are happier, healthier and have lower rates of various mental disorders than the single, widowed or divorced. The excessive mortality of the unmarried relative to the married has generally been increasing over the past two to three decades, and it seems that divorced (and widowed) people in their 20s and 30s have particularly high risks of dying compared to people of the same age (Cramer, 1995). According to Eysenck and Wakefield (1981), measures of marital adjustment indicate that agreement between partners on various issues (a measure of marital compatibility) is positively correlated with other components of relationship adjustment such as satisfaction, affection and doing various activities together.

Bee (1994) has argued that the greatest beneficiaries of marriage are men, partly because they are less likely than women to have close confidants outside marriage and partly because wives provide more emotional warmth and support for husbands than husbands do for wives. Marriage is less obviously psychologically protective for women, not because a close, confiding and harmonious relationship is any less important for them (indeed, if anything it is more important), but because (a) many marriages do not provide such a relationship and (b) other consequences of marriage are different between the sexes. Although our attitudes towards education and women's careers have changed, Rutter and Rutter (1992), echoing the idea of men and women's 'dreams' being different (see Chapter 11, page 138), have proposed that:

> 'the potential benefits of a harmonious relationship may, for a woman, be counterbalanced by the stresses involved in giving up a job or in being handicapped in a career progression or promotion through having to combine a career and parenthood'.

According to Turnbull (1995), divorce rates are highest during the first five years of marriage and then peak again after couples have been married for 15 to 25 years. Divorce is a stressor for both men and women, since it involves the loss of one's major attachment figure and source of emotional support. However, men appear to experience more stress than women. We should also note that various studies have shown that divorce can have serious effects on the psychological adjustment of those children whose parents are separating (see, for example, Amato, 1993; Cockett and Tripp, 1994; Richards, 1995: see Chapter 2).

Duck (1988) has identified a number of antecedents of divorce and marital unhappiness. One of these is *age*. Marriages in which the partners are younger than usual tend to be unstable. Marriages also tend to be less stable when couples are from *lower socio-economic groups* and have *lower educational levels*. This is also true for marriages between partners of *different demographic backgrounds* (race, religion and so on). Finally, marriages tend to be more unstable between people who have experienced *parental divorce* or have had a *wider variety of sexual experiences/partners* than average before marriage. Relationships are, of course, highly complex and it is important to remember that these factors on their own cannot completely explain why marriage break-ups occur (Duck, 1995).

As we noted in Chapter 2 (see page 18), there is emerging evidence to suggest that divorce can *benefit* both children and their mothers. According to Woollett and Fuller (cited in Cooper, 1996b), mothers who have been through a divorce often report experiencing a sense of achievement in their day-to-day activities and a feeling of 'a job well done'. This is because they use their experiences of divorce in a positive way to 'galvanise' them into taking charge of their lives. According to Woollett:

> 'when the marriage breaks down, the mother is thrown into all sorts of things that are unfamiliar. There are new areas, new decisions, and she is forced to cope'.

Things like getting the car repaired at a garage may sound trivial, but can fill mothers with a sense of self-confidence. Charlie Lewis at the University of Lancaster (cited in Cooper, 1996b) has suggested that the findings from research such as Woollett and Fuller's be treated with caution. Lewis argues that:

> 'we must be careful about thinking about the positive changes (divorced women report) because we are always comparing a positive change against the negative feeling that went before. The positive is only relative'.

Parenthood

For most people, parenthood and child-rearing represent key transitions. According to Bee (1994), 90 per cent of adults will become parents, and most will be in their 20s and 30s when they do so. Parenthood, however, varies in meaning and impact more than any other life transition. It may occur at any time from adolescence to middle age, and in the case of some men, may even occur in late adulthood! Parenthood may also be planned or unplanned, wanted or unwanted, and there may be many motives for having children.

Traditionally, parenthood is the domain of the married couple. However, it may involve a single woman, a homosexual couple, a cohabiting couple or couples who adopt or foster children. Since the 1950s, there has been a greater acceptability of sexuality among young people, and this has been accompanied by a marked rise in the number of teenage pregnancies. Equally, though, the increasing importance of work careers for women has also led to more and more couples postponing starting a family so that the woman can become better established in her career. As a result of this, there is a new class of middle-aged parents with young children (Turnbull, 1995).

Parenthood brings with it a number of psychological adaptations. For example, many women worry that their babies may be abnormal. They also worry about the changes in their bodies and how they will cope with parenthood. Another concern is the way in which the relationship with the husband or partner will be

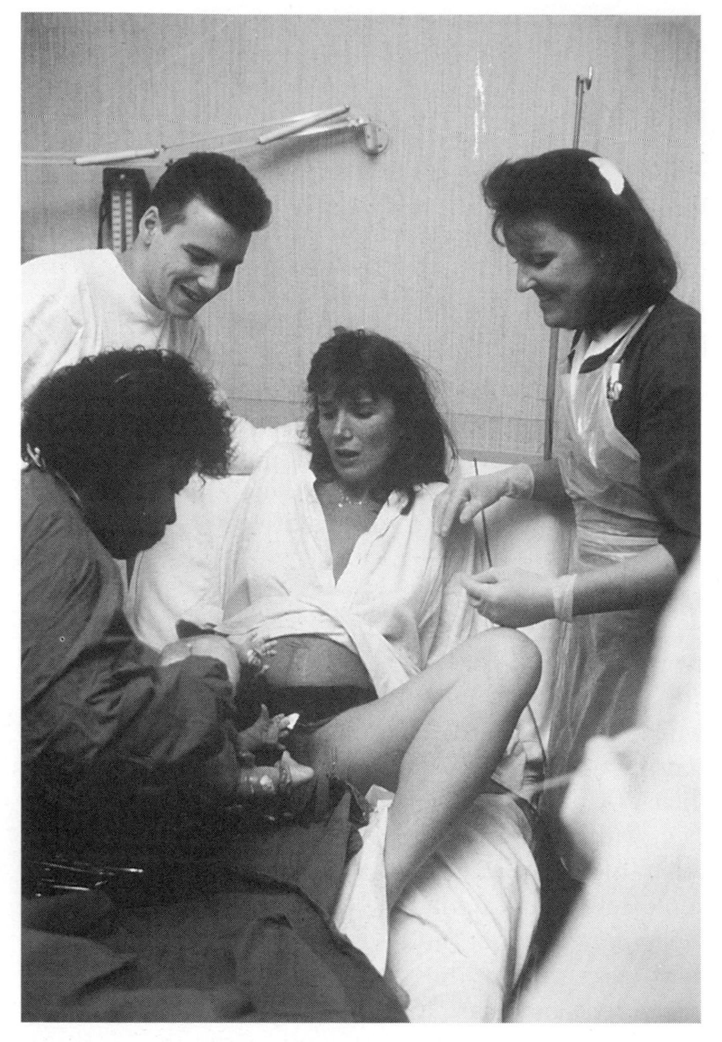

Figure 12.4 Being at the birth of his child can help to counteract a father's feelings of being excluded during the pregnancy – and afterwards. It can also help him to form an emotional bond with the baby

affected. Certainly, pregnancy brings many couples closer together, but most men take longer than women to become emotionally involved in the pregnancy, and some men feel left out. This feeling of exclusion may continue after the baby has been born, as the mother becomes preoccupied with it. If the father does not wish, or is unable, to share in this, the baby may pull the parents further apart. Marital satisfaction tends to be highest before children arrive. It then drops and remains relatively low as long as there are dependent children in the home. Finally, it rises again during the 'post-parental' and retirement stages. For new parents, the roles of parent and spouse are at least partially incompatible. Bee (1994) found that new parents report they have less time for each other, whether it be conversing, having sex, being affectionate or carrying out routine chores that used to be done together.

Parents are, of course, attachment figures for their dependent children. Unlike the relationship with a partner, the relationship with a child is *asymmetrical*. As Durkin (1995) has noted, this new form of responsibility can be very stressful and has implications for how parents adapt to these new role demands and the quality of their interactions with the child. Unhappy couples sometimes stay together not 'just for the kids' sake', but because the parental role has sufficient meaning and value for each partner to outweigh the dissatisfaction with their marriage (Levinson et al., 1978).

In Chapter 11 (see page 138), we mentioned *empty-nest distress*. The evidence (Durkin, 1995) suggests that most parents do not find their children's departure from home a distressing time. Indeed, many report that the end of child-rearing responsibilities is a 'liberating experience', and they welcome new opportunities for a closer relationship with their partner, personal fulfilment through work, a return to education and so on. Durkin (1995) has proposed that the extent to which women report empty-nest distress may be cohort-related, that is, it may be more typical of women who reached maturity during historical periods when traditional roles were stressed. The *crowded nest* (Datan et al., 1987) can, however, be a source of stress. This occurs when grown-up children opt *not* to leave home, which defies the demands of the 'social clock' established by preceding generations. Parents find it difficult to adjust to 'adult children' living at home, especially if the parents themselves are still doing much of the material providing.

Bereavement

As we saw in Chapter 11, the older we become, the more likely it is that we will suffer the loss, through death, of loved ones, parents, husbands or wives, siblings, friends and even our children. We refer to such losses as *bereavement*. The psychological and bodily reactions that occur in people who suffer bereavement are termed *grief*. What Parkes and Weiss (1983) have termed the 'observable expression of grief' is called *mourning*, although mourning is often used to refer to the social conventions surrounding death such as funerals, wearing dark clothes and so on.

There appear to be characteristic stages or phases of the

grieving process. Engel (1962) sees *griefwork*, that is, the process of mourning through which a bereaved person adjusts to a loss, as being comprised of three stages. These are shown in Box 12.4.

Box 12.4 The three phases of 'griefwork'

1 **Disbelief and shock:** This phase can last for a few days and involves the refusal to accept the truth of what has happened.
2 **Developing awareness:** This is the gradual realisation and acknowledgement of what has happened. This phase is often accompanied by feelings of guilt, apathy, exhaustion and anger.
3 **Resolution:** In this phase, the bereaved individual views the situation realistically, begins to cope without the deceased, establishes a new identity and comes to accept fully what has happened. This phase marks the completion of 'griefwork'.

(based on Engel, 1962)

Although researchers differ in terms of what the components of the stages or phases of the grieving process are, they all agree that grief must follow some sort of natural progression which must be experienced if healthy adjustment to the loss is to be achieved. However, instead of stages or phases, some researchers prefer to talk about the *components* of grief. Ramsay and de Groot (1977), for example, have identified nine components, some of which occur early and some late in the grieving process. These are shown in Box 12.5.

Box 12.5 Ramsay and de Groot's nine components of grief

1 **Shock:** Usually the first response, most often described as a feeling of 'numbness'. Can also include pain, calm, apathy, depersonalisation and derealisation. It is as if the feelings are so strong that they are 'turned off'; can last from a few seconds to several weeks.
2 **Disorganisation:** The inability to do the simplest thing or, alternatively, organising the entire funeral and then collapsing.
3 **Denial:** Behaving as if the deceased were still alive, a defence against feeling too much pain, usually an early feature of grief but one that can recur any time. A common form of denial is searching behaviour, e.g. waiting for the deceased to come home, or having hallucinations of them.
4 **Depression:** Emerges as the denial breaks down but can occur, usually less frequently and intensely, at any point during the grieving process. Either 'desolate pining' (a yearning and longing, an emptiness 'interspersed with waves of intense psychic pain') or 'despair' (feeling of helplessness, the blackness of the realisation of powerlessness to bring back the dead).
5 **Guilt:** Can be both real and imagined, for actual neglect of the deceased when they were alive or for angry thoughts and feelings.
6 **Anxiety:** Fear of losing control of one's feelings, of going mad or more general apprehension about the future (changed roles, increased responsibilities, financial worries, etc.).
7 **Aggression:** Irritability towards family and friends, outbursts of anger towards God or fate, doctors and nurses, the clergy or even the person who has died.
8 **Resolution:** An emerging acceptance of the death, a 'taking leave of the dead and an acceptance that life must go on'.
9 **Reintegration:** Putting acceptance into practice by reorganising one's life in which the deceased has no place. (However, pining and despair, etc. may reappear on anniversaries, birthdays, etc.).

(taken from Gross, 1996)

Whether everyone experiences all of the components identified by Ramsay and de Groot is questionable, and there are wide individual differences in grieving patterns. As Stroebe et al. (1993) have noted, grief is not a simple, universal process through which we all go.

Distinguishing normal from pathological grief is difficult. Parkes and Weiss (1983) identify prolonged, incapacitating grief (or *chronic grief*) as the most common variant of the usual pattern of grieving. In addition to this, Hinton (1975) has identified three other abnormal patterns. The first is an exaggeration of the *numbness* associated with the shock of the loss. The second is the 'shading' of some of the more immediate responses into *neurotic forms of emotional distress.* These include fears of being alone, enclosed spaces, of one's own death, and feelings of depersonalisation (that is, a sense of being unreal or unfamiliar to oneself). The third pattern is the appearance of *physical symptoms*. Sometimes these accompany, and sometimes overshadow, the emotional disturbance. Such symptoms include fatigue, insomnia, loss of appetite and weight, headaches and palpitations.

According to Parkes (1964), widows consult GPs much more often than usual during the first six months of widowhood for both physical and psychological symptoms. According to Stroebe et al. (1993), both widows and widowers have a greater risk of suffering illness and dying following the death of a spouse than is the case for married people of a similar age. Parkes et al. (1969) see this risk as being largely confined to the first six months after the bereavement and identify *self-neglect*, *suicide* and *cardiac disease* (a 'broken heart') as the important factors. In the case of widowers, death sometimes occurs through a disease similar to that experienced by the wife.

Lieberman (1993) has criticised traditional measures used in bereavement research (which include the symptoms and variations of grief and social adjustment) for their underlying assumption that bereavement is a stressor that upsets a person's equilibrium and requires a return to a normal and balanced state. As Weiss (1993) has observed, recovery is not a simple 'return to baseline' level of functioning. Both Lieberman and Weiss see 'adaptation' to bereavement as being a better term to use than 'recovery' from bereavement. Whilst the majority of bereaved people do stop grieving intensely after a year or two, a minority continue to do so for longer, and aspects of grief may never end for some otherwise normally adjusted and bereaved individuals. For Stroebe et al. (1993):

> 'if there has been a strong attachment to a lost loved one, emotional involvement is likely to continue, even for a lifetime'.

We should also note that adjustment is more difficult when a death is 'off time', as is the case in sudden accidents (Lopata, 1988).

Most adolescents and young adults rarely think about their own death, since it is an event far removed in time. Barrow and Smith (1979) have suggested that some people even engage in an *illusion of immortality* and completely avoid confronting the fact that their own days are numbered. As people age, however, so their thoughts become increasingly preoccupied with death. Our attitude towards death is ambivalent: sometimes we shut it out and deny it, and sometimes we

Figure 12.5 Looking through old photographs represents a form of *reminiscing*, part of the *life review* in which the elderly person tries to come to terms with his/her death

desperately want to talk about it and share our fears of the unknown. Kübler-Ross (1969) uses the term *anticipatory grief* to describe how the terminally ill come to terms with their own understanding of imminent death. One common feature of this is *reminiscing*. This may be a valuable way of 'sorting out' the past and present (Butler, 1963). The recognition of impending death allows us to re-examine old conflicts, consider how we have treated others, and come to some conclusion about our lives. This *life review* may result in a new sense of accomplishment, satisfaction and peace (and corresponds to Erikson's *ego-integrity*: see Chapter 10, page 125).

Coming to terms with our own death is a crucial *task* of life which Peck (1968) calls *ego-transcendence* versus *ego-preoccupation*. We may review our lives privately (or internally) or we may share our memories and reflections with others. By helping us to organise a final perspective on our lives for ourselves, and leaving a record that will live on with others after we have died, sharing serves a double purpose.

Conclusions

A large number of marker events (or critical life events) or processes have been identified. These include unemployment, retirement, marriage, divorce, parenthood and bereavement. Psychological research has told us much about the effects of these and the ways in which they help us to understand adjustment to adulthood.

Summary

- There is conflicting evidence regarding the predictability of changes in adult life or **psychobiosocial transitions**. Hetherington and Baltes distinguish between **normative age-graded influences**, **normative history-graded influences** and **non-normative influences**.
- Age-graded and non-normative influences are also called **marker events** (Levinson) and **critical life events**. These include marriage and parenthood, which tend to happen early in adulthood, retirement, which marks the entry into late adulthood, and bereavement and unemployment, which can occur at any age. Studying the impact of these events is another way of looking at how we adjust to adulthood.
- According to Argyle, **unemployment** produces both physical and psychological effects, which occur some time after the individual has been made unemployed. Not only is depression more prevalent among the unemployed, but its severity is strongly correlated with the **length** of unemployment: the long-term unemployed seem to develop a sense of **learned helplessness**. Depression, along with poverty and reduced social support, contributes to **suicide**, which is far more common among the unemployed.
- Unemployment is also associated with a **loss of self-esteem**. The material hardships of low income produce financial strain, especially when there are dependent children, and this represents a source of emotional distress.
- Distress is increased amongst those most **committed** to their jobs, who lack **social support**, whose **level of activity** is low and who **perceive the cause of unemployment** as personal incompetence.
- The initial response to unemployment is **shock**, **anger** and **incomprehension**, followed by **optimism**. As job searching fails and the length of unemployment increases, **pessimism** takes over, giving way to **fatalism**.
- Unemployment can **cause** anxiety, negative affect, self-reported cognitive difficulties, worry about the future, demoralisation, resignation and powerlessness. The mental health of relatives of the unemployed person is also put at risk.
- Evidence for the detrimental effects of unemployment on physical health is more mixed than that for mental health. While Warr found some evidence of an **improvement** in physical health, Moser et al. found much higher death rates over a ten-year period among unemployed men compared with the general male population. Their wives were also more likely to die prematurely.
- Unlike unemployment, **retirement** is an inevitable, often acceptable, anticipated loss of work which many people experience without undue psychological upheaval. However, if we see ourselves as being 'too young' to stop work, retirement may be unacceptable. Following an initial celebration, emptiness, frustration and a sense of 'uselessness' gradually set in, which may produce an angry and irritable response to the world.
- According to Atchley, retirement is a **process** and **social role** which proceeds through six phases, each requiring a different adjustment: **pre-retirement phase**, **honeymoon phase**, **disenchantment phase**, **reorientation phase**, **stability phase** and **termination phase**. These are not related to chronological age, do not occur in a fixed order, and not everyone experiences all six phases.
- People who retire **voluntarily** have little or no difficulty in adjusting, compared with those who retire because they have reached retirement age (although they eventually adapt) or those whose health is poor (which might be the reason for retiring).
- According to Bromley, it is the transition between employment and retirement that causes adjustment problems. Academics, whose retirement is continuous with their jobs, and those who discover satisfying leisure activities, adjust best, along with those who choose early retirement.
- Women may have to adjust both to their own retirement and their husband's, or to widowhood. However, since home and family still occupy a major part of a working woman's time, she may see retirement as less of a change in lifestyle than does her husband.
- Compared with unemployment, retirement is an accepted and 'honourable' social status, a proper reward for a hard life's work.
- Over 90 per cent of adults marry at least once, making it a normative age-graded influence. The lasting personal commitment to another person, financial and, perhaps, family responsibilities represent an important transition, but it cannot be the same type of transition for everyone, as illustrated by **arranged marriages**.
- The evidence that exists suggests that couples who **cohabit** before marriage are **more** likely to

divorce later or be dissatisfied with their marriage than those who don't cohabit; they are also quite likely not to marry. The higher rate of divorce could reflect the more unconventional attitudes of cohabitees as a group compared with the 'more traditional' non-cohabitees.

- Not only do married people tend to live longer, they are also happier, healthier and have lower rates of mental disorder than unmarried people. The greater mortality of the unmarried has been increasing in recent decades, and divorced and widowed people in their 20s and 30s are particularly prone to dying.
- According to Bee, men benefit most from marriage, partly because they are less likely than women to have close confidants outside marriage, and partly because wives provide more emotional warmth and support for their husbands than vice versa.
- Despite the fact that a close, confiding and harmonious relationship is probably more important for women, they are less obviously psychologically protected by marriage than are men. Its potential benefits may be counterbalanced by the stresses involved in giving up career progression or promotion through having to combine a career and parenthood.
- Divorce rates peak during the first five years of marriage, then again after 15 to 25 years. Divorce is a stressor for both men and women, involving the loss of one's major attachment figure and source of emotional support; it can also seriously affect the psychological adjustment of the children involved.
- Marriages between **younger-than-usual** partners tend to be unstable, as are those involving couples from **lower socio-economic groups** and with **lower educational levels**. Partners from **different demographic backgrounds**, who have experienced **parental divorce** or who have had a **wider-than-average variety of sexual experiences** and **partners** before marriages also face more unstable marriages.
- Divorce may be **beneficial** for both children and their mothers. Mothers who have been through a divorce often report a sense of achievement in their day-to-day activities: divorce seems to galvanise them into taking charge of their lives and forces them to cope with previously unfamiliar tasks and decision-making, which induces self-confidence.
- About 90 per cent of adults will become parents, mostly in their 20s and 30s. However, parenthood has greater variability in meaning and impact than any other life transition.
- Parenthood requires many psychological adaptations. While pregnancy can bring couples closer together, men can feel excluded, especially after the baby has been born, thus pulling the parents further apart.
- Marital satisfaction tends to peak before children arrive, then drops and remains relatively low until the 'post-parental' and retirement stages, when it rises again. At first, the roles of parent and spouse are at least partially incompatible.
- Parents are attachment figures for their dependent children, the relationship being **asymmetrical**, unlike that with a partner. This new form of responsibility can be very stressful, but unhappy couples sometimes stay together because the parent role has sufficient meaning and value for each partner to compensate for the poor marriage.
- According to Durkin, there is little support for **empty-nest distress**, which may be cohort-related. Many parents report that the end of child-rearing responsibilities is a 'liberating experience', providing opportunities for a closer relationship with their partner and personal fulfilment.
- More stressful than the empty nest may be the **crowded nest**, which occurs when 'adult children' opt **not** to leave home.
- As we grow older, the more likely we are to suffer **bereavement**. **Griefwork** comprises three stages: **disbelief** and **shock**, **developing awareness** and **resolution**. While researchers disagree about the specific components, there is general agreement that people must pass through a series of stages or phases of grief for healthy adjustment to the loss to be achieved.
- Ramsay and deGroot prefer to talk about the **components** of grief: **shock**, **disorganisation**, **denial**, **depression**, **guilt**, **anxiety**, **aggression**, **resolution** and **reintegration**. These do not occur in a fixed order and not everyone necessarily experiences all of them; there are wide individual differences in grieving patterns and grief is not a simple, universal process.
- Perhaps the most common form of pathological grief is **chronic grief**. Other abnormal patterns include an exaggeration of the **numbness** associated with the shock of the loss, **neurotic forms of emotional distress** and **physical symptoms**.
- Widows consult GPs much more often than usual during the first six months following their husband's death for both physical and psychological symptoms, and both widows and widowers are

more likely to suffer illness and die compared with married people of a similar age.

- Traditional measures used in bereavement research assume that bereavement is a stressor that upsets a person's equilibrium and requires a return to normal ('baseline') functioning ('recovery'). Some researchers prefer the term 'adaptation' to 'recovery', arguing that a minority of bereaved people continue to grieve intensely for more than a year or two.
- A common feature of **anticipatory grief** is reminiscing, a valuable way of sorting out our life and relationships. This **life review** may produce a new sense of achievement, satisfaction and peace (corresponding to Erikson's **ego-integrity**).
- Coming to terms with our own death is a crucial task of life (ego-transcendence vs. ego-preoccupation). We may review our lives privately and internally or by sharing our memories and reflection with others, the latter helping us to organise a final perspective on our lives and leave a record that will live on after we have died.

ADJUSTMENT TO LATE ADULTHOOD

Introduction and overview

'Growing up' is normally taken to be something desirable and almost an end in itself. By contrast, 'growing old' has traditionally had negative connotations. The negative view of ageing is based on what is called the *decrement model* which sees ageing as a process of decay or decline in physical and mental health, intellectual abilities and social relationships. An alternative to the decrement model is the *personal growth model* which stresses the potential advantages of late adulthood or 'old age', and this much more positive attitude is the way in which ageing has been studied within the life-span approach. Kalish (1982), for example, emphasises the increase in leisure time, the reduction in many day-to-day responsibilities, and the ability to pay attention only to matters of high priority among the elderly. Older people respond to the reality of a limited and finite future by ignoring many of life's inconsequential details and instead channel their energies into what is really important.

Our aim in this chapter is to look at some of the theories and research concerned with the adjustment to late adulthood or old age. We will begin, however, by looking at what is meant by the term 'old' and at some of the physical and psychological changes that occur in late adulthood.

The meaning of 'old'

People today are living longer and retaining their health better than any previous generation (Baltes and Baltes, 1993). The proportion of older people in the British population has increased dramatically in recent years. In 1961, two per cent of the population (one million people) were aged 80 or over. In 1991, almost four per cent of the population (2.2 million) were aged over 80, and the projected percentage for 2001 is even higher. Because of this *demographic imperative* (Swensen, 1983), developmental psychologists have become increasingly interested in our older years. But what do we mean by 'old'? In his book *Growing Old – Years of Fulfilment*, Robert Kastenbaum (1979) devised a questionnaire called 'The ages of me'. This assesses how we see ourselves at the present moment in time in relation to our age. Box 13.1 illustrates Kastenbaum's approach.

Box 13.1 Kastenbaum's 'Ages of me' questionnaire

- My *chronological* age is my actual or official age, dated from my time of birth. My chronological age is . . . . . .
- My *biological* age refers to the state of my face and body. In other people's eyes, I *look* as though I am about . . . . . years of age. In my own eyes, I judge my body to be like that of a person of about . . . . . years of age.
- My *subjective* age is indicated by how I feel. Deep down inside, I really feel like a person of about . . . . . years of age.
- My *functional* age, which is closely related to my *social* age, refers to the kind of life I lead, what I am able to do, the status I believe I have, whether I work, have dependent children and live in my own home. My thoughts and interests are like those of a person of about . . . . . years of age, and my position in society is like that of a person of about . . . . . years of age.

(adapted from Kastenbaum, 1979)

The evidence suggests that few people, irrespective of their chronological age, describe themselves *consistently*. In other words, we often give different responses to the ages identified by Kastenbaum. One finding that has emerged is the difference between subjective and chronological age. People in their 20s and above usually describe themselves as feeling younger than their chronological age, and this is also true for many people in their 70s and 80s. People also prefer to 'be younger', that is, we generally consider ourselves to be *too* old. Very few people over the age of 20 say that they want to be older.

It seems, then, that knowing a person's chronological age isn't particularly helpful in terms of allowing us to say anything meaningful about the sort of life that person leads. However, one of the dangerous aspects of *ageism* is that chronological age *is* assumed to be an accurate indicator of all the other ages. Put another way, there is a tendency for us to infer that people over the age of 60 have certain characteristics which, taken together, make up the decrement model we mentioned in the introduction to this chapter. Terms like 'past it' and 'over the hill' are examples of this. By recognising that there are different 'ages of me', the idea of ageing as decaying should be dispelled and lead to a more analytical and positive approach to old age (cf. Kalish, 1982). The danger of inferring what an elderly person is like and what he or she is likely to be experiencing (or not) based simply on external appearance is dramatically illustrated by the poem 'Crabbit old woman', which appears in Box 13.2.

One description of 'the elderly' has been provided by Burnside et al. (1979). Their decade-by-decade approach is illustrated in Box 13.3.

Box 13.3 A decade-by-decade description of 'the elderly'

The young old (60–69): This marks a major transition. Most adults must adapt to a new role structure in an effort to cope with the losses and gains of the decade. Income is reduced due to retirement. Friends and colleagues start to disappear. Although physical strength wanes somewhat, a great many 'young old' have surplus energy and seek out new and different activities.

The middle-aged old (70–79): This is often marked by loss or illness. Friends and family may die. The middle-aged old must also cope with

Box 13.2 Crabbit old woman

What do you see nurses
What do you see?
Are you thinking
When you are looking at me,
A crabbit old woman
not very wise,
Uncertain of habit
with far-away eyes,
Who dribbles her food
and makes no reply,
When you say in a loud voice
'I do wish you'd try'
Who seems not to notice
the things that you do,
And forever is losing
a stocking or shoe,
Who unresisting or not
lets you do as you will
with bathing and feeding
the long day to fill,
Is that what you're thinking,
is that what you see?
Then open your eyes nurse,
You're not looking at me.
I'll tell you who I am
as I sit here so still,
I'm a small child of ten
with a father and mother,
Brothers and sisters who
love one another,
A young girl of sixteen
with wings on her feet,
Dreaming that soon now
a lover she'll meet;
A bride soon at twenty,
my heart gives a leap,
Remembering the vows
that I promised to keep;
At twenty-five now
I have young of my own
Who need me to build
a secure happy home.
A young woman of thirty
my young now grow fast,
Bound to each other
with ties that should last;
At forty my young ones
now grown will soon be gone,
But my man stays beside me
to see I don't mourn;
At fifty once more
babies play round my knee,
Again we know children
my loved one and me.
Dark days are upon me,
my husband is dead,
I look at the future
I shudder with dread,
For my young are all busy
rearing young of their own,
And I think of the years
and the love I have known.
I'm an old woman now
and nature is cruel,
'Tis her jest to make
old age look like a fool.
The body it crumbles,
Grace and vigour depart,
There now is a stone
where once I had a heart:
But inside this old carcase
a young girl still dwells,
And now and again
my battered heart swells,
I remember the joys
I remember the pain,
And I'm loving and living
life over again,
I think of the years
all too few – gone too fast,
And accept the stark fact
that nothing can last.
So open your eyes nurses
Open and see,
Not a crabbit old woman
look closer – see ME.

This poem was found following the death of a resident of an old people's home

Figure 13.1 While (c) might depict someone's *chronological age*, (a) might correspond to his *biological age* and (b) might represent his *subjective age* (see Box 13.1, page 156)

reduced participation in formal organisations which can lead to restlessness and irritability. Their own health problems become more severe. The major developmental task is to maintain the personality re-integration achieved in the previous decade.

The old old (80–89): The old old show increased difficulty in adapting to and interacting with their surroundings. They need help in maintaining social and cultural contacts.

The very old old (90–99): Although health problems become more acute, the very old old can successfully alter their activities to make the most of what they have. The major advantage of old age is freedom from responsibilities. If previous crises have been resolved satisfactorily, this decade may be joyful, serene and fulfilling.

(based on Burnside et al., 1979, and Craig, 1992)

As Craig (1992) has noted, the aged are not in fact one cohesive group. Rather, they are a collection of subgroups, each of which has unique problems and capabilities, but all of them share to some degree the age-related difficulties of reduced income, failing health and the loss of loved ones. For Craig, however:

> 'having a problem is not the same as being a problem, and the all-too-popular view of those over age 65 as needy, non-productive, and unhappy needs revision'.

Echoing Craig, Dietch (1995) has commented that:

> 'life's final stage is surrounded by more myths, stereotypes and misinformation than any other developmental phase'.

Exactly why there seems to be an upper limit as to how long humans can live for is not known. According to *genetic clock* or *programmed theory*, ageing is built into every organism through a genetic code that informs cells when to stop working. This theory is supported by the finding that rare human conditions involving accelerated ageing are the result of defective genes, and also by the observation that identical twins have very similar life-spans. *Accumulated damages theory*, by contrast, sees ageing as a consequence of damages that result from the wear-and-tear of living. Like a machine, a body eventually wears out as a result of accumulated damage from continued, non-stop use. As we grow older, our cells lose the capability to replace or repair damaged components and they eventually cease to function.

Physical and psychological changes in old age

PHYSICAL CHANGES

Bee and Mitchell (1980) have summarised the major physical changes that occur in old age. These are shown in Box 13.4.

Box 13.4 Physical changes in old age

Smaller: Connective tissues holding the long bones together become compressed and flattened. As a result, height tends to decrease. Changes in calcium metabolism lead to a smaller total body weight than in younger people. Muscle mass is reduced, and some organs (e.g. the bladder) get smaller.

Slower: Since nerve impulses travel more slowly to and from the brain, response or reaction time is slower. Older people recover more slowly under stressful conditions since the immune system functions less effectively. Fractures take longer to heal, and the renewal of liver and skin cells also slows down.

Weaker: Because of gradual changes in calcium metabolism, bones become brittle and break more easily. Muscles also become weaker. In general, the senses become less efficient.

Lesser: The gradual lessening of elastic tissue in the skin causes wrinkling and sagging. The ear drum and lens of the eye lose some of their elasticity, producing problems in hearing and seeing. Blood vessels also become less elastic which can give rise to circulatory problems. In women, the ovaries stop producing eggs and so reproductive ability (fertility) is lost.

Fewer: Body hair becomes more sparse, and the number of teeth and taste buds is reduced (hence food does not taste as good to older people).

(adapted from Bee and Mitchell, 1980)

Although the data presented in Box 13.4 may paint a gloomy picture, we should remember that many of the declines that occur in old age can be compensated for. Moreover, regular exercise can significantly reduce the deterioration of many bodily functions, since tissue *disuse* accounts for about half the functional decline between the ages of 30 and 70.

PSYCHOLOGICAL CHANGES

It is commonly believed that old age is associated with a decrease in cognitive abilities. Until recently, it was believed that intellectual capacity peaked in the late-teens or early 20s, levelled off, and then began to decline fairly steadily during middle age and more rapidly in old age. The evidence on which this claim was based came from *cross-sectional studies*. These involve studying *different* age groups at the *same* time. However, the main problem with this sort of methodology comes from what is known as the *cohort effect*. Although there may be age differences in intelligence, we cannot draw firm conclusions from cross-sectional studies because the age groups compared represent different cohorts who have had different *experiences*. Unless we know how 60-year-olds, say, performed when they were 40 and 20, it is impossible to say whether or not intelligence declines with age.

An alternative methodology is the *longitudinal study*. This is not liable to cohort effects since the *same* people are tested and re-tested at various times during their life. A number of such studies have produced data which contradict the results of cross-sectional studies, and indicate that at least some people retain their intellect well into middle age and beyond (see, for example, Holahan and Sears, 1995). However, the evidence does suggest that some changes in different *kinds* of intelligence do appear to be age related.

Changes in intelligence

Although the definition of intelligence has always been a matter of disagreement among psychologists, it is generally accepted that intelligence is *multi-dimensional*, that is, composed of a number of different abilities. Psychologists distinguish between *crystallised* and *fluid* intelligence. Crystallised intelligence results from accumulated knowledge, including a knowledge of how to reason, language skills and an understanding of technology. This type of intelligence is linked to education, experience and cultural background, and is measured by tests of general information. Fluid intelligence refers to the ability to solve novel and unusual problems, that is, problems that have not been encountered before. Fluid intelligence allows us to perceive and draw inferences about relationships among patterns of stimuli and to conceptualise abstract information, which aids problem-solving. It is measured by tests which use novel and unusual problems. Fluid intelligence, then, is not based on specific knowledge or any particular previous learning.

Horn (1982) has shown that crystallised intelligence *increases* with age and that people tend to continue improving their performance until near the end of their lives. Using the *cross-longitudinal* method, in which different groups of people of different ages are followed up over a long period of time, Schaie and Hertzog (1983) reported that fluid intelligence declines for all age groups over time, having peaked between the ages of 20 and 30. The decline of fluid intelligence with age but the relative constancy (and improvement) of crystallised intelligence is difficult to explain. It could be that our tendency to continue to add to our knowledge as we grow older accounts for the constancy of crystallised intelligence. The decline in fluid intelligence may be an inevitable part of the ageing process which is related to the reduced efficiency of neurological functioning. Alternatively, it may be that we are more likely to maintain our crystallised abilities because we exercise them on a regular basis (Denney and Palmer, 1981). In old age, however, we may be less frequently challenged to use our fluid abilities (Cavanaugh, 1995).

Changes in memory

As far as memory is concerned, the evidence suggests that some aspects of memory decline with age, possibly because we become less effective at processing information (and this may underlie cognitive changes in general: Stuart-Hamilton, 1994). On tests of recall, older adults *generally* perform more poorly than younger adults. In some cases, however, the reverse is true, as was shown by Maylor (1994) in a study of the performance of older contestants on the television programme *Mastermind*. On tests of recognition, the differences between younger and older people are less apparent and may even disappear. As far as *everyday memory* is concerned, the evidence does indicate that the elderly do have trouble recalling events from their youth and early life (see, for example, Miller and Morris, 1993).

Significant memory deficits are one feature of *dementia*, the most common form of which is *Alzheimer's disease*. Despite the wide publicity received by this disease in recent years, the data actually indicate that over 90 per cent or more of people over the age of 65 show *little* deterioration (Diamond, 1978). Diamond argues that the loss of cortical neurons is minimal in most humans until very late in life, and that even in old age, such neurons seem capable of responding to enriched conditions by forming additional functional connections with other neurons. Support for this comes from Rogers et al.'s (1990) finding that those who keep mentally active are those who maintain their cognitive abilities.

TED WHO?
SIR TED AT 80
Peter Brookes
11 vii 96
WOMEN BECOME FORGETFUL WHILE MEN GET GRUMPIER (REPORT ON AGEING)

Figure 13.2 Former Conservative Prime Ministers, Margaret Thatcher and Edward Heath, are well known for their political disagreements. If recent reports on ageing are to be believed, Thatcher will have difficulty remembering them, while Heath will remember them with irritation

Figure 13.3 The Reverend Richard Sturch, a recent winner of *Mastermind*, which requires high levels of recall ability

The view that decline is wired into the nervous system has also been challenged by those who believe that *negative cultural stereotypes* of ageing actually *cause* memory decline in the elderly. In one study, Levy and Langer (1994) investigated the memory capabilities of hearing Americans, members of the American deaf community and people from mainland China. The researchers chose members of the deaf community because they were assumed to be less likely to have been exposed to negative cultural stereotypes. People from mainland China were chosen because of the high esteem in which Chinese society holds its aged members. The results showed that the older American deaf participants and the Chinese participants performed much better on memory tasks than the older American hearing participants. The results also showed that younger hearing Americans held less positive views of ageing than any of the other groups. Amongst the older participants, attitudes towards ageing and memory performance were positively correlated. According to Levy and Langer, negative stereotypes about ageing may become *self-fulfilling prophecies* in which low expectations mean that people are less likely to engage in activities that will help them maintain their memory abilities. They may also fail to seek medical attention for disease-related symptoms of forgetfulness.

Social changes in old age

A number of theories of social development in old age have been advanced. In this section, two of these theories will be discussed.

SOCIAL DISENGAGEMENT THEORY

In *Growing Old – The Process of Disengagement*, Cumming and Henry (1961) attempted to describe what happens to us socially when we grow old. *Social disengagement theory* was based on a five-year study of 275 50- to 90-year-olds in Kansas City, USA. Bromley (1988) has defined disengagement as:

> 'a systematic reduction in certain kinds of social interaction. In its simplest and crudest form, the theory of disengagement states that diminishing psychological and biological capacities of people in later life necessitates a severance of the relationships they have with younger people in the central activities of society, and the replacement of these older individuals by younger people. In this way, society renews itself and the elderly are free to die.'

According to Cumming (1975), social disengagement is the withdrawal of society from the individual, which takes place in the form of compulsory retirement, children growing up and leaving home, the death of a spouse and so on. Social disengagement also refers to the withdrawal from society of the individual, which takes place in the form of reduced social activities and a more solitary life. Hence, the withdrawal is mutual.

Cumming sees disengagement as having three aspects. The first (*shrinkage of life space*) refers to the fact that as we age we tend to interact with fewer and fewer others, and begin to occupy fewer and fewer roles. The second aspect is *increased individuality*. What this means is that in the roles that remain, older people are less and less governed by strict rules and expectations. The third aspect is *acceptance (and even embrace) of these changes*. In this, the healthy, older adult actively disengages from roles and relationships and turns more and more inward and away from interactions with others, as if preparing for death. Put another way, withdrawal is seen as being the most appropriate and successful way to age.

Bee (1994) sees the first two aspects identified by Cumming as being beyond dispute. However, the third is more controversial. This is because of its view of disengagement as being a natural and *inevitable* process rather than an imposed one, and because it may not accurately describe and account for what happens. Bromley (1988) has offered three main criticisms of social disengagement theory. The *practical* criticism is that such a view of ageing encourages a policy of segregation, even indifference, to the elderly and the very destructive belief that old age has no value. The *theoretical* criticism is that disengagement is not actually a true theory, but more a *proto-theory*, that is, a collection of loosely related assumptions and arguments. Bromley's most serious criticism is *empirical*. It is this criticism that Bromley and others have focused on, and concerns whether *everyone* actually does disengage.

Although retirement does bring losses in social relationships (as when children leave home or a spouse dies), relationships with others (in particular grandchildren, neighbours and friends) go some way to replacing them. In later life, the *quality* of activities and relationships may become more important than their *quantity*. As a result, older people are more likely to seek engagement and activity. Evidence supporting this came from Havighurst et al.'s (1968) follow-up of about half of the sample originally studied by Cumming and Henry (1961). Although there was evidence that increasing age was accompanied by increasing disengagement, at least some of those studied remained active and engaged. Havighurst et al. found that amongst the active and engaged there were high levels of contentment and that those who were the most active were the happiest. The fact that those who disengage the least are the happiest, have the highest morale and live the longest goes against social disengagement theory's view that the tendency to withdraw from mainstream society is natural and an inherent part of the ageing process (Bee, 1994). Whilst some people do choose to lead a socially isolated life and find contentment in it, such disengagement does not appear to be necessary for overall mental health in old age.

Rather than speaking of 'social' disengagement, Bromley (1988) believes that it is generally more accurate to speak of 'industrial' disengagement and increased socio-economic dependence. In this way, the origins and circumstances of retirement are kept in focus and the theory is more closely linked to empirical and common-sense impressions. Turner and Helms (1989), for example, have pointed out that many of the past social conditions forcing adults into restricted environments have changed. For example, improved health care, earlier retirement age, higher educational levels and so on have opened up new areas of pursuit for the elderly and made more active life-styles possible. In Kermis' (1984) view:

> 'disengagement represents only one of many possible paths of ageing. It has no blanket application to all people.'

It is also possible that disengagement may be *cohort specific*, that is, it may have been adaptive to withdraw from an ageist society in the 1950s, but in a more enlightened culture this might not be the case. We should also note that as well as there being differences between people with respect to disengagement, an individual rarely disengages from *all* roles to the same degree. Psychological disengagement may not, therefore, coincide with disengagement from social roles. According to Bromley (1988), the disposition to disengage is a *personality dimension* as well as a characteristic of ageing. Havighurst et al.'s (1968) follow-up of Cumming and Henry's study identified a number of different personality types. These included *reorganisers*, who were involved in a wide range of activities and reorganised their lives to substitute for lost activities, and the *disengaged* who voluntarily moved away from role commitments. Consistent with disengagement theory, the disengaged reported low levels of activity but high 'life satisfaction'.

ACTIVITY (OR RE-ENGAGEMENT) THEORY

The major alternative to disengagement theory is activity (or re-engagement) theory (Havighurst, 1964; Maddox, 1964). Activity theory says that except for inevitable changes in biology and health, older people are the same as middle-aged people, with essentially the same psychological and social needs. Decreased social interaction in old age results from the withdrawal by society from the ageing person and happens against the wishes of most elderly people. Contrary to social disengagement theory, then, activity theory proposes that the withdrawal is *not* mutual.

Optimal ageing involves staying active and managing to resist the 'shrinkage' of the social world. This can be achieved by maintaining the activities of middle age for as long as possible, and then finding substitutes for work or retirement and for spouse and friends upon their deaths. Activity theory claims that it is important for older adults to maintain their *role count*, that is, to ensure that they always have several different roles to play.

There are, however, many exceptions to the 'rule' that the greater the level of activity, the greater the level of satisfaction. As we mentioned in our discussion of social disengagement theory, there are some elderly people who seem satisfied with disengagement. This suggests that activity theory *alone* cannot explain successful ageing. Something else that could be involved is personality, which seems to play a crucial role in determining the relationship between activity levels and life satisfaction. Neugarten and Neugarten (1987) suggest that people will select a style of ageing that is best suited to their personality and past experience or lifestyle, and there is no single way to age successfully. Some people may develop new interests or pursue in earnest those they did not have time enough for during their working lives. Others will be developing relationships with grandchildren or even great-grandchildren, remarrying or perhaps getting married for the first time. Yet others will go on working part time or in a voluntary capacity in their local community.

As a counterbalance to disengagement theory, activity theory sees the natural tendency of most elderly people as associating with others, particularly in group and community affairs, although this is often blocked by present-day retirement practices. Whilst disengagement enables or obliges older people to relinquish certain roles (namely those they cannot adequately fulfil), activity or re-engagement prevents the consequences of disengagement from going too far in the direction of isolation, apathy and inaction.

An evaluation of disengagement and activity theories

According to Hayslip and Panek (1989), both disengagement and activity theories refer to a legitimate process through which some people come to terms with the multitude of changes that accompany ageing. Viewed in this way, they are *options*. Just as disengagement may be involuntary (as in the case of poor health, for example), so we may face involuntarily high levels of activity (as in looking after grandchildren, for example). Both disengagement and activity may, therefore, be equally maladaptive. Quite possibly, disengagement theory actually underestimates, and activity theory overestimates, the degree of control people have over the 'reconstruction' of their lives. Additionally, both theories see ageing as being essentially the same for all people. For Turner and Helms (1989), however:

> 'personality is the pivotal factor in determining whether an individual will age successfully, and activity and disengagement theories alone are inadequate to explain successful ageing'.

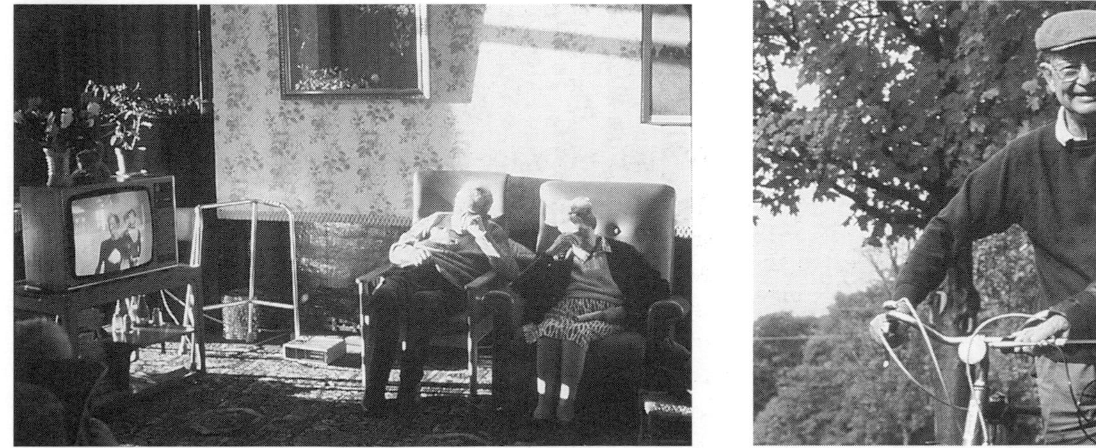

Figure 13.4 The elderly couple on the left seem to fit the stereotype of the withdrawn, isolated, 'disengaged' person, while the couple on the right illustrate an alternative, but less common, stereotype, of the person who remains as active in old age as when he/she was middle-aged

As Baltes (1987) has observed, it is increasingly the case that development is seen as a life-span phenomenon by theorists, and therefore adjustments to old age or late adulthood are an extension of personality styles. Theoretical emphasis is therefore placed on the *continuity* between earlier and later phases of life. Reedy (1983) believes that satisfaction, morale and adaptations in later life generally appear to be closely related to a person's life-long personality style and general way of dealing with stress and change. As Reedy notes:

> 'In this sense, the past is the prologue to the future. While the personality changes somewhat in response to various life events and changes, it generally remains stable throughout all of adult life'.

One of the major criticisms that has been made of activity theory is that it oversimplifies the issues involved in adjusting to late adulthood. Also, there is little empirical support for it. As we have seen, activity can decline without seriously affecting morale. Indeed, a more leisurely lifestyle, with fewer responsibilities and so on, can be seen as one of the *rewards* of old age. This view is at the centre of the *social exchange theory* of late adulthood. According to Dyson (1980), both disengagement and activity theories can be criticised for failing to take sufficient account of the physical and economic factors which might limit people's choices about how they age. Rather than accounting for how most people do age, both theories tell us what the elderly *should* be doing during this stage of life and are therefore *prescriptive.* As Hayslip and Panek (1989) have noted, disengagement and activity theories also involve *value judgements* about what it is to age successfully.

For Dyson, a more useful approach is to see the process of adjusting to ageing in general, and retirement in particular, as a sort of *contract* between the individual and society. As Dowd (1975) has observed, we give up our role as an economically active member of society when we retire, but in *exchange* we receive increased leisure time, take on fewer responsibilities and so on. For the most part, the contract is unwritten and not enforceable. However, most people will probably conform to the expectations about being elderly which are built into social institutions and stereotypes.

Yet another alternative to disengagement and activity theories is provided by Erik Erikson, whose psychosocial theory was examined in Chapter 11 (see pages 132–4). By its very nature, of course, Erikson's theory applies to late adulthood. In contrast to disengagement and activity theories, a more valid and useful way of looking at what all elderly people have in common might be to examine the importance of old age as a stage of development, albeit the last we will go through (which is where its importance lies). This brings us back to the personal growth model we mentioned in the introduction to this chapter, which stresses the advantages and positive aspects of ageing. As Table 10.1 shows (see page 125), in old age there is a conflict between what Erikson terms *ego-integrity* (the positive force) and *despair* (the negative force). Our task is to end this stage, and hence our life, with greater ego-integrity than despair. The achievement of this represents successful ageing. However, as with the other stages identified by Erikson, we cannot avoid the conflict which occurs as a result of inevitable biological, psychological and social forces. For Erikson, the important thing is how successfully this is resolved. Therefore, the task of ageing is to take stock of one's life, to look back over it and assess and evaluate how worthwhile and fulfilling it has been. The characteristics of ego-integrity are shown in Box 13.5.

Box 13.5 The characteristics of ego-integrity

- Life does have a purpose and makes sense.
- Within the context of our lives as a whole, what happened was somehow inevitable and could only have happened when and how it did.
- A belief that all of life's experiences offer something of value. We can learn from everything that happens to us. Looking back, we can see how we have grown psychologically as a result of life's ups and downs, triumphs and failures, calms and crises.
- Seeing our parents in a new light and being able to understand them better because we have lived through our own adulthood and have probably raised children of our own.
- Seeing that what we share with other humans, past, present and future, is the inevitable cycle of birth and death. Whatever the differences (be they historic, cultural, economic and so on), all of us have this much in common. In the light of this, death 'loses its sting'.

Lack or loss of ego-integrity is signified by a fear of death, which is the most conspicuous symptom of despair. In despair, we express the feeling that it is too late to undo the past and put the clock back in order to right wrongs or do what hasn't been done. Life is not a 'rehearsal' and this is the only chance we get.

Conclusions

Several theories concerned with adjustment to late adulthood or old age have been advanced. Of these, two that have attracted a great deal of research interest are social disengagement theory and activity (or re-engagement) theory. Research indicates that, whilst there is some evidence consistent with both of these theories, neither is a completely satisfactory account and that a number of factors not considered by the theories appear to contribute to 'successful ageing'.

Summary

- While 'growing up' has positive connotations, 'growing old' has traditionally had negative ones, reflecting the **decrement model**, which sees ageing as a process of physical, intellectual and social decline. An alternative, more positive view is the **personal growth model** which is how ageing has been studied within the life-span approach.
- The personal growth model stresses the potential advantages of old age, such as increase in leisure time, reduction in everyday responsibilities and ability to attend only to things that really matter, ignoring many of life's unimportant details.
- The proportion of older people (e.g. over 80) in the British population has increased dramatically over the last 30 years or so and is expected to go on increasing. This **demographic imperative** has made developmental psychologists much more interested in late adulthood.
- According to Kastenbaum, age can be defined in different ways, specifically **chronological**, **biological**, **subjective** and **functional** (closely related to **social**). Based on his 'ages of me' questionnaire, Kastenbaum has found that few people, regardless of chronological age, describe themselves **consistently**. People in their 20s and over (including many in their 70s and 80s) usually describe themselves as feeling younger (subjective age) than their actual (chronological) age; they also rarely say they want to be older.
- While it seems that chronological age tells us little about a person's life-style, one of the dangerous features of **ageism** is the assumption that chronological age is an accurate indicator of biological, subjective, functional and social ages (i.e. the decrement model).
- Burnside et al. identify four categories of 'the elderly': **the young old** (60–69), **the middle-aged old** (70–79), **the old old** (80–89) and **the very old old** (90–99). This is a way of seeing the aged as a collection of sub-groups, each with its own problems and capabilities, while also sharing age-related difficulties of reduced income, failing health and loss of loved ones. However, we need to change our stereotypes of the elderly as all being needy, non-productive and unhappy.
- According to **genetic clock** or **programmed theory**, ageing is genetically built into every organism, whereas **accumulated damages theory** sees ageing as the result of damages due to wear-and-tear of the body during a person's lifetime.
- According to Bee and Mitchell, physical changes in old age include: **smaller** height, total body weight, muscle mass and organ size, **slower** reaction time, recovery time from stress, healing of fractures and renewal of liver and skin cells, **weaker** bones, muscles and senses, **lesser** elasticity of the skin, ear drum, lens of the eye, blood vessels and female fertility, **fewer** teeth and taste buds and less body hair.
- Many of these changes can be compensated for, and regular exercise can significantly reduce the deterioration of many bodily functions; tissue **disuse** accounts for about half the functional decline between ages 30 and 70.
- A common belief is that **intelligence** and intellectual capacity peaks in the late-teens and early 20s, then levels off before declining fairly steadily during middle age and more rapidly in old age. This is based on **cross-sectional studies**, in which **different** age groups are studied at the **same** time. But this methodology faces the problem of the **cohort effect**, whereby different age groups have had different **experiences**.
- An alternative methodology is the **longitudinal study**, in which the **same** people are tested and re-tested at various times during their life. These studies indicate that at least some people retain their intellect well into middle age and beyond, although some changes in different **kinds** of intelligence appear to be age-related.

- It is generally agreed that intelligence is **multidimensional**. There is evidence that **crystallised intelligence increases** with age, while, based on the **cross-longitudinal** method, it has been shown that **fluid intelligence declines** for all age groups over time, peaking between 20 and 30.
- Our tendency to continue gaining knowledge as we grow older might explain the constancy and improvement of our crystallised intelligence; these abilities also tend be used on a regular basis. The decline in our fluid intelligence may reflect the inevitable reduction in the efficiency of neurological functioning, although we may be less often challenged to use these abilities in old age.
- Some aspects of **memory** decline with age, perhaps due to less effective information processing. Older adults **generally** perform more poorly than younger adults on tests of recall, but when tests of recognition are used, the differences are reduced or may even disappear. Regarding **everyday memory**, the elderly have trouble recalling events from their early life.
- Over 90 per cent of people over 65 show **little** memory deficit of the kind involved in **Alzheimer's disease**, the most common form of **dementia**. Loss of cortical neurons is minimal in most humans until very late in life, when they are still capable of forming new functional links with other neurons. This is supported by evidence that those who keep mentally active maintain their cognitive abilities.
- Levy and Langer's study of the memory abilities of hearing and deaf Americans and people from mainland China supports the view that **negative cultural stereotypes** of ageing actually **cause** memory decline in the elderly. Negative stereotypes about ageing may become **self-fulfilling prophecies**.
- **Social disengagement theory** refers to the withdrawal **of** society **from** the individual (compulsory retirement, children growing up and leaving home, death of spouse) and the withdrawal **from** society **of** the individual (reduced social activities, more solitary life).
- According to Cumming, disengagement involves **shrinkage of life space**, **increased individuality** and **acceptance (and even embrace) of these changes**, so that withdrawal is seen as the most appropriate and successful way to age. While the first two aspects are beyond dispute, the third is more controversial: it sees disengagement as a natural and **inevitable** process rather than an imposed one and may not be an accurate account of what happens.
- According to Bromley, disengagement encourages segregation of the elderly and a view of old age as valueless. Most seriously, he challenges the claim that **everyone** actually does disengage: although losses in certain relationships do occur, these are replaced to some degree by others, with **quality** becoming more important than **quantity**.
- Havighurst et al.'s follow-up of Cumming and Henry's original sample found that, although increasing age was accompanied by increasing disengagement, at least some of those studied remained active and engaged. Those who were the most active were also the happiest, had the highest morale and lived the longest, contradicting the claim that disengagement is natural and an inherent part of the ageing process.
- Bromley believes that 'industrial' disengagement and increased socio-economic dependence is more accurate than social disengagement, thereby linking the theory more closely with past and present circumstances of retirement.
- Disengagement may be **cohort-specific**, so that in a more enlightened and less ageist society, it may no longer be adaptive to withdraw. Not only does disengagement represent only one of many possible ways of ageing, but individuals rarely disengage from **all** roles to the same degree.
- The disposition to disengage is a **personality dimension** as much as a characteristic of ageing. Havighurst et al. identified **reorganisers** and the **disengaged**, the latter reporting low levels of activity but high levels of satisfaction (thus supporting disengagement theory).
- The major alternative to disengagement theory is **activity** or **re-engagement theory**, according to which older people are psychologically and socially essentially the same as middle-aged people. Contrary to disengagement theory, activity theory sees the withdrawal of society and the individual as **not** mutual.
- Optimal ageing involves staying active, maintaining the activities of middle age for as long as possible and resisting the 'shrinkage' of the social world; it is important to maintain one's **role count**.
- However, activity theory **alone** cannot explain successful ageing, since some elderly people seem satisfied with disengagement. According to Neugarten et al., people will select a style of ageing that is best suited to their personality and past experience and life-style: there is no single way to age successfully.
- Both disengagement and activity theories refer to

options. Just as disengagement may be involuntary, so we may face involuntarily high levels of activity; both may be equally maladaptive.

- Both theories see ageing as being essentially the same for everyone; personality is all-important as far as successful ageing is concerned. In the context of a life-span approach, adjustment to old age is increasingly being seen as **continuous** with earlier phases of life.
- According to **social exchange theory**, a more leisurely lifestyle and fewer responsibilities can be seen as among the **rewards** of old age. Adjusting to old age in general and retirement in particular involves a mainly unwritten and unenforceable **contract** between the individual and society, whereby we give up our role as an economically active member of society in **exchange** for increased leisure time and fewer responsibilities, etc.
- Dyson criticises both disengagement and activity theories for failing to take into account the physical and economic factors which limit people's choices about how they age. They are both **prescriptive** theories and involve **value judgements** about successful ageing.
- Erikson's psychosocial theory is an example of the personal growth model. Old age involves a conflict between **ego-integrity** and **despair**, and successful ageing involves the former outweighing the latter.
- The task of ageing is to take stock of one's life, to look back over it and assess and evaluate its value and meaning. Ego-integrity consists of seeing the purpose and inevitability of our life, concluding that all experiences, positive and negative, are valuable, reaching a better understanding of our parents, and seeing what we have in common with all other human beings, namely the cycle of birth and death.
- Despair is characterised by a fear of death and a feeling that it is too late to undo the past and right the wrongs. We cannot put the clock back and this life is the only one we get.

REFERENCES

ADEY, P., SHAYER, M. & YATES, C. (1989) Cognitive acceleration: The effects of two years of intervention in science classes. In P. Adey (Ed.) *Adolescent Development and School Science*. Lewes: Falmer Press.

AINSWORTH, M.D.S. (1985) Patterns of infant-mother attachments: Antecedents and effects on development. *Bulletin of the New York Academy of Medicine*, 61, 771–791.

AINSWORTH, M.D.S., BELL, S.M.V. & STAYDON, D.J. (1971) Individual differences in strange-situation behaviour of one-year-olds. In H.R. Schaffer (Ed.) *The Origins of Human Social Relations*. New York: Academic Press.

AINSWORTH, M.D.S., BLEHAR, M.C., WATERS, E. & WALL, S. (1978) *Patterns of Attachment: A Psychological Study of the Strange Situation*. Hillsdale, NJ: Lawrence Erlbaum Associates Inc.

ALEXANDER, R.D. (1985) A biological interpretation of moral systems. *Zygon*, 20, 3–18.

ALLPORT, G.W. (1955) *Becoming – Basic Considerations for a Psychology of Personality*. New Haven, CT: Yale University Press.

AMATO, P.R. (1993) Children's adjustment to divorce: Theories, hypotheses and empirical support. *Journal of Marriage and the Family*, 55, 23–28.

AMICE, V., BERCOVI, J., NAHOUL, K., HATAHET, M. & AMICE, J. (1989) Increase in H-Y antigen positive lymphocytes in hirsute women: Effects of cyproterone acetate and estradiol treatment. *Journal of Clinical Endocrinology and Metabolism*, 68, 58–62.

ARGYLE, M. (1983) *The Psychology of Interpersonal Behaviour* (4th edition). Harmondsworth: Penguin.

ARGYLE, M. (1989) *The Social Psychology of Work* (2nd edition). Harmondsworth: Penguin.

ARMSBY, R.E. (1971) A re-examination of the development of moral judgement in children. *Child Development*, 42, 1241–1248.

ARONFREED, J. (1963) The effects of experimental socialisation paradigms upon two moral responses to transgression. *Journal of Abnormal and Social Psychology*, 66, 437–438.

ARONFREED, J. (1976) Moral development from the standpoint of a general psychological theory. In T. Lickona (Ed.) *Moral Development and Behaviour*. New York: Holt, Rinehart & Winston.

ASHER, J. (1987) Born to be shy? *Psychology Today*, April, 56–64.

ATCHLEY, R.C. (1982) Retirement: Leaving the world of work. *Annals of the American Academy of Political and Social Science*, 464, 120–131.

ATCHLEY, R.C. (1985) *Social Forces and Ageing: An Introduction to Social Gerontology*. Belmont, California: Wadsworth.

ATCHLEY, R.S. & ROBINSON, J.L. (1982) Attitudes towards retirement and distance from the event. *Research on Ageing*, 4, 288–313.

AUSUBEL, D.P. (1968) *Educational Psychology: A Cognitive View*. New York: Holt, Rinehart & Winston.

BAILLARGEON, R. (1987) Object permanence in $3\frac{1}{2}$- and $4\frac{1}{2}$-month-old infants. *Developmental Psychology*, 33, 655–664.

BALTES, P.B. (1987) Theoretical propositions of life-span developmental psychology: On the dynamics of growth and decline. *Developmental Psychology*, 23, 611–626.

BALTES, P.B. & BALTES, M.M. (1993) *Successful Ageing: Perspectives from the Behavioural Sciences*. Cambridge: Cambridge University Press.

BANDURA, A. (1977) Self-efficacy: Toward a unifying theory of behaviour change. *Psychological Review*, 84, 191–215.

BANDURA, A. & WALTERS, R. (1959) *Social Learning and Personality Development*. New York: Holt.

BANDURA, A., ROSS, D. & ROSS, S.A. (1961) Transmission of aggression through imitation of aggressive models. *Journal of Abnormal and Social Psychology*, 63, 575–582.

BANDURA, A., ROSS, D. & ROSS, S.A. (1963) Imitation of film-mediated aggressive models. *Journal of Abnormal and Social Psychology*, 66, 3–11.

BARBER, M. (1996) The long shadow of the IQ empire. *Times Educational Supplement*, September 13th, 152.

BARON-COHEN, S. (1990) Autism: a specific cognitive disorder of 'mind-blindness'. *International Review of Psychiatry*, 2, 79–88.

BARON-COHEN, S. (1995) Infantile autism. In A.A. Lazaras & A.M. Colman (Eds.), *Abnormal Psychology*. London: Methuen.

BARROW, G. & SMITH, P. (1979) *Aging, Ageism and Society*. St. Paul, MN: West.

BARRY, H. (1980) Description and uses of the Human

Relations Area Files. In H.C. Triandis & J.W. Berry (Eds.) *Handbook of Cross-Cultural Psychology, Volume 2, Methodology.* Boston: Allyn & Bacon.

BARRY, H., CHILD, I. & BACON, M. (1959) Relation of child training to subsistence economy. *American Anthropologist*, 61, 51–63.

BAUMRIND, D. (1967) Child care practices anteceding three patterns of preschool behaviour. *Genetic Psychology Monographs*, 75, 43–88.

BAUMRIND, D. (1971) Current patterns of parental authority. *Developmental Psychology Monograph*, 4 *(1, Part 2)*.

BAUMRIND, D. (1975) Early socialisation and adolescent competence. In S.E. Dragustin & G.H. Elder (Eds.) *Adolescence in the Life Cycle.* Washington, DC: Hemisphere.

BAUMRIND, D. (1983) Rejoinder to Lewis' reinterpretation of parental firm control effects: Are authoritative families really harmonious? *Psychological Bulletin*, 94, 132–142.

BAUMRIND, D. (1991) Parenting styles and adolescent development. In R. Lerner, A.C. Petersen & J. Brooks-Gunn (Eds.) *The Encyclopaedia of Adolescence.* New York: Garland.

BAYLEY, N. (1969) *Bayley Scales of Infant Development.* New York: Psychological Corporation.

BEALES, H.L. & LAMBERT, R.S. (1934) *Memoirs of the Unemployed.* London: Victor Gollancz.

BEAUMONT, P. (1996) Thirtysomethings who won't grow up. *The Observer*, May 19th, 11.

BEE, H. (1994) *Lifespan Development.* New York: HarperCollins.

BEE, H. & MITCHELL, S.K. (1980) *The Developing Person: A Lifespan Approach.* New York: Harper & Row.

BELL, S.M. & AINSWORTH, M.D.S. (1972) Infant crying and maternal responsiveness. *Child Development*, 43, 1171–1190.

BEM, S.L. (1985) Androgyny and gender schema theory: A conceptual and empirical integration. In T.B. Sonderegger (Ed.) *Nebraska Symposium on Motivation.* Nebraska, NE: University of Nebraska Press.

BERRY, J.W., POOTINGA, Y.H., SEGALL, M.H. & DASEN, P.R. (1992) *Cross-Cultural Psychology: Research and Applications.* Cambridge: Cambridge University Press.

BERTENTHAL, B.I. & FISCHER, K.W. (1978) Development of self-recognition in the infant. *Developmental Psychology*, 14, 44–50.

BIFULCO, A., HARRIS, T. & BROWN, G.W. (1992) Mourning or early inadequate care? Re-examining the relationship of maternal loss in childhood with adult depression and anxiety. *Development and Psychopathology*, 4, 433–449.

BLASI, A. (1980) Bridging moral cognition and moral action: A critical review of the literature. *Psychological Bulletin*, 88, 1–44.

BLOCK, J. (1978) Review of H.J. Eysenck and S.B.G. Eysenck, The Eysenck Personality Questionnaire. In O. Buros (Ed.) *The Eighth Mental Measurement Yearbook.* Highland Park, NJ: Gryphon.

BLOCK, J. (1979) Another look at sex differentiation in the socialisation behaviours of mothers and fathers. In F. Denmark & J. Sherman (Eds.) *Psychology of Women: Future Directions of Research.* New York: Psychological Dimensions.

BLOOM, B.S. (1964) *Stability and Change in Human Characteristics.* New York: Harcourt Brace Jovanovich.

BOOTH, A. & AMATO, P.R. (1994) Parental marital quality, parental divorce and relations with parents. *Journal of Marriage and the Family*, 55, 21–34.

BORKE, H. (1975) Piaget's mountains revisited: Changes in the egocentric landscape. *Developmental Psychology*, 11, 240–243.

BORNSTEIN, M.H. (1989) Sensitive periods in development: Structural characteristics and causal interpretations. *Psychological Bulletin*, 105, 179–197.

BOTVIN, G.J. & MURRAY, F.B. (1975) The efficacy of peer modelling and social conflict in the acquisition of conservation. *Child Development*, 46, 796–799.

BOUCHARD, T.J. & McGUE, M. (1981) Familial studies of intelligence: A review. *Science*, 212, 1055–1059.

BOUCHARD, T.J. & SEGAL, N.L. (1988) Heredity, environment and IQ. In *Instructor's Resource Manual* to accompany G. Lindzey, R. Thompson & B. Spring, *Psychology* (3rd edition). New York: Worth Publishers.

BOUCHARD, T.J., LYKKEN, D.T., McGUE, M., SEGAL, N.L. & TELLEGEN, A. (1990) Sources of human psychological differences: The Minnesota study of twins reared apart. *Science*, 250, 223–228.

BOWER, T.G.R. (1976) Repetitive processes in child development. *Scientific American*, 235, 38–47.

BOWER, T.G.R. (1977) *The Perceptual World of the Child.* London: Fontana.

BOWER, T.G.R. & WISHART, J.G. (1972) The effects of motor skill on object permanence. *Cognition*, 1, 28–35.

BOWLBY, J. (1946) *Forty-Four Juvenile Thieves.* London: Balliere Tindall and Cox.

BOWLBY, J. (1951) *Maternal Care and Mental Health.* Geneva: World Health Organisation.

BOWLBY, J. (1953) *Child Care and the Growth of Love.* Harmondsworth: Penguin.

BOWLBY, J. (1969) *Attachment and Loss. Volume 1: Attachment.* Harmondsworth: Penguin.

BOWLBY, J. (1973) *Attachment and Loss. Volume 2: Separation.* Harmondsworth: Penguin.

BOWLBY, J. (1980) *Attachment and Loss. Volume 3: Loss, Sadness and Depression.* London: Hogarth Press.

BOWLBY, J., AINSWORTH, M., BOSTON, M. &

ROSENBLUTH, D. (1956) The effects of mother-child separation: A follow-up study. *British Journal of Medical Psychology*, 29, 211.
BRADLEY, R.H. & CALDWELL, B.M. (1976) The relation of infants' home environments to mental test performance at 54 months: A follow-up study. *Child Development*, 47, 1172–1174.
BRADLEY, R.H. & CALDWELL, B.M. (1984) The relation of infants' home environments to achievement test performance in first grade: A follow-up study. *Child Development*, 55, 803–809.
BRAINERD, C.J. (1978) Neo-Piagetian training experiments revisited: Is there any support for the cognitive-developmental stage hypothesis? *Cognition*, 2, 349–370.
BRAINERD, C.J. (1983) Modifiability of cognitive development. In S. Meadows (Ed.) *Development of Thinking*. London: Methuen.
BRETHERTON, I. (1985) Attachment theory: Retrospect and prospect. In I. Bretherton & E. Walters (Eds.) Growing points of attachment theory and research. *Child Development Monographs*, 50 (Serial No. 209), 1–2.
BROMLEY, D.B. (1988) *Human Ageing: An Introduction to Gerontology* (3rd edition). Harmondsworth: Penguin.
BRONFENBRENNER, U. (1979) *The Ecology of Human Development*. Cambridge, MA: Harvard University Press.
BROWN, B. & GROTBERG, J.J. (1981) Headstart: A successful experiment. *Courrier* (Paris International Children's Centre).
BRUNER, J.S. (1957) On perceptual readiness. *Psychological Review*, 64, 123–152.
BRUNER, J.S. (1963) *The Process of Education*. Cambridge, MA: Harvard University Press.
BRUNER, J.S. (1966) On the conservation of liquids. In J.S. Bruner, R.R. Oliver & P.M. Greenfield (Eds.) *Studies in Cognitive Growth*. New York: Wiley.
BRUNER, J.S. (1983) *Child's Talk: Learning to Use Language*. Oxford: Oxford University Press.
BRUNER, J.S. & KENNEY, H. (1966) *The Development of the Concepts of Order and Proportion in Children*. New York: Wiley.
BRUNER, J.S., OLIVER, R.R. & GREENFIELD, P.M. (1966) *Studies in Cognitive Growth*. New York: Wiley.
BRYDEN, M. & SAXBY, L. (1985) Developmental aspects of cerebral lateralisation. In J. Obrzat & G. Hynd (Eds.) *Child Neuropsychology, Volume 1: Theory and Research*. Orlando, FLA: Academic Press.
BURMAN, E. (1994) *Deconstructing Developmental Psychology*. London: Routledge.
BURNSIDE, I.M., EBERSOLE, P. & MONEA, H.E. (1979) *Psychological Caring Throughout the Lifespan*. New York: McGraw-Hill.
BURR, V. (1995) *An Introduction to Social Constructionism*. London: Routledge.
BURT, C.L. (1966) The genetic determination of differences in intelligence: A study of monozygotic twins reared together and apart. *British Journal of Psychology*, 57, 137–153.
BUSS, A.H. & PLOMIN, R. (1984) *Temperament: Early Developing Personality Traits*. Hillsdale, NJ: Erlbaum.
BUSS, D.M. (1994) Mate preference in 37 cultures. In W.J. Lonner & R.S. Malpass (Eds.) *Psychology and Culture*. Boston: Allyn & Bacon.
BUTLER, R. (1963) The life review: An interpretation of reminiscence in the aged. *Psychiatry*, 26, 65–76.
CAMPBELL, A. (1981) *The Sense of Well-Being in America*. New York: McGraw-Hill.
CAMPBELL, A. & MUNCER, S. (1994) Men and the meaning of violence. In J. Archer (Ed.) *Male Violence*. London: Routledge.
CAMPBELL, R. (1996) Cognitive skills and domain-specificity. Report on the Piaget-Vygotsky centenary conference. *The Psychologist*, 9, 369.
CAPRON, C. & DUYME, M. (1989) Assessment of effects of socio-economic status on IQ in full cross-fostering study. *Nature*, 340, 552–554.
CAREY, S. (1988) Are children fundamentally different kinds of thinkers and learners than adults? In K. Richardson & S. Sheldon (Eds.) *Cognitive Development to Adolescence*. Milton Keynes: Open University Press.
CARLSON, N.R. (1988) *Discovering Psychology*. London: Allyn & Bacon.
CASE, R. (1985) *Intellectual Development*. London: Methuen.
CAVANAUGH, J.C. (1995) Ageing. In P.E. Bryant & A.M. Colman (Eds.) *Developmental Psychology*. London: Longman.
CHUMLEA, W. (1982) Physical growth in adolescence. In B. Wolman (Ed.) *Handbook of Developmental Psychology*. Englewood Cliffs, NJ: Prentice-Hall.
CLARKE, A.M. & CLARKE, A.D.B. (1976) *Early Experience: Myth and Evidence*. New York: Free Press.
CLOPTON, N.A. & SORELL, G.T. (1993) Gender differences in moral reasoning: Stable or situational? *Psychology of Women Quarterly*, 17, 85–101.
COCKETT, M. & TRIPP, J. (1994) Children living in disordered families. *Social Policy Research Findings, No.* 45. Joseph Rowntree Foundation.
COLBY, A., KOHLBERG, L., GIBBS, J. & LIEBERMAN, M. (1983) A longitudinal study of moral development. *Monographs of the Society for Research in Child Development*, 48, (1–2, Serial No. 200).
COLEMAN, J.C. (1980) *The Nature of Adolescence*. London: Methuen.
COLEMAN, J.C. (1995) Adolescence. In P.E. Bryant & A.M. Colman (Eds.) *Developmental Psychology*. London: Longman.
COLEMAN, J.C. & HENDRY, L. (1990) *The Nature of Adolescence* (2nd edition). London: Routledge.

COLES, R. (1986) *The Moral Life of Children.* Boston: The Atlantic Monthly Press.

COLLINS, R.C. (1983) Headstart: An update on program effects. *Newsletter of the Society for Research in Child Development.* Summer, 1–2.

CONDRY, J.C. & ROSS, D.F. (1985) Sex and aggression: The influence of gender label on the perception of aggression in children. *Child Development,* 56, 225–233.

CONSTANZO, P.R., COIE, J.D., GRUMET, J.F. & FARNHILL, D. (1973) Re-examination of the effects of intent and consequence of children's moral judgements. *Child Development,* 44, 154–161.

COOLEY, C.H. (1902) *Human Nature and the Social Order.* New York: Shocken.

COOPER, G. (1996a) How nursery breeds bad behaviour. *Independent,* September 13th, 3.

COOPER, G. (1996b) The satisfying side of being home alone. *Independent,* September 13th, 3.

COOPER, R. & ZUBEK, J. (1958) Effects of enriched and restricted early environments on the learning ability of bright and dull rats. *Canadian Journal of Psychology,* 12, 159–164.

COOPERSMITH, S. (1967) *The Antecedents of Self-Esteem.* San Francisco: Freeman.

COWAN, P.A. (1978) *Piaget with Feeling.* New York: Holt, Rinehart & Winston.

CRAIG, G.J. (1992) *Human Development* (6th edition). Englewood Cliffs, NJ: Prentice-Hall.

CRAMER, D. (1994) Personal relationships. In D. Tantam & M. Birchwood (Eds.) *Seminars in Psychology and the Social Sciences.* London: Gaskell Press.

CRAMER, D. (1995) Special issue on personal relationships. *The Psychologist,* 8, 58–59.

CRATTY, B.J. (1970) *Perceptual and Motor Development in Children.* New York: MacMillan.

CRIDER, A.B., GOETHALS, R.D., KAVANAUGH, R.D. & SOLOMON, P.R. (1989) *Psychology* (3rd edition). Glenview, Il: Scott, Foresman and Company.

CROOKS, R.L. & STEIN, J. (1991) *Psychology: Science, Behaviour and Life* (2nd edition). London: Holt, Rinehart & Winston Inc.

CSIKSZENTMIHALYI, M. & LARSON, R. (1984) *Being Adolescent: Conflict and Growth in the Teenage Years.* New York: Basic Books.

CUMMING, E. (1975) Engagement with an old theory. *International Journal of Ageing and Human Development,* 6, 187–191.

CUMMING, E. & HENRY, W.E. (1961) *Growing Old: The Process of Disengagement.* New York: Basic Books.

CURTISS, S. (1977) *Genie: A Psycholinguistic Study of a Modern-Day 'Wild Child'.* London: Academic Press.

DACEY, J.S. (1982) *Adolescents Today* (2nd edition). Glenview, Illinois: Scott, Foresman & Company.

DAMON, W. & HART, D. (1988) *Self-Understanding in Childhood and Adolescence.* Cambridge: Cambridge University Press.

DARLING, N. & STEINBERG, L. (1993) Parenting style as context: an integrative model. *Psychological Bulletin,* 113, 487–496.

DASEN, P.R. (1994) Culture and cognitive development from a Piagetian perspective. In W.J. Lonner & R.S. Malpass (Eds.) *Psychology and Culture.* Boston: Allyn & Bacon.

DATAN, N., RODEHEAVER, D. & HUGHES, F. (1987) Adult development and ageing. *Annual Review of Psychology,* 38, 153–180.

DAVIES, D.L. (1956) Psychiatric illness in those enagaged to be married. *British Journal of Preventive and Social Medicine,* 10, 123–127.

DAVIS, D., CAHAN, S. & BASHI, J. (1977) Birth order and intellectual development: The confluence model in the light of cross-cultural evidence. *Science,* 196, 1470–1472.

DAVIS, K. (1940) Extreme isolation of a child. *American Journal of Sociology,* 45, 554–565.

DAVIS, R.B. (1984) *Learning Mathematics: The Cognitive Science Approach to Maths Education.* London: Croom Helm.

DENNEY, N. & PALMER, A. (1981) Adult age differences on traditional problem-solving measures. *Journal of Gerontology,* 36, 323–328.

DENNIS, W. (1960) Causes of retardation among institutional children: Iran. *Journal of Genetic Psychology,* 96, 47–59.

DENZIN, N.K. (1995) Symbolic interactionism. In J.A. Smith, R. Harre & L.V. Langenhove (Eds.) *Rethinking Psychology.* London: Sage Publications.

DIAMOND, M. (1978) Sexual identity and sex roles. *The Humanist,* March/April.

DIAMOND, M. (1982) Sexual identity, monozygotic twins reared in discordant roles, and a BBC follow-up. *Archives of Sexual Behaviour,* 11, 181–186.

DIETCH, J.T. (1995) Old age. In D. Wedding (Ed.) *Behaviour and Medicine* (2nd edition). St Louis, MO: Mosby-Year Book.

DONALDSON, M. (1978) *Children's Minds.* London: Fontana.

DOOLEY, D. & PRAUSE, J. (1995) Effect of unemployment on school leavers' self-esteem. *Journal of Occupational and Organisational Psychology,* 68, 177–192.

DORNER, G. (1976) *Hormones and Brain Differentiation.* Amsterdam: Elsevier.

DOWD, J.J. (1975) Ageing as exchange: A preface to theory. *Journal of Gerontology,* 30, 584–594.

DOWNEY, D.B. & POWELL, B. (1993) Do children in single-parent households fare better living with same sex parents? *Journal of Marriage and the Family,* 55, 65–71.

DUCK, S. (1988) *Relating to Others.* Milton Keynes: Open University Press.

DUCK, S. (1995) Repelling the study of attraction. *The Psychologist,* 8, 60–63.

DURKIN, K. (1995) *Developmental Social Psychology: From Infancy to Old Age.* Oxford: Blackwell.

DWORETZKY, J.P. (1981) *Introduction to Child Development.* St Paul, Minnesota: West Publishing Co.

DYER, C. (1996) Parents could face new restrictions on smacking children. *The Guardian,* September 10th, 1.

DYSON, J. (1980) Sociopolitical influences on retirement. *Bulletin of the British Psychological Society,* 33, 128–130.

EAGLY, A.H. (1983) Gender and social influence: A social psychological analysis. *American Psychologist,* September.

EASTERBROOKS, M. & GOLDBERG, W. (1984) Toddler development in the family: Impact of father involvement and parenting characteristics. *Child Development,* 55, 74–752.

ECKENSBERGER, L.H. (1994) Moral development and its measurement across cultures. In W.J. Lonner & R.S. Malpass (Eds.) *Psychology and Culture.* Boston: Allyn & Bacon.

EDLEY, N. & WETHERELL, M. (1995) *Men in Perspective: Practice, Power and Identity.* Hemel Hempstead: Harvester Wheatsheaf.

EISENBERG, N. (1986) *Altruistic Emotion, Cognition and Behaviour.* Hillsdale, NJ: Erlbaum.

ELARDO, R., BRADLEY, R.H. & CALDWELL, B.M. (1975) The relation of infants' home environments to mental test performance from 6 to 36 months: A longitudinal analysis. *Child Development,* 46, 71–76.

ELKIND, D. (1970) Erik Erikson's eight ages of man. *New York Times Magazine,* April 5th.

ELKIND, D. (1976) *Child Development and Education: A Piagetian Perspective.* Oxford: Oxford University Press.

ELLIOTT, B.J. & RICHARDS, M.P.M. (1991) Children and divorce: educational performance before and after parental separation. *International Journal of Law and the Family,* 5, 258–278.

ENGEL, G. (1962) *Psychological Development in Health and Disease.* Philadelphia: Saunders.

ERIKSON, E.H. (1963) *Childhood and Society* (2nd edition). New York: Norton.

ERLENMEYER-KIMLING, L. & JARVIK, L.F. (1963) Genetics and intelligence: A review. *Science,* 142, 1477–1479.

EYSENCK, H.J. (1964) *Crime and Personality.* London: Routledge & Kegan Paul.

EYSENCK, H.J. & WAKEFIELD, J.A. (1981) Psychological factors as predictors of marital satisfaction. *Advances in Behaviour Research and Therapy,* 3, 151–192.

FAGOT, B.I. (1978) The influence of sex of child on parental reactions to toddler children. *Child Development,* 49, 459–465.

FAGOT, B.I. (1985) Beyond the reinforcement principle: Another step toward understanding sex-role development. *Developmental Psychology,* 21, 1097–1104.

FARBER, S.L. (1981) *Identical Twins Reared Apart.* New York: Basic Books.

FAUST, M.S. (1977) Somatic development of adolescent girls. *Monographs of the Society for Research on Child Development,* 42, (1, Serial No. 169).

FELDMAN, D.H. (1986) How development works. In I. Levin (Ed.) *Stage and Structure, Reopening the Debate.* Norwood, NJ: Ablex.

FIELD, T. (1978) Interaction behaviours of primary versus secondary caretaker fathers. *Developmental Psychology,* 14, 183–184.

FISKE, M. (1980) Changing hierarchies of commitment in adulthood. In N.J. Smelser & E.H. Erikson (Eds.) *Themes of Work and Love in Adulthood.* Cambridge, MA: Harvard University Press.

FLANAGAN, C. (1996) *Applying Psychology to Early Child Development.* London: Hodder & Stoughton.

FLAVELL, J.H. (1971) First discussant's comments: What is memory development the development of? *Human Development,* 14, 272–278.

FLAVELL, J.H. (1982) Structures, stages and sequences in cognitive development. In W.A. Collins (Ed.) *The Concept of Development: The Minnesota Symposia on Child Development,* Volume 15. Hillsdale, NJ: Erlbaum.

FLAVELL, J.H., SHIPSTEAD, S.G. & CROFT, K. (1978) *What young children think you see when their eyes are closed.* Unpublished report, Stanford University.

FOGELMAN, K. (1976) *Britain's Sixteen-Year-Olds.* London: National Children's Bureau.

FOOT, H.C. (1994) *Group and Interactive Learning.* Computational Mechanics Publications.

FOOT, H.C. & CHEYNE, W. (1995) Collaborative learning: Putting theory into practice. *Psychology Review,* 1, 16–19.

FREUD, A. & DANN, S. (1951) An experiment in group upbringing. *Psychoanalytic Study of the Child,* 6, 127–168.

FREUD, S. (1924) The passing of the Oedipus complex. In *Collected Papers of Sigmund Freud* (Volume 5) edited by E. Jones. New York: Basic Books.

FREUD, S. (1926) Inhibitions, symptoms and anxiety. In *Standard Edition of the Complete Psychological Works of Sigmund Freud.* London: Hogarth Press.

FREUD, S. (1933) *New Introductory Lectures on Psychoanalysis.* New York: Norton.

FRYER, D. (1992) Signed on at the 'beroo': Mental health and unemployment research in Scotland. *The Psychologist,* 5, 539–542.

FRYER, D. (1995) Benefit agency? *The Psychologist,* 8, 265–272.

GALLUP, C.G. (1977) Self-recognition in primates. *American Psychologist,* 32, 329–338.

GARBER, H.L. (1988) *The Milwaukee Project: Preventing Mental Retardation in Children at Risk.* Washington, DC: American Association on Mental Retardation.

GARLAND, C. & WHITE, S. (1980) *Children and Day Nurseries.* London: Grant McIntyre.

GELMAN, R. (1978) Counting in the pre-schooler: What does and does not develop. In R.S. Siegler (Ed.) *Children's Thinking: What Develops?.* Hillsdale, NJ: Erlbaum.

GELMAN, R. (1979) Preschool thought. *American Psychologist,* 34, 900–905.

GELMAN, R. & BAILLARGEON, R. (1983) A review of some Piagetian concepts. In J.H. Flavell & E.M. Markman (Eds.) Cognitive development, Vol. 3 in P.H. Mussen (Ed.) *Handbook of Child Psychology* (4th edition). New York: Wiley.

GESCHWIND, N. & BEHAN, P. (1984) Laterality, hormones and immunity. In N. Geschwind & A. Galaburda (Eds.) *Cerebral Dominance: The Biological Foundations.* Cambridge, MA: Harvard University Press.

GIBBS, J.C. & SCHNELL, S.V. (1985) Moral development 'versus' socialisation. *American Psychologist,* 40, 1071–1080.

GILLIE, O. (1976) Pioneer of IQ faked his research. *The Sunday Times,* October 29th, H3.

GILLIGAN, C. (1982) *In a Different Voice: Psychological Theory and Women's Development.* Cambridge, MA: Harvard University Press.

GINSBERG, H.P. (1981) Piaget and education: The contributions and limits of genetic epistemology. In K. Richardson & S. Sheldon (Eds.) *Cognitive Development to Adolescence.* Milton Keynes: Open University Press.

GOFFMAN, E. (1959) *The Presentation of Self in Everyday Life.* Harmondsworth: Penguin.

GOLDBERG, S. & LEWIS, M. (1969) Play behaviour in the year-old infant: Early sex differences. *Child Development,* 40, 21–31.

GOLDFARB, W. (1943) The effects of early institutional care on adult personality. *Journal of Experimental Education,* 12, 106–129.

GOLDWYN, E. (1979) The fight to be male. *The Listener,* May 24th, 709–712.

GOLOMBOK, S., SPENCER, A. & RUTTER, M. (1983) Children in lesbian and single-parent households: Psychosexual and psychiatric appraisal. *Journal of Child Psychology and Psychiatry,* 24, 551–572.

GOTTFRIED, A. (Ed.) (1984) *Home Environment and Early Cognitive Development: Longitudinal Research.* Orlando, FLA: Academic Press.

GOULD, R.L. (1978) *Transformations: Growth and Change in Adult Life.* New York: Simon & Schuster.

GOULD, R.L. (1980) Transformational tasks in adulthood. In S.I. Greenspan & G.H. Pollock (Eds.) *The Course of Life: Psychoanalytic Contributions Toward Understanding Personality Development, Volume 3: Adulthood and the Ageing Process.* Washington, DC: National Institute for Mental Health.

GREENBERG, M. & MORRIS, N. (1974) Engrossment: The newborn's impact upon the father. *American Journal of Orthopsychiatry,* 44, 520–531.

GREENOUGH, W.T. & BLACK, J.E. (1992) Induction of brain structure by experience: substrates for cognitive development. In M. Gunnar & C.A. Nelson (Eds.) *Behavioural Developmental Neuroscience, Volume 24, Minnesota Symposia on Child Psychology.* Hillsdale, NJ: Erlbaum.

GROSS, R. (1992) *Psychology: The Science of Mind and Behaviour* (2nd edition). London: Hodder & Stoughton.

GROSS, R. (1994) *Key Studies in Psychology* (2nd edition). London: Hodder & Stoughton.

GROSS, R. (1996) *Psychology: The Science of Mind and Behaviour* (3rd edition). London: Hodder & Stoughton.

GROSS, R. & MCILVEEN, R. (1996) *Abnormal Psychology.* London: Hodder & Stoughton.

GUNTER, B. (1986) *Television and Sex-Role Stereotyping.* London: IBA and John Libbey.

GUNTER, B. & McALEER, J.L. (1990) *Children and Television – The One-Eyed Monster?* London: Routledge.

GUTHRIE, E.R. (1938) *Psychology of Human Conflict.* New York: Harper & Row.

HALL, G. S. (1904) *Adolescence.* New York: Appleton & Company.

HAMBURG, D. & TAKANISHI, R. (1989) Preparing for life: The critical transition of adolescence. *American Psychologist,* 44, 825–827.

HAMPSON, S.E. (1995) The construction of personality. In S.E. Hampson & A.M. Colman (Eds.) *Individual Differences and Personality.* London: Longman.

HARGREAVES, D., MOLLOY, C. & PRATT, A. (1982) Social factors in conservation. *British Journal of Psychology,* 73, 231–234.

HARLOW, H.F. (1959) Love in infant monkeys. *Scientific American,* 200, 68–74.

HARLOW, H.F. & SUOMI, S.J. (1970) The nature of love – simplified. *American Psychologist,* 25, 161–168.

HARLOW, H.F. & ZIMMERMAN, R.R. (1959) Affectional responses in the infant monkey. *Science,* 130, 421–432.

HARRÉ, R. (1985) The language game of self-ascription: a note. In K.J. Gergen & K.E. Davis (Eds.) *The Social Construction of the Person.* New York: Springer-Verlag.

HARRÉ, R. (1989) Language games and the texts of identity. In J. Shotter & K.J. Gergen (Eds.) *Texts of Identity.* London: Sage.

HARTSHORNE, H. & MAY, M. (1930) *Studies in the Nature of Character.* New York: MacMillan.

HASSETT, J. & WHITE, M. (1989) *Psychology in Perspective* (2nd edition). Cambridge: Harper & Row.

HAVIGHURST, R.J. (1964) Stages of vocational development. In H. Borrow (Ed.) *Man in a World of Work.* Boston: Houghton Mifflin.
HAVIGHURST, R.J., NEUGARTEN, B.L. & TOBIN, S.S. (1968) Disengagement and patterns of ageing. In B.L. Neugarten (Ed.) *Middle Age and Ageing.* Chicago: University of Chicago Press.
HAYSLIP, B. & PANEK, P.E. (1989) *Adult Development and Ageing.* New York: Harper & Row.
HEARNSHAW, L. (1979) *Cyril Burt: Psychologist.* Ithaca, NY: Cornell University Press.
HENDRIX, L. (1985) Economy and child training reexamined. *Ethos,* 13, 246–261.
HESS, E.H. (1958) Imprinting in animals. *Scientific American,* March, 71–80.
HETHERINGTON, E.M. (1967) The effects of familial variables on sex-typing, on parent-child similarity, and on imitation in children. In J.P. Hill (Ed.) *Minnesota Symposium on Child Psychology (Volume 1).* Mineapolis, MN: University of Minnesota Press.
HETHERINGTON, E.M. & BALTES, P.B. (1988) Child psychology and life-span development. In E.M. Hetherington, R. Lerner, & M. Perlmutter (Eds.) *Child Development in Life-Span Perspective.* Hillsdale, NJ: Erlbaum.
HIGHFIELD, R. (1996) X Factor is 'key to intelligence'. *The Daily Telegraph,* 24 June, 1.
HINTON, J. (1975) *Dying.* Harmondsworth: Penguin.
HOBBS, N. & ROBINSON, S. (1982) Adolescent development and public policy. *American Psychologist,* 49, 15–19.
HODGES, J. & TIZARD, B. (1989) Social and family relationships of ex-institutional adolescents. *Journal of Child Psychology and Psychiatry,* 30, 77–97.
HODGKIN, J. (1988) Everything you always wanted to know about sex. *Nature,* 331, 300–301.
HODGSON, J.W. & FISHER, J.L. (1979) Sex differences in identity and intimacy development. *Journal of Youth and Adolescence,* 8, 37–50.
HODKIN, B. (1981) Language effects in assessment of class-inclusion ability. *Child Development,* 52, 470–478.
HOFFMAN, M.L. (1970) Conscience, personality and socialisation techniques. *Human Development,* 13, 90–126.
HOFFMAN, M.L. (1975) Altruistic behaviour and the parent-child relationship. *Journal of Personality and Social Psychology,* 31, 937–943.
HOFFMAN, M.L. (1976) Empathy, role-taking, guilt and development of altruistic motives. In T. Lickona (Ed.) *Moral Development and Behaviour.* New York: Holt, Rinehart & Winston.
HOGG, M.A. & VAUGHN, G.M. (1995) *Social Psychology: An Introduction.* Hemel Hempstead: Harvester Wheatsheaf.
HOLAHAN, C.K. & SEARS, R.R. (1995) *The Gifted Group in Later Maturity.* Stanford, CA: Stanford University Press.
HONZIK, M.P., MacFARLANE, H.W. & ALLEN, L. (1948) The stability of mental test performance between two and eighteen years. *Journal of Experimental Education,* 17, 309–324.
HOPSON, B. & SCALLY, M. (1980) Change and development in adult life: Some implications for helpers. *British Journal of Guidance and Counselling,* 8, 175–187.
HORGAN, J. (1993) Eugenics revisited. *Scientific American,* June, 92–100.
HORN, J.L. (1976) Human abilities: A review of research and theory in the early 1970s. *Annual Review of Psychology,* 27, 437–485.
HORN, J.L. (1982) The ageing of human abilities. In B. Wolman (Ed.) *Handbook of Developmental Psychology.* Englewood Cliffs, NJ: Prentice-Hall.
HOUSTON, J.P., HAMMEN, C., PADILLA, A. & BEE, H. (1989) *Introduction to Psychology* (3rd edition). New York: Harcourt Brace Jovanovich.
HOWE, M. (1990) *The Origins of Exceptional Abilities.* Oxford: Blackwell.
HOWE, M. (1995) Hothouse tots: Encouraging and accelerating development in young children. *Psychology Review,* 2, 2–4.
HOWE, M. & GRIFFEY, H. (1994) *Give Your Child a Better Start.* London: Michael Joseph.
HOYENGA, K.B. & HOYENGA, K.T. (1979) *The Question of Sex Differences.* Boston: Little Brown.
HU, Y. & GOLDMAN, N. (1990) Morality differentials by marital status: An international comparison. *Demography,* 27, 233–250.
HUMPHREYS, N. (Ed.) (1975) *Vital Statistics: A Memorial Volume of Selections From the Reports and Writings of William Farr.* Metuchen, NJ: Scarecrow Press.
HUNT, J. McVicker (1961) *Intelligence and Experience.* New York: Ronald Press.
HUNT, J. McVicker (1969) Has compensatory education failed? Has it been attempted? *Harvard Educational Review,* 39, 278–300.
HUNT, J. McVicker (1982) Towards equalising the developmental opportunities of pre-school children. *Journal of Social Issues,* 38, 163–191.
HUSTON, A.C. (1983) Sex-typing. In E.M. Hetherington (Ed.) Socialisation, personality and social development, Volume 4 in P.H. Mussen (Ed.) *Handbook of Child Psychology.* New York: Wiley.
HYDE, J.S. & LINN, M.C. (1988) Gender differences in verbal ability: A meta-analysis. *Psychological Bulletin,* 104, 53–69.
HYDE, J.S., FENNEMA, E. & LAMON, S. (1990) Gender differences in mathematics performance: A meta-analysis. *Psychological Bulletin,* 107, 139–155.
IMPERATO-McGINLEY, J., PETERSON, R.,

GAUTIER, T. & STURLA, E. (1979) Androgens and the evolution of male-gender identity among pseudohermaphrodites with 5–alpha-reductase deficiency. *New England Journal of Medicine*, 300, 1233–1237.

INHELDER, B. & PIAGET, J. (1958) *The Growth of Logical Thinking*. London: Routledge & Kegan Paul.

INTONS-PETERSON, M.J. & REDDEL, M. (1984) What do people ask about a neonate? *Developmental Psychology*, 20, 358–359.

JAHODA, M. (1958) *Current Concepts of Positive Mental Health*. New York: Basic Books.

JAMES, W. (1890) *Principles of Psychology*. New York: Holt.

JENSEN, A. (1969) How much can we boost IQ and scholastic achievement? *Harvard Educational Review*, 39, 1–23.

JUEL-NIELSEN, N. (1965) Individual and environment: A psychiatric and psychological investigation of monozygous twins raised apart. *Acta Psychiatrica et Neurologica Scandinavia*, (Suppl. 183).

KADUSHIN, A. (1970) *Adopting Older Children*. New York: Columbia University Press.

KAGAN, J. (1984) *The Nature of the Child*. New York: Basic Books.

KAGAN, J. (1989) *Unstable Ideas: Temperament, Cognition and Self*. Cambridge, MA: Harvard University Press.

KAGAN, J. & KLEIN, R.E. (1973) Cross-cultural perspectives on early development. *American Psychologist*, 28, 947–961.

KAGAN, J., KEARSLEY, R. & ZELAGO, P. (1978) *Infancy: Its Place in Human Development*. Cambridge, MA: Harvard University Press.

KAGAN, J., KEARSLEY, R.B. & ZELAZO, P. (1980) *Infancy: Its place in Human Development* (2nd edition). Cambridge, MA: Harvard University Press.

KAIL, R.V. & NIPPOLD, M.A. (1984) Unrestrained retrieval from semantic memory. *Child Development*, 55, 944–951.

KALISH, R.A. (1982) *Late Adulthood: Perspectives on Human Development*. Monterey, CA: Brooks-Cole.

KAMIN, L.J. (1974) *The Science and Politics of IQ*. Harmondsworth: Penguin.

KARMILOFF-SMITH, A. (1986) Stage/structure versus phase/process in modeling linguistic and cognitive development. In I. Levin (Ed.) *Stage and Structure, Reopening the Debate*. Norwood, NJ: Ablex.

KARNIOL, R. (1978) Children's use of intention cues in evaluating behaviour. *Psychological Bulletin*, 85, 76–85.

KASTENBAUM, R. (1979) *Growing Old – Years of Fulfilment*. London: Harper & Row.

KEIL, F.K. (1986) On the structure-dependent nature of stages in cognitive development. In I. Levin (Ed.) *Stage and Structure, Reopening the Debate*. Norwood, NJ: Ablex.

KENRICK, D.T. (1994) Evolutionary social psychology: From sexual selection to social cognition. *Advances in Experimental Social Psychology*, 26, 75–121.

KERMIS, M.D. (1984) *The Psychology of Human Ageing*. Boston: Allyn & Bacon.

KIMURA, D. (1992) Sex differences in the brain. *Scientific American*, September, 80–87 (Special Issue).

KLAUS, H.M. & KENNELL, J.H. (1976) *Maternal Infant Bonding*. St Louis: Mosby.

KOHLBERG, L. (1963) The development of children's orientations toward a moral order: 1. Sequence in the development of moral thought. *Human Development*, 6, 11–33.

KOHLBERG, L. (1969) Stage and sequence: The cognitive developmental approach to socialisation. In D.A. Goslin (Ed.) *Handbook of Socialisation Theory and Research*. Chicago: Rand McNally.

KOHLBERG, L. (1975) The cognitive-developmental approach to moral development. *Phi Delta Kappa*, June, 670–677.

KOHLBERG, L. (1978) Revisions in the theory and practice of moral development. *Directions for Child Development*, 2, 83–88.

KOHLBERG, L. (1984) *Essays on Moral Development: The Psychology of Moral Development (Volume 2)*. New York: Harper & Row.

KOHLBERG, L. & ULLIAN, D.Z. (1974) Stages in the development of psychosexual concepts and attitudes. In R.C. Van Wiele (Ed.) *Sex Differences in Behaviour*. New York: Wiley.

KOLUCHOVA, J. (1972/1976) Severe deprivation in twins: A case study. *Journal of Child Psychology and Psychiatry*, 13, 107–114.

KOTELCHUCK, M. (1976) The infant's relationship to the father: Experimental evidence. In M.E. Lamb (Ed.) *The Role of the Father in Child Development*. New York: Wiley.

KREBS, D. & BLACKMAN, R. (1988) *Psychology: A First Encounter*. London: Harcourt Brace Jovanovich.

KROGER, J. (1985) Separation-individuation and ego identity status in New Zealand university students. *Journal of Youth and Adolescence*, 14, 133–147.

KRUGER, A.C. (1992) The effect of peer and adult-child transactive discussions on moral reasoning. In M. Gauvain & M. Cole (Eds.) *Readings on the Development of Children*. New York: W.H. Freeman & Company.

KÜBLER-ROSS, E. (1969) *On Death and Dying*. London: Tavistock/Routledge.

KUHN, H.H. (1960) Self attitudes by age, sex and professional training. *Sociology Quarterly*, 1, 39–55.

KUHN, H.H. & McPARTLAND, T.S. (1954) An empirical investigation of self attitudes. *American Sociology Review*, 47, 647–652.

LABOUVIE-VIEF, G. (1980) Beyond formal operations:

uses and limits of pure logic in life-span development. *Human Development*, 22, 141–161.

LAMB, M.F. (1976) Twelve-month-olds and their parents: Interactions in a laboratory playroom. *Developmental Psychology*, 12. 237–244.

LAMB, M.E., THOMPSON, R.A., GANDER, W. & CHARNOV, E.L. (1985) *Infant-mother Attachment: The Origins and Significance of Individual Differences in Strange Situation Behaviour.* Hillsdale, NJ: Earlbaum.

LAMBERT, W.E., HAMERS, J. & FRASURE-SMITH, N. (1979) *Child Rearing Values.* New York: Praeger.

LANSKY, L.M., CRANDALL, V.J., KAGAN, J. & BAKER, C.T. (1961) Sex differences in aggression and its correlates in middle-class adolescents. *Child Development*, 32, 45–58.

LARSEN, R.J. & DIENER, E. (1987) Affect intensity as an individual difference characteristic: A review. *Journal of Research in Personality*, 21, 1039.

LAURANCE, J. (1996) Psychologists extol the benefits of divorce for all the family. *The Times*, September 16th, 6.

LEACH, M.P. (1993) Should parents hit their children? *The Psychologist*, 6, 216–220.

LeFRANCOIS, G.R. (1986) *Of Children: An Introduction to Child Development.* Belmont, CA: Wadsworth.

LERNER, R.M. (1975) Showdown at generation gap: Attitudes of adolescents and their parents towards contemporary issues. In H.D. Thornburg (Ed.) *Contemporary Adolescences: Readings* (2nd edition). Belmont, CA: Brooks/Cole.

LERNER, R.M. & SHEA, J.A. (1982) Social behaviour in adolescence. In B.B. Wolman (Ed.) *Handbook of Developmental Psychology.* Englewood Cliffs, NJ: Prentice-Hall.

LEVINSON, D.J. (1986) A conception of adult development. *American Psychologist*, 41, 3–13.

LEVINSON, D.J., DARROW, D.N., KLEIN, E.B., LEVINSON, M.H. & McKEE, B. (1978) *The Seasons of a Man's Life.* New York: A.A. Knopf.

LEVY, B. & LANGER, E. (1994) Ageing free from negative stereotypes: successful memory in China and among the American deaf. *Journal of Personality and Social Psychology*, 66, 989–997.

LEWIS, C. (1981) The effects of parental firm control: A reinterpretation of findings. *Psychological Bulletin*, 90, 547–563.

LEWIS, M. & BROOKS-GUNN, J. (1979) *Social Cognition and the Acquisition of Self.* New York: Plenum.

LEWONTIN, R. (1976) Race and intelligence. In N.J. Block & G. Dworkin (Eds.) *The IQ Controversy: Critical Readings.* New York: Pantheon.

LIEBERMAN, M.A. (1993) Bereavement self-help groups: review of conceptual and methodological issues. In M.S. Stroebe, W. Stroebe & R.O. Hansson (Eds.) *Handbook of Bereavement: Theory, Research and Intervention.* New York: Cambridge University Press.

LIGHT, P. (1986) Context, conservation and conversation. In M. Richards & P. Light (Eds.) *Children of Social Worlds.* Cambridge: Polity Press.

LIGHT, P. & GILMOUR, A. (1983) Conservation or conversation? Contextual facilitation of inappropriate conservation judgements. *Journal of Experimental Child Psychology*, 36, 356–363.

LIGHT, P., BUCKINGHAM, N. & ROBBINS, A.H. (1979) The conservation task as an interactional setting. *British Journal of Educational Psychology*, 49, 304–310.

LINN, R.L. (1982) Admissions testing on trial. *American Psychologist*, 29, 279–291.

LLEWELLYN SMITH, J. (1996) Courses for gifted children are often 'a waste of time'. *The Sunday Telegraph*, September 8th, 5.

LOPATA, H.Z. (1988) Support systems of American urban widowhood. *Journal of Social Issues*, 44, 113–128.

LORENZ, K.Z. (1935) The companion in the bird's world. *Auk*, 54, 245–273.

LUMSDEN, C.J. & WILSON, E.O. (1983) *Promethean Fire.* Cambridge, MA: Harvard University Press.

LYTTON, H. & ROMNEY, D.M. (1991) Parents' differential socialisation of boys and girls: A meta-analysis. *Psychological Bulletin*, 109, 267–296.

MACCOBY, E.E. (1980) *Social Development – Psychological Growth and the Parent-Child Relationship.* New York: Harcourt Brace Jovanovich.

MACCOBY, E.E. & HAGEN, J.W. (1965) cited in S.A. Rathus (1990) *Psychology* (4th edition). Orlando, FLA: Holt, Rinehart & Winston.

MACCOBY, E.E. & JACKLIN, C.N. (1974) *The Psychology of Sex Differences.* Stanford, CA: Stanford University Press.

MACCOBY, E.E. & MARTIN, J.A. (1983) Socialisation in the context of the family: Parent-child interaction. In E.M. Hetherington (Ed.) *Handbook of Child Psychology: Socialisation, Personality and Social Development, Volume* 20. Orlando, FLA: Academic Press.

MADDOX, G.L. (1964) Disengagement theory: A critical evaluation. *The Gerontologist*, 4, 80–83.

MAIN, M. (1991) Metacognitive knowledge, metacognitive monitoring, and singular (coherent) versus multiple (incoherent) models of attachment: Findings and directions for future research. In C.M. Murray Parkes, J.M. Stephenson-Hinde & P. Marris (Eds.) *Attachment Across the Life-Cycle.* London: Routledge.

MANDLER, J. (1990) cited in P.G. Zimbardo & A.L. Weber (1994) *Psychology.* New York: HarperCollins.

MARCIA, J.E. (1980) Identity in adolescence. In J. Adelson (Ed.) *Handbook of Adolescent Psychology.* New York: Wiley.

MARCUS, D.E. & OVERTON, W.F. (1978) The

development of cognitive gender constancy and sex-role preferences. *Child Development*, 49, 434–444.
MARSLAND, D. (1987) *Education and Growth*. London: Falmer.
MARTIN, B. (1975) Parent-child relations. In F.D. Horowitz (Ed.) *Review of Child Development Research (Volume 4)*. Chicago: University of Chicago Press.
MARTIN, C.L. (1991) The role of cognition in understanding gender effects. *Advances in Child Development and Behaviour*, 23, 113–149.
MARVIN, R.S. (1975) Aspects of the pre-school child's changing conception of his mother. Cited in C.G. Morris (1988) *Psychology: An Introduction* (6th edition). Englewood Cliffs, NJ: Prentice-Hall.
MASON, M.K. (1942) Learning to speak after six and one half years of silence. *Journal of Speech and Hearing Disorders*, 7, 295–304.
MATTHEWS, R. (1996) Parents blamed for tantrums of Terrible Twos. *The Sunday Telegraph*, September 8th, 3.
MAURER, D. & SALAPATEK, P. (1976) Developmental changes in the scanning of faces by young infants. *Child Development*, 47, 523–527.
MAYALL, B. & PETRIE, P. (1983) *Childminding and Day Nurseries: What Kind of Care?* London: Heinemann Educational Books.
MAYLOR, E.A. (1994) Ageing and the retrieval of specialised and general knowledge: Performance of ageing masterminds. *British Journal of Psychology*, 85, 105–114.
McCALL, R.B., APPLEBAUM, M.I. & HOGARTY, P.S. (1973) Developmental changes in mental test performance. *Monographs for the Society of Research in Child Development*, 38, (3, Whole No. 150).
McCARTNEY, J. (1996) Yes it hurts . . . No, it doesn't work. *The Sunday Telegraph*, September 8th, 22.
McGARRIGLE, J. & DONALSON, M. (1974) Conservation accidents. *Cognition*, 3, 341–350.
McGHEE, P.E. (1976) Children's appreciation of humour: A test of the cognitive congruency principle. *Child Development*, 47, 420–426.
McGLONE, J. (1980) Sex differences in human brain asymmetry: A critical survey. *Behaviour and Brain Sciences*, 3, 215–227.
McGOWAN, R.J. & JOHNSON, D.L. (1984) The mother-child relationship and other antecedents of childhood intelligence: A causal analysis. *Child Development*, 55, 810–820.
McGURK, H. (1975) *Growing and Changing*. London: Methuen.
McILVEEN, R.J., LONG, M. & CURTIS, A. (1994) *Talking Points in Psychology (Teacher's Guide)*. London: Hodder & Stoughton.
MEAD, G.H. (1934) *Mind, Self and Society*. Chicago: Chicago University Press.
MEADOWS, S. (1993) *The Child as Thinker: The Acquisition and Development of Cognition in Childhood*. London: Routledge.
MEADOWS, S. (1995) Cognitive development. In P.E. Bryant & A.M. Colman (Eds.) *Developmental Psychology*. London: Longman.
MEILMAN, P.W. (1979) Cross-sectional age changes in ego identity status during adolescence. *Developmental Psychology*, 15, 230–231.
MELTZOFF, A. & MOORE, M. (1983) Newborn infants imitate adult facial gestures. *Child Development*, 54, 702–709.
MILLER, E. & MORRIS, R. (1993) *The Psychology of Dementia*. Chichester: Wiley.
MINTURN, L. & LAMBERT, W.W. (1964) *Mothers of Six Cultures*, New York: Wiley.
MISCHEL, W. (1973) Toward a cognitive social learning reconceptualisation of personality. *Psychological Review*, 80, 252–283.
MISCHEL, W. & MISCHEL, H.N. (1976) A cognitive social learning approach to morality and self-regulation. In T. Lickona (Ed.) *Moral Development and Behaviour: Theory, Research and Social Issues*. New York: Holt, Rinehart & Winston.
MONEY, J. (1974) Prenatal hormones and postnatal socialisation in gender identity differentiation. In J.K. Cole & R. Dienstbier (Eds.) *Nebraska Symposium on Motivation*. Lincoln: University of Nebraska Press.
MONEY, J. & EHRHARDT, A. (1972) *Man and Woman, Boy and Girl*. Baltimore: Johns Hopkins University Press.
MONTEMAYOR, R. (1983) Parents and adolescents in conflict: All families some of the time and some families most of the time. *Journal of Early Adolescence*, 3, 83–103.
MOORE, C. & FRYE, D. (1986) The effect of the experimenter's intention on the child's understanding of conservation. *Cognition*, 22, 283–298.
MORRIS, C.G. (1988) *Psychology: An Introduction*. Englewood Cliffs, NJ: Prentice Hall.
MOSCOVICI, S. (1985) Social influence and conformity. In G. Lindzey & E. Aronson (Eds.) *Handbook of Social Psychology* (3rd edition). New York: Random House.
MOSER, K.A., FOX, A.J. & JONES, D.R. (1984) Unemployment and mortality in the OPCS longitudinal study. *Lancet*, 2, 1324–1329.
MOSHMAN, D.A., GLOVER, J.A. & BRUNING, R.H. (1987) *Developmental Psychology: A Topical Approach*. Boston: Little, Brown & Company.
MUIR, H., SHAW, T. & SYLVESTER, R. (1996) Major vows to defend smacking. *The Daily Telegraph*, September 16th, 1–2.
MUNROE, R.H., SHIMMIN, H.S. & MUNROE, R.L. (1984) Gender understanding and sex-role preference in four cultures. *Developmental Psychology*, 20, 673–682.
MUNSINGER, H. (1975) The adopted child's IQ: A critical review. *Psychological Bulletin*, 82, 623–659.

MURDOCK, G.P. (1975) *Outline of World Cultures* (5th edition). New Haven: Human Relations Area Files.
MURDOCK, G.P., FORD, C.S. & HUDSON, A.E. (1971) *Outline of Cultural Materials* (4th edition). New Haven: Human Relations Area Files.
MURPHY, G. (1947) *Personality: A Bio-Social Approach to Origins and Structure.* New York: Harper & Row.
MYERS, B. (1984) Mother-infant bonding: The status of the critical period hypothesis. *Developmental Review*, 4, 240–274.
MYERS, D.G. (1990) *Exploring Psychology.* New York: Worth.
NEEDLEMAN, H.L., SCHELL, A., BELLINGER, D., LEVITON, A. & ALLRED, E. (1990) Lead-associated intellectual deficit. *New England Journal of Medicine*, 322, 83–88.
NELSON, S.A. (1980) Factors influencing young children's use of motives and outcomes as moral criteria. *Child Development*, 51, 823–829.
NEUGARTEN, B.L. (1975) The future of the young-old. *The Gerontologist*, 15, 4–9.
NEUGARTEN, B.L. & NEUGARTEN, D.A. (1987) The changing meanings of age. *Psychology Today*, 21, 29–33.
NEWMAN, H.H., FREMAN, F.N. & HOLZINGER, K.J. (1937) *Twins: A Study of Heredity and the Environment.* Chicago, ILL: University of Chicago Press.
NEWSWEEK (1990) Living together. *Special edition*, Winter/Spring.
NOLLER, P. & CALLAN, V.J. (1990) Adolescents' perceptions of the nature of their communication with parents. *Journal of Youth and Adolescence*, 19, 349–362.
NOVAK, M.A. (1979) Social recovery of monkeys isolated for the first years of life: 2. Long-term assessment. *Developmental Psychology*, 15, 50–61.
NOVAK, M.A. & HARLOW, H.F. (1975) Social recovery of monkeys isolated for the first years of life: 1. Rehabilitation and therapy. *Developmental Psychology*, 11, 453–465.
OAKHILL, J.V. (1984) Why children have difficulty reasoning with three-term series problems. *British Journal of Developmental Psychology*, 2, 223–230.
O'BRIEN, M., HUSTON, A.C. & RISLEY, T. (1983) Sex-typed play of toddlers in a day-care centre. *Journal of Applied Developmental Psychology*, 4, 1–9.
OFFER, D. (1969) *The Psychological World of the Teenager.* New York: Basic Books.
OFFER, D., OSTROV, E., HOWARD, K.I. & ATKINSON, R. (1988) *The Teenage World: Adolescents' Self-Image in Ten Countries.* New York: Plenum Press.
OLWEUS, D. (1980) Familial and temperamental determinants of aggressive behaviour in adolescent boys: A causal analysis. *Developmental Psychology*, 16, 644–666.
PAGE, D., MOSHER, R., SIMPSON, E., FISHER, E., MARDON, G., POLLOCK, J., McGILLIVRAY, B., CHAPPELLE, A. & BROWN, L. (1987) The sex-determining region of the human Y-chromosome encodes a finger protein. *Cell*, 51, 1091–1104.
PAPERT, S. (1980) *Mindstorms: Children, Computers and Powerful Ideas.* Brighton: Harvester.
PARKE, R.D. (1981) *Fathering.* London: Fontana.
PARKE, R.D. & SWAIN, D.B. (1980) The family in early infancy. In F.A. Pederson (Ed.) *The Father-Infant Relationship: Observational Studies in a Family Context.* New York: Praeger.
PARKES, C.M. (1964) Recent bereavement as a cause of mental illness. *British Journal of Psychiatry*, 110, 198–204.
PARKES, C.M., BENJAMIN, B. & FITZGERALD, R.G. (1969) Broken heart: A statistical study of increased mortality among widowers. *British Medical Journal*, 1, 740–743.
PARKES, C.M. & WEISS, R.S. (1983) *Recovery From Bereavement.* New York: Basic Books.
PASCUAL-LEONE, J. (1976) Metasubjective problems of constructive cognition: Forms of knowing and their psychological dimensions. *Canadian Psychological Review*, 17, 110–125.
PASCUAL-LEONE, J. (1980) Constructive problems for constructive theories: The current relevance of Piaget's work and a critique of information-processing simulation psychology. In R.H. Kluwe & H. Spads (Eds.) *Developmental Models of Thinking.* New York: Academic Press.
PATTERSON, G.R. (1982) *Coercive Family Process.* Eugene, OR: Catalia Press.
PEARLIN, L.I. (1980) Life strains and psychological distress among adults. In N.J. Smelser & E.H. Erikson (Eds.) *Themes of Work and Love in Adulthood.* Cambridge, MA: Harvard University Press.
PECK, R.C. (1968) Psychological developments in the second half of life. In B.L. Neugarten (Ed.) *Middle Age and Ageing.* Chicago, Ill.: University of Chicago Press.
PEEL, E.A. (1972) *The Nature of Adolescent Judgement.* London: Staples Press.
PERRY, D.G. & BUSSEY, K. (1979) The social learning theory of sex differences: Imitation is alive and well. *Journal of Personality and Social Psychology*, 37, 1699–1712.
PETKOVA, B. (1995) New views on the self: Evil women – witchcraft or PMS? *Psychology Review*, 2, 16–19.
PHILLIPS, J.L. (1969) *The Origins of Intellect: Piaget's Theory.* San Francisco: W.H. Freeman.
PIAGET, J. (1932) *The Moral Judgement of the Child.* London: Routledge and Kegan Paul.
PIAGET, J. (1952) *The Origins of Intelligence in Children.* New York: International Universities Press.
PIAGET, J. (1973) *The Child's Conception of the World.* London: Paladin.
PIAGET, J. & INHELDER, B. (1956) *The Psychology of the Child.* London: Routledge & Kegan Paul.

PIAGET, J. & SZEMINSKA, A. (1952) *The Child's Conception of Number.* London: Routledge & Kegan Paul.

PLOMIN, R. (1988) The nature and nurture of cognitive abilities. In R.J. Sternberg (Ed.) *Advances in the Psychology of Human Intelligence* (Volume 4). Hillsdale, NJ: Erlbaum.

PLOMIN, R. & DeFRIES, J.C. (1980) Genetics and intelligence: Recent data. *Intelligence*, 4, 15–24.

PLOMIN, R., DeFRIES, J. & FULKER, D. (1988) *Nature and Nurture During Infancy and Early Childhood.* Cambridge: Cambridge University Press.

POTTER, J. & WETHERELL, M. (1987) *Discourse and Social Psychology: Beyond Attitudes and Behaviour.* London: Sage Publications.

QUINTON, D. & RUTTER, M. (1988) *Parental Breakdown: The Making and Breaking of Intergenerational Links.* London: Gower.

RAMSAY, R. & de GROOT, W. (1977) A further look at bereavement. Paper presented at EATI conference, Uppsala. Cited in P.E. Hodgkinson (1980) Treating abnormal grief in the bereaved. *Nursing Times*, 17 January, 126–128.

RAPHAEL, B. (1984) *The Anatomy of Bereavement.* London: Hutchinson.

RATHUS, S.A. (1990) *Psychology* (4th edition). London: Holt, Rinehart & Winston.

REBOK, G.W. (1987) *Life-Span Cognitive Development.* New York: Holt, Rinehart & Winston.

REEDY, M.N. (1983) Personality and ageing. In D.S. Woodruff & J.E. Birren (Eds.) *Ageing: Scientific Perspectives and Social Issues* (2nd edition). Monterey, CA: Brooks/Cole.

REST, J.R. (1983) Morality. In J.H. Flavell & E. Markman (Eds.) *Handbook of Child Psychology (Volume 3).* New York: Wiley.

REST, J.R. & THOMA, S.J. (1986) Relation of moral judgement development to formal education. *Developmental Psychology*, 21, 709–714.

RICHARDS, M.P.M. (1987) Children, parents and families: Developmental psychology and the re-ordering of relationships at divorce. *International Journal of Law and the Family*, 1, 295–317.

RICHARDS, M.P.M. (1995) The International Year of the Family – family research. *The Psychologist*, 8, 17–20.

RIEGEL, K.F. (1976) The dialectics of human development. *American Psychologist*, 31, 689–700.

ROBERTS, R. & NEWTON, P.M. (1987) Levinsonian studies of women's adult development. *Psychology and Ageing*, 39, 165–174.

ROGERS, C.R. (1951) *Client-Centred Therapy – Its Current Practices, Implications and Theory.* Boston: Houghton Mifflin.

ROGERS, J., MEYER, J. & MORTEL, K. (1990) After reaching retirement age physical activity sustains cerebral perfusion and cognition. *Journal of the American Geriatric Society*, 38, 123–128.

ROGOFF, B. (1990) *Apprenticeship in Thinking: Cognitive Development in a Social Context.* New York: Oxford University Press.

ROSE, S.A. & BLANK, M. (1974) The potency of context in children's cognition: an illustration through conservation. *Child Development*, 45, 499–502.

ROSENBERG, M. (1965) *Society and the Adolescent Self-Image.* Princeton, NJ: Princeton University Press.

ROSENHAN, D. (1973) *Moral Development.* CRM-McGraw-Hill Films.

RUBIN, J.Z., PROVENZANO, F.J. & LURIA, Z. (1974) The eye of the beholder: Parents' views on sex of newborns. *American Journal of Orthopsychiatry*, 44, 512–519.

RUBLE, D.N. (1984) Sex-role development. In M.C. Bornstein & M.E. Lamb (Eds.) *Developmental Psychology: An Advanced Textbook.* Hillsdale, NJ: Erlbaum.

RUTTER, M. (1981) *Maternal Deprivation Reassessed* (2nd edition). Harmondsworth: Penguin.

RUTTER, M. (1989) Pathways from childhood to adult life. *Journal of Child Psychology and Psychiatry*, 30, 23–25.

RUTTER, M., GRAHAM, P., CHADWICK, D.F.D. & YULE, W. (1976) Adolescent turmoil: Fact or fiction? *Journal of Child Psychology and Psychiatry*, 17, 35–56.

RUTTER, M. & RUTTER, M. (1992) *Developing Minds: Challenge and Continuity Across The Life-Span.* Harmondsworth: Penguin.

RYAN, S. (1974) *A Report on Longitudinal Evaluations of Pre-school Programs: Volume 1: Longitudinal Evaluations.* (DHEW Publications No. OHD 74–24). Washington, DC: Office of Human Development.

SAMEROFF, A.J. & SEIFER, R. (1989) *Social Regulation of Developmental Communities.* Paper presented at the annual meeting of the American Association for the Advancement of Science, San Francisco.

SAMUEL, J. & BRYANT, P. (1984) Asking only one question in the conservation experiment. *Journal of Child Psychology and Psychiatry*, 25, 315–318.

SANGIULIANO, I. (1978) *In Her Time.* New York: Morrow.

SANTROCK, J.W. (1986) *Psychology: The Science of Mind and Behaviour.* Dubuque, IA: William C. Brown.

SARAFINO, E.P. & ARMSTRONG, J.W. (1980) *Child and Adolescent Development.* Glenview, Ill.: Scott, Foresman and Company.

SAYERS, J. (1982) *Biological Politics: Feminist and Anti-Feminist Perspectives.* London: Tavistock.

SCARR, S. (1984) *Mother Care/Other Care.* New York: Basic Books.

SCARR, S. & WEINBERG, R. (1976) IQ test performance of black children adopted by white families. *American Psychologist*, 31, 726–739.

SCARR, S. & WEINBERG, R. (1978) Attitudes, interests, and IQ. *Human Nature*, April, 29–36.

SCHAFFER, H.R. (1966) The onset of fear of strangers and the incongruity hypothesis. *Journal of Child Psychology and Psychiatry*, 7, 95–106.

SCHAFFER, H.R. (1971) *The Growth of Sociability.* Harmondsworth: Penguin.

SCHAFFER, H.R. (1996) Is the child father to the man? *Psychology Review*, 2, 2–5.

SCHAFFER, H.R. & EMERSON, P.E. (1964) The development of social attachments in infancy. *Monographs of the Society for Research in Child Development*, 29, (Whole No. 3).

SCHAIE, K.W. & HERTZOG, C. (1983) Fourteen-year cohort-sequential analysis of adult intellectual development. *Developmental Psychology*, 19, 531–543.

SCHIFF, N., DUYME, M., DUMARET, A., STEWART, J., TOMKIEWICZ, S. & FEINGOLD, J. (1978) Intellectual status of working-class children adopted early into upper-middle-class families. *Science*, 200, 1503–1504.

SCHLOSSBERG, N.K., TROLL, L.E. & LEIBOWITZ, Z. (1978) *Perspectives on Counselling Adults: Issues and Skills.* Monterey, CA: Brooks/Cole.

SCHWEINHART, L.J. & WEIKART, D.P. (1980) Young children grow up: The effects of the Perry Preschool Program on youths through age 15. *Monographs of the High/Scope Educational Research Foundation* (Series No. 7).

SEARS, R.R., MACCOBY, E.E. & LEVIN, H. (1957) *Patterns of Child Rearing.* New York: Harper & Row.

SELIGMAN, M.E.P. (1975) *Helplessness: On Depression, Development and Death.* San Francisco: W.H. Freeman.

SHAFFER, D.R. (1985) *Developmental Psychology.* Monterey, CA: Brooks/Cole.

SHATZ, M. (1994) *A Toddler's Life: Becoming a Person.* Oxford: Oxford University Press.

SHEEHY, G. (1976) *Passages – Predictable Crises of Adult Life.* New York: Bantam Books.

SHEEHY, G. (1996) *New Passages.* New York: HarperCollins.

SHIELDS, J. (1962) *Monozygotic Twins Brought Up Apart and Brought Up Together.* London: Oxford University Press.

SHWEDER, R.A. (1991) *Thinking Through Cultures: Expeditions in Cultural Psychology.* Cambridge, MA: Harvard University Press.

SHWEDER, R.A., MAHAPATRA, M. & MILLER, J.G. (1987) Culture and moral development. In J. Kagan & S. Lamb (Eds.) *The Emergence of Morality in Young Children.* Chicago: University of Chicago Press.

SIDDIQUE, C.M. & D'ARCY, C. (1984) Adolescence, stress and psychological well-being. *Journal of Youth and Adolescence*, 13, 459–474.

SIMMONS, R. & BLYTH, D.A. (1987) *Moving Into Adolescence.* New York: Aldine de Gruyter.

SIMMONS, R. & ROSENBERG, S. (1975) Sex, sex-roles and self-image. *Journal of Youth and Adolescence*, 4, 229–256.

SINCLAIR-de-ZWART, H. (1969) Developmental psycholinguistics. In D. Elkind & J. Flavell (Eds.) *Handbook of Learning and Cognitive Processes* (Volume 5). Hillsdale, NJ: Erlbaum.

SKEELS, H.M. (1966) Adult status of children with contrasting early life experiences. *Monographs of the Society for Research in Child Development*, 31, (Whole no. 3).

SKEELS, H.M. & DYE, H.B. (1939) A study of the effects of differential stimulation on mentally retarded children. *Proceedings of the American Association of Mental Deficiency*, 44, 114–136.

SKINNER, B.F. (1969) *Contingencies of Reinforcement: A Theoretical Analysis.* New York: Appleton Century Crofts.

SKUSE, P. (1984) Extreme deprivation in early childhood – I. Diverse outcome for three siblings from an extraordinary family. *Journal of Child Psychology and Psychiatry*, 25, 523–541.

SLABY, R.G. & FREY, K.S. (1975) Development of gender constancy and selective attention to same-sex models. *Child Development*, 46, 839–856.

SLUCKIN, W. (1965) *Imprinting and Early Experiences.* London: Methuen.

SMEDSLUND, J. (1961) The acquisition of conservation of substance and weight in children. *Scandinavian Journal of Psychology*, 2, 11–20.

SMETENA, J.G. (1990) Morality and conduct disorders. In M. Lewis & S.M. Miller (Eds.) *Handbook of Developmental Psychopathology.* New York: Plenum.

SMITH, C. & LLOYD, B.B. (1978) Maternal behaviour and perceived sex of infant. *Child Development*, 49, 1263–1265.

SMITH, L. (1982) Class inclusion and conclusions about Piaget's theory. *British Journal of Psychology*, 73, 267–276.

SMITH, P.B. & BOND, M.H. (1993) *Social Psychology Across Cultures: Analysis and Perspectives.* Hemel Hempstead: Harvester Wheatsheaf.

SMITH, P.K. & COWIE, H. (1991) *Understanding Children's Development* (2nd edition). Oxford: Basil Blackwell.

SMITH, P.K. & DAGLISH, L. (1977) Sex differences in parent and infant behaviour in the home. *Child Development*, 48, 1250–1254.

SNAREY, J.R. (1987) A question of morality. *Psychology Today*, June, 6–8.

SOBESKY, W. (1983) The effects of situational factors on moral judgements. *Child Development*, 54, 575–584.

SPITZ, R.A. (1945) Hospitalisation: An inquiry into the

genesis of psychiatric conditions in early childhood. *Psychoanalytic Study of the Child*, 1, 53–74.

SPITZ, R.A. (1946) Hospitalism: A follow-up report on investigation described in Vol. 1, 1945. *Psychoanalytic Study of the Child*, 2, 113–117.

SPITZ, R.A. & WOLF, K.M. (1946) Anaclitic depression. *Psychoanalytic Study of the Child*, 2, 313–342.

SPOCK, B. (1946) *Baby and Child Care.* New York: Pocket Books.

SROUFE, L.A., FOX, N.E. & PANCAKE, V.R. (1983) Attachment and dependency in developmental perspective. *Child Development*, 54, 1615–1627.

STACEY, M., DEARDEN, R., PILL, R. & ROBINSON, D. (1970) *Hospitals, Children and Their Families: The Report of a Pilot Study.* London: Routledge & Kegan Paul.

STAUB, E. (1979) Understanding and predicting social behaviour – with emphasis on prosocial behaviour. In E. Staub (Ed.) *Personality: Basic Issues and Current Research.* Englewood Cliffs, NJ: Prentice-Hall.

STERN, D. (1977) *The First Relationship: Infant and Mother.* Cambridge, MA: Harvard University Press.

STERNBERG, R.J. (1986) Cognition and instruction: Why the marriage sometimes ends in divorce. In R.F. Dillon & R.J. Sternberg (Eds.) *Cognition and Instruction.* London: Academic Press.

STERNBERG, R.J. (1990) *Metaphors of Mind.* Cambridge: Cambridge University Press.

STOCK, M.B. & SMYTHE, P.M. (1963) Does malnutrition during infancy inhibit brain growth and subsequent intellectual development? *Archives of Disorders in Childhood*, 38, 546–552.

STROEBE, M.S., STROEBE, W. & HANSSON, R.O. (1993) Contemporary themes and controversies in bereavement research. In M.S. Stroebe, W. Stroebe & R.O. Hansson (Eds.) *Handbook of Bereavement: Theory, Research and Intervention.* New York: Cambridge University Press.

STUART-HAMILTON, I. (1994) *The Psychology of Ageing: An Introduction* (2nd edition). London: Jessica Kingsley.

SUGARMAN, L. (1986) *Life-Span Development.* London: Methuen.

SUOMI, S.J. & HARLOW, H.F. (1977) Depressive behaviour in young monkeys subjected to vertical chamber confinement. *Journal of Comparative and Physiological Psychology*, 80, 11–18.

SUTHERLAND, P. (1992) *Cognitive Development Today: Piaget and his Critics.* London: Paul Chapman Publishing.

SWENSEN, C.H. (1983) A respectable old age. *American Psychologist*, 46, 1208–1221.

SYLVA, K. (1996) Education: Report on the Piaget-Vygotsky centenary conference. *The Psychologist*, 9, 370–372.

TAKAHASHI, K. (1990) Are the key assumptions of the strange situation procedure universal?: A view from Japanese research. *Human Development*, 33, 23–30.

TANNER, J.M. (1978) *Fetus into Man: Physical Growth from Conception to Maturity.* Cambridge, MA: Harvard University Press.

TANNER, J.M. & WHITEHOUSE, R.H. (1976) Clinical longitudinal standards for height, weight, height velocity, weight velocity and stages of puberty. *Archives of Disorders in Childhood*, 51, 170–179.

TAVRIS, C. & WADE, C. (1995) *Psychology in Perspective.* New York: HarperCollins.

THATCHER, R., WALKER, R. & GUIDICE, S. (1978) Human cerebral hemispheres develop at different rates and ages. *Science*, 236, 1110–1113.

THOMAS, R.M. (1985) *Comparing Theories of Child Development* (2nd edition). Belmont, CA: Wadsworth Publishing Company.

THOMPSON, R. (1985) *The Brain.* San Francisco: Freeman.

THOMPSON, L.A., DETTERMAN, D.K. & PLOMIN, R. (1991) Associations between cognitive abilities and scholastic achievement: Genetic overlap but environmental differences. *Psychological Science*, 2, 158–165.

THORNTON, D. & REID, D.L. (1982) Moral reasoning and type of criminal offence. *British Journal of Social Psychology*, 21, 231–238.

TIZARD, B. (1977) *Adoption: A Second Chance.* London: Open Books.

TIZARD, B. & HODGES, J. (1978) The effects of early institutional rearing on the development of eight-year-old children. *Journal of Child Psychology and Psychiatry*, 19, 99–118.

TIZARD, B. & REES, J. (1974) A comparison of the effects of adoption, restoration to the natural mother and continued institutionalisation on the cognitive development of four-year-old children. *Child Development*, 45, 92–99.

TOMLINSON-KEASEY, C. (1985) *Child Development: Psychological, Sociocultural, and Biological Factors.* Chicago: Dorsey Press.

TRABASSO, T. (1977) The role of memory as a system in making transitive inferences. In R.V. Kail & J.W. Hagen (Eds.) *Perspectives on the Development of Memory and Cognition.* Hillsdale, NJ: Erlbaum.

TREDRE, R. (1996) Untitled article. *Observer Life*, May 12th, 16–19.

TRISELIOTIS, J. (1980) Growing up in foster care and after. In J. Triseliotis (Ed.) *New Developments in Foster Care and Adoption.* London: Routledge & Kegan Paul.

TRONICK, E., ALS, H., ADAMSON, L., WISE, S. & BRAZELTON, T.B. (1978) The infant's response to entrapment betwen contradictory messages in face-to-face interaction. *Journal of the American Academy of Child Psychiatry*, 17, 1–13.

TRYON, R.C. (1940) Genetic differences in maze-learning abilities in rats. In *39th Yearbook, Part* 1. National Society for the Study of Education. Chicago: University of Chicago Press.

TURNBULL, S.K. (1995) The middle years. In D. Wedding (Ed.) *Behaviour and Medicine* (2nd edition). St. Louis, MO: Mosby-Year Book.

TURNER, J.S. & HELMS, D.B. (1989) *Contemporary Adulthood* (4th edition). Fort Worth, FL: Holt, Rinehart & Winston.

UNGER, R.K. (1979) *Female and Male*. London: Harper & Row.

VAN LEHN, K. (1983) On the representation of procedures in repair theory. In H.P. Ginsburg (Ed.) *The Development of Mathematical Thinking*. London: Academic Press.

VAUGHN, B.E., GOVE, F.L. & EGELAND, B.R. (1980) The relationship between out-of-home care and the quality of infant-mother attachment in an economically disadvantaged population. *Child Development*, 51, 1203–1214.

VYGOTSKY, L.S. (1962) *Thought and Language*. Cambridge, MA: MIT Press.

VYGOTSKY, L.S. (1978) *Mind in Society*. Cambridge, MA: Harvard University Press.

VYGOTSKY, L.S. (1981) The genesis of higher mental functions. In J.V. Wertsch (Ed.) *The Concept of Activity in Soviet Psychology*. Armonk, NY: Sharpe.

WADE, C. & TAVRIS, C. (1993) *Psychology* (3rd edition). New York: HarperCollins.

WALLACE, P. (1974) Complex environments: Effects on brain development. *Science*, 185, 1035–1037.

WARR, P.B. (1984) Work and unemployment. In P.J.D. Drenth (Ed.) *Handbook of Work and Organisational Psychology*. Chichester: Wiley.

WARR, P.B. (1987) *Work, Unemployment and Mental Health*. Oxford: Clarendon Press.

WATSON, J.B. (1928) *Psychological Care of Infant and Child*. New York: Norton.

WEINBERG, R. (1989) Intelligence and IQ: Landmark issues and great debates. *American Psychologist* 44, 98–104.

WEISFELD, G. (1994) Aggression and dominance in the social world of boys. In J. Archer (Ed.) *Male Violence*. London: Routledge.

WEISS, R.S. (1993) Loss and recovery. In M.S. Stroebe, W. Stroebe & R.O. Hansson (Eds.) *Handbook of Bereavement: Theory, Research and Intervention*. New York: Cambridge University Press.

WHITE, B.L. (1971) *Human Infants: Experience and Psychological Development*. Englewood Cliffs, NJ: Prentice-Hall.

WHITE, B.L. (1985) *The First Three Years of Life* (revised edition). New York: Prentice-Hall.

WHITE, K.M. & FERSTENBERG, A. (1978) Professional specialisation and formal operations: The balance task. *Journal of Genetic Psychology*, 133, 97–104.

WHITEHURST, G.J., FALCO, F.L., LONIGAN, C.J. & FISCHEL, J.E. (1988) Accelerating language development through picture-book reading. *Developmental Psychology*, 24, 552–559.

WHITING, B.B. (Ed.) (1963) *Six Cultures: Studies in Child Rearing*. New York: Wiley.

WHITING, J.W. & CHILD, I. (1953) *Child Training and Personality*. New Haven: Yale University Press.

WILLIAMS, J.E. & BEST, D.L. (1994) Cross-cultural views of women and men. In W.J. Lonner & R.S. Malpass (Eds.) *Psychology and Culture*. Boston: Allyn & Bacon.

WILSON, C.O. (1996) Children are out of control, says Spock. *Sunday Telegraph*, October 20th, 22.

WILSON, E.O. (1978) *On Human Nature*. Cambridge, MA: Harvard University Press.

WILSON, R.S. (1983) The Louisville Twin Study: Developmental synchronies in behaviour. *Child Development*, 54, 298–316.

WOBER, J.M., REARDON, G. & FAZAL, S. (1987) *Personality, Character Aspirations and Patterns of Viewing Among Children*. London: IBA Research Papers.

WOOD, D.J., BRUNER, J.S. & ROSS, G. (1976) The role of tutoring in problem-solving. *Journal of Child Psychology and Psychiatry*, 17, 89–100.

WRIGHT, D. (1971) *The Psychology of Moral Behaviour*. Harmondsworth: Penguin.

YOGMAN, M., DIXON, S., TRONICK, E., ALS, H. & BRAZELTON, T.B. (1977) The goals and structure of face-to-face interaction between infants and fathers. *Paper presented at the biennial meetings of the Society for Research in Child Development*, New Orleans (March).

YUSSEN, S.R. & SANTROCK, J.W. (1982) *Child Development* (2nd edition). Dubuque, IA: Wm. C. Brown.

ZAJONC, R.B. & MARKUS, G.B. (1975) Birth order and intellectual development. *Psychological Review*, 82, 74–88.

ZIGLER, E., ABELSON, W.D., TRICKETT, P.K. & SEITZ, V. (1982) Is an intervention program necessary to improve economically disadvantaged children's IQ scores? *Child Development*, 53, 340–348.

ZIMBARDO, P.G. & WEBER, A.L. (1994) *Psychology*. New York: HarperCollins.

INDEX

Page numbers in **bold** refer to definitions and main explanations of particular concepts.

PICTURE CREDITS

The authors and publishers would like to thank the following copyright holders for their permission to reproduce illustrative materials in this book:

Photo Almasy - D.F. for Figure 5.1 (p. 55, top); **Edward Arnold/© Antony McAvoy** for Figure 7.2 (p. 82); **Ashgate Publishing Limited** for Figure 2.4 (p. 22); **Associated Press/Topham** for Figure 2.3 (p. 20) and Figure 7.3 (p. 83, left); **BBC** for Figure 11.1 (p. 134), Figure 12.1 (p. 146) and Figure 13.3 (p. 161); **Concord Films Council** for Figure 2.1 (p. 17); **The Ronald Grant Archive** for Figure 2.2 (p. 18) © 1979 Columbia Pictures Industries, Inc. and Figure 11.3 (p. 137); **Sally and Richard Greenhill** for Figure 1.6 (p. 10) and Figure 7.5 (p. 86, top) © Sally Greenhill, Figure 8.3 (p. 102, bottom) © Kate Mayers, Figure 12.4 (p. 150), Figure 12.5 (p. 152) and Figure 13.4 (p. 163, right); **Harlow Primate Laboratory, University of Wisconsin**, for Figure 1.3 (p. 7); **HarperCollins Publishers** for Box 7.4 (p. 87), an example of a moral dilemma from *Essays on Moral Development: The Psychology of Moral Development* (Vol. II) by Lawrence Kohlberg, copyright © 1984 by Lawrence Kohlberg, reprinted by permission of HarperCollins Publishers, Inc.; **Hulton Getty** for Figure 1.4 (p. 8); **The Johns Hopkins University Press** for Figure 8.2 (p. 99) from Money, J. and Ehrhardt, A., *Man and Woman, Boy and Girl* © 1972 The Johns Hopkins University Press; **The Kobal Collection** for Figure 10.2 (p. 123); **Dennis Krebs and Roger Blackman** for Figure 1.1 (p. 3); **Life File/© Nicola Sutton** for Figure 8.3 (p. 102, top); **LWT** for Figure 8.4 (p. 104); **The McGraw-Hill Companies** for Figure 11.6 (p. 140) from John W. Santrock, *Psychology the Science of Mind and Behavior*, copyright © 1986 The McGraw-Hill Companies, Inc., reprinted by permission, all rights reserved; **Newsweek** for Figure 12.3 (p. 148) from Newsweek-'Living Together', special edition Winter/Spring 1990 © 1990 Newsweek, Inc., all rights reserved, reprinted by permission; **Paul Chapman Publishing Ltd** for the figure in Box 5.2 (p. 57) reprinted with permission from Sutherland, P. (1992) *Cognitive Development Today: Piaget and his Critics*, copyright © 1992 Paul Chapman Publishing Ltd, London; **Popperfoto** for Figure 8.1 (p. 96); **Rex Features Ltd** for Figure 6.1 (p. 69) and Figure 6.3 (p. 74); **Routledge** for Figure 10.3 (p. 129) from Coleman, J.C. and Hendry, L. *The Nature of Adolescence*, 2nd edition, published 1990 by Routledge; **S & G Press Agency Ltd** for Figure 7.3 (p. 83, right) and Figure 7.4 (p. 85); **Scientific American** for Figure 1.5 (p. 8); **The Telegraph Group Limited** for Figure 3.2 (p. 33); **Times Newspapers Limited** for Figure 13.2 (p. 160) © Peter Brookes/The Times, 11th July 1996; **Topham Picture Point** for Figure 7.3 (p. 83, middle) and Figure 13.4 (p. 163, left); **ZEFA** for Figure 7.5 (p. 86, bottom), Figure 9.1 (p. 113) and Figure 12.2 (p. 147) © R. Halin-ZEFA.

Every effort has been made to obtain necessary permission with reference to copyright material. The publishers apologise if inadvertently any sources remain unacknowledged and will be glad to make the necessary arrangements at the earliest opportunity.

Index prepared by Frank Merrett, Cheltenham, Gloucs.